Dōgen and the Kōan Tradition

SUNY Series in Philosophy and Psychotherapy
Edited by Sandra A. Wawrytko

Dōgen
and the
Kōan Tradition

A Tale of Two *Shōbōgenzō* Texts

Steven Heine

STATE UNIVERSITY OF NEW YORK PRESS

Published by
State University of New York Press, Albany

© 1994 State University of New York

For information, address State University of New York Press,
State University Plaza, Albany, N.Y., 12246

Production by Cathleen Collins
Marketing by Dana Yanulavich

Library of Congress Cataloging in Publication Data

Heine, Steven, 1950–
    Dōgen and the Kōan tradition: a tale of two Shōbōgenzō texts
Steven Heine.
        p. cm. — (SUNY series in philosophy and psychotherapy)
    Includes bibliographical references and index
    ISBN 0–7914–1773–5. — ISBN 0–7914–1774–3 (pbk.)
    1. Dōgen, 1200–1253. 2. Dōgen, 1200–1253, Shōbō genzō.
3. Dōgen, 1200–1253, Mana Shōbō genzō. 4. Koan. I. Title.
II. Series
BQ9449.D657H45   1993
294.3'927'092—dc20   93-18446
                                                            CIP

10 9 8 7 6 5 4 3 2 1

Contents

Illustrations

Tables

Preface

THIS BOOK HAS three major goals in critically examining the historical and philosophical relation between the writings of Dōgen and the Zen kōan tradition. First, it introduces and evaluates recent Japanese scholarship concerning Dōgen's two *Shōbōgenzō* texts, the Japanese (*Kana*) collection of ninety-two fascicles on Buddhist topics and the Chinese (*Mana*) collection of three hundred kōan cases also known as the *Shōbōgenzō Sanbyakusoku*. The authenticity of the *Mana Shōbōgenzō*, long considered spurious, has recently been convincingly demonstrated, and now this text can be seen as a bridge linking Dōgen's Japanese Sōtō Zen to Sung era Zen in China, where Dōgen studied and attained enlightenment. Second, this book develops a new methodology for clarifying the development of the kōan tradition and the relation between multifarious interpretations of kōan cases based on postmodern literary criticism and intellectual history. Referred to here as "discourse analysis," the method integrates the notions of intertextuality and genre criticism, which focus on the formation of texts, with narratology and tropology, which highlight their rhetorical meaning and function. Discourse analysis demonstrates how Dōgen's unconventional handling of Zen anecdotes, such as Bodhidharma's "skin, flesh, bones, marrow," Chao-chou's *Mu*, Te-shan's "rice cake," and Ma-tsu's "polishing the tile," are based on polysemy and continuing hermeneutics in connection to the trope of metonymy in a way that is just as consistent with the tropological structure of the source dialogues as interpretations based on abbreviation and silence in connection to irony. Third, the book's emphasis on a literary critical methodology challenges the conventional reading of kōans stressing exclusively the role of psychological impasse culminating in silence. Without negating the significance of the psychological implications in kōan practice, discourse analysis reorients the issue of the effectiveness of kōans as a religious symbol in terms of textuality and rhetorical strategies.

This is my third book on Dōgen studies. The first book, *Existential and Ontological Dimensions of Time in Heidegger and Dōgen* (1985), is a comparative philosophical study of Dōgen's notions of time, impermanence, and death in relation to Heidegger's phenomenological analysis of temporality, finitude, and dying in *Being and Time*. It includes a translation of Dōgen's "Uji" ("Being-Time") fascicle. The second book, *A Blade of Grass: Japanese Poetry and Aesthetics in Dōgen Zen* (1989), is the first complete translation of Dōgen's Japanese poetry collection ("Dōgen Zenji Waka Shū" or "Sanshōdōei") with an introductory essay on Dōgen's connection to the medieval Japanese religio-aesthetic tradition. The underlying theme of these works is the issue of impermanence in Dōgen's thought: how and why he challenges some traditional doctrines concerning Buddha-nature and original enlightenment that he feels overlook or betray the basic Buddhist understanding of the ephemerality of all human and natural phenomena by locating enlightenment as a realm beyond the vicissitudes of everyday time. In these books, I analyze Dōgen's approach to impermanence in light of Heidegger's overcoming of Western eternalist metaphysics as well as in terms of how Dōgen absorbs and transforms influences from Japanese literary ideals, including *aware* (poignant sadness) and *yūgen* (profound mystery). One of the main topics in the background of these works is the issue of language and symbolism, that is, how Dōgen crafts his philosophical and poetic writings in a literary style appropriate to conveying his religious message.

This book shifts the focus to the question of language by undertaking an examination of the role of kōans and philosophy of language in Dōgen's Japanese or *Kana Shōbōgenzō*. It discusses recent discoveries and research by Dōgen specialists in Japan concerning Dōgen's kōan collection written in Chinese, or *Mana Shōbōgenzō*, in connection to the kōan tradition that developed in the texts of Sung China that recorded Zen dialogues. The current study deals with the stylistic and thematic influences Dōgen absorbed from several genres of Zen writings, including the *dentōroku* (transmission of the lamp), *goroku* (recorded sayings), and kōan collection genres. It also shows how influences from Japanese religiosity and literature helped steer Dōgen toward an an emphasis on the efficacious and polysemous nature of religious discourse. Part I explores fundamental methodological issues in Dōgen and kōan studies concerning the apparent conflict within Zen writings between voluminous textuality and irreverent antitextuality as well as between mythological/hagiographical and demythological/philosophical ideals. Part II applies discourse analysis to a deconstruction of the conventional polarities between Dōgen's zazen-only approach and the Rinzai (particularly Ta-hui) emphasis on kōan introspection. It discusses the open-ended quality of the source dialogues or roots of the tradition which give rise to multiple branches, including both narratological chronicles and tropological kōan cases. The final chapter situates Dōgen's approach to continuing hermeneutics in comparison with two other branches of the tradition: the wraparound commentary of the *Hekiganroku* and Ta-hui's shortcut method of the *watō* or head-word technique. Appendix I includes translations of several *Shōbōgenzō* fascicles that highlight the issue of kōan interpretation, including "Kattō" and "Ōsakusendaba," both of which treat the Bodhidharma "skin, flesh, bones, marrow" kōan, and "Shinfukatoku," on Te-shan's "rice cake" kōan. Appendix II cross-lists the titles of the *Mana Shōbōgenzō* kōans with other works by Dōgen, especially the Japanese *Shōbōgenzō*, that cite the same cases as well as the Sung texts which probably served as the sources for Dōgen's citations.

In hearing of this topic some readers may initially consider the question, "*Is* there any relation between Dōgen and the kōan tradition?", since Dōgen is generally portrayed as one of the main detractors rather than contributors to the use of kōan study from the standpoint of emphasizing zazen-only. One of my goals is to demonstrate that the sense of ideological conflicts and contrasts implicit in this kind of question reflect an attitude that has been overly influenced by sectarian polarization and polemic in Zen discourse in a way that obscures a genuine understanding of Dōgen's Japanese and Chinese texts in their appropriate historical and ideological setting. Dōgen's thought and writings were very much immersed in kōans, and his work can be seen as one of the culminative peaks in the development of the kōan tradition, which at the same time must be characterized as multiformed and diverse, supporting diverging paradigms including the approaches in the texts of of Dōgen, Ta-hui, and the *Hekiganroku*, among others.

Acknowledgments

I express my deepest gratitude to several professors at Komazawa University in Tokyo, Yoshizu Yoshihide, Kawamura Kōdō, and Ishii Shūdō. During numerous interviews and informal discussions in the summer of 1992, as well as other correspondences, they generously answered my questions concerning the formation of Dōgen's texts in relation to Zen recorded sayings and medieval Sōtō commentaries. I especially appreciate Prof. Ishii's comments regarding Figure 4.6. Also, Matsunaga Kandō provided valuable assistance in examining texts at the Komazawa University Library. Research on this project was made possible by several funding sources. The main source was a 1992–93 Research Initiation Grant from Pennsylvania State University that enabled me to travel to Japan and to collections at the University of California, Berkeley and the University of Hawaii. In addition, a 1992 research fellowship from the Northeast Asia Council of the Association for Asian studies allowed me to extend my travels in Japan. The third source was a summer 1991 faculty grant from LaSalle University that provided an opportunity for library research at the University of California, Los Angeles. I also thank a number of colleagues and friends who discussed key aspects of this project, including Masao Abe, David Barnhill, Richard DeMartino, Charles Wei-hsun Fu, Paul Groner, Ken Inada, Stephen Kaplan, Hee-Jin Kim, Miriam Levering, Dan Lusthaus, Charles Prebish, Jackie Stone, Sandra Wawrytko, and Dale Wright. As always, my wife Rhonda was enormously insightful and supportive.

In addition, Frank Cook was kind enough to show me his unpublished translation of the titles of the Mana Shōbōgenzō cases, which was extremely helpful in preparing Appendix II. I also thank Profs. Kawamura and Ishii for permission to translate material from their books in Appendix II, and I am grateful to Prof. Kawamura for permision to use a reproduction of material for the book cover from the 1287 Kanazawa Bunko manuscript of the Mana Shōbōgenzō that appears in his Ei-in-bon Shōbōgenzō. In addition, some of the passages in this book are included in my papers: "Does the Kōan Have Buddha-Nature? The Zen Kōan as Religious Symbol," Journal of the American Academy of Religion 58/3 (1990), 357–87; and "History, Transhistory, and Narrative History: A Postmodern View of Nishitani's Philosophy of Zen," Philosophy East and West 44/2 (1994).

Note on Transliteration

This book deals to a large extent with T'ang and Sung era Chinese texts from the standpoint of their impact on Japanese Zen and in light of modern Japanese scholarship. I have used Japanese pronunciation for terminology and titles throughout the book, and I also refer to the entire religious tradition as "Zen" although I preserve the use of "Ch'an" (or "Chan" in Pinyin) when quoting passages from other scholars' writings. The one exception to this rule involves the use of the names of Chinese masters. The glossary provides Japanese/Chinese equivalents when appropriate. Also, Far Eastern names are written with family names first unless they are cited for English language writings.

Chinese and Japanese Eras

China

Sui 589–618
T'ang 618–907
Wu-tai 907–960
Sung
  (North) 960–1127
  (South) 1127–1279
Yüan 1280–1368
Ming 1368–1644
Ch'ing 1644–1912

Japan

Asuka 555–710
Nara 710–784
Heian 794–1185
Kamakura 1185–1333
Muromachi 1333–1600
Tokugawa 1600–1868
Meiji 1868–1912

Abbreviations

CZW   Ishii Shūdō, *Chūgoku Zenshūshi Wa: Mana Shōbōgenzō ni Manabu* (Kyoto: Zen Bunka Kenkyūjō, 1988).

DKK   Kagamishima Genryū, *Dōgen Zenji to In'yō Kyōten-Goroku no Kenkyū* (Tokyo: Mokujisha, 1974).

DR   Ta-hui, *Daie Goroku*, in TSD 47, 811–943.

DZZ   *Dōgen Zenji Zenshū*, 2 volumes, ed. Ōkubo Dōshū (Tokyo: Chikuma Shobō, 1969 and 1970).

EK   Dōgen, *Eihei Kōroku*, 10 fascicles, ed. Yokoi Yūhō (Tokyo: Sankibō, 1978) [also in DZZ II].

EK-9   *Eihei Kōroku*, ninth fascicle [containing *juko* commentary on 90 *kosoku-kōan*, DZZ II, 167–85].

HR   Yüan-wu, *Hekiganroku* in TSD 48, 139–225, and Iriya Yoshitaka, Mizoguchi Yūzō, Sueki Fumihiko, Itō Fumio, ed. (Tokyo: Iwanami Shoten, 1992); trans. Thomas Cleary and J.C. Cleary, *The Blue Cliff Record*, 3 volumes (Boulder: Shambala, 1977).

IH   *Ichiya Hekiganroku*, attributed to Dōgen, photo-fascimile edition in Komazawa University Library.

KB   MS Kanazawa Bunko text (1287), in SSK.

KD   *Keitoku Dentōroku*, in TSD 51, 196–467.

KS   Dōgen, *Kana Shōbōgenzō*, up to 95 fascicles, in *Dōgen*, 2 volumes, ed. Terada Tōru and Mizuno Yaoko (Tokyo: Iwanami Shoten, 1970 and 1972) [also in DZZ I and TSD 82, 7–309).

MMK   *Mumonkan* in TSD 48, 292–99, and in Hirata Takashi in *Zen no Goroku* 18 (Tokyo: Chikuma Shobō, 1969); trans. with commentary by Zenkei Shibayama, *Zen Comments on the Mumonkan* (New York: Mentor, 1974).

MS   Dōgen, *Mana Shōbōgenzō* (*Shōbōgenzō Sanbyakusoku*), 300 cases, in DZZ II, 201–52 [also in SSK].

NS   *Nempyō Shōbōgenzō Sanbyakusoku Funogo*, attributed to Shigetsu Ein in *Zoku Sōtō Shū Zensho* (Tokyo: Kōmeisha, 1929–39).

SH   *Shōyōroku*, in TSD 48, 226–92, and ed. Yasutani Hakuun (Tokyo: Shunjūsha, 1973); trans. Thomas Cleary, *The Book of Serenity* (Hudson, NY: Lindisfarne Press, 1990).

SR   *Shūmon Rentōeyō* (1183), in ZZ 2:9.3–5.

SSK   Kawamura Kōdō, *Shōbōgenzō no Seiritsu Shiteki no Kenkyū* (Tokyo: Shunjūsha, 1987).

ST   *Shūmon Tōyōshū* (1133), Tōyō Bunka edition, photo-fascimile edition in Komazawa University Library.

SZ   Dōgen, *Shōbōgenzō Zuimonki*, 6 fascicles, ed. Mizuno Yaoko (Tokyo: Chikuma Shobō, 1963) [also included in DZZ II].

SZK   Ishii, *Sōdai Zenshūshi no Kenkyū* (Tokyo: Daitō Shuppansha, 1987).

SZS   Yanagida Seizan, *Shoki Zenshū Shisho no Kenkyū* (Kyoto: Hōzōkan, 1967).

TSD   *Taishō Shinshū Daizōkyō* (Tokyo: 1914–22).

ZD   Isshū Miura and Ruth Fuller Sasaki, *Zen Dust: The History of the Kōan and Kōan Study in Rinzai (Lin-chi) Zen* (New York: Harcourt, Brace and World, 1966).

ZZ   *Dainihon Zoku Zōkyō* (Kyoto: 1905–12).

PART I

Methodological Issues

ONE

Text and Untext

On the Significance of Kōans

Introduction to the Two Texts

In considering Dōgen's relation to the kōan tradition, a number of conflicting perspectives must be confronted. First, Dōgen, who is generally known as a strong critic of kōans, emphasized the importance of zazen-only and referred to kōan training as misguided and deficient. Yet, Dōgen is also cited as playing a central role in introducing kōans to Japan, and it is said that he brought back to his native country the first copy of the most prominent kōan collection, the *Hekiganroku*, which he copied in a single night just before his return from China as the epitome of what he had studied there. Second, Dōgen's *Shōbōgenzō* is prized for its philosophical commentary on Buddhist doctrines written in Japanese, mainly in the period in the early and mid-1240s as he was leaving the Kyoto area and was settling in the Echizen mountains. But Dōgen also composed another text known as *Shōbōgenzō* that is a collection of three hundred kōan cases without commentary culled from Chinese Zen texts and written in Chinese in 1235 while he was still in Kyoto. Third, the Chinese monk Ta-hui was the main target of Dōgen's criticisms of what had gone wrong with Buddhism in Sung China primarily because he was the foremost proponent of kōan practice that was based on the teachings of his master, Yüan-wu, compiler of the *Hekiganroku* (hereafter HR), and that continued to spread to Japan and Korea. However, Ta-hui also apparently opposed the excessive use of kōans, and he is said to have burned in protest the xylographs of the HR so that it was lost in China for nearly two hundred years. Fourth, the aim of kōan

3

training is to foster a psychological process of suppressing and transcending ordinary consciousness and language to realize a nonconceptual truth without reliance on words. Yet, kōans can also be interpreted as rhetorical devices or literary symbols that utilize fully the resources of language in highly creative and original ways indicating that verbal expression supports rather than obstructs the attainment of Zen enlightenment. Fifth, Zen writings containing kōan cases express an essentially demythological standpoint that takes an irreverent, iconoclastic attitude toward Buddhist rituals and symbols. But many of the same Zen works are also highly mythical and hagiographical in their accounts of the lives of the leaders of the sect, and kōans themselves often seem to function in the Zen monastic institution as basically ritual exercises seemingly devoid of philosophical meaning.

Dealing with these conflicting perspectives raises fundamental questions in Dōgen studies and Zen studies as a whole: What is the nature and function of a kōan? Is it a psychological device that defeats language or a literary tool that fosters textuality? What is Dōgen's attitude toward kōans and kōan interpretation in Zen training? Does he really intend to support or refute the use of kōans? The complex hermeneutic context underlying this set of questions is highlighted in considering Dōgen's novel, even radical, reinterpretation of one of the most famous kōan cases, Bodhidharma's "skin, flesh, bones, and marrow." The original case cited by Dōgen deals with the first Chinese patriarch's process of selecting his successor from among his top four disciples. The dialogue first appears in the seminal Sung Chinese Zen work, the *Keitoku Dentōroku* (hereafter KD), which traces the "transmission of the lamp" of patriarchal succession beginning with the seven primordial buddhas culminating in Śākyamuni and continuing through and beyond the first and sixth patriarchs in China. Prior to the KD version, there were over half a dozen less embellished versions of the tale in earlier texts, with some of these referring to only three disciples and all of them lacking the full dialogue.[1] Dōgen cites the Bodhidharma dialogue as case no. 201 in his Chinese collection, and he comments extensively on it in the "Kattō" fascicle of the Japanese *Shōbōgenzō*. He also mentions it in the "Ōsakusendaba" fascicle and in several lectures included in the *Eihei Kōroku* (hereafter EK) collection.

This Bodhidharma dialogue is particularly significant because it seems to epitomize the fundamental view of kōans and of the role of language in general that is held not only by the first patriarch but by the mainstream of Zen thought from the classical period to the present based on the ideal of a "special transmission outside the teachings (or scriptures)" (*kyōge betsuden*). According to the source dialogue, Bodhidharma, sensing that his time has come, asks his disciples to succinctly state their understanding of the Dharma. The first three disciples use some kind of metaphorical or philosophical expression, and the master's response is that they express, in succession, his "skin," his "flesh," and his "bones," thereby indicating a progression of understanding from superficiality to depth, or from exteriority to interiority, that still falls somewhat short of disclosing the ultimate truth. The final disciple, Hui-k'o, who in another dialogue is said to have begun his training under Bodhidharma by demonstrating his commitment to Zen by cutting off his arm as "heaven sends down a snow," bows three times and remains silent. Bodhidharma responds, "You express my marrow," apparently granting approval of the deepest and most interior level of understanding to Hui-k'o, who in traditional accounts goes on to become the second patriarch. Thus, according to conventional interpretations, silence prevails over speech, and there is a clear distinction and sense of hierarchy concerning the first three and the last of the disciples. Therefore, the kōan, and by implication all discourse and uses of language, functions as a dispensable tool of psychological transformation, or as a trigger mechanism for spiritual insight that has no validity in and of itself. By culminating in the termination of discourse the dialogue creates a double-bind that forces language, as well as the ego sustained by it, to "expend itself and actualize its ultimate limit not in terms of its external failures or impossibilities, but in terms of its inner structural antimony."[2]

However, Dōgen challenges and reverses this reading of the kōan on several grounds. First, he argues for the *equalization* of each of the four responses as fully valid expressions of the Dharma if interpreted in the appropriate context and, while allowing for provisional distinctions, he refutes any final sense of hierarchy or superiority: "You should realize," he writes, "that the first patriarch's expression 'skin, flesh, bones, and marrow' does not refer to the superficiality or depth [of understanding]. Although there may remain a [provisional] distinction between superior and inferior understanding, [each of the four disciples] expresses the first patriarch in his entirety."[3] Furthermore, Dōgen maintains, in contrast to an exclusive emphasis on the priority of silence, that language is a necessary and effective means of conveying the Dharma. He reinterprets the term *kattō* (literally "vines," but by implication "entanglements," "complications," or "word-tangles"), which is often understood as an illusion and therefore an impediment to enlightenment, to suggest a *self-entangling/dis-entangling vehicle* for expressing spiritual realization that is never free from the need to be expressed:

> Generally, although all Buddhist sages in their training study how to cut off entanglements (*kattō*) at their root, they do not study how to cut off entanglements by using entanglements. They do not realize that entanglements entangle entanglements. How little do they know what it is to transmit entanglements in terms of entanglements. How rarely do they realize that the transmission of the Dharma is itself an entanglement.[4]

In numerous examples, Dōgen's characteristically unconventional interpretations of traditional cases are frequently aimed at defeating their author's apparent intentions in the belief that all expressions are fair game for the creative interpreter. In another interesting rereading of the tradition, he subverts a kōan almost always seen as advocating a classic pro-kōan/anti-zazen position so that it takes on a reverse meaning supporting meditation. Based on a KD anecdote, Nan-yüeh likens his disciple Ma-tsu's practicing zazen in order to become a buddha to the futility of polishing a tile to create a mirror, apparently to point out the limitation of meditation as a gradual means of attaining enlightenment.[5] Dōgen, who in contrast to the tradition maintains that Ma-tsu is already enlightened *before rather than after* the dialogue begins,[6] subverts and remythologizes this understanding by arguing that the act of polishing does create a mirror, just as zazen brings about a realization of the potential illumination of Buddha-nature. "We truly know," he writes, "that when we make a mirror by polishing a tile, Ma-tsu becomes a buddha. When Ma-tsu becomes a buddha, Ma-tsu immediately becomes Ma-tsu. When Ma-tsu becomes Ma-tsu, zazen immediately becomes zazen."[7] Dōgen argues that the kōan legitimates his view of zazen as the method of "practice in realization" (*shōjō no shu*) and thus can be interpreted as refuting the very point it is supposed to establish concerning the prioritizing of kōans in relation to zazen. However, such a reversal of meaning or contradictory interpretation represents the kind of self-subverting process that typifies and enhances the kōan tradition even as it criticizes the standard understanding of one of the cases.

What do these examples indicate about Dōgen's view of kōans? Is he supporting or denying their usefulness? It is clear that Dōgen frequently cites kōans and uses them as the basis for articulating a philosophy of Zen.

Yet it is also apparent that he often deliberately deviates from the standard interpretation. But then the question becomes, How is the standard view established, and where is the line drawn between convention and deviation? Dōgen's view is that the kōan as the raw material for philosophical commentary related to religious praxis has an innate flexibility and open-endedness of utility that does not stand in contrast to but derives from within the very rhetorical structure of the source dialogue itself to generate diverse and multidimensional implications. He seems to suggest that the kōan should be seen not as a psychological tool that brings one to a labyrinthine impasse based on the paradoxicality of speech and silence, but as a *discursive means of generating shifting, self-displacing (and thereby self-correcting) parallactical perspectives.*

In recent years, modern scholarship has begun rewriting much of the history of Zen Buddhist thought and institutional development by reexamining many of the stereotypical conflicts in a way that is free of sectarian polarization and traditional polemics. In the case of Dōgen, the stereotypical view of his support for zazen in opposition to Ta-hui's defense of kōans has been called into question, particularly in light of recent discoveries of medieval manuscripts of Dōgen's Chinese *Shōbōgenzō*, also known as the *Shōbōgenzō Sanbyakusoku* (or collection of three hundred kōans), long considered apocryphal. The Chinese text is now seen as a significant influence on Dōgen's Japanese *Shōbōgenzō*, which cites and interprets several hundred kōan cases in its philosophical discussions. According to Manabe Shunshō, co-editor with Kawamura Kōdō of an extraordinary new forty-one-volume "photo-fascimile" edition (*ei-in-bon*) that contains three manuscripts each of the Chinese and Japanese *Shōbōgenzō* texts: "The text in [Japanese] *kana* syllables is a work related by Dōgen himself of his experience of profound enlightenment on the basis of the ancient principles of the Chinese text."[8] Therefore, the new understanding of the historical and interpretative relation between Dōgen's two *Shōbōgenzō* texts helps clarify an understanding of the importance of kōans in his teachings in a way that compels a rethinking and reevaluation of the unfolding of the entire kōan tradition, the history of which has generally been told without reference to Dōgen's approach.

Questioning the Conventional View

The central concern of this book is to provide an interpretation of the writings of Dōgen, particularly his two works known as *Shōbōgenzō* written in Chinese and in Japanese, in relation to the historical and philosophical development of the Zen kōan tradition during the T'ang and Sung eras in China. As founder of Sōtō Zen in Kamakura era Japan, Dōgen traveled to China to study Zen for four years (1223–27) and ultimately to attain enlightenment under the guidance of his mentor, Sōtō master Ju-ching, who was known for his strict adherence to meditation and refutation of kōan studies. According to his traditional biographies and other sources, Dōgen rejected studying with Rinzai priests before being instructed by Ju-ching that the only way to attain enlightenment in Zen training is through just-sitting or zazen-only (*shikantaza*).[9] In several passages of his writings Dōgen explicitly refutes the use of kōans, and he is at times harshly critical of the Chinese priest Ta-hui, a leading Rinzai proponent of kōans known for his approach emphasizing the exclusive use of "head-words" (*watō*) or main phrases extracted from traditional kōan cases. Ta-hui's teacher, Yüan-wu, compiled the most prestigious of the Sung kōan collections, the HR. Therefore, Dōgen is generally associated with a pro-zazen and anti-kōan standpoint that seems antithetical to and isolated from the mainstream of the kōan tradition. When Dōgen does deal in his writings with the issue of the meaning and importance of the kōan, he seems to prefer the doctrine of *genjōkōan* (spontaneous manifestation of the kōan in concrete activities) to the Rinzai approach known as *kanna-zen* (introspecting the kōan), which involves examining and contemplating *kosoku-kōan* (old sayings or paradigmatic cases) included in kōan collections.

The linchpin of the conventional view of the tradition is that there is a diametrical opposition between two approaches that emerged by the southern Sung/early Kamakura period: Ta-hui's iconoclastic attitude toward language and thought following the ideal of Zen as a "special transmission outside the teachings (or scriptures)," and the view that seems to be supported by Dōgen of continuing hermeneutic reflection on scripture, sometimes referred to as the "oneness of Zen and teachings (or scriptures)" (*kyōzen itchi*) as seen from the standpoint of sustained zazen meditation. However, while there is no question that Dōgen and Ta-hui were quite different and even opposed in many respects, the context of interrelations between Dōgen, Ta-hui, the HR, as well as numerous other key Zen texts and thinkers of this period is quite complex and indicates that the stereotypical polarization is misleading. A close look at Dōgen's life and teachings reveals that he did have a strong connection to kōans and kōan collections in several ways. For example, there is a tradition that it was Dōgen himself who introduced to Japan the HR, which he is said to have copied in a single night just before leaving China to return home. Even if reports of the "one-night HR" (*Ichiya Hekiganroku*) (hereafter IH) are legendary or mistaken, it is clear that Dōgen's main philosophical work, the ninety-two fascicle *Shōbōgenzō* written in Japanese, is thoroughly grounded in the use of kōans.[10] The *Shōbōgenzō* consists of novel interpretations, sometimes in several different versions, of dozens of kōans attributed to masters who were leaders of the tradition, including some of the most famous cases like Chao-chou's "*Mu*" and "oak tree in the garden," Te-shan's "rice cake," Ma-tsu's "polishing the tile," Bodhidharma's "skin, flesh, bones, marrow," and Pai-chang's "fox." Furthermore, the standard hermeneutic procedure in Dōgen's Japanese *Shōbōgenzō* is to justify philosophical arguments by citing, often with critical, interlinear commentary in a way that resembles the hermeneutic style of kōan collections like the HR, the sayings of prominent Zen masters that served as the source material for kōan cases. The Japanese *Shōbōgenzō* relies heavily on standard Sung era Zen texts, especially the KD and the *Shūmon Rentōeyō* (hereafter SR) as well as the recorded sayings of Ta-hui, Hung-chih, Ju-ching, and Yüan-wu for its references and citations.

In addition, recent scholarship has demonstrated the authenticity of Dōgen's own collection of three hundred kōan cases for centuries regarded as spurious, the *Shōbōgenzō Sanbyakusoku*, also referred to as the *Mana* or *Shinji Shōbōgenzō* (*Shōbōgenzō* in Chinese) (hereafter MS) to distinguish it from the *Kana* or *Kaji Shōbōgenzō* (*Shōbōgenzō* in Japanese) (hereafter KS). The MS text, which may have been very important for the training of monks at Eiheiji temple in Dōgen's lifetime and for a substantial period thereafter, was apparently kept in limited circulation in several Sōtō branch temples from the Muromachi period to the Tokugawa period, and was not known even by many leaders of the sect. In the mid-1700s a version of the *Sanbyakusoku* was discovered and commented on with prose commentary by a Sōtō scholastic, Shigetsu Ein, and it was published posthumously with additional commentary by his disciple, Honkō Katsudō, who was well-known for his own KS commentaries.[11] The Shigetsu/Honkō text, the *Nempyō Sanbyakusoku Funogo* (hereafter NS), was actually produced, somewhat ironically, at a time when the general atmosphere of sectarian polarization between the Rinzai kōan and Sōtō zazen methods was escalating. However, the NS *Sanbyakusoku* along with a subsequent Edo poetic commentary, the *Sanbyakusoku Juko* (from 1787 by Taigen Ryōnin) gained considerable popularity among Sōtō followers and became prominent texts within the sect well into modern times. Yet many Dōgen specialists were still unwilling to accept the authenticity of the *Sanbyakusoku*, largely because its existence tended to contradict the standard image of Dōgen's approach to Zen practice as being fundamentally anti-kōan. The general attitude was that since Dōgen did not value kōan practice he could not have been involved in compiling a kōan collection. Consequently, the main Tokugawa commentaries on the MS were not included in the early twentieth century major collections of the Sōtō sect.[12]

Then, in 1934, the earliest known manuscript containing a portion of the *Sanbyakusoku* dating back to 1287 was discovered by the library of the Kanazawa Bunko Buddhist Institute, where a number of classical Buddhist texts have been found.[13] The Kanazawa text (hereafter KB) contains only the *chūkan* section (cases no. 101 to 200), or the middle of three sections containing one hundred cases each; the first and third sections as well as the preface (*jobun*) are not available in the KB. Although it is incomplete and differs in the exact wording and sequence of some cases from the NS text, the existence of the KB text confirmed that the MS was extant as early as the Kamakura era, and it thus reawakened speculation about the status of Dōgen's kōan collection. The real breakthrough, however, came during the 1980s, when Kawamura Kōdō, a professor at Komazawa University in Tokyo researching textual and historical issues in the formation of Dōgen's Japanese KS text, discovered three complete printed manuscripts of the *Sanbyakusoku* from the Muromachi era (each contained three sections of one hundred cases plus the preface), as well as what appeared to be a Tokugawa period handwritten version of the NS text.[14] There are several important historical questions remaining concerning the status of the Chinese MS text, which will be discussed in the final section of Chapter 3. Yet Kawamura's examination of the Muromachi versions of the MS in comparison with the KB and NS manuscripts, and in light of the KS and Dōgen's collected writings as a whole, has made an exceptionally strong case supporting the view that the *Sanbyakusoku* was a genuine Dōgen text.

According to the studies of Dōgen specialists Kawamura, Ishii Shūdō, Kagamishima Genryū, as well as other scholars of Japanese Zen, including Yanagida Seizan, who have been studying the relation between the two *Shōbōgenzō* texts, the *Sanbyakusoku* was probably compiled by Dōgen in Chinese around 1235 or during his stay at Kōshōji temple in Uji outside Kyoto. This was the period about eight years after Dōgen returned to Japan but before he began composing most of the fascicles that came to form the more prominent Japanese KS, one of the first works of Buddhism in Japan to be written in the vernacular. The title for these main works by

Dōgen—the *Mana* and the *Kana Shōbōgenzō* (Treasury of the True Dharma-Eye, C. *Cheng-fa yen-tsang*), as well as the *Shōbōgenzō Zuimonki* (hereafter SZ)—was apparently borrowed from the title of Ta-hui's kōan collection of over six hundred and fifty cases.[15] Unlike the HR and other prominent Sung Chinese kōan collections, Dōgen's Chinese MS is a listing of cases without any interpretation. Kawamura and Ishii maintain that Dōgen's Japanese work consisting primarily of philosophical essays must now be evaluated in terms of its relation to the Chinese compilation of paradigmatic cases. Each considers several possibilities about the relationship between the two texts. For example, it is quite likely that the KS was created initially to provide prose commentary on, and thus it grew directly out of the Chinese collection. As Kawamura observes:

> After the compilation of this *Shōbōgenzō Sanbyakusoku* in Chinese literary style, Dōgen Zenji began to write many chapters of *Shōbōgenzō* in *kana* successively. So the existence of the former, the *Sanbyakusoku*, began to be overshadowed by the latter, the *Shōbōgenzō* in *kana*, and gradually [the former] was transmitted [only] among a very limited number of people.[16]

According to Kawamura and Ishii, the MS was a preparatory work eventually used as notes or memos for the composition of the KS, which was written over a span of twenty years, from 1231 ("Bendōwa") to just before Dōgen's death in 1253 ("Hachidainingaku"). During the years that the KS was still being produced by Dōgen, the MS may have been given to new acolytes at Eiheiji temple as a textbook for their Zen studies until they were ready to tackle the more challenging philosophical work, the KS. Another possibility is that the MS represented a crystallization—without the need for extensive commentary—of the ideas expressed in the KS.

This debate to a large extent revolves around two factors: the status of the preface to the MS, which is not included in the Kanazawa text so that its authenticity is still questioned, and the otherwise rather obscure *Shūmon Tōyōshū* (hereafter ST) text. According to Ishii, the ST was the single main source contributing over one-third of the cases in the MS, but it was also apparently a relatively minor influence on the KS text especially when compared to other Sung texts, such as the KD, that are cited in the MS.[17] However, the overriding point is that Kawamura and Ishii demonstrate convincingly that the composition of the Chinese text highlights the way in which the Japanese KS text fundamentally and extensively draws upon Sung Chinese kōan collections and commentaries. According to Ishii, the KS reflects the fact that "Dōgen's thought is part of a continuum of Sung Chinese Zen thought," and it should be studied as another though distinctive text in the series of T'ang and Sung Zen kōan texts that include, among others, the *Hōrinden* (801), *Keitoku Dentōroku* (1004), *Setchō* (C. *Hsüeh-tou*) *Juko Hyakusoku* (1026), *Shūmon Tōyōshū* (1133), *Engo* (C. *Yüan-wu*) *Goroku* (1136), *Shūmon Rentōeyō* (1183), and *Wanshi* (C. *Hung-chih*) *Kōroku* (1201), among others.[18] Kawamura, who tends to see some of these texts, especially the KD and the SR, as more influential on the MS than the ST, strongly agrees that in either case Dōgen was steeped in reading and interpreting a remarkably wide variety of Sung era sources.

Based on these findings several conclusions become clear supporting the depth of Dōgen's involvement in the kōan tradition. First, the authenticity of Dōgen's kōan collection shows the importance of kōans in his thought and writings, especially during the first ten or twelve years after his return from China. Second, the two *Shōbōgenzō* texts very much depend upon and reinforce one another, so that the Japanese work can only be understood properly in connection to or as initially deriving from and eventually overshadowing the Chinese text. Third, Dōgen played a great role in introducing and disseminating the voluminous Sung Zen literature containing kōans and kōan commentaries, including recorded sayings texts and transmission of the lamp histories, into early medieval Japan. He developed the literary style of the KS, which departs from the Chinese textual models, as a way of accomplishing this task quickly and effectively in response to Japanese cultural and religious influences. Both of Dōgen's *Shōbōgenzō* texts—in addition to the ninth chapter of his *Eihei Kōroku* collection (hereafter EK-9), which contains verse commentaries on ninety traditional kōan cases (over two-thirds of these are included in the MS)— must be seen in terms of their interrelatedness, not only to each other, but to the kōan tradition from which they sprang. Therefore, the MS text's real significance is not only for Dōgen studies and Dōgen's approach to kōans, but for an understanding of the kōan tradition itself. The MS represents a bridge between Dōgen and the kōan tradition. As a "missing link" in the connection between Sung and Kamakura, and Rinzai and Sōtō Zen, the MS also functions as a window opening up a very different view of what the development of kōans from their origin in the T'ang era to their flourishing in the Sung era was like, now seen from a perspective no longer excluding but rather pointing to Dōgen's hermeneutical approach. In fact, Dōgen's method of interpreting kōans in the KS, understood in light of the MS and its relation to Sung texts, can be interpreted as a logical outcome

and perhaps even a culminating stage in the formation of kōans as a Zen
literary genre.

At the same time that Dōgen's role is reevaluated, it is important to
recognize that Ta-hui's attitude toward kōans is much more complex, and
perhaps not nearly as favorable or supportive as it first appears. Ta-hui was
a tremendously important figure in the twelfth century who had a great
impact on the development of Rinzai Zen in China, Japan, and Korea. He
was an extremely innovative and prolific author who, in addition to
proposing the *watō* "shortcut" method and writing extensive collections of
recorded sayings and kōan commentaries, developed two Zen genres primarily aimed at laypersons: sermons (*fusetsu*) used as a way of preaching
the Dharma during times of mourning or other personal hardships; and
letters (*tegami*) of instruction pedagogically suited to the particular person's
situation and level of learning. While he lectured and wrote extensively
on kōans, Ta-hui is said to have burned the HR out of fear that it would
lead to a rigid formalization of Zen instruction. Even if that report is fictive,
Ta-hui's central doctrine of citing only the main phrase of cases suggests
that the basic content of kōans and kōan commentaries is superfluous and
even counter-productive for his method of training, which leads to the
suppression of ordinary consciousness.

Ta-hui and Dōgen in the twelfth and thirteenth centuries, respectively, appeared toward the end of the classical period of the development
of kōans that is said to have had its roots in the sayings and dialogues of
the eminent Zen masters of the eighth and ninth centuries. They were
equally eager to restore a lost sense of spontaneity and vitality to the kōan
tradition, so that these leaders of Chinese Rinzai and Japanese Sōtō cannot
be appropriately understood as standing for monolithic ideologies that
somehow co-existed in polarized and antithetical fashion. The historicity
of the accounts that Ta-hui burned and that Dōgen copied the HR may
well be in doubt. Yet the irony in the symbolism that the supposed
proponent destroyed while the avowed critic salvaged the main kōan text
cannot be unnoticed. In some ways Dōgen's KS *Shōbōgenzō* is closer in style
and content to the seminal kōan texts, including the HR and *Mumonkan*
(hereafter MMK), than are some of Ta-hui's writings. It is probably these
issues involving the overlooked connections as well as the overemphasized
discrepancies between Dōgen, Ta-hui, and kōan collections that prompted
Taizan Maezumi, a contemporary Sōtō abbot in America who has used
kōans extensively as a training method, to comment in his preface to an
English translation of the HR that there is "an unfortunately widespread

impression nowadays that Dōgen Zenji and the Sōtō School represent a non-kōan or even anti-kōan orientation within Zen. In fact, nothing could be further from the truth."[19] Maezumi and others have been calling for a reorientation of our understanding and appreciation of Dōgen's work in relation to the practices of zazen meditation and kōan studies.

Postmodernism and Zen Discourse

The single, overriding issue in modern Dōgen studies has been an examination of the nature and significance of the Japanese KS, including textual and historical topics concerning how and when it was written and compiled in relation to Chinese Buddhist thought and medieval Japanese religion, as well as philological and philosophical concerns dealing with the value and impact of its use of language and literary symbolism for religious life and spiritual attainment. As Heinrich Dumoulin writes, "The Japanese Shōbōgenzō shows a fluency of style of unmistakable uniqueness. Dogen's thought is branded with his own language. Even when he takes over expressions from colloquial Chinese of the Sung period, he renders them in Japanese constructions suited to his own style. He labored for special effects through the repetition of certain expressions and a liberality of grammar and syntax."[20] Dōgen's text needs to and frequently has been studied from a variety of methodologies and perspectives to evaluate the full range of religious, literary, and cultural factors impacting on its formation. For example, the KS has been analyzed in terms of how it absorbs and reflects influences from Japanese Buddhism, literature, aesthetics, and views of nature in addition to Chinese Buddhist doctrines of Buddha-nature, time, or meditation. Furthermore, methodologies in Dōgen studies range from positivist historiography and linguistic studies to comparisons with modern Japanese or European phenomenological and analytic philosophy.[21] The aim here is to draw on recent Japanese scholarship on the relation between the two Shōbōgenzō texts, which demonstrates the great importance kōans had for Dōgen's writings and approach to Zen. Without overlooking the many other angles from which the KS can be viewed, the current study seeks to situate and highlight the creation and the use of language in Dōgen's text in terms of the role of kōans and kōan collections in twelfth- and thirteenth-century China and Japan.

Therefore, the significance of this topic is to carry out a reconsideration of the conventional view in sectarian and modern studies that one-sidedly stresses Dōgen's rejection and tends to obscure his profound relation to the kōan tradition. Revising the standard interpretation of Dōgen's approach to kōans necessarily involves reexamining and rethinking the kōan tradition itself, because its history is generally explained in a way that excludes Dōgen since he is seen as one of its main detractors rather than participants. That is, a work on Dōgen's understanding of the meaning and function of kōans must at the same time be a study of the philosophical, literary, and psychological implications in kōan collections and kōan training in Zen as a whole. This issue involves clarifying why Dōgen has been defined as standing outside the tradition and in opposition to Ta-hui in terms of the historically and culturally rooted differences between these thinkers, despite their use of common textual materials and sources. One of the key points is to lead the discussion away from the polarity of Dōgen vs. Ta-hui, or at least to explain the relative appropriateness of this contrast, and toward an appreciation of the affinities between the KS *Shōbōgenzō* and kōan collections, including the HR and MMK in addition to the kōan commentaries in the recorded sayings of Ta-hui and other Sung thinkers. Accomplishing this requires, in turn, examining the origins of the kōan tradition in T'ang era dialogues and recorded sayings in order to see how a number of divergent styles for presenting and interpreting the source dialogues emerged during the Sung period. Thus, rewriting the history of Dōgen Zen is a matter of rewriting the history of kōan Zen, and vice versa, to demonstrate how these areas of study are interconnected in many crucial respects concerning views of language in relation to religious practice and enlightenment.

On "Discourse Analysis"

The interpretive method that will be used in this study is referred to as a "discourse analysis," which incorporates some of the main categories of postmodern literary criticism and intellectual history. These categories include intertextuality and genre criticism, which pertain to the formation and organization of interrelated yet distinctive styles of texts, and narrative theory and tropology, which help disclose the function and meaning of a text's rhetorical images and ideals.[22] Discourse analysis, the categories of which will be explained more fully near the end of Chapter 2, focuses on the historical context and literary implications in the ways that Zen, as a religious tradition, has created a cluster of linguistic and visual symbols as well as symbolic actions—or discourse—to communicate its vision of spiritual fulfillment. Discourse refers to an historically determined totality of utterances and references, signifiers and significations that appear in oral and written form constituting texts.[23] Rather than echo the partisan polemics and apologetics of the kōan vs. zazen, or Rinzai vs. Sōtō debates that all too often cloud an appreciation of the development of Zen, the ultimate goal of discourse analysis is to formulate a methodology that goes beyond a sense of Dōgen's "relation" to kōans in a way that assumes that these are separate and independent texts. The aim is to make use of postmodern notions of the insubstantiality of author, the inseparability of creator and audience, and the intertextuality linking the formation of texts, in order to demonstrate a profound interdependence of the texts of Dōgen and the kōan tradition.

Discourse analysis takes a different approach than and has several advantages over the two prevalent Western models of interpreting Zen kōans: psychology or psychotherapy, and comparative philosophy of mysticism. A key difference involves the way that these other methods focus on the mind, or the internal, mental processes involved in the attainment of enlightenment. Psychology and mysticism generally presuppose bifurcations between self and other, mind and reality, conscious and unconscious, or sacred and secular, such that one category is deemed to have priority over its polar opposite. For example, Erich Fromm finds a parallel between psychoanalysis and the function of kōans in that both attempt therapeutically to "make the unconscious conscious."[24] D. T. Suzuki, in comparing Zen and Christian mysticism, notes affinities between Zen's notion of intuitive wisdom (Skt. *prajñā*) and Christian conceptions of the trinity, particularly in Meister Eckhart's view of the ultimate human experience as being one with "the love with which God loves himself." According to Suzuki, these words referring to the mystic's union with God and final full identification with the divine perspective "sound unfamiliar to Buddhist ears but when they are read with a certain insight we will find [they are the] same [as enlightenment]."[25] Postmodern criticism, however, stemming from the disciplines of semiotics, poststructuralism, and deconstruction, primarily examines the role of language and symbols in terms of the form and function conditioning the way texts are generated and come to be interrelated. For example, Jacques Derrida tries to subvert conventional bifurcations when he maintains that "nothing exists outside of the text"[26]— an holistic, non-logocentric approach that appears to be in accord with the nondualistic foundations of Zen philosophy. Also, the postmodern notion of intertextuality, which argues that every text is a "mosaic of citations . . . the absorption and transformation of other texts,"[27] suggests the possibility of a nonhierarchical and decentric means of explaining the mutuality of influences and reverberating reactions within the Zen tradition. Thus, psychotherapy and comparative mysticism highlight the development and transformation of the "self," or a profound subjectivity that presupposes a contrast between subject and object. Postmodernism, on the other hand, discloses the "*stereographical plurality* of the signifiers that weave [the text]," which is entirely open-ended and dynamically created, and "must not be thought of as a defined object,"[28] for it is beyond the subject/object dichotomy.

Another methodological difference is that when psychotherapy and mysticism are applied to comparative studies, they tend to be somewhat ahistorical in taking up cross-cultural representatives of thought without regard for sequence or diachronic determination. For example, they may harbor an implicit assumption that a medieval Chinese or Japanese Zen thinker can be compared to a post-Reformation Christian mystic or to a contemporary psychotherapist without taking into account fully the relevant historical discrepancies. This often results in an uncritical acceptance of the romanticized and mythologized hagiographies that are pervasive in Zen chronicles apparently under the guise of biography.[29] Discourse analysis, on the other hand, tries to be sensitive to the view expressed by Foucault and others that modes of discourse are never far removed from bids for power and approval, and are therefore very much historically conditioned. According to Edward Said, "Too many exceptions, too many historical, ideological, and formal circumstances implicate the text in actuality. . . . Texts are a system of forces institutionalized at some expense by the reigning culture, not an ideal cosmos of ideally equal [writings]."[30] Discourse analysis is also responsive to recent developments in historiographical studies that have questioned the veracity of Zen's own historical accounts. It therefore takes a neutral stance toward the truth-claims that are posited by a tradition by seeking through an archaeology of knowledge, which deals with the way that ideologies are shaped by social, political, and economic concerns, to uncover amidst levels of sedimentation the *fundamental literary structure of the texts* in question. This structure consists of two interconnected components which in tandem establish the literary symbolism of religious texts: *narratology*, or the use of narrative elements involving temporal sequencing and character development contributing to a sacred emplotment that depicts the historical development of the sect and its leading personalities; and *tropology*, or the use of rhetoric and wordplay— the "tropics of discourse,"[31] including metaphor, metonymy, synechdoche, and irony—to create a base of philosophical insight that stimulates spiritual awakening and enhances the experience of religious freedom. Discourse analysis, therefore, looks holistically (that is, intertextually) at the major trends in Zen theory and practice in the appropriate time frame— eighth- to thirteenth-century China and Japan—out of which Dōgen's KS and other interpretations of kōans emerged as literary variations on a common spiritual theme of attaining and expressing Zen enlightenment. It asks how the similarities and differences in the literary forms of these works reflect underlying affinities and disparities in religious conviction.

A key advantage of discourse analysis is that it seeks to be more open-ended than other methodologies that have portrayed kōans almost exclusively in terms of the function of silence and abbreviation informing the choice of words used in the dialogical exchanges between master and disciple. Psychotherapy and mysticism are very useful but also somewhat problematic methodologies in this regard. In defining kōans as a form of abbreviated, paradoxical communication harboring an underlying silence and rejection of language and leading to a personal transformation from conscious to unconscious, or from a state of diffusion to unification with the sacred, these interpretive methods often fail to come fully to grips with how the multifaceted significance of language and symbols contribute to the way that kōans accomplish their religious aims or contribute to the goal of spiritual liberation. An emphasis on the priority of silence has been so strong and pervasive that it has greatly influenced most of the psychological-mystical, or self-oriented, as well as many of the literary-historical, or text-oriented, accounts of the history and meaning of kōans. For example, Suzuki and Garma Chang, among others, have categorized kōan rhetoric as being deliberately "irrational," "illogical," and "nonsensical." Also John McRae maintains that "ineffability" is the key to the Zen dialogues. "Ch'an is more emphatic," he writes, "than any other Buddhist School in its position that the ultimate goal of religious practice cannot be understood with words. Elsewhere [in Buddhist thought] this ineffability is taken to mean that the words of the scriptures point at some higher, more abstract truth, but in Ch'an those very words are perceived as impediments to understanding."[32] In a genre critical account of recorded sayings (goroku), Judith Berling argues that Zen discourses are "puzzling because their stance toward language is that all thought, all language or silence, all conventional ways of communicating and responding are incapable of conveying the substance of Zen."[33] This conclusion emphasizing ineffability and silence probably derives in part from a twofold tendency: first, an overreliance on

Ta-hui's shortcut *watō* approach, which is set up as the norm or standard by which to evaluate all other aspects of kōan studies leading up to or competing with it; and at the same time an almost complete neglect of the role of Dōgen's hermeneutics in interpreting kōans.

Part of the reason that some interpreters of Zen discourse emphasize exclusively the role of silence may be that they are overly informed by certain modern myths about supposedly unique features of Japanese (and East Asian) intellectual life and cultural identity, resulting in a vicious cycle of (mis)interpretation. In this trend, a traditional Zen notion such as *ishin-denshin* (mind-to-mind understanding without the need for external communication or words, i.e., "the less said the better") is first taken out of its Zen context for somewhat inappropriate or misleading reasons, such as to support the *nihonjinron* ("Japanism") thesis of Japanese uniqueness.[34] *Ishin-denshin* is applied to an understanding of modern Japanese society as being founded on silent communication, and from this contemporary vantage point it is projected retrospectively to interpreting various traditional literary phenomena, including kōans, that have actually helped inform the modern standpoint.[35] According to Roy Miller, when the myth, or "antimyth," that silence is the distinctive feature of Japanese expression is applied to problems in literary history and criticism (often stemming from Chinese sources), "it is not the texts themselves that are important. To [these critics], texts are valuable only because they represent 'violations of silence,'"[36] that is, interruptions or exceptions that somehow prove the rule of cultural uniformity.

Silence and abbreviation are indeed significant but simply do not exhaust all the levels of meaning in Zen discourse. For example, these forms of expression can be seen as contributing, along with ambiguity, ellipsis, and nonverbal gestures, to the function of the trope of irony. But it must be recognized that there are also numerous examples in kōans in which irony is challenged, undercut, or displaced within the bounds of discourse by a metonymic wordplay, as in Dōgen's frequent punning, or some other tropical mode, such as the metaphor of comparing *samādhi* to an ocean, the synechdoche of referring to the moon as Buddha-nature, or the deceptively non-literal mimetic, or tautological, assertion that "mountains are mountains." For example, Dale Wright argues that Zen claims like "no dependence or reliance on words or letters, or on language and text" (*furyū monji*) are themselves linguistically constituted, textually transmitted strategies of discourse aimed at explaining and initiating experiences they identify and categorize in Buddhist thought. Furthermore, he argues that "Far from

being a transcendence of language, this process would consist in a fundamental reorientation within language . . . [that] require[s] training to a
level of fluency in distinctive, nonobjectifying, rhetorical practices."[37]
Kōans utilize decentric signs and signifiers—or it could be said that *the
kōans themselves represent the process of the decentering of all signs*—so that
they function flexibly and provisionally as symbolic discourse without
reference to an absolute or transcendental Signified. When the kōan is
seen holistically in terms of the overall discourse of Zen, it becomes clear
that there are many aspects of literary symbolism other than paradox and
silence in operation. Zen discourse encompasses a kind of seamlessly woven
structure combining narratology stressing the trope of metaphor to depict
and legitimate the transmission of lineage as well as numerous other
tropological elements that deliberately subvert or reorient the mythical
narrative. Thus it is important to analyze the use of tropical discourse in
Zen dialogues and kōans as a whole in order to clarify more specifically the
contrast between Dōgen's emphasis on metonymic wordplay in interpreting kōan cases and Ta-hui's stress on silence as an example of irony.

Yet discourse analysis is intended to be complementary rather than in
conflict with other interpretive models, particularly psychotherapy. Both
approaches recognize how the dynamics of the interrelated psychological
and linguistic dimensions contribute to the effectiveness of the kōan as the
single main symbol of Zen enlightenment. Psychotherapy is useful in
describing the process of inner, psychological transformation, that is, the
experience of *satori* or "great death" (*taishi*) that takes place as a result of
using kōans, especially the *watō* method in which head-words catalytically
stimulate the "great doubt" (*taigi*) of anxiety and despair as a necessary
preparatory stage for awakening. Discourse analysis emphasizes the literary
devices such as metaphor and wordplay used in creating and disseminating
the kōans through various literary genres. On the other hand, some
approaches to postmodern criticism, including Lacan, Bloom, Kristeva,
and Ricoeur, also integrate key aspects of psychoanalytic theory, such as
the role of anxiety, oedipal confrontation, and emotional displacement, in
their studies of the complexities of the creative process of text formation.
For example, Lacan's work explains the relation between signifier and
signified as functioning parallel to the relation between conscious and
unconscious states. Bloom examines the role of anxiety and of the inevitability of oedipally generated misreading and rewriting in establishing an
author's originality in relation to the intertextual influences he or she has
absorbed from a mentor or other strong predecessors. Therefore, psycho-

therapy can be used in relation to discourse analysis to explain not only the attainment of Zen enlightenment, but some of the reasons for the discord and conflict between the diverse, often competing philosophical positions that claim to represent it.

Satori Dialogues in Relation to Sung Zen Genres

A central aim of discourse analysis is to examine the ways in which the choices reflected in a text concerning style and form announce its under-lying intentions. For example, decisions about whether to emphasize prose or poetry, autobiography/subjectivity or history/objectivity, or philosophy or mythology in making an argument or establishing a position can indicate the text's fundamental orientation. It is important to try to recognize how a literary style or genre reflects the relation between and value attached to orality and writing, individual interpretation and traditional ideology, liberalism and orthodoxy. Whether or not Ta-hui burned the xylographs of the HR, or Te-shan several centuries before him destroyed the copies of his prized *Diamond Sūtra* commentaries, the fact that these masters are said to have done so, and the narrative patterns in the way such assertions are made, become crucial indicators of the intentionality of the tradition.

In the case of Zen in Sung China, nearly all written texts present and interpret dialogues that were originally based on an oral context for which the mutuality of interacting participants leading to the realization of authentic subjectivity was decisive. Therefore, one of the most important points to keep in mind for an understanding of Dōgen's use of kōans is that the KS and the Sung era kōan collections appeared near the final stages of a long tradition of recording oral dialogues. Zen dialogues, according to traditional accounts, were initially spontaneous utterances attributed to T'ang era (eighth and ninth centuries) masters delivered in a specific existential context for the sake of liberating a disciple from a particular psychological fixation or philosophical delusion that impeded the quest for enlightenment. In the early Sung (eleventh and twelfth centuries) there were several important new genres of Zen literature attempting to trans-form oral utterances into written scriptures. The major kōan collections, which select and comment on paradigmatic cases culled from other textual materials of the period, include the HR, the *Shōyōroku* (hereafter SH), and the MMK. These were published in 1128, 1224, and 1229, respectively, though the first two works were initially composed nearly a century before (1026 and 1166) and then were reissued with amplified commentary by new editors/authors. The first text that can be considered a kōan collection was the *Fun'yō Roku* by Fen-yang (J. Fun'yō) in 1024 only twenty years after the most prominent transmission of the lamp history. The HR is a collection of one hundred cases with prose and poetic commentary first compiled by Hsüeh-tou in the early eleventh century with additional prose commentary, including some discussion of Hsüeh-tou's original remarks, supplied by Yüan-wu. The SH has a parallel structure and development, but was first compiled by Hung-chih, a Chinese Sōtō predecessor of Dōgen, and then further commented on by Wan-sung. The MMK contains briefer prose and poetic comments on forty-eight cases provided by a Rinzai monk, Mumon. Dōgen's MS text seems to fit into the mold of the kōan collections in that it represents a selection and listing of paradigmatic cases, but it obviously lacks the multileveled commentary that is characteristic of the prominent collections. One of the main subdivisions of the kōan collection genre involves the distinction between commentaries on old or paradigmatic (*ko*) cases (*soku*) that are written in either poetry (*juko*) or prose (*nenko*). While the main collections including the HR, SH, and MMK contain prose and poetic materials, the root of their interlinear commentary appears to be the *juko* style. The *nenko* style is the basis of Yüan-wu's *Gekisetsuroku* collection and of Hung-chih's *Shinekiroku* collection.

There were also two other main genres composed during the Sung era containing *satori* dialogues that served as sources for the kōan collection genre. One of the genres is "transmission of the lamp" histories (*dentōroku*) that trace the origin and development of the genealogy of the sect through several stages. The *dentōroku* texts begin with the seven primordial buddhas culminating in Śākyamuni, then continue through the twenty-eight Indian masters leading up to Bodhidharma, who was also the first patriarch in China, and go on to include the first six Chinese patriarchs leading up to Hui-neng, and conclude with the succession of fifteen or more generations of subsequent Chinese masters. Most of the main ingredients of the transmission theory, as well as many anecdotes concerning prominent Zen masters, were already present in T'ang works, such as the *Rekidai Hōbōki* (date uncertain but before 779) and especially the *Hōrinden* (801). However, these elements did not become popular until they were given systematic and comprehensive treatment in Sung transmission texts that were composed after the 845 suppression of Buddhism, including the *Sodōshū* (952) and especially the seminal lamp-transmission historical text, the KD. Shortly after the KD, there was a flurry of lamp histories, including the *Tenshō Kōtōroku* (1036), the *Kenchū Seikoku Zokutōroku* (1101), and the SR

(1183), in addition to numerous other works composed in the early Sung.[38] Dōgen's MS text was especially influenced by the KD and the ST (1133), an obscure Sung text which was probably a precursor of the more prominent SR.[39] Many of the *dentōroku* texts tend to replicate one another, but each contains some novel and unique materials (i.e., new or revised kōan cases) and stylistic features in terms of balancing historical concerns with a listing of paradigmatic cases. It is also important to note that the *dentōroku* genre is not static but tends to change by the twelfth century in the direction of putting a structural emphasis on the collecting of kōans rather than on biography. For example, section twenty-seven (out of thirty) of the KD switches from a strict lineage format to a collection of miscellaneous materials, including a listing of cases with prose and poetic commentaries.[40] Subsequent *dentōroku* texts, particularly the ST and SR, nearly abandon the twenty-eight patriarch theory altogether in favor of the recording of *kosoku-kōan*. The *Kenchū Seikoku Zokutōroku* text begins with the transmission theory, but sections two through twenty-six are devoted to kōan collections.

The third important Sung genre is "recorded sayings" (*goroku*), which contains the dialogues, sermons, legends, and biographical anecdotes attributed to a single master as collected by his disciples. A prominent example of this genre is the *Shike Goroku* (from the end of the tenth century) covering four masters in the Hung-chou school lineage: Ma-tsu, the founder, Pai-chang, Huang-po, and Lin-chi. In addition, there are independent versions of the *goroku* texts of each of these masters, as well as records of many other T'ang masters crucial to the kōan tradition, including Chao-chou and Tung-shan, in addition to Sung masters, such as Yüan-wu, Ta-hui, Hung-chih, and Ju-ching, among others. The *goroku* genre is quite diversified and complex, and it can be subdivided in several ways according to content and style. Some records of T'ang masters are primarily concerned with tracing lineage (*dentō*) and contain a biographical section that explains the master's training in relation to his teacher and disciples. Others emphasize individual (*kojin*) methods of instruction and are more concerned with philosophical commentary. The Lin-chi record is an example of a text that contains both philosophy and biographical materials; the story of the master's personal struggle to attain enlightenment is in the final section. The philosophical section of the *goroku* texts contain two kind of records: brief, formal lectures (*daisan* or *jōdō*) often dealing with kōan cases that were first presented by the Zen master to his disciples in the Dharma Hall (*hattō*);[41] and informal, lengthier, and more candid discussions of the implications in a specific case (shōsan or jishu)[42] for a select group of monks in the abbot's quarters (shitsunai or hōjō). According to the Zen-en Shingi (1103), the earliest remaining listing of rules for Sung Zen monasteries, the requirements for conducting jōdō and shōsan according to the monthly calendar are very strictly laid out. The jōdō, for which the master ascends (jō) the high or elevated Dharma seat in the great hall (dō) before the whole assembly of monks, must be held six times a month on specified days during daytime hours; and the shōsan is required at least six times on another schedule of specified days during the evening.[43]

Dōgen's EK and SZ texts, particularly the former, can be considered examples of the jōdō style of goroku. As in Sung goroku, most of the passages are introduced by the phrase "the master enters the Dharma Hall and ascends the hight seat," and they also have a rather short length and a formal ambience in terms of master-disciples relations that recalls the Chinese texts. But there is no clear, single model or precedent for the kinds of philosophical essays found in the KS. By the twelfth century—the time of Ta-hui and Hung-chih—there is a sense that much of the goroku material was beginning to be written down in advance of the oral delivery and edited by the masters themselves rather than only being recorded or gathered, often posthumously, by their disciples. The oral context or background for the sessions in which the shōsan were delivered—of either the disciples' asking advanced, challenging questions or expressing confusion or misunderstanding—was increasingly not preserved in the recorded material, so that the lectures often come across as unilateral presentations of ideas rather than mutual, existential exchanges. The KS can be compared in style to the shōsan or jishu, which have a rather open-ended and freewheeling exegetical approach to getting across the essential meaning of kōan cases to both advanced and confused students that resembles Dōgen's hermeneutics.[44] Indeed, the term jishu appears in the colophon of a majority of KS fascicles, which were probably first written by Dōgen as lecture notes and recorded by his main diciples, especially Ejō, at the end of his lecture and then further edited at least once each by Dōgen, Ejō, and other disciples such as Gien. Unlike the Sung goroku texts, Dōgen continued to edit and/or rewrite many of the KS fascicles throughout his career, apparently, according to Ejō's postscript to the "Hachidainingaku" fascicle, in hopes of creating a one hundred fascicle edition. There is some confusion today as to which version of the fascicles Dōgen really intended by the end of his life to be taken as the authentic one. There is also considerable debate about the number of fascicles, which in various editions can range from as few as twelve to twenty-eight, sixty, seventy-five, ninety-two, or to as many as ninety-five fascicles in the Tokugawa edition that attempted to be comprehensive by including all known KS writings. There are also editions representing various combinations of the other versions, such as one combining seventy-five and twelve fascicles or another version combining sixty and twenty-eight fascicles.[45]

The *goroku* genre as a whole puts more emphasis on philosophical interpretation of Zen dialogues and is less concerned with a systematic presentation of transmission theory than the *dentōroku* genre. Therefore it seems to stand somewhere between the *dentōroku* texts and the kōan collections. The kōan collections depend on both genres, citing cases from *dentōroku* with *goroku* style commentary. They were generally compiled around the same time as the texts of the other genres, and represent an alternative way of presenting and interpreting the source dialogues. In contrast to *goroku* texts, which were compiled as disciples tried to gather comprehensively all of their teacher's words, *the kōan collections reflect a master's deliberate decision to select and interpret specific dialogues*; this seems to be a major influence on the KS's interpretive style. When compared with kōan collections, the *dentōroku* as well as many of the *goroku* texts dealing with T'ang masters' lives can be considered narratives or chronicles that are primarily historical and biographical: the lamp histories trace genealogy in a refined, classical style, and the lineage-oriented recorded sayings focus on the life and teachings of remarkable individual masters using a more rustic, colloquial style.[46] Modern biographical studies of leading Zen masters, therefore, require investigating references scattered throughout both genres. For instance, it is not sufficient to look only at Lin-chi's recorded sayings to understand his life and teaching, for that text must be coordinated with numerous anecdotes about Lin-chi in *dentōroku* and *goroku* texts. Since these genres contain many examples of the dialogues used in kōan cases, they tend to complement and to be very closely intertextually connected with the kōan collections, which are primarily theoretical or philosophical texts that highlight the pedagogical significance of paradigmatic anecdotes with prose and poetic commentaries.

One way of sorting out the lines of continuity and discontinuity among the three genres is to divide them into two categories, which will be examined more fully in Chapter 4. The first category can be labelled *tōshi-roku*, or records of lamp history, which covers the texts that are primarily narratives or chronicles committed to transmission theory and recounting the lineage of sects and schools.[47] This category includes, among others, the KD from the *dentōroku* genre and the *Shike Goroku* from the *goroku* genre. The second category is labelled *kōan-roku*, or kōan records, and covers texts that are mainly concerned with preserving and/or interpreting *kosoku-kōan*. This category includes examples from all three genres; in addition to the kōan collections it includes many of the *goroku* texts of Sung masters that primarily contain *daisan* and *shōsan* lectures dealing with paradigmatic cases, and even some of the *dentōroku* texts, such as the ST and the *Kenchū Seikoku Zokutōroku*, that are more concerned with listing cases than with presenting lamp history.

In addition to the three major Sung Zen genres divided into two categories, as just described, there are still two other key genres of the period which contain *satori* dialogues and other exegetical materials often cited in kōan collections, but which are not as directly related to the kōan tradition as the *dentōroku* and *goroku* genres. One genre is monk biographies, the oldest of all the genres involving the T'ang dialogues that became prevalent in Sung texts. The biography genre dates back to the *Kōsōden* text of the pre-T'ang (519), which deals with many sorts of leaders and luminaries from other Buddhist sects in addition to the Zen lineage, including "translators, commentators, scholars, Vinaya-followers, masters of meditation, possessors of miraculous virtues, etc."[48] While the approach is somewhat more objectively historiographical than the lineage-transmission polemic found in the Zen chronicles, the *Kōsōden* also contains many legendary reports of magical or supernatural feats that sometimes filter into one of the other Zen genres.[49] Yanagida Seizan has traced the important transition from the two main early biography texts, the *Kōsōden* and its sequel, the *Zoku Kōsōden* (between 645 and 667), to the Sung version, the *Sō Kōsōden* (988). In the T'ang text Zen patriarchs play a limited role in relation to other Buddhist schools, so that even Bodhidharma is given only brief mention as a meditation master. But by the time of the Sung version, Zen had become the dominant sect in China, and the monk biography genre was significantly more devoted to Zen masters and had thus become closely connected to the transmission of the lamp literature.[50] The other genre that influences kōans is the poetry collections of Zen masters that were often integrated into one of the other literary forms. Often, the more lyrical Zen verse dealing with themes such as contemplation of nature or the relation between monastic life and aesthetic appreciation appeared as one of the main sections of a master's recorded sayings.[51] Also, didactic verse commentaries on traditional cases were used either independently or in combination with prose commentaries in the kōan collections, and in addition *satori* and death *gāthā* verses were used at appropriate junctures in the *dentōroku* portrayals of masters' lives.

As Yanagida has shown, the literary unit that forms the basis for the three main Sung genres—lamp histories, recorded sayings, and kōan collections—is the "transmission or *satori* dialogic exchange" (*kien-mondō*) (issues in translating and defining this key term will be discussed in Chapter 4). The Zen dialogue is a spontaneous face-to-face encounter apparently first associated with the teaching of Ma-tsu, and then perfected by his followers in the Hung-chou lineage, in which an enlightened master displays an uncanny knack for exposing and overcoming the conceptual impasse of a disciple, often by using a rhetorical device, such as homophone, punning, paradox, or non sequitur, or some nonverbal gesture such as the iconoclastic, anti-authoritarian "sticks and shouts" of Te-shan and Lin-chi.[52] The dialogues, which capture and convey the living word of orality expressing a realization beyond the *sūtras* or written texts, became the primary means of transmitting the Dharma from teacher to pupil, and thus the link of continuity binding the tradition over the course of generations. The dialogues form the basis of kōans, which isolate and highlight a key passage in the conversation that represents an important existential turning point, generated in a way that often defies logical analysis, in the spiritual transformation of the disciple. Thus, historical studies of the development of the kōan tradition necessarily involve an examination of how each of the Zen genres attempted a formalization of kōan learning by organizing and interpreting the source dialogues along with sermons, anecdotal materials, and commentaries culled from T'ang and later writings.

The argument to be put forth here is that Dōgen's KS *Shōbōgenzō* should not be considered separate and independent from the other main Zen genres. Rather, it is integral to the development of the tradition of Zen dialogues and kōans—dependent upon, yet often offering compelling reinterpretations of the source material of T'ang *satori* dialogues—in which all the Sung Zen literary forms participated. Thus Dōgen's Japanese work, especially when it is seen in conjunction with his MS *Shōbōgenzō*, could be viewed as a fourth Zen genre of the Sung/Kamakura eras. Or, perhaps it can be interpreted even more fruitfully as an offshoot or subdivision of the kōan collection genre, or even as a kind of synthesis of *goroku* and kōan collection texts that falls into the *kōan-roku* category.

Interpreting the KS as integral to the kōan tradition and as an important part of the kōan collection literary genre significantly alters our perception of the other Zen writings contributing to the tradition. Dōgen and the compilers of the kōan collections, lamp histories, and recorded sayings took part in the effort to restore a lost sense of spontaneity and immediacy to the tradition of recording dialogues. However, in seeking to recapture and reveal the essence of the so-called golden age of T'ang Zen, probably all of the Sung texts, to varying extents, inevitably concealed and defeated the original spontaneity. But they made the effort with very different ideological concerns and literary styles. The chronicles or *tōshi-roku* created a narratological structure to recount and legitimate the genealogy of the sect, emphasizing the differences in style among the "five houses" (*goke*),[53] and they used the *satori* dialogues to reflect important points of transition and transformation in the lives of Zen patriarchs that helped preserve the continuity of transmission. The kōan-centered texts or *kōan-roku*, including many Sung *goroku* texts and the HR, highlighted and interpreted the tropological structure of the dialogues, that is, the way they revolve around the use of rhetoric including irony and metaphor to elicit a subitaneous awakening from the participants. The KS stands closer to the kōan collections, especially the HR, as well as to the *goroku* of Sung Zen masters, than to the chronicles in its hermeneutic method of interpreting the dialogues. The KS is stylistically innovative in a manner that is different than and yet parallel to the creativity of interpretation in the MMK and the HR. Like the kōan collections, the KS gives an interlinear exegesis that glosses key words and phrases from the source dialogues based on the holistic metaphysical view that penetrating a single discourse is equivalent to penetrating all possible discourses. The KS and the kōan collections seek to uncover the "deep structure" of kōans from the standpoint of a free, decentric samadhic association of ideas, images, and figures of speech reflecting an all-encompassing Zen insight.

Classifying the KS as an example of *kōan-roku* is intended to highlight rather than obscure some of the main differences between Dōgen's text and the kōan collections: First, the KS is organized around (that is, nearly all KS fascicles are entitled and deal with) a *specific topic in Zen thought*, citing cases as well as other examples of Buddhist literature as interpretive tools to clarify the topic. Second, and following from the previous point, the KS *cites Mahayana sūtras* much more frequently than other Zen texts as a source or authority of truth, without necessarily abandoning the notion of *kyōge betsuden*, and it mixes together rather than separates out prose and poetic commentary. Third, Dōgen's commentaries tend to *equate master and disciple*, question and answer, by seeing all Buddhist practitioners and expressions as reflective of original enlightenment rather than setting up a process of transforming delusion into correct understanding. Fourth, and this point must be clarified in relation to the previous one, Dōgen seems much more assertive than earlier Zen masters, perhaps because of the influence of T'ien-t'ai/Tendai exegetical methods, in *criticizing and recommending changes* in what the kōans actually say. Therefore, while the kōan collections provide multilayered verse and prose commentaries about kōans, the KS *Shōbōgenzō* is notable in that its commentaries attempt to genuinely recreate or to essentially become kōans. Dōgen frequently suggests modifications of the original cases, or argues about what a master could or should have said differently in a given context. That is, Dōgen's text, perhaps to a greater extent than Sung *goroku* or kōan collections, *represents an erasure of difference between source and interpretation, or between encounter dialogue and interlinear commentary.*

The trademark of the *kōan-roku* category of texts is the attempt to create a literary form that recaptures the original creative spirit that engendered the oral dialogues in order to bridge the gap between source and commentary, or orality and writing. Some of the disparities in the style and structure of the texts are due to differences in the social-historical settings at the time of their composition as well as the audiences to which they were addressed. The kōan collections of Sung China like the HR and MMK, which are quite different from each other in many ways, were intended for monks in training who had a ready knowledge and understanding of other Zen records. But in seeking to justify the role of Zen as the main survivor of the 845 suppression of Buddhism, they were also aimed at attracting the attention of the Neo-Confucian scholar-officials (*shih-tai-fu*) who dominated Sung culture. Ta-hui's monosyllabic *watō* method, growing out of and yet in some ways negating the HR, was specifically designed to entice the scholar-officials away from a doctrinaire adherence to the priority of reason in Neo-Confucian morality and metaphysics, and to offer them a simplified access to Zen enlightenment. Dōgen's work attempted, in a quick, decisive, and democratizing way, to acquaint Japanese Buddhists in the thirteenth century with the vast storehouse of Zen dialogues recorded in the Sung literature with which they were largely unfamiliar. Many of the fascicles of the KS sought to be persuasive for an audience of disillusioned literati at the Court who were also attracted to Tendai esoteric (*taimitsu*) Buddhism and Shinto religiosity. Although fifteen years after his return to Japan Dōgen abandoned the secularized court life in Kyoto for the natural splendor of the Echizen mountains, his writings in the KS draw extensively on the polysemous wordplay, punning, and homophones used by the literati in Japanese court poetry and other Kamakura era religio-aesthetic works.

The result is that the KS *Shōbōgenzō*, the HR, the MMK, and Ta-hui's records or *Daie Roku* (hereafter DR), in addition to each master's other collected commentaries, including his *goroku*, kōan collections, sermons, and letters, represent numerous alternative strategies for presenting, as well as views on interpreting, the efficacy of kōans. But despite discrepancies, the approaches of these texts more or less equally derive from common textual sources. According to the conventional account of the kōan tradition, however, the kōan collections like the HR, as well as their commentators, developed in a single, inevitable progression toward an emphasis on the method of abbreviation of the source dialogues. This method involves selecting increasingly brief or condensed portions of the dialogue—a key word or phrase, or even just a single syllable uttered at just the right contextual moment, which is considered to contain the meaning of the entire conversation—in order to approximate ever more closely the goal of maintaining a noble silence and discarding the use of language altogether. Probably the main example of abbreviation is the shortcut to enlightenment in the *watō* or main phrase technique perfected by Ta-hui, whose theories were especially crucial to the development of Rinzai Zen in Japan and Korea. Abbreviation does play a key role in Dōgen's glossing of key words and phrases, but Dōgen's views are generally excluded from an account of the kōan tradition's history because he sees the kōan, in a way seemingly opposite to Ta-hui's use of abbreviation, as a means of ongoing hermeneutic disclosure of enlightenment experience based on a principle akin to Paul Ricoeur's notion of the "surplus of meaning" or the "fullness of language."[54] For Dōgen, the aim of kōan studies is not to abbreviate and cut off speech, but to expand and multiply the diverse levels and implications of meaning embedded though sometimes also concealed by the polysemy of words. The style of commentary in the HR appears to stand somewhere between Dōgen and Ta-hui on the issue of abbreviation in relation to polysemy, and thus it at once clarifies and undercuts the sense of polarity between these texts.

Dōgen's Hermeneutics and Ta-hui's Iconoclasm

The disparities between Ta-hui's shortcut and Dōgen's "scenic route" approach revolve around issues concerning the use of language and symbolism in relation to religious vision. Thus, an interpretation of the kōan as a religious symbol consisting of a multivalent literary discourse seems to be a way of opening up the differences and affinities in the respective interpretations that is impartial and free of conventional polarization. For example, discourse analysis allows for an even-handed analysis of how Dōgen and Ta-hui comment extensively on one of the most famous kōans, in which Chao-chou paradoxically answers Mu (literally, "no") and U ("yes") in response to the query, "Does the dog have Buddha-nature?" From the standpoint of intertextuality it is important to note that Chao-chou's kōan is probably best known as the first case in the MMK, but it also appears in Chao-chou's recorded sayings (Chao-chou lu or Jōshū Roku), the kōan collection of Hung-chih, as well as numerous other Sung texts, usually with at least minor variations in the wording. A similar version of the dialogue featuring master Ikan is also included in the KD. Ta-hui mentions Chao-chou's Mu over two dozen times in his collected writings.[55] Dōgen discusses the dialogue primarily in the "Busshō" fascicle of the KS, but he also interprets the kōan in other works, including the "Gakudōyōjinshū" and the EK. In contrast to Dōgen and some other commentators, such as Hung-chih and Yüan-wu, Ta-hui focuses exclusively on the Mu response and ignores the U answer. The key element in Ta-hui's approach is to interpret Mu as a prime example of the shortcut head-word that creates a sudden breakthrough to enlightenment. The watō technique, also known as kanna-zen (introspecting the kōan) captures an abbreviated essence or succinct kernel of the traditional case, a "tasteless" yet "live" word beyond intellect and conceptualization. It functions as both a hindrance to illumination and a sword cutting through all obstacles. For Ta-hui, the Mu response is an iconoclastic antisymbol pointing to a nonconceptual, nondifferentiable, and ineffable truth. Ta-hui's interpretation seems to be supported by the MMK's prose comments stressing an abbreviated view of the case:

> Don't you want to pass this barrier? Then concentrate yourself into the "Mu," with your 360 bones and 84,000 pores, making your whole body one great inquiry. Day and night work intently at it. Do not attempt nihilistic or dualistic interpretations. It is like having bolted a red hot iron ball. You try to vomit it but cannot.[56]

According to Dōgen, the entire question-and-answer process leading up the Mu and U responses demonstrates that kōans are effective as a means of expressing realization. They are not to be condensed but rather expanded as a continuing hermeneutic revelation and elaboration of the multiple dimensions of insight into the doctrines from which the articulation of the original cases derive. Thus, the *Mu* is not seen as a tasteless syllable defying thought, but a symbolic disclosure that

> the nothingness (*mu*) of all the various nothings (*shomu*) must be learned in the nothingness of no-Buddha-nature (*mu-bisshō*).[57]

Dōgen stresses not the barrier but the gateless and ever-flexible nature of discourse and interpretation in conveying the fathomable depths of "nothingness-nothingness" (*mu-mu*) from the standpoint of *genjōkōan*, or the direct and immediate yet perpetual realization of the kōan in concrete human affairs and natural existence. Seen in terms of the tropics of discourse, Ta-hui uses *Mu* as a supreme example of irony undermining all attachment to words and letters, whereas Dōgen values it as exemplary of metonymy opening the verbal door to a multiplicity of meanings found in associative wordplay or a decentric, semiotic playfulness with language. The degree of importance of *Mu* is the same for both approaches, but there are clearly serious disagreements in terms of how it should be applied to the relation between speech and silence, and thinking and non-thinking.

The "Shinfukatoku" fascicle of the KS also illustrates how Dōgen reinterprets traditional dialogues based on their symbolic power to highlight his view of the role of language in terms of silence and quietism. Here, Dōgen examines a well-known case involving master Te-shan's attempt to purchase rice cakes from an old woman while traveling in a quest to find an authentic master. This anecdote is cited in the commentary in HR case no. 4 and in a number of other Zen texts, so that intertextuality is an important factor in assessing the different genres, including the KS, in which the dialogue appears. Intertextuality is also helpful in appreciating how the dialogue contributes to the overarching narrative quality surrounding the development of the personality of Te-shan and the distinctiveness of his spiritual quest as portrayed in the chronicles. After Te-shan became an enlightened master and uncompromising teacher, he was especially known for his ruthless pedagogical method of wielding a stick during training sessions with his disciples, warning them, "Whether you can say a word or not, it's all the same: Thirty blows of my stick!" But Te-shan began his Buddhist career as an expert on the *Diamond Sūtra*, and since he always carried his notes and commentaries on the scripture in a backpack he was often referred to as "Diamond Chou" (Chou was his family name). According to traditional accounts, the rice cake incident became a key turning point leading him away from a reliance on scripture, and he eventually took a radically iconoclastic stance by burning his copy of the *Diamond Sūtra*. Te-shan's journey to self-discovery culminated with a decisive encounter with his master, Lung-t'an, resulting in his *satori*. This occurred when Te-shan was subitaneously awakened as Lung-t'an, after a lengthy and intense discussion, blew out the candle he was just about to offer Te-shan to illuminate a dark pathway on his way home. The Lung-t'an anecdote takes place subsequent to the rice cake incident and extends the Te-shan narrative, but it has also been separated out to function as a paradigmatic case on its own—it appears as case no. 28 in the MMK and case no. 104 in Dōgen's MS kōan collection (which cites Te-shan three times).[58]

Furthermore, a tropological analysis of the passage is useful because the source dialogue revolves around one of the more intriguing wordplays used in Zen discourse, which specializes in puns, paradoxes, and extended conceits. This wordplay is significantly elaborated upon in Dōgen's commentary. In the original passage, Te-shan, carrying his copies and commentaries on the *Diamond Sūtra*, was offended in hearing about the Southern school Hung-chou lineage because of its refutation of scriptural exegesis, and he traveled south to see first-hand the deficiencies he suspected must be prevalent in its approach. A bit weary while on his journey, Te-shan stopped to buy some refreshments (*ten-shin*) at a roadside stand in what would appear to represent an insignificant pause in his lengthy travels. But the woman selling rice cakes, an apparently uneducated elderly layperson, made an ingenious pun while interrogating Te-shan to test his understanding of a key line from the *Diamond Sūtra*. She asked him,

> According to the *Diamond Sūtra*, the past mind is ungraspable (*fukatoku*, Skt. *anupalambha*), the present mind is ungraspable, and the future mind is ungraspable. So, where is the mind (*shin*) that you now seek to refresh (*ten*) with rice cakes?[59]

Te-shan was rendered speechless, outsmarted by the woman whose clever philosophical insight into the impermanence and insubstantiality of mind apparently led his scholastically oriented mentality to an impasse in confronting nonconceptuality and silence that requires the abandonment of thought and discourse. Looked at in terms of tropology, the woman's pun constitutes a metonymy, a rhetorical device in which meaning emerges based on "the accidental association or linkage of words,"[60] which dislodges the scriptural specialist from his fixation with the literal meaning of texts and introduces him to a decentric, polysemous semiotic field. Te-shan's reputation for scriptural exegesis is defeated, and he has no choice but to abandon the *sūtra* as a primary source of truth. This dialogue places him on the verge of attaining *satori* that is soon culminated in his encounter with Lung-t'an, which demonstrates that expert instruction can potentially come from a variety of sources, and at any and every opportunity. A seemingly innocuous situation or a very unlikely rendezvous can stimulate the highest degree of insight, perhaps just when a seeker has temporarily suspended his quest and does not even appear to be looking for enlightenment at that particular moment. This incident reinforces the Zen view, expressed in the *Vimalakīrti Sūtra* and in the recorded sayings of Layman P'ang, both of which valorize the teaching of non-monks, that an awakened person serendipitously discovered represents a higher authority than formal ritual, clerical hierarchy, or scripture.

What is the key lesson to be learned from the Te-shan dialogue? The conventional Rinzai interpretation admires the woman's verbal feat in putting an end to words, or in using wordplay as a catalyst for the self-dissolution of Te-shan's tendency to conceptualize and verbalize. For Ta-hui, the term *ten-shin* might function as a *watō* grounded in an ironic undercutting of any possible meaning conveyed by words. To Dōgen, however, an exclusive emphasis on the silence and the barrier to speech that concludes the dialogue, rather than on the rhetorical skills that produced the transformative effect for Te-shan through metonymy, reflects the deficiencies in the Ta-hui approach to kōans. In his commentary, Dōgen criticizes both the woman and Te-shan for not bringing the conversation to a more productive conclusion by building on the tropology in the conversation instead of allowing it to vanish. "Currently in Sung China," he writes, "many dimwitted [monks] are quite superficial and foolish in responding so unfavorably to Te-shan while at the same time lavishly praising the old woman's wisdom. But it is not unreasonable to doubt [her understanding]."[61] Dōgen goes on to create a continuation of the dialogue, first suggesting that Te-shan should turn the woman's deliberate use of metonymy back on itself by demanding, "If the past, present, and future minds are ungraspable, where is the mind (*shin*) that now makes the rice cakes used for refreshment (*ten*)?"[62] Only such a retort, at once extending and undermining the woman's wordplay, could prove that Te-shan truly grasped her teaching. Dōgen then recommends that the woman reply to Te-shan's hypothetical comment by indicating that the mind is neither an entity nor nonentity but is actively engaged in self-liberation:

> You know only that one cannot refresh the mind with a rice cake.
> But you do not realize that the mind refreshes the rice cake, or
> that the mind refreshes (or liberates) the mind (*kokoro no kokoro
> o tenzuru*).[63]

Dōgen concludes that the woman should reward Te-shan with three cakes, one for each of the temporal occasions—past, present, and future—of the mind. But he continues to maintain that both Te-shan and the old woman have failed in their attenuated dialogue according to the conventional interpretation. "Therefore," he writes, "neither the old woman nor Te-shan were able to hear adequately or to express the past ungraspable mind, the present ungraspable mind, or the future ungraspable mind."[64]

Neither Rinzai Zen nor Dōgen take the source dialogue at face value. The Rinzai Zen of Ta-hui's shortcut approach interprets the woman's pun as a barrier of language and a pathway to silence, whereas Dōgen sees it as a hermeneutic vehicle for the continual unfolding of the multiple levels of self-critical symbolism and understanding: the mind liberating the mind through discourse and symbolic disclosure of experiential truth. Rinzai stresses the anti-symbolic quality revealed at the turning point in the dialogue, and argues that the real aim of discourse and symbolism is to defeat themselves. Dōgen maintains that discourse is liberated through literary symbols, which should be explored for their multidimensional and polysemous ability to evoke various aspects and perspectives of truth. Rinzai reduces the source dialogue to the vanishing point, whereas Dōgen builds upon and extends the dialogue to what he considers its translogical conclusion.

Arborescent Metaphor

In examining diverging interpretations of the *Mu* and rice cake kōans thinkers within the Zen school have often asked, What was the original intention of the dialogue and whose viewpoint does it support, Rinzai or Sōtō, Ta-hui or Dōgen? From the decentric, intertextual postmodern perspective, however, it is important to interpret the material not in terms of sectarian polarization but from a standpoint that takes into account the full range of possibilities in the tradition based on the flexibility and open-endedness of the dialogues. Therefore, questions concerning correct interpretation are misleading and must be transmuted into another set of inquiries: What are the common semiotic indicators and thematic images and patterns underlying the seemingly opposite approaches? How do each of the various Zen genres represent diverging interpretations branching out from the same literary roots? Thus the key to understanding the connection between Dōgen and kōans is to refer constantly back and forth to the complex sources and multiple manifestations of the tradition. This enables a reconstruction of how kōan collections evolved in relation to the forms of Zen literature, especially the chronicles, that as part of the "branches" of the tradition were also working with the source dialogues or "roots." At the same time, it establishes a means of situating the distinctiveness of Dōgen's work, as one more of the branches, in terms of its interaction with and contribution to the full historical and literary setting (the entire organism, or "tree").

Therefore, the arborescent metaphor indicates that there are multiple branches emerging from common sources so that Dōgen's approach should be seen as one of many possible outcomes in cultivating and refining the roots, or original forms of expression.[65] The metaphor also suggests, according to a view expressed in the Confucian text, the Ta-hsüeh (The Great Learning), that the roots and branches of the tree grow simultaneously though in opposite directions. Thus, it is equally important to understand the development of the roots (the T'ang satori dialogues) by looking nonsequentially at the branches (Sung interpretations on which our knowledge of the dialogues is largely based) as it is to do the reverse, that is, to follow sequentially the growth of the branches beginning with the roots. Viewing the tradition in this fashion acts as a corrective for the tendency prevalent in both Sung texts and in Western scholarship to see Zen discourse moving inevitably, in teleological fashion, toward a single comprehensive conclusion—as if, for example, there were an internal and invariably logical progression from the source dialogues through the paradigmatic cases leading directly and finally to the watō method. In an otherwise impeccable article tracing the historical development of kōans from the T'ang to the Sung, for example, Robert Buswell comes to a somewhat misleading conclusion that distillation and abbreviation is the key to this teleological progression. He maintains that the shortcut form of the watō is the necessary result of the terseness of the dialogues and the expression of subitaneous enlightenment: "[Kōan and watō] may more fruitfully be viewed," he writes, "as the products of an internal dynamic within [Zen] that began in the T'ang and climaxed in the Sung. [Kōan-introspection Zen] may thus be seen as the culmination of a long process of evolution in [Zen] whereby its subitist rhetoric came to be extended to pedagogy and finally to practice . . . [it is] a consummation of forces set in motion centuries before."[66] Buswell, an expert in the appropriation of Zen by Korea from China, explains the history of the kōan from a standpoint that presupposes the merits of Ta-hui's approach—as seen through the lens of Korean monk Chinul—since Ta-hui is considered the leading Zen spokesman by the mainstream of Korean Rinzai. Similarly, Rinzai Zen in Japan, especially as advocated by Hakuin during the Tokugawa era, regards Ta-hui's shortcut method as a culminative peak in the history of Chinese Zen.

However, such a view of the history of Zen reflects a tendency to evaluate retrospectively the intent of the source dialogues by presupposing the priority of only one of several later interpretations. That is, it looks back from a vantage point that itself became sedimented centuries later at what the T'ang *satori* encounters, which may indeed have been for the most part invented or manufactured during the Sung, were supposedly really about. But if that procedure is altered by seeing Dōgen's approach to expansive hermeneutics rather than, or even in addition to, Ta-hui's shortcut or abbreviation as the consummation of the tradition, then it becomes necessary to reexplore the essential meaning of the source dialogues which gave rise to these seemingly opposite interpretations. In at least one important respect, Dōgen's approach appears closer to the structure of the T'ang dialogues than the shortcut technique. That is because in the *watō* method the conversational quality, as well as the background atmosphere accompanying it, is deliberately removed as a distraction and obstacle to enlightenment. Dōgen, however, creates a writing style that is dialogical, or at least an approximation of oral dialogue, in that he explores, rather than cuts off, through interlinear commentary the multiple implications suggested by the original encounter. As Kazuaki Tanahashi writes in the introduction to his translation of the KS, "Dōgen is unique both as a thinker and as a Buddhist teacher. Like his predecessors, he presents paradoxical statements; but unlike them, he makes continuous and systematic efforts to verbalize the process of his thinking. He demonstrates the extraordinary quality of intuitive logic in Zen tradition. . . . at the same level of insight as the Chinese Zen masters, who were trying to express a logic beyond normal logic."[67] Thus, if the dialogues are seen as leading directly to Dōgen instead of or in addition to Ta-hui, the issue of the relation between T'ang sources, or roots, and Sung interpretations, or branches, becomes much more complex and open-ended.

Multiple Implications of the Term "Kōan"

Part of the difficulty in coming to grips with the issue of the relation between roots and branches is the fact that the term "kōan" is not always clearly distinguished in meaning from numerous other terms that are often used—sometimes appropriately, and sometimes not—interchangeably with it. These terms include *kien-mondō*, *watō*, *kanna-zen*, *kosoku*, *juko*, *nen-ko*, *kikan* (pedagogical opportunities), *kattō* (dialogical entangling "vines"), and *kufū* (meditative technique).[68] Furthermore, the terms kōan and *watō* are sometimes connected with two other abbreviated forms of studying the dialogues that became popular during the Sung and later periods: *jakugo* (capping words), perfected by Daitō Kokushi, by which a dialogue is capped off, culminated, or succinctly epitomized; and *tengo* (turning words), which represent the primary catalytic verbal agents in a dialogue. Beyond this, kōans are sometimes conflated with *jōdō* and *shōsan* sermons that cite dialogues as a source of truth, and it also happens that the oral and written as well as the formal and performative dimensions of kōan practice are not always clearly distinguished. Generally, "kōan" is used in at least three overlapping yet distinct ways. The term can refer in the most general sense to the spontaneous T'ang dialogues, eventually recorded in the chronicles, from which the traditional cases were usually drawn; this significance more or less corresponds to the meanings of *kien-mondō*, *kikan*, and *kattō*. It has been said by Japanese Rinzai master Daiō Kokushi, who helped introduce kōan training into Japan, that there are seventeen-hundred kōans, which is a rough approximation of the number of masters discussed in the KD.[69] But in a stricter sense, "kōan" refers only to the formal, paradigmatic cases serving as the basis of instruction and included in the Sung kōan collections—these are the "public (*kō*) records (*an*)," or *kosoku*, usually accompanied by *nenko* and *juko* commentaries. And in its most limited meaning, "kōan" is sometimes considered identical with the shortcut method (*kufū*) of the *watō*, or with *kanna-zen*. But it is crucial to avoid conflating these levels of meaning because kōans in the second and third senses—that is, as catechistic and shortcut techniques, respectively—were probably relatively late developments that involved interpreting the dialogues in a certain though by no means necessarily predetermined direction.

One way of sorting out the significance of the term kōan is to associate these three levels of meaning with three of five main stages in the historical unfolding of Zen writings. The first historical stage is the formative or early period of Bodhidharma and Hui-neng and the establishment of the dominant Southern school. Although their dialogues are catalogued in the chronicles, and several kōans each are attributed to the illustrious early patriarchs in the kōan collections, the writings given their signatures were for the most part formal and didactic. Therefore, this historical period is generally considered to anticipatively precede the formation of kōans even in the general dialogical sense. The second stage marks the origin of the *satori* dialogues beginning with Ma-tsu and the Hung-chou school in the eighth and ninth centuries. During this period some of the most radically individualistic and anti-authoritarian Zen masters, such as Chao-chou, Te-shan, and Lin-chi, came to represent a concrete existential embodiment of the Dharma. They spoke the "living word" of human realization which alone carried the inspiration of the transmission of Zen enlightenment. The Zen emphasis on a "special transmission outside the scriptures/without reliance on words and letters" (*kyōge betsuden/furyū monji*), supposedly originated by Bodhidharma, probably came into prominence as the dominant mode of Zen discourse during the second stage, although the saying itself was not actually formulated until the third stage. This motto, which has come to be seen as definitive of the kōan tradition, is found in its earliest extant form in a text from 1108, and is attributed retrospectively to the first patriarch. The motto, however, did not indicate an outright rejection of *sūtra* literature, for in the same passage according to some versions it is said that monks who are stubbornly silent are like "dumb sheep" who show an attachment to the words and letters of nonattachment precisely in disdaining words and letters.[70] Rather, the motto "signified a return to [Zen's] vital essence, which cannot be replaced by any texts. . . . a new time spirit, in which man as an individual had been assigned the central focus, together with a general appreciation for the spoken word."[71] The next two stages are marked by the flourishing during the early part of the Sung era of the Zen chronicles (third stage) and kōan texts (fourth stage), both of which formally recorded and interpreted the *kosoku-kōan*. According to the conventional, teleological view, the third and fourth stages are separable yet sequentially linked. But for a variety of reasons to be discussed more fully in Chapter 4, particularly the issue of dating the chronicle and kōan texts which actually first appeared not in sequence but around the same time during the Sung, it seems more plausible to combine these stages into one stage. In either case, the period of early Sung, which represented a new self-reflective historical awareness in Zen, helped maintain the integrity and popularity of the sect with the demise of scholasticism after the suppression of Buddhism in 845. However, compared to the radical iconoclasm of

the T'ang style, Zen now "had become an authoritative, established tradition and was no longer the revolutionary or renegade movement it had
once been."[72]

The fifth and final stage in the history of Zen kōans in medieval China
was the attempt to condense the theory and practice of the catechistic
kōans formalized in the fourth stage through a distillation of the paradigmatic cases into the *watō* method. From the conventional standpoint, this
historical sequence has a kind of inner logic based on the necessity for abbreviation. But as soon as Dōgen's text is put into the picture, the sequential
understanding needs to be revised. That is because Dōgen's text could be
seen either as fourth or fifth stage, or as fitting in between the two stages,
and this negates a sense that there is a logical progression from one stage
to the next. Although Dōgen lived a century after the HR was composed,
and fifty years after Ta-hui, the KS *Shōbōgenzō* and its *genjokōan* approach
were an attempt to create a new kōan text for Japan. The KS text was not
so much a fifth stage effort to reflect back on—let alone to negate, as
conventionally portrayed—the fourth stage as it was a Japanized alternative expanding upon the multiple implications of the second stage source
dialogues.

Which historical stage and corresponding level of meaning represents
the true significance of the term kōan? Is it the T'ang or the Sung that
constitutes the "golden age" of Zen in China? If the T'ang is the classical
period, should the Sung be considered a "post-classical" or a "baroque"
period? The answers to these questions are based to a large extent on how
one evaluates the fourth of the historical stages (corresponding to the
catechistic meaning of the kōan collections, including the KS) in relation
to the second stage (or dialogical meaning). The fourth stage may be seen
as marking either a period of decline or a process of refinement in terms of
the way kōans had been formed in the original, spontaneous sense. The
view that the catechistic kōan cases represented a decline in creativity and
spontaneity is expressed by Zenkei Shibayama in his modern commentary
on the MMK. He notes that by the time of the Sung dynasty [collections]
the kōan tradition seemed to take on a "reminiscent, traditional character"
that tried to recapture the spirit of "Zen [that] was most creative and vital
in the T'ang dynasty."[73] That is, kōans in the formal sense reflected a
nostalgic, retrospective glance at the spontaneous atmosphere, then lost,
out of which the dialogues were created. Similarly, John Wu and John
McRae refer to the second stage Ma-tsu era as the "golden age" or classical
period of Zen which dominates all subsequent developments. On the other

hand, the argument can be reversed in that the prose and poetic commentaries in the fourth stage kōan collections represent from a "literary point of view . . . a pinnacle in the history of [Zen] literature."[74] This is because Yüan-wu's HR absorbs and reflects in its multifaceted structure the full development of Zen thought by developing a six-layered literary form (including commentaries and annotations based on kosoku cases) and a three-tiered historical fabric (encompassing the T'ang dialogues and an earlier version of the collection of one hundred cases compiled by Hsüeh-tou). Heinrich Dumoulin refers to the HR as the "epitome of poetic composition in Zen literature . . . [and] one of the foremost examples of religious world literature."[75] In a similar vein, Buswell maintains that the fourth stage Sung kōan collections (rather than the second stage T'ang dialogues) represent the true golden age in that a "more complex genre of literature can hardly be imagined, rivaling any of the exegetical commentaries of the doctrinal [Buddhist] schools."[76] In support of an identification of the Zen golden age with the fourth stage, it can also be pointed out that the KS, if placed in this stage, has been frequently cited by Watsuji Tetsurō, Tanabe Hajime, Nishitani Keiji, and Nakamura Hajime as the single most important text in Japanese intellectual history that also occupies a firm position at the forefront of international philosophy in its creative means of expressing ultimate reality.

However, there is another fundamental problematical issue that affects all these matters of understanding the history and terminology of kōans. This hermeneutic problem pertains to the dating and evaluation of Zen writings, which probably do not follow the sequential ordering or have the step-by-step relation to one another that the conventional view ascribes. Many of the dialogues attributed to T'ang dynasty masters subsequent to Ma-tsu were probably initially contained in T'ang works such as the Hōrinden. But recent historiographical studies show that these dialogues actually did not become prominent until the T'ang writings were absorbed into and given a systematic application in the transmission of the lamp histories and other texts that developed rapidly during the early Sung.[77] There is very little evidence in T'ang sources themselves for the picture of T'ang era Zen we now have; most of this picture in painted in Sung sources. As McRae points out, "We simply do not have any texts relevant to the earliest period of classical Ch'an [second stage above] that did not pass through the hands of Sung dynasty editors, who either knowingly or unknowingly homogenized the editions they produced."[78] That is, nearly all of the works recording the second stage T'ang conversations are actually of third or fourth stage Sung origin, at least as far as can be told. It is impossible to make an accurate assessment of how much was lost or changed in the interim, or whether in fact the Sung writings fabricated, perhaps deliberately so, the nature and content of T'ang era Zen. Griffith Foulk argues in his study of the arising and development of Chinese Zen monastic institutions that "the dearth of materials explicitly describing T'ang 'Ch'an' monasteries is striking, especially when one considers, again by way of comparison, that a tremendous quantity of hagiographical material pertaining to the lives and teachings of various T'ang Ch'an masters has come down to us mostly in Sung compilations."[79] Foulk concludes that "the Ch'an lineage in the T'ang existed primarily as *a conceptual entity, not a distinctive institutional establishment.*"[80]

The key T'ang transmission text, the *Hōrinden* (much of which appears to be irretrievably lost) can be described as "partially a creation and partially a 'historical' arrangement of many old and new legends about the Indian and Chinese patriarchs and Ch'an masters, starting with the Seven Buddhas of the Past up to Ma-tsu inclusively." Concerning its usefulness for examining the life of Ma-tsu, however, it is evident that "the report about Ma-tsu's own role . . . has been lost; *we are therefore dependent on later works which are presumably based on the [Hōrinden].*"[81] Furthermore, a textual archaeology that tries to discover an authentic classical base substantiating the historicality of the third stage chronicles will undoubtedly prove fruitless. This is due to the exaggerations and the general unreliability and hagiographical excesses in the biographical material contained in all the Sung chronicles, especially the lamp histories, which remain the only available historical sources. As Kenneth Ch'en points out, "The standard Ch'an history, *Record of the Transmission of the Lamp* [KD], was written almost four centuries after the events, and during that interval numerous Ch'an legends must have been fabricated and inserted into the account."[82] The conventional view of a sequential development of the kōan tradition becomes even more skewed since the second stage did not exist independently of the third stage. In fact, the second stage may not have preceded the third stage at all in the sense that it is possible, as Foulk suggests, that the second stage was a conceptual fabrication manufactured by third-stage texts. The third-stage chronicles operate as a kind of screen or veil determining our access to the relation between the second-stage dialogues and fourth-stage catechisms. Therefore, rather than argue about the lines of progression from classical to post-classical periods, it seems preferable to see the various Zen genres of the second through fourth stages as a kind of case study in the intertextuality of sources and responses, or roots and branches. The Sung genres were characterized by an ongoing give-and-take and consequent multilayered quality in the fabric or the texturing of texts and textual components.

Significance of the Kōan as a Zen Symbol

The main date in Chinese religious history that separated T'ang and Sung Zen, as well as the second and third stages in the unfolding of the kōan tradition according to the conventional view, was 845. At this point, after years of imperial support and the flourishing of Buddhism as a social and economic as well as religious institution, Emperor Wu-tsung began the temporary (three-year) but severe suppression of Buddhism causing nearly 5,000 monasteries and 40,000 temples to be destroyed and well over a quarter of a million monks and nuns to be returned to the laity. This eventually led to the demise of the scholastic, *sūtra*-oriented sects (although T'ien-t'ai continued to compete with Zen as a meditation tradition through the Sung). This period of suppression, also known as the Hui-chung persecution, was recorded in detail by Ennin, the Japanese priest who was traveling and observing Buddhism in China at the time. It transpired due to a variety of personal, political, and economic factors, particularly the emperor's exclusive leanings for rather questionable (and even obsessive) personal reasons toward a corrupted form of religious Taoism, as well as the desire of the government to confiscate the vast wealth and resources in Buddhist temples.[83] Probably much of the success Zen enjoyed in surviving the otherwise devastating impact of this event for Buddhism as a whole probably lay in the oral transmission of kōans as an alternative form of communication to formal scriptures that would defy censorship or external supervision. According to Ch'en, the survival of Zen "might be attributed to . . . its lack of dependence on the external paraphernalia of the religion, such as the scriptures, images, and so forth, [which] enabled it to function and carry on even after the destruction of such externals."[84] Actually, Zen did rely on rituals and images based on patterns of imperial succession to propogate lineage, but these features of religious praxis were deliberately cultivated to contribute to the rhetoric of spontaneous oral teaching.

Therefore, to a large extent Zen's rhetoric and sense of explaining its own history should be seen as an attempt to circumvent the forces of censorship and persecution. Before examining more fully in the following chapters how the problematics involved in understanding the development of the kōan tradition from the T'ang to the Sung pertain to interpreting Dōgen's texts, it is important to consider the general significance of kōans in contributing to the prominence attained by the Zen sect. An overview of the unfolding of Zen from its origins in T'ang China and throughout its development in medieval and modern Japan (as well as Korea and Vietnam) indicates that the kōan (in both the general, or dialogical, and the specific, or catechistic, senses) stands out as the single most characteristic and important aspect defining the sect's history and practice. The kōan is certainly not the only religious symbol for which Zen is well known. But it seems to have a greater distinctiveness than many other doctrines that can be seen more readily as a natural outgrowth of earlier Buddhist theories and practices. For example, zazen (sitting meditation) is an extension of various forms of traditional Buddhist meditative techniques, and the notions of *satori* (sudden awakening) and *kenshō* (seeing into [one's own-] nature) are elaborations on the central goal of attaining the spiritual transformation of *nirvāṇa*. The kōan is a psycholinguistic puzzle that leads to the exhaustion of the ego and fosters a dynamic and dramatic insight based on the unity of self and reality, humans and nature, subject and object. It is unique in the way that it captures the essential spirit of the *personalization*, *subitization* (or emphasis on sudden awakening), and *sinitization* (as well as *Japanization*) of enlightenment, which are the main factors contributing to the special status of Zen in the post-845 period.

Personalization

By the early Sung era Zen had become the dominant praxis sect of Chinese Buddhism, and nearly the only one (along with Pure Land devotionalism) to thrive after the 845 persecutions. Very shortly thereafter Zen was transmitted by Dōgen and Eisai, among others, to early Kamakura era Japan where it again assumed a prominent position in religious and cultural life. During the Sung era kōans came to epitomize Zen's success in fashioning a discourse of oral and written, verbal and nonverbal signs and symbols to communicate a unique vision of religious fulfillment. This vision, known as "patriarchal Zen" (*soshi-zen*) represented a "special transmission outside the *sūtras*" based on the concrete human embodiment of ultimate truth rather than on scriptural exegesis or sacramental authority as was typical of many other Mahayana Buddhist schools, from Hua-yen and T'ien-t'ai holistic metaphysics to Pure Land popular worship and esoteric movements. The aim of the truth of "absolute subjectivity" (*zettai shukan*), as the modern Kyoto school thinker Hisamatsu Shin'ichi characterizes Zen enlightenment, is to bring the image of buddha back "down to earth" (as Judith Berling puts it) from the excesses of supernatural speculation and superstitious worship found in some forms of early Chinese Mahayana practice. It identifies the Buddha Dharma with the "flesh and bones" of particular persons who authentically realize and live out its meaning in everyday activities. There are many examples of the iconization and deification of Zen masters. According to the patriarchal transmission, however, these are to be interpreted in demythological fashion as symbolizing the concrete, here-and-now experience of realizing enlightenment instead of the attainment of suprahuman or supernatural powers. The truth of realized buddhahood, according to the tradition, can be carried on only through the direct person-to-person transmission of the essence of the enlightenment experience from the teacher in one generation to his foremost disciple in the next. Dōgen's thought is very much in accord with the notion of patriarchal transmission in that he constantly refers to the two paradigmatic moments of master transmitting the Dharma to disciple: the primordial scenario of Śākyamuni's handing a flower, while winking, to the wondrously smiling Mahākāśyapa; and Bodhidharma's transmitting his sacred clerical robe directly to Hui-k'o, who attained the first patriarch's essence or "marrow."[85] In the KS "Kattō" and other fascicles, Dōgen maintains that each and every occasion that awakening is attained, and that the Dharma is appropriately transmitted, is fundamentally the self-same moment experienced by Mahākāśyapa and Hui-k'o in receiving the transmission from their masters.[86]

Therefore, personalization in Zen has two implications, one concerning the existential authenticity of realized masters, and the other involving the masters' method of targeting instruction for particular disciples. First, patriarchal transmission is an "ecce homo" approach to religion in the Nietzschean sense of a radically independent individual attaining a state of supreme self-confidence deriving from personal spiritual triumph over all delusions and a willingness to defy any ideological convention. The attained Zen master is often referred to as the "true person" (*shinjin*). For Lin-chi, this is further defined as the "true person of no rank" (*mui no shinjin*), to highlight his or her flexibility and open-endedness of thought, but for Dōgen it is designated as the "true person with rank" (*ui no shinjin*), which stands as a corrective for what might be considered the nihilistic or relativist implications in Lin-chi's notion. In either case, true personhood is characterized by intense dedication and determination to the overcoming of any obstacle or gate (*kan*) to the quest for a religious attainment of gatelessness (*mumon*). This does not, however, refer to a strictly anthropocentric or humanistic notion in a way that would violate the basic Buddhist principle of interdependent origination or the East Asian emphasis on naturalism.[87] Zen is highly individualistic in that spiritual attainment can be reached only through one's own personal effort or self-power (*jiriki*). But such an accomplishment is theoretically grounded on the doctrine articulated in various forms of Mahayana Buddhism, particularly *tathāgatagarbha* thought, of the universal potentiality for enlightenment or Buddha-nature (*busshō*) encompassing self and other, humans and nature. Dōgen is particularly known for stressing the all-embracing unity of Buddha-nature in his rewriting of the Zen saying "All things *have* the Buddha-nature," which may suggest that the fundamental reality of original enlightenment is a human possession, as "All things *are* the Buddha-nature," which indicates an identity of essence and existence, the one and the many, and means and end. That is, from out of an holistic spiritual context of the universality of potential buddhahood, only the most highly skilled and trained individual seekers can reach the ultimate truth. According to Chang Chung-yüan, "In both the T'ien-t'ai and the Hua-yen schools [preceding the development of Zen] an interfusion of appearance and reality is strongly maintained. But this interfusion and identification are present in the abstract, in terms of philosophical principles. Ch'an maintains, however, that these principles are never fully grasped by the intellect alone but must be personally experienced through one's own efforts . . . for the Ch'an Buddhist nothing is transcendental apart from the concrete. In other words, the man of Ch'an engages in ordinary daily activities and simultaneously transcends them, so that the concrete and the transcendental in his life are one and the same."[88]

The second implication of personalization refers to the way Zen pedagogy is geared toward the particular needs of the specific disciple being instructed. Originally, in the early T'ang, the transmission dialogues were apparently truly spontaneous occasions of profound existential encounter that took place at an opportune moment in the student's training. In these conversations there was a strong emphasis on the spiritual meeting between two persons. Enlightenment is considered in Zen to be a matter of self-power (*jiriki*) attained by Bodhidharma through "wall-gazing" (*menpeki*), which is not so much a matter of gazing at an objectified wall in way that betrays duality as attaining an undistracted, balanced, nonobjectifying perspective. Yet the Ma-tsu style dialogues also indicate that genuine awareness must come through an active engagement with another person who helps illumine the self. Ideally, in this encounter both parties become equalized without a sense of priority or hierarchy in the relationship between master and disciple. As Lin-chi maintains, "killing the buddha" requires eliminating the gap between superiority and inferiority, or objective instruction and inner realization. Dōgen further develops the theme of teacher-student identity in his interpretation of the doctrines of *kannō dōkō* (spiritual communion between self and other) and *yuibutsu-yobutsu* (transmission only between a buddha and a buddha). Thus, the *mondō* or dialogical aspect of Zen discourse indicates that realization is actual and active in the sense that it is only attained through concrete lived-experience, as well as oral and mutual in that it occurs on the basis of verbal and nonverbal exchange between two existentially, dynamically engaged persons.[89] The *goroku* style of literature contains both a recording of the dialogical exchanges and individual commentary on their meaning and significance for instructing disciples.

However, Zen became an increasingly popular movement during the late T'ang and early Sung, and direct one-on-one contact by a student with the most eminent teacher was prohibited by sheer numbers. At that stage, the formalized, catechistic kōan began to represent a shift from originality and creativity to the performance and ritualistic quality in terms of how the disciple delivered to the master in ceremonial fashion an already known response to a paradigmatic case. This ritual was performed in an introverted setting, sequestered from external exposure and review, yet it probably appealed to the spiritual concerns of the elite class of scholar-officials who were somewhat dissatisfied with Neo-Confucian morality and metaphysics. The face-to-face, usually private, dialogical encounter between liberated master and deluded disciple eventually became, according to Philip Kapleau's interpretation of modern Zen training, a decisive kind of "testing [which] is vital because there is a fine line between a profound intellectual awareness (based on a conceptual insight) and a genuine awakening . . . [for] the gradations are many and subtle."[90]

This method of psychological testing is designed to compel an ever deepening process of self-reflection in order to distinguish between mere intellectual understanding and genuine transformative wisdom. Often taking place through body language and gestures as much as words and speech, the atmosphere of testing helps make the kōan a verbal/nonverbal symbol appropriate for the personalization or existentialization of enlightenment in Zen. The master therapeutically disentangles the "vines" of misunder-standing of the disciple by a challenging—often enigmatic, irreverent, nonsensical, contradictory, incongruous, redundant, or non-sequitured—expression or gesture that is intended to be appropriate pedagogically only to a particular fixation. The kōan is a direct, immediate, and intensely personal form of speech often accompanied by some outrageous action, like shouting or beating with a bamboo stick. As Isshū Miura and Ruth Fuller Sasaki explain, "In energetic and vivid language, much of it the colloquial idiom of the time, interspersed with quotations from the *sūtras* and other Buddhist writings, the old masters relentlessly drove their message home."[91]

To accomplish this, the Zen master might take up any topic he considered suitable to the occasion. While citing scripture, for example, the master could offer a radically unconventional interpretation of key terms or contexts, or support the standard view but for seemingly contra-dictory reasons. Or he could turn for inspiration to a concrete object, such as a lantern or cypress tree, to an action, including bowing or refusing to bow, or to a situation, like a journey or meeting.[92] Often these illustrations are seemingly irrelevant, exceedingly mundane, or altogether out of con-text in terms of the high-minded ideal of enlightenment. But the examples are chosen in order to offer some special insight in a way that might deliberately confound the disciple and thus place him at the doorway of the proverbial gateless gate: stymied and unable to move forward or backward and yet, since losing ground by simply standing still, compelled to act. The very incomprehensibility or absurdity helps force the disciple into what the Tokugawa era Zen master Hakuin calls the "great doubt" (*taigi*), or what Karl Jaspers refers to as an existential "boundary situation." Yet the usefulness of the kōan encounter goes beyond liberating the delusion in the specific setting for which it was originally devised, and it takes on a timeless and universal quality as it becomes a tool in the kōan collections for instruction and transformation of others at any and all times. Therefore, while kōan dialogues and testing scenarios are often private, eyeball-to-eyeball occasions, the catechistic kōan is established as a "public record" in the sense of providing a precedent or standard for future instruction or evaluation. As Chung-feng Ming-pen explains in his early yet definitive Sung era explication of the meaning of the kōan, "The kōans may be compared to the case records of the public law court. . . . There have never been rulers who did not have public law courts, and there have never been public law courts that did not have case records which are to be used as precedents of laws in order to stamp out injustice in the world.

When these public case records (kōans) are used, then principles and laws will come into effect... "[93] Thus, the catechistic kōans allowed the disciple's level of insight to be judged against the paradigmatic case as a kind of universal standard.

Subitization

Another factor that makes the kōan so effective and important is that its terse and dramatic literary style is well-suited to the attainment and expression of sudden awakening, which is a eureka-like spiritual event or fundamentally spontaneous and transformative turning point that represents the culmination of Zen training. One of the oldest and most basic issues throughout the history of Buddhist thought involves the relation between the third and fourth of the Four Noble Truths: extinction (*nirodha*) and the path (*mārga*); or, to put this in a broader context, soteriology and psychology, theory and practice, end and means, or goal and method. The key question is to clarify when the practice of the path leaves off and the attainment of the soteriological goal begins. A main contribution of Zen to Buddhist thought is the way it resolves this issue in terms of the subitization of the awakening process, which emphasizes that enlightened realization is not to be awaited as a futural event but transpires with here-and-now immediacy. The doctrine of subitaneous awakening stems from the early stages of Zen, particularly the *Platform Sūtra*. Dōgen, Ta-hui, and other Sung thinkers are in accord in stressing the importance of spontaneous dynamism rather than a counter-productive waiting for enlightenment. But the terms "subitaneous" and "immediate" can have two implications, of which Zen strongly emphasizes that only the second is authentic. These terms can refer to *quickness* or rapidity in terms of linear, sequential time, which implies an anticipation of enlightenment in the future; or to *spontaneity* in a transtemporal sense that at once goes beyond linearity and yet is realized at this very moment.

Subitaneous awakening as initially expounded by Tao-sheng, prior to Hui-neng's emphasis on the notion, was still an abstract, intellectual concept, something that was explained in a logical, systematic way. Ma-tsu's *satori* dialogues in the second stage of Zen brought into harmony in an holistic moment of actualization the method and goal of realization. Carl Bielefeldt points out, "The old forms of cultivation were superseded—at least in the imagination of the tradition—by the revolutionary methods of beating and shouting or spontaneous dialogues, and explicit discussion of no-thought and sudden practice gave way to suggestive poetry, enigmatic saying, and iconoclastic anecdote,"[94] by which sudden practice was no longer an abstract ideal but concrete reality. The sudden approach of the Hui-neng/Ma-tsu Southern school lineage was traditionally contrasted with the Northern school's gradual method. Dōgen sought to surpass the dichotomy of subitaneity and gradualism in doctrines such as the "oneness of practice and realization" (shushō ittō), the simultaneity of Buddha-nature and Buddha-attainment, and the inseparability of moment (nikon) and continuity (kyōryaku) in terms of the holistic unity of being-time (uji). His approach to the continuing hermeneutics of kōan commentary is an attempt to coordinate a training method with the sustained or perpetually renewed enlightenment process beyond present and future, now and then, and sudden and gradual.

It has often been argued that the identification of the sudden teaching with the Zen sect in the early T'ang was directly related to "the transformation of Zen from a little-known and isolated phenomenon into a large scale movement whose ramifications affected the course of Chinese Buddhism as a whole."[95] Although the formalized Sung kōan can be seen as a diminishing of T'ang spontaneity, it can also be considered to represent a finely honed linguistic tool growing out of the satori dialogues for adroitly and abruptly stimulating an awareness of the multiple meanings of nothingness. It records and establishes a method of speaking that compels the conversation to culminate in an unveiling of the unspeakable, thereby catapulting the recipient in the dialogue into a state of nonconceptualizable liberation. The key to the strategy is to embed the insight that the dialogue is seeking to offer in a literary form that deliberately conceals it, so that one must keep searching and scratching beneath the superficial layers that both obstruct and offer a potential glimpse of the underlying message. When the non-fixated truth is finally disclosed, it comes across much more forcefully and intensely as something surprising in a humorous or even shocking way based on the discontinuity, incongruity, or absurdity of the mismatched contexts of presentation and message.

The recorded cases often conclude suddenly and dramatically in order to catch the disciple offguard and unable to resort to the defense mechanisms of ordinary thinking. John Wu explains that the dialogues and kōans are characterized by "breath-taking abruptness, blinding flashes, deafening shouts, shocking outbursts . . . rocket-like soarings beyond the sphere of reason, tantalizing humor and whimsicality, unaccountable beatings . . ."[96] They might end, for example, with a single syllable (i.e., Mu), a non sequitur (the oak tree in the garden), an instance of absurd or even destructive behavior (cutting off a disciple's finger, or jumping off a one-hundred-foot pole), or a tremendous impasse (the command to interpret without resorting to words or silence). According to Nishitani Keiji, kōans embody an ability to constantly rise above presuppositions and expectations in a way that places Zen discourse in an "excelsior" (kōjō), or self-surpassing, position in relation to all other philosophical and religious viewpoints, including even earlier Buddhist doctrines, which are seen as inherently one-sided and partial. Thus Buswell's comment cited above—despite the disagreement expressed here about its conclusions concerning the watō method—appears on target when he maintains that the kōan does not signify a decline from an earlier stage but "the culmination of a long process of evolution in Zen *whereby its subitist rhetoric came to be extended to pedagogy and finally to practice.*" Through the formation of the kōan as a means of at once heightening and undercutting expectations of imminent truth, Zen created a vehicle by which the practice and the attainment of the transformational event of *satori* occur simultaneously and thus become equalized.

The key to the experience of subitization lies in the use of language which can be explained, as will be discussed more fully in Chapter 4, in terms of the complex interrelations between the four "master" tropes of discourse: metaphor, metonymy, synecdoche, and irony. The dialogues represent a sudden, often radical, shifting back and forth of tropical levels of discourse, for example, from literal to figurative, metaphorical to ironic, concrete to abstract, ideal to material, and vice versa, in order to defeat expectations and assumptions, heighten the intensity of doubt and anxiety, and compel a spontaneous breakthrough or liberation from one-sided views. Truth does not reside in or behind, so to speak, any of one or another particular trope, but is activated in the discursive process which frees a deluded mind from its fixation with centrism, hierarchy, or authority. Truth does not pertain to one specific signified, but evolves (or "devolves") out of the open, decentric play of signifiers devoid of an objective referent of signification. If a disciple seems to be attached to one trope, then another trope must be evoked, though not necessarily in sequence or order. Zen questions and statements should not be seen as assertions of an exclusive path to truth, but as by-products or side effects of the juxtaposition of tropes which create a constructive conflict resulting in a spiritual release from fixation and delusion. In this process of tropical shifting and displacement there are numerous possible contexual emphases, including paradox, ambiguity, contradiction, and reticence, which reflect a withholding of meaning, along with incongruity and absurdity in which everyday meanings are twisted and distorted.

Sinitization and Japanization

Another main element contributing to the kōan's power of communication is that it fully reflects the sinitization of Buddhism, and the utilization of the special resources of the Chinese language in terms of the style or method of religious discourse. For it seems clear that the success of Zen "was purely due to its adaptation to Chinese culture . . . with the result that a distinctly Chinese style of teaching was adopted merely as a didactic device."[97] Arthur F. Wright further argues, "In [the Zen] writings the style, the metaphors, the form of argument bear a closer relation to Chinese philosophic traditions than to any Indian Buddhist text or school. And the methods of imparting their doctrine—the homely analogy, the concrete metaphor, the paradoxical question, the bibliophobic directness—all lack any Indian prototype."[98] The kōan as a technique for spiritual attainment with "no reliance on words and letters" is deeply rooted in the basic Buddhist approach to silence on unedifying queries, and can be understood as a Chinese way of perfecting that method of contextualizing the relation between speech and silence. According to the original Pali passage, the Buddha's silence or refusal to answer his disciple Māluṅkyaputta's queries about eternity, infinity, the identity of body and soul, and the afterlife of the Tathāgata, is not based on stubbornness, ignorance, or arbitrary reticence. Rather, the silence has a profoundly diagnostic and therapeutic quality in that the Buddha carefully analyzes the questions into sets of dilemmas and quadrilemmas to point out to his disciple the unsatisfactory nature of each alternative. He makes clear that any response—whether affirmation (yes), negation (no), or some combination (both yes and no, or neither yes nor no)—falls short of an adequate reply.

The Buddha's aim is twofold: to expose and root out the psychological cause of the questioning process, that is, the longing or greed for one-sided, partial views (Skt. dṛṣṭi) that haunts the inquirer; and to reveal the deficiency of any and every metaphysical assertion and negation in describing the basis of human existence. The Buddha's silence, like the Mu kōan, does not indicate absence or nonexistence in contrast to presence or existence, but a transcendental awareness beyond these distinctions. The Buddha also shows that silence should be understood only as a means to the goal of correcting the tendency to philosophical one-sidedness, and not as an end in itself, when he makes a fundamental and all-important distinction between "what I have explained as explained, and what I have not explained as unexplained."[99] What is not explained by the Buddha are unedifying opinions because these are not "connected with the spiritual holy life . . . not conducive to aversion, detachment, cessation, tranquillity, deep penetration, full realization, nirvāṇa." On the other hand, what is explained by the Buddha systematically and in great detail are those topics "connected to the spiritual life," including duḥkha, its causes, and the possibilities for its extinction. Therefore, the Buddha seeks an appropriate balance between words and no-words; while reticent concerning dṛṣṭi in order therapeutically to uproot and refute them, he deals eloquently and elaborately with appropriate or edifying questions that lead directly to the attainment of nirvāṇa.[100]

The issue that becomes crucial throughout the history of Buddhist thought is how to formulate a cogent style of discourse concerning the arising and eradication of the causes of suffering—a process that is coterminous with the attainment of nirvāṇa—in light of the injunction to remain silent about that which is not conducive to religious pursuit. That is, Buddhism continually tries to develop what Kierkegaard refers to as an "indirect communication," or to convey the truth of subjectivity by creating a style of expression that can suggest just enough to get the appropriate message across, but not too much in a way that might obfuscate or distort through objectification the fundamental subjectivity of spiritual attainment. Like other religious traditions that are based on an inner, gnoseological realization rather than supernatural revelation or objectifiable truth, the Pali texts often use poetry and parables to fulfill this goal. For example, the Buddha's parables of the "discardable raft" and "poisoned arrow" suggest the provisional nature of language and point out its limitations in expressing a solution to the problem of suffering. In later forms of Buddhism, there are several key doctrines that refine these themes, including: the Mādhyamika dialectical negation and theory of two truths, which systematically point out the relativity of all presuppositions projected into metaphysical positions, as well as the interdependence of the ultimate and provisional standpoints; the Prajñāpāramita Sūtras' sustained use of paradoxical language to disclose the meaning of emptiness (śunyatā); the Lotus Sūtra's notion of using words as "skillful means" (hōben) to remedy a particular spiritual ailment; the Mahayana view of language as a "finger pointing to the moon" that must not be confused with the moon itself, or as a symbol distinct from what is symbolized; and the *Vimalakīrti Sūtra*'s advocacy of speaking "no-words about no-words" to ensure that silence is not superficial or one-sided.

Yet, for the most part, Buddhist thought tends to be rather abstract and systematic in terms of its manner or style of presentation. The Buddha's own teaching stresses a logical analysis of the five aggregates (Skt. *skandha*) of human existence, twelve links of dependent origination (*pratītya-samut-pada*), and eighteen phenomenological fields (*dhātu*) of subject-object interaction. This style is continued in much of Indian Buddhism, particularly in the methodological emphasis on epistemology in the Abhidharma analysis of the experiential factors of existence (*dharma*) in terms of the categories of conditioned (*saṃskṛta*) and unconditioned (*asaṃskṛta*) reality, and the Yogacara revision of this analysis by focusing on the states of consciousness (*vijñāna*) in relation to the fundamental storehouse consciousness (*ālaya-vijñāna*). Based on the Indian model, early Chinese Mahayana writings are often technical, scholastic exercises in which an ultimately nonconceptualizable truth is presented in a logical, systematic fashion, as in Mādhyamika philosopher Chi-tsang's dialectical negation in terms of the "four levels of the two truths." This also seems to be the case in Hua-yen and T'ien-t'ai explications of an all-embracing monistic principle in such doctrines as the interpenetration of form and form (*jiji muge*), three thousand dharmas in a single thought (*ichinen sanzen*), the threefold cessation and contemplation (*shikan*), and the ten levels of *dharmadhātu*.[101] Even early Zen works, including seminal texts such as Bodhidharma's "Treatise on the Two Gates" and Hui-neng's *Platform Sūtra*, are relatively straightforward and didactic in presentation. There thus appears to be a subtle but important gap between medium and message, or style and content in the writings at the formative stage of Zen.

The aim of straightforward, systematic writings is to create a manner of exposition that strives for clarity, precision, and persuasion. However, the point of an indirect communication in religious discourse is to be deliberately cryptic, ironic, and obscure, if necessary, in order to stimulate a "leap" into the realm of pure subjectivity. This leap of Zen awakening (rather than a leap of faith in the Kierkegaardian Christian sense) is symbolized by MMK case no. 46, which urgently demands that when climbing to the top of a one-hundred-foot pole one must immediately jump or leap forward in order "to manifest the whole body throughout the ten directions of the universe." Straightforward analysis, however intellectually appealing, may fall short of inspiring an awakening of genuine wisdom, or it may even go a long way toward subverting and obstructing the goal of Zen. The opacity of indirect discourse is illuminative because it invites and remains open to the active participation of the audience/reader in the processes of thought and expression. This frequently stimulates what Roland Barthes refers to as the "pleasure of the text," a process of ec-static reading whereby the reader enters into and becomes as important for the creation of the text as the author. From that vantage point, there is an erasure of difference between reader and author. A parallel to Barthes' view is Dōgen's notion that the fertile, eminently engaged imagination contributes to, and indeed is ultimately responsible for, all expressions of enlightenment. In the KS "Gabyō" Dōgen interprets the term for painted rice cake (gabyō), which conventionally referred to false or illusory conceptions in contrast to reality, as an image for self-reflection and self-understanding:

> If there is no painted rice cake, there is no remedy to satisfy hunger. If there is no painted hunger, there is no satisfaction for people. If there is no painted satisfaction, there is no capacity [to satisfy]. Furthermore, satisfying hunger, satisfying no-hunger, not satisfying hunger, and not satisfying no-hunger can be neither attained nor expressed without painted hunger.[102]

Thus, the painting of the rice cake as well as the hunger for it, which are both aspects of creative expression, are more satisfying or fulfilling than the tangible rice cake or physical sensation of hunger.

Kōans in general represent a highly imaginative, poetic form of indirect expression that has absorbed the influence of the anecdotal, aphoristic, and epigrammatic style of edifying instruction typical of indigenous Chinese religions. Berling remarks that in comparing the role of encounter dialogues in Sung works with T'ang texts, including the Platform Sūtra in addition to the collected sayings of Pai-chang and Huang-po, "we see that a shift has occurred in the presentation of Zen teachings for posterity. . . . A master was judged by his prowess in the paradoxical, intuitive interchanges of Zen dialogues . . . rather than homilies or more straightforward doctrinal statements."[103] McRae further notes, "Where early [Zen] texts contain a wide variety of doctrinal formulations, practical exhortations, and ritual procedures, the texts of classical Zen [Ma-tsu dialogues] are more uniform in their dedication to the transcription of encounter dialogue incidents, and they delight in baffling paradoxes, patent absurdities, and instructive vignettes of nonconformist behavior . . . [and] are alternately charming, informative, and baffling."[104]

Scholars seem to be in general agreement about the distinctively Chinese features of Zen discourse, as suggested in the following comments by Peter Gregory: "Chinese Buddhists continually adapted Buddhism to forms of expression and modes of practice more suited to their own cultural experience. [Kōan Zen] represents the shedding of the final trappings of Indian Buddhist doctrinal terminology and meditation practices in the creation of what was both a uniquely Ch'an and a uniquely Chinese style of Buddhism."[105] However, there is far less agreement about what constitutes the fundamental factor of Chinese influence on Zen. For example, Paul Demiéville has argued that the rise of kōans reflects the priority of the impact on Buddhism of Taoist intuitionism, mysticism, and naturalism over Confucian orderliness and social hierarchical concerns. Philosophical Taoism is certainly a key, and perhaps even the single most important influence on Zen. The open-ended, demythologizing tropological quality of Zen discourse reflects the influence of Taoist creativity and intuition, particularly the poetic eloquence and naturalism epitomized in Chuang Tzu's "fishnet of words"—that is, using language with great flexibility and rhetorical skill as a net to catch fish, symbolizing ideas, and then discarding the tool or net.

On the other hand, it seems to be more appropriate to consider that the Chinese influences on the kōan style are multiple and diverse, encompassing many elements from both Confucian and Taoist thought in addition to popular Buddhism and folk religiosity as well as basic Chinese culture and language. First, while verse and parable often do appear in earlier forms of Indian and Chinese Buddhism, Zen seems unique in exploiting the multivalent quality of the Chinese language to disclose a vast storehouse of philosophical ambiguity, nuance, and multidimensionality through the use of paradox, sustained wordplay, metaphor, and tautology. Kōans are to a large extent the product of the distinctive features of Chinese language in relation to philosophical investigation that is grounded in everyday phenomenal experience (rather than an abstract ideal such as rationalism). According to Charles Wei-hsun Fu, "because Chinese philosophy [as a whole, not only Taoism] itself never presupposes any bifurcation whatsoever between theory and practice, philosophy and religion, natural language and ideal language, everyday lived-experience and metaphysical thinking, etc., it never deviates from depicting the everyday form of life involving the philosophers' employment of natural language for the sake of a metaphysical adventure that liberates the common folk. . . . [Philosophers] are able to dis-cover or create a deeper philosophical, especially metaphysical, implication of an [everyday] word, a phrase, or a sentence while common folks are mostly unaware of such a deeper implication in everyday discourse."[106] Examples of this as cited by Fu are the *Mu* and *ten-shin* kōans also discussed above.

In addition, the personalized and existential pedagogical style of Zen discourse reflects the importance of dialogical encounter in Confucian, Neo-Confucian, and Neo-Taoist traditions. For example, Zen instruction shared the attitude expressed in the subtle yet highly demanding and uncompromising psychology of the master-disciple relationship in Confucian teaching. In the *Analects*, Confucius establishes a standard based on the injunction that is also cited by many Zen masters, including Yüan-wu in the HR: "If I show a disciple one corner of the room, I do not expect to have to show him the other three." This helps give Zen kōan teaching a pragmatic, goal-oriented focus in terms of shifting responsibility for soteriological attainment from an other-worldly power to dialogically stimulated introspection and self-discovery. As Suzuki writes, "The *practical imagination of the Chinese people* came thus to create Zen, and developed it to the best of their abilities to suit their own religious requirements."[107] Also, the Zen dialogues were influenced by Neo-Taoist philosophical conversations or colloquies known as *ch'ing-t'an* (elevated talk, J. *seidan*), which were initially considered a key access to truth but eventually became a sophisticated way of killing time and were "transformed from a speculative instrument into the drawing room pastime of an disillusioned aristocracy."[108] Zen dialogues as transcribed in the recorded sayings genre were also very much interactive with similar Neo-Confucian texts created during the Sung by "thinkers [who] associated the popularity of Ch'an with the freshness, simplicity, and accessibility of the Ch'an *yü-lu* [J. *goroku*] texts and so adopted the genre for their own use."[109] Thus, dialogical pedagogy was a main part of Zen's appeal to Neo-Confucian scholar-officials.

Yet another aspect of Chinese influence involves the way that kōans represent a syncretization of several elements of popular and folk religion with Zen philosophical ideals. First, the kōan in its catechistic function resembles the *nembutsu* chant of the Pure Land sect, which also became popular during the Sung, as a succinct linguistic device supporting meditative awareness. Both the kōan and *nembutsu* seek to provide a direct access to enlightenment in which a single practice thoroughly performed is considered to contain the complete truth. In addition, many kōans integrate folk legends and myths into a fundamentally demythological message. There are several examples of such syncretism in the MMK, including case no. 2, which uses a shamanistic tale of trance possession by a fox to comment on the doctrines of karma and causality; no. 35, which uses a tragic legend of the bilocation of a woman whose soul is divided into two equally viable bodies to convey a philosophy of nonduality; and no. 42, which highlights the role of discipline and dedication in meditation through the myth of Mañjuśrī, whose countless supernatural powers are unable to stir a woman from her profoundly contemplative state.

Dōgen's approach to kōans was also influenced by a number of aspects, which will be explained more fully in Chapter 3, in Japanese religiosity and aesthetics emphasizing the efficacy of language in expressing religious truth. When compared with Chinese, Japanese seems to support an even greater degree of polysemy giving rise to multiple interpretations. For instance, David Pollack contrasts the two languages by using the astrophysical analogy of a "black hole" for Chinese, which creates a deficit of meaning, and a "supernova" for Japanese, which incessantly generates a plurality of meanings.[110] Some of the Japanese influences on Dōgen include traditional Shinto ritualistic emphasis on the power of the word, and the affinity between words (*kotoba*) and things (*koto*); Kūkai's Shingon view of the unity of sound, word, and reality, a philosophical elaboration on Buddhist esotericism from Indian and Chinese sources; medieval literary ideals based on methods of using homonyms, puns, and other forms of wordplay to demonstrate the innate connection between words and the mind (*kokoro*), which suffuses verbal expressions with intention and meaning; and the Tendai sect's (as taken over from Chih-yi's Chinese T'ien-t'ai commentaries) emphasis on the interpretive power of "explaining through contemplation of mind" (*kanjin-shaku*). Thus, one of the keys to the success of Dōgen's KS text is that it represents a Japanization of Zen discourse that builds on Chinese models by integrating Japanese ritualistic, poetic, and philosophical forms of expression.

Furthermore, a number of modern Dōgen specialists have commented on how Dōgen was able to use Japanese influences and sources to free Chinese Ch'an from what he considered misleading, non-Buddhistic tendencies, especially a misleading Taoistic emphasis on a naturalist acceptance of phenomenal reality. Although Dōgen emphasizes the value of nature as model and mirror for human activity, he also argues that without sufficient stress on the need for spiritual authentication through meditation and monastic discipline the naturalist view can betray substantialist presuppositions that violate the basic Buddhist approach to impermanence and insubstantiality. Dōgen also consistently emphasizes the significance of insubstantiality in his major doctrines such as impermanence-Buddha-nature (mujō-busshō) and being-time. While maintaining on the one hand that Dōgen's view of kōans must be seen in light of Sung era texts, Ishii also argues that there are fundamental "differences . . . between Chinese Ch'an, constructed according to the traditions of China, and Dōgen Zen, formed in a completely different tradition than China. When Dōgen tried to establish his reformed Zen in Japan. . . . This purification may also, I think, be referred to as Japanization. When Buddhism was acclimatized in China, it incorporated non-Buddhist, indigenous Chinese ideas. Dōgen, being Japanese and not Chinese, successfully eliminated these."[111]

A Zen Problematic: Textuality and Untextuality

Despite general agreement on its significance, however, an understanding of the role of the kōan is still controversial and clouded by a variety of historical and methodological concerns. Eido T. Shimano cautions, "In the West today the meaning of the word kōan remains unclear or even mysterious."[112] Part of the reason for this is that the kōan is a deliberately elusive and enigmatic kind of expression, a "mysterious gate" to enlightenment often relying on "strange words and extraordinary gestures" (kigen kiko), that is intended to defy easy explanation and that cannot be reduced to a ready-made analysis. Indeed, a kōan that is clearly understandable is probably one that fails in its aim of challenging and undermining the presuppositions of conventional, discriminative thinking. The kōan has been portrayed, for example, as "the weapon which smashes all types of wrong knowledge and wrong conceptualization."[113] According to Chung-feng Ming-pen, "It cannot be understood by logic; it cannot be transmitted in words; it cannot be explained in writing; it cannot be measured by reason. It is like the poisoned drum that kills all who hear it, or like a great fire that consumes all who come near it."[114] Zen does not want to be pinned down by verbal expression, and some kōans could be seen as an expression of contempt or an act of defiance against the unenlightened need to categorize and compartmentalize thought (while other kōans have a humorous dimension in their use of absurdity and nonsensicality). The kōan is a mute affront to those who presume not just the superiority of a particular view, but the adequacy of any ideology to depict reality. Commentators who have labelled Zen discourse irrational or counter-logical are apparently somewhat justified by the fact that the MMK refers to the Mu kōan as a "red hot iron ball" that is impossible to swallow.

Zen maintains that its continuity is based on a "mind-to-mind transmission" (*ishin-denshin*), or is actualized by means of oral, existential encounters between master and disciple rather than the authority of any
written scriptural or commentatorial text. Perhaps the paradigmatic example of this emphasis on humanistically based orality is the anecdote cited
in HR case no. 1 (originally appearing in the KD) concerning Bodhidharma's interview with Emperor Wu of the Liang dynasty, in which the
first patriarch repeatedly defeats the pressupositions underlying the emperor's questions. When asked by the emperor how much merit is to be
gained by doing good deeds (building stupas, copying *sūtras*, etc.) Bodhidharma succinctly responds, "No merit." When then pressed to explain the
"sacred truth's first principle" he contradicts the question by quipping, "Just
emptiness, nothing sacred" (*kakuzen mushō*). And when finally asked about
his name or identity ("Who is this who faces me?") since nothing else is
established with certainty, the first patriarch retorts simply, "I don't know."
That is, transformative and transmissive spiritual insight for Zen seems to
be primarily intuitive rather than exegetical, and a matter of silence instead
of speech. But Miura, paraphrasing Chung-feng, adds an important note:
"Zen is 'without words, without explanation, without instruction, without
knowledge.' Zen is self-awakening only. Yet if we want to communicate
something about it to others, we are forced to fall back upon words."[115] If
communicated, Zen truth tends to be expressed through oxymoronic or
self-contradictory utterances in an oral setting rather than the declaration
of propositional claims in scriptures or in commentaries on scriptures. This
paradoxical juxtaposition of textuality and untextuality, or of words and
no-words, has been referred to as using "poison to counteract poison" or a
"thorn (of words) to extract another thorn (of words)." It is the method of
the "wordless word" (*muji no ji*).

However, to explain Zen by highlighting wordlessness at the expense
of words may support the view that the kōan is destined toward abbreviation as the closest possible approximation of an original reticence, which
is the Ta-hui *watō* position Dōgen refutes. Furthermore, the history of the
entire kōan tradition seems to move in the other direction—toward
amplification and extensive commentary—so that the chronicles and
collections in which the kōans are housed are anything but brief and simple
antitexts. Rather, they are complex, sophisticated, and often voluminous
texts despite, or perhaps because of, the fact that the kōan itself deliberately
runs counter to and continually seeks to undo textuality. When kōans are
functioning in harmony with their source of authentic subjectivity, they

are an example of Chuang Tzu's "goblet words" or "no-words." According to Chuang Tzu, "With words that are no-words, you may speak all your life long and you will never have said anything. Or you may go through your whole life *without* speaking them, in which case you will never have stopped speaking."[116] The main factor that contributes to the effectiveness of the kōan as a means of spiritual training is not a matter of setting up a contrast between words and wordlessness, speech and silence, or prolixity and brevity. Rather, the key is that the interpretation of the kōan resists being turned into a formula, conceptual crutch, or object of dependence, that is, ritualized so that mere repetition diminishes spontaneity. This can happen, however, just as easily through the abbreviated *watō* method as with another commentator's polysemous interpretive method. But it is clear that in the kōan tradition a significant element of ritualization invariably does take place, particularly by the Sung era. In many cases this result transpires with the tacit support of the religious institution, which mythologizes its leaders and ceremonializes the performance of catechistic kōans in ways that seem to overlook or even violate its own ideal of demythologization as the key to spiritual liberation. When ritualization does occur, there must be a turning over and fertilization of the soil of oral spontaneity based on genuine subjectivity from which the kōans spring. This is something that Dōgen, the kōan collections, and Ta-hui, who is said to have burned the HR, all sought in different written contexts to regain.

On Intertextuality

Therefore, the kōan could be considered an "untext" embedded in the elaborate texts it seeks to subvert in order to defeat any lingering expectation of or dependence on textuality in accord with the notion of "no reliance on words and letters." Dōgen refers to this interaction between text and untext as a process of "tangled vines disentangling tangled vines"—his interpretation of the term *kattō*—by which the source of the problem transmutes itself into the self-generating resolution of the obstacles that it has caused. In contrast to some other traditions of oral teaching that were eventually turned into writing, such as the Talmud in Jewish thought, Zen realization does not refer to an "ultimate Text"[117] (i. e., Torah), but to an intuitive gnoseological insight at once undermining and sustaining textuality. In many forms of Mahayana Buddhism, scriptures such as the *Lotus Sūtra*, the *Awakening of Faith*, the *Laṅkāvatāra Sūtra*, the *Saṃdhinirmocana Sūtra*, or the *Sukhāvatīvyūha Sūtra* may serve as an irreproachable textual

authority, but in Zen the dialogue based on spontaneous existential encounter challenges and replaces an authoritative text. For example, a
well-known T'ang Zen line evoked by Dōgen stresses in KS "Immo" the
priority of human awareness over any form of verbal expression: "If you
want such a thing, you must be such (*immo*) a person; if you are such a
person, why do you worry about such a thing?"[118] Because of the untextual
or detextualizing element inherent in kōans, it may not be effective to
transfer to an analysis of Zen some of the interpretive models typical in
Western thought that examine the claims of theological or metaphysical
assertions, such as many forms of textual criticism or linguistic analysis.
That is why it is fruitful to consider alternative methodologies that have
been used to focus on the relation between language and nonconceptualizable truth, including comparative mysticism, which views language in
terms of expressing the "groundless ground" (*Ungrund*) of a trans-theologi-
cal reality, and psychotherapy, which analyzes how verbal expressions both
reveal and conceal the unconscious source of language. However, discourse
analysis, which is complementary rather than in conflict with the insights
offered by these methods, sets out to achieve another aim, that is, to
examine the delicate relation between textuality and untextuality in Zen
discourse by focusing on the complexity of the chronicles and kōan texts
in connection with the stark simplicity of the defiantly untextual oral
dialogues.

   To accomplish this, the notion of intertextuality understands the term
"text" to mean something much more comprehensive than a written
document. Rather, "text" refers to the entire creative process, encompassing oral and written, conscious and unconscious, grounded and groundless
dimensions.[119] Postmodern criticism highlights in a nonlogocentric way
the edges and unnoticed borders of texts, or the conceptual and stylistic
cracks and crevices, the fault lines and fissures, so to speak, underlying the
fabrication of literary forms. A text is not a fixed and finite entity, nor is
the author an independent, discrete subject with a clear-cut agenda based
on personal intentionality. Rather, the text is the product of a fluid and
flexible continuing process of creativity in which the relativity and mutuality of author and reader contribute to the "mosaic of citations." As Mark
C. Taylor comments:

> The fabric(ation) of intertextuality not only lacks beginning and
> middle; it has no end. Texts forever cross and crisscross in a
> perpetual process of interweaving. . . . Rather than stable and

static, texts are insubstantial and transitory. Unavoidably entangled in an excentric web that neither begins nor ends, texts cannot be unified or totalized. The meaning of a text, therefore, is never fully present. Meaning is always in the process of forming, deforming, and reforming.[120]

Therefore, discourse analysis assumes that text and untext are always interrelated and interpenetrating, and that the aim of criticism is to "reveal hidden division, dispersion, multiplicity, alterity as silences, displacements, or supplements *within* what presents itself as unitary, selfsame, and self-present, indeed as its constitutive and engendering core."[121]

According to Harold Bloom, one of the main factors responsible for the engendering of texts is the inevitability of creative "misreading" or "misprision" caused by anxiety and other psychological defense mechanisms. This occurs when a strong author's work is greatly influenced or intertextually determined by, and yet at the same time is dedicated to trying to overcome its mentor's equally significant work in order to establish its creative independence and integrity.[122] Bloom's view seems to be a good way of explaining the psycholinguistic nature of Zen discourse in which a disciple constantly strives to surpass his master. For example, Bloomian "oedipal confrontation" may account for Ta-hui's destruction of Yüan-wu's kōan collection, as well as Dōgen's complex relations to his rivals and predecessors, including his attacks on Ta-hui, his creative rewriting of the poetry of Hung-chih, a prominent predecessor of Ju-ching, as well as his subtle criticisms of his Chinese mentor.

The following chapter continues to explore methodological issues in Dōgen and kōan studies by focusing on two themes. First, it examines more fully the problematics of Zen based on the apparent conflict in its discourse between ritualization and liberation, or mythology and demythology. Second, to help resolve these problematics, it clarifies the role of intertextuality, as well as other aspects of discourse analysis dealing with literary and historical issues, in comparison with psychological interpretations of kōans. This discussion sets the stage for Part II, which applies discourse analysis to a rethinking and overcoming of the conventional opposition between Dōgen and the kōan tradition by exploring the underlying intertextual connections as well as distinctive aims of the various genres of Sung Zen *satori* dialogue texts in order to situate and highlight the role of language and kōans in the KS text.

TWO

Mythology and Demythology

The Aporetics of Kōan Studies

Two Sets of Problematical Issues

Postmodern literary criticism, especially the notion of intertextuality, seems to offer an effective means of coming to grips with the basic problematical issue concerning the contradictory juxtaposition of textuality and untextuality that operates at the heart of Zen discourse and that is necessarily confronted when interpreting Dōgen's relation to the kōan tradition. But, as indicated in the previous chapter, it is also necessary to consider another very important problematic in Zen studies concerning the dating of the voluminous texts in which kōans are contained. The T'ang masters to whom the vast majority of *satori* dialogues are attributed are primarily known only through works originated during the Sung era, that is, after the considerable political impact and the upheaval of Buddhism caused by the persecutions of 845. Furthermore, a close look at the post-845 writings, especially the chronicles designed to transcribe the genealogy of sectarian transmission, opens up an even more complex set of problematics pertaining to the history of the Zen masters who created kōans, and the role of discourse analysis must be seen in terms of how it can contribute to a clarification of these issues.

Indeed, much of the misunderstanding concerning the function of kōans that Eido Shimano has warned us of is by no means due only to the phenomenon of "orientalism," that is, to the failure in the Western tendency to presuppose the need for an analysis of objectifiable truth to grasp the supposed inscrutability of Eastern wisdom. Rather, a great deal of the difficulty in interpreting kōans is based on an inverse cause: problematics or aporetics (in the sense of *aporia*, apparently unresolvable paradoxes) lurking within Zen's self-presentation and sense of its own historicality, which is rife with inconsistencies, contradictions, and outright inaccuracies. In this case, Western-influenced methodologies including positivist historiography and philosophical hermeneutics have been especially helpful in exposing the extent of the problematical issues. These methodologies have been introduced and incorporated into Zen studies by Hu Shih, Ui Hakuju, Sekiguchi Shindai, and Kagamishima Genryū (in Dōgen studies) in addition to Yanagida Seizan, among many others, and further developed in recent years by a host of Western scholars. As a result, it is possible to welcome the fact that current developments in research "have forced scholars to become sensitive to textual and historical problems and gradually to recognize the extent to which our view of Ch'an and Zen history has been informed by sectarian traditions . . . [so that scholars are] embarked on a wide-ranging reevaluation of the history and literature of the school."[1]

Many of the recent revisionist studies make it clear that in addition to the issue of untextuality, the traditional accounts of the history of Zen have long been haunted by at least two separable but very much interconnected problematics. One problem concerns the seemingly unchecked use throughout Zen history of a mythical-legendary "pseudohistoricizing"[2] about the leaders of the sect. Zen writings by no means overlook or sidestep the issue of history; in fact, it is the primary concern of the chronicles, especially the transmission of the lamp genre and, to a lesser extent, the lineage-oriented recorded sayings. Of course, it is not unusual in Chinese religious biography, a genre that has been greatly influenced by Taoist tales of immortality, to attribute to sages supernatural qualities and miraculous acts. But it is important to recognize that the more extensively and comprehensively that Sung Zen texts deal with historical topics, the more elaborate the mythology and hagiography becomes, and that *the accelerated pace of this pseudohistory after 845 co-exists with the tendency toward abbreviation and iconoclasm in many kōan texts.* This extensive use of hagiography does not seem to be simply a matter of naivete or a failure to understand historical methodology on the part of Zen authors and compilers. Rather, it represents a deliberate choice reflecting a certain religious vision to explain the lives of individual Zen masters in mythical rather than historiographical terms, and to encase the act of transmission from master to disciple in ritualistic rather than strictly existential fashion. The second problem is the extent to which partisan polemics has infiltrated Zen discourse, so that it becomes difficult to draw the line between the use of legitimate argumentation based on the goal of refuting deluded viewpoints and the outright exaggeration of a rival's position in order to set up a straw man so as to advance a particular set of doctrines in a sectarian bid for power. The initial controversy during the formative years of Zen between the Southern and Northern schools, in which the former asserted its subitist position over and against the latter's apparently misportrayed gradualism, eventually became paradigmatic for subsequent debates, including the Rinzai vs. Sōtō and kōan vs. zazen controversies in which the rhetoric of Dōgen's era was embroiled.

The two issues concerning pseudohistory and partisanship constitute one set of aporetics that is complementary to the problematic of untextuality discussed in Chapter 1. Therefore, it is necessary to formulate a methodology that can clarify and coordinate the relation between these two sets of problematical issues, which underlie and could undermine any attempt to situate Dōgen's approach to kōans in the context of the development of Sung Zen literature. The first set of problematics involves the juxtaposition of text and untext, symbol and antisymbol, and it creates a challenge for Western methodology to locate the appropriate means of appreciating, without further obscuring, the subtlety and elusiveness of Zen discourse. However, the second set of issues surrounding the seemingly excessive use of idealized and polemicized historical references in Zen literature presents a challenge for Zen to justify the inconsistencies concerning its own history. The first set represents the strength of the eloquence, flexibility, and utility of Zen discourse that seems to surpass many of the most sophisticated uses of language in world religious philosophy and thus defies facile analysis. But the second set reflects a weakness of inaccuracy based on sectarianism that seems to betray the perhaps overstated merits of Zen discourse and remains badly in need of clarification if not necessarily correction.

The topic of relating the two sets of problematical issues is crucial because it may appear that the second set of problems is severe enough to generate an image of inconsistency that undermines Zen's claim to religio-philosophical transcendence involved in the first set of issues. For example, in assessing Dōgen's doctrines in light of recent scholarship that demonstrates how he seems to have changed his positions over the years in response to sectarian debates and other partisan concerns, Bielefeldt argues that these issues raise "considerable doubt about the adequacy of the shōbō genzō not only as a historical but also as a theoretical model for interpreting his Zen."[3] The same kind of question could well be raised in regard to the

Zen tradition as a whole. Robert Sharf contends, for instance, that "'Enlightenment,' far from being a trans-cultural and trans-historical subjective experience, is constituted in elaborately choreographed and eminently public ritual performances." Further, Sharf argues that to see kōans as being exclusively aimed at fostering a spontaneous realization of a philosophical eternal now is "a woeful misreading of traditional Zen doctrine, and is altogether controverted by the lived contingencies of Zen monastic practice. Classical Zen ranks among the most ritualistic forms of Buddhist monasticism."[4] These comments point to the need for an interpretive standpoint that represents a compromise between traditional (as well as modern) apologetics and contemporary skepticism.

In attempting to resolve this matter, it is important to note that postmodern philosophers of history have shown that religious symbols, as part of an ideological system, should not be considered to represent pure, abstract, and unconditioned ideals. Rather, symbols of soteriological attainment are historically conditioned by a variety of factors, some having to do with intellectual, doctrinal debates within the tradition, and others with social and political forces exerting an impact from outside it. For example, Martin Heidegger maintains that all philosophical truth-claims are bound by their historical epoch and undergo a continuing process of concealment or hiddenness (*lethe*) of their essence in relation to their periodic revealment or coming-out-of-concealing (*a-letheia*). That is, all truths must be seen not as independent but as relative to the ontological-historical context from which they emerge. Foucault further argues that truth never exists in and of itself removed from the effort to gain, establish, and perpetuate power: "'Truth' is linked in a circular relation with systems of power which produce and sustain it, and to effects of power which it induces and which extend it. [There is only] A 'regime' of truth."[5]

In religious traditions, it is often the case not only that truths are conditioned by history, but also that the view of history itself is determined and sculpted in accord with what the past is dictated to have been in terms of the religion's current truth-claims. Therefore, it is not necessarily unusual or surprising to find that a tradition has "invented"[6] itself by writing its history backwards, or that a religion mythologizes and hagiologizes its leaders in order to contribute to this imaginative retrospection so as to legitimate its bid for power. The tendency to mythicization generally occurs when symbols are stripped of their status as figures of speech and are extended by way of conflation to cover and replace factual history. This problematic is tropological in origin in that the original metaphor gets severed from its rhetorical base and is mistakenly understood as a literal or mimetic representation: figurative symbol is reduced in a fundamentally misleading way to literal sign. As Nietzsche writes, "truths are illusions whose illusionary nature has been forgotten, metaphors that have been used up and have lost their imprint and that now operate as mere metal, no longer as coins."[7] Therefore, sacred myths about the past, as misplaced symbols, or misportrayed signs, are illusions substituting as truths. Yet if they are deliberately so used, and if they are interpreted in their appropriate context, they may still be able to function as legitimate symbols of religious vision or soteriological fulfillment. One pitfall is to accept myths inauthentically at face value, while the problem of the other extreme is to reject them altogether as unfactual. However, in the case of Zen the tendency to mythization may be particularly disconcerting because it seems to go against the grain of the masters' oft-repeated aim of nonreliance on words and letters. Typically the singleminded goal of their instruction is just the opposite of myth-making and requires a Nietzschean refutation of all illusion, a remarkable ability to at once make use of and penetrate to the arbitrary and one-sided quality of the tropes of discourse. Thus, the coexistence of mythology and demythology may foster a kind of "credibility gap" in that, on the one hand, Zen places itself in a privileged position of transcending and critiquing any attachment to symbols while at the same time its rhetoric succumbs to some of the very dangers it vigorously warns and protests against.

Nishitani's View of "Self-Surpassing" Zen

One way of clarifying the significance of this credibility gap is to consider the writings of Nishitani Keiji, a modern Kyoto school thinker who situates Zen's approach to history and related issues of time, death, and impermanence in the context of international religion and philosophy. Nishitani's main aim in *Religion and Nothingness* (original Japanese title: *Shūkyō to wa nanika*, or What is Religion?) is to explicate the transhistorical perspective of Zen in the philosophical context of analyzing the ways that traditional religion, especially Christianity, encounters and responds to several forces in modern society which conflict with and challenge it. These forces include science, which seeks to replace religion by explaining the origin and structure of the universe based on reason rather than revelation; nihilism, which negates all truth-claims, particularly otherworldly or supernatural ones; and secularism, which represents a gradual undermining of traditional spiritual values and customs by giving priority to finite, material pursuits.

Nishitani considers that genuine spirituality has been kept alive in the West not so much through mainstream religiosity but through what could be called the suprareligious mystical longing for divine unity in Eckhart and St. Francis as well as the extrareligious philosophical quest for existential authenticity in Sartre and Nietzsche. Yet he also maintains that Zen is an ideal tool with which to survey critically and to overcome self-reflectively Western thought because it represents a self-surpassing attitude not bound to any particular viewpoint, even its own historical or ideological background in Buddhist doctrine.[8] Therefore, Zen is not merely an alternative to Christianity but the paradigmatic, nonfixated ideology that exposes the origin of the forces that contradict and stifle the vitality of religion.

In asking which of the these forces—science, nihilism, or secularism—has the most devastating impact on religion, Nishitani's response is that, ironically, Christianity itself lies at the root and must bear responsibility for creating the very trends that threaten to negate it. Nihilism may seem to be the most significant challenge to religion because it denies any possibility of finding meaning, even in scientific investigation. Yet Nishitani sees nihilism as a by-product of the scientific assertion of lifeless matter; he agrees with Heidegger that nihilism arose as an historical stage in connection with the onset of—and it is therefore a unique response to—modernization. On the other hand, secularism, which seems to be another consequence of the scientific, technologized era, severely undermines religion because unlike science it does not even attempt to engage in the kind of dialogue that may in the end strengthen the ideology of religion; secularism has the deteriorating effect of "rust," caused by indifference, that eats away slowly but surely at the very structure of traditional religious life. Science appears to oppose religious faith in the supernatural with its logical approach to natural law, but for Nishitani scientism is the converse of religion which is still fundamentally of the same origin as Christianity.

The key to understanding the connection between religion and science is to see that both are a product of the Christian view of time and history. Christianity developed its linear teleology as a way of going beyond the primal, mythical sense of circular time. Mythical circularity is based on externally arranged cycles such as seasonal rotation determining the fertility, growth, and harvest of crops, and it must be distinguished from the circular time of Buddhist thought which is subjectively realized through meditative awareness of an "eternal now."[9] For Christianity, time begins with creation caused by a transhistorical being (God), and the unfolding of history is a sequence of dramatic events from the sins of Adam through the death and resurrection of Christ building toward a final eschatological culmination guided by a new, desperately needed transhistorical intervention (the Second Coming). Scientific and secular approaches to history may deny the role of a transhistorical power, but in seeking to discover and explain the origin or cause of things in the past and the attainment of progress in the future they represent a projection of the teleological position seeming to go outside of but still operating within the linear framework of Christianity. Nishitani writes:

> Although the views of history found in Christianity and in the Enlightenment represent diametrically opposed points of view, they both concur in recognizing a meaning in history. From its standpoint of *theocentric* faith, Christianity sees a divine providence . . . operative in history; the Enlightenment, from its *anthropocentric* standpoint of reason, locates the *telos* of history in the consummate rationalization of human life.[10]

Nishitani agrees that Nietzsche's "creative nihilism" attempts to encompass the totality of new creations in history. But he also seems to concur with Heidegger's critique of eternal recurrence as the ceaseless perpetuation of the will to will based on an infinite regression into the past. Thus, eternal recurrence does not fully capture the bottomless present moment in which, according to Buddhism, the circularity of past and future are contained. In order to revitalize Christianity in terms of the genuine ground of circular time, Nishitani recommends a radical existentialization and demythologization of the main events of Christian cosmology and teleology. In this way, "the most solemn moments of Christianity . . . [including] the *metanoia* to faith that represents the solemn moment when the solemnity of those other moments is truly realized" are transformed by way of demythologizing linear, teleological history into a sense of "gathering all those times within the home-ground of the present." Furthermore, this home-ground is a matter not of external time but authentic existential realization in that "Dasein [human existence] realizes the solemnity of the present as a monad of eternity, and thereby realizes all times in their solemnity."[11] As Masao Abe explains in his analysis of Nishitani, this monad moves neither backward nor forward but "can be properly realized only by overcoming both the regressive and the progressive movements together with the very dimension on which these two opposing movements are taking place."[12]

A prime example of true awareness of circular time in Zen is Dōgen's doctrine of the unity of practice and realization, or the inseparability of

continuing, sustained exertion and fundamental awakening: "As one practices," Dōgen writes, "one must not anticipate realization apart from
practice in that practice points directly to original realization."[13] Dōgen
also maintains the "unceasing circulation of continuous practice" (gyōji-
dōkan), such that "the Way [of buddhas and patriarchs] is circulating
ceaselessly without even the slightest gap between resolution, practice,
enlightenment, and nirvāṇa."[14] Perhaps the most striking parallel in Western thought to this understanding of the transhistorical eternal now is the
William Blake verse:

> To see a world in a Grain of Sand
> And a Heaven in a Wild Flower
> Hold Infinity in the palm of your hand
> And Eternity in an hour.[15]

Nishitani's strategy in using Zen to critique the West is to elevate the
issue of history to a higher, metaphysical level in terms of the dynamic,
transhistorical unity of time and eternity allowing for the uniqueness of
particular events. But a credibility gap is opened up because recent inves-
tigations have raised serious questions about the historicity of the leading
figures depicted in Zen literature on a lower, more practical level of
factuality and verifiability. The gap, perhaps long hidden from view, comes
to the fore in considering the relation between the ideal presentation of
Zen transcendental philosophy in the writings of traditional and modern
exponents like Nishitani and the actual content of Zen chronicles that
seem to violate or betray this ideal. This issue is crucial for an understanding
of how Dōgen's text is related to other Zen genres because the demythological kōans are contained in the mythical chronicles that were composed just
prior to or in some cases even at the same time as the compilation of the
kōan collections (see table 4.1). That is, the philosophical commentary on
kōans that Nishitani evokes appeared in the fourth stage of Zen history but
actually emerged coterminous with the hagiography in third stage chronicles whose aim was to gather and disseminate the second-stage source
dialogues for the purpose of legitimating sectarian interests.

Five Main Aporetics of Zen Studies

In order to deal comprehensively with the literary and historical connections between the genres in these various stages, it is necessary to clarify

five main aporetics generated by the credibility gap in that Zen pseudohistorical writings pass off mythology under the guise of reporting historical occurrences. The Zen chronicles, which became prominent during the Sung dynasty but deal primarily with T'ang dynasty leaders, purport to trace the origins and development of the sect, yet in these works factuality is nearly obliterated by sacred myth and hagiography. According to McRae, "except for Shen-hsiu, Shen-hui, and a few other individuals, the extant body of primary sources does not indicate one-to-one correspondences between individual masters and specific doctrines. Rather, the bulk of our doctrinal information can be identified only as having been valid in a certain general context at a certain time."[16] The chronicles consist largely of fabrications and legends attributed retrospectively to famous patriarchs and falsely projected as factual. Zen chronicles not only exaggerate and defy common sense but are often based on claims of prophecies and oracles, heavenly signs and portents, premonitions and predestinations, infant superawareness and fateful encounters. They are primarily concerned with using legendary anecdotes expressed in terms of mythic themes of pilgrimage, supernatural intervention, temptation, and heroic attainment to hagiologize the lives of leading Zen teachers, including the seminal figures Bodhidharma and Hui-neng, as well as post-Ma-tsu figures such as Lin-chi and Te-shan. Some of the prominent examples reflecting the use of mythemes include the snow falling from the heavens as Bodhidharma's disciple, Hui-k'o, who eventually exchanges skeletons with his teacher, offers to cut off his arm as a sign of his dedication; Hui-k'o's ability to cure a lay follower of a disease equally severe as leprosy by uttering a few phrases on the nonduality of mind; the supernatural elements accompanying the death of fourth patriarch Tao-hsin, who passes away "to the accompaniment of strange natural phenomena: the ground trembled and the earth was enveloped in mists . . . [and] three years after he died the doors to his stone mausoleum opened of themselves, and his body was revealed, retaining still the natural dignity it had possessed while he was alive";[17] and the prophetic dreams and visions experienced by both parties foretelling the fateful encounters of Lin-chi, Dōgen, and other masters-to-be with their preordained teachers. In addition to revelatory dreams, in KS "Gyōji" Dōgen refers to a guardian deity protecting Hung-chih and in KS "Kokyō" he cites the importance of traditional Shinto images of mirror, sword, and jewel, which are emblems of divine protection of the state.

Recent historical studies seriously question the historicity in the traditional accounts of the major patriarchs. It seems clear that Bodhidharma and Hui-neng, though not necessarily totally fabricated, can no longer be understood as the substantive historical personages portrayed in the chronicles. From a deconstructivist perspective, the illustrious names of the first and sixth patriarchs may represent no more than convenient designations of which texts and doctrines crucial for the advancement of the sect have been attributed by subsequent generations.[18] Probably the foremost case in which the two problematics of mythicization and partisanship have converged to obfuscate any clear sense of factual history involves Hui-neng. The historicity of the sixth patriarch is now questioned to the point that his life-story may indeed be a fictive device invented by Shen-hui, who was interested in perpetrating a sectarian debate between the dominant Southern school and the misrepresented Northern school. The names of these schools are not accurate geographically and do not even represent real institutional entities, but constitute rhetorical devices for the legitimation of a particular ideology. While the basic historicity of Dōgen does not appear to be in question, the traditional accounts of his life and teachings are by no means immune to these problematics. The medieval, sectarian biographies of Dōgen such as the *Kenzeiki*, which was composed over one hundred and fifty years after his death, have clearly embellished the details of his aristocratic birth and noble upbringing so that they must be read as hagiography rather than historiography. They clearly place more importance on exaggeration and idealization of the founder of Japanese Sōtō Zen than on fact or verifiability.[19] In addition, it must be acknowledged that some percentage of the writings attributed to Dōgen are not completely his own in that they were at least partially modified by scribes, including his first disciple, Ejō. Even if they are accepted as authentic, Dōgen's records of the history of Zen ideology at times delve into partisan attacks, perhaps smuggled into the texts by his editors, on a variety of positions supposedly antithetical to his own, especially Ta-hui's *kanna-zen*. The combined impact of the problematical tendencies is that Zen historicality is clouded if not altogether distorted under the pretext of an ostensible history. Who is the real Dōgen, and what are his concerns? Is there in fact a Hui-neng, and if not how and why was he invented?

The Sung was marked by a proliferation of multiple forms of expression when, according to Yün-hua Jan, "we find a large and unprecedented number of [historical] works."[20] Because of the gap between the supposed time of the T'ang oral sources and the written compositions, some scholars view the Sung works—both the chronicles and the kōan collections which in different ways *give priority to precedent over creativity*—as a sign of decline and a nostalgic hope for recapturing the lost spontaneity of a bygone classical period. Others interpret the Sung as the period of genuine creativity for synthesizing the otherwise disparate materials of an earlier time, and accord it the label of "golden age."[21] A third standpoint, borrowing from either positivism or deconstructionism, finds the Sung writings to be a time of inventing, or at least fancifully remembering, an essentially forgotten tradition which may or may not have ever existed in the pure form depicted in the chronicles.

While the pace of composition reached the accelerated rate of one major chronicle written every eight years, the concern for accuracy did not improve and probably was severely diminished, so that this apparently was the time Zen was busy creatively writing its history backwards.[22] Therefore, *the first aporetic is that the more Zen writings are preoccupied with history the less accurate they are historiographically.* As Jan points out, "the main objective of these works was naturally in defence of the genealogy of the Ch'an sect . . . [they] omitted the definite dates relating to patriarchs, and only recorded them in dynastic order. . . . Their works possessed brilliant literary expression but [were] not so reliable regarding the authenticity of some historical facts."[23] Philip B. Yampolsky sums up the approach to history found in Zen chronicles by arguing, "In the manufacture of this history, accuracy was not a consideration. . . . The few facts that are known can, perhaps, also be molded into a nice story, but it is one surrounded by doubts, lacunae, and inconsistencies . . . [and] almost certainly untrue."[24]

Contributing to this problematic is the basic consideration that Zen chronicles were not composed at a stage in the history of civilization that might be considered mythical in the sense that epic narrative was the primary form of expression. On the contrary, China already had a thousand year-old tradition, to which Zen undoubtedly thought it contributed, of sophisticated and extremely subtle philosophical analysis. According to Buswell, however, many Buddhist chronicles of this period (including Zen and other sects) were deliberately

> (c)ouched in thaumaturgy and theurgy, [for] Buddhist hagiography was designed for the edification of the faithful and the proselytization of the unconverted, not the imparting of biographical fact. Hagiography was ultimately a composite of . . . the life of the person himself, the retained memories of him within the religious community, and his value as a personification of certain spiritual ideals, cultural symbols, or religious accomplish-

ments. The paradigmatic elements present in sacred biography tend to interfere with attempts to reconstruct historically the "facts" about important spiritual figures.[25]

But this trend seems to subvert the attainment of enlightenment, which in Zen requires a Nietzschean demythologization, as Nishitani portrays it, through intense, personal dialogical encounter with an attained master. Zen indulges in mythology at the same time that it demands the deconstruction of any conceptual fixation or delusion in the mind of disciples by pointing directly to a spiritual fulfillment expressed through concrete particulars, such as "mountains are mountains, rivers are rivers," "when tired I eat, when hungry I sleep," and "everyday mind itself is buddha." Thus, there appears to be a gap between the truth of the enlightenment experience Zen proposes in master-disciple dialogues and the method of depicting its leading representatives in the chronicles. In other words, *the second, and perhaps fundamental, aporetic pervading Zen literature concerning the source dialogues is that Zen mythologizes, at times perhaps excessively so, precisely about the ability of its masters to demythologize pedagogically through face-to-face dialogue at any opportunity*. Yet modern exponents of Zen, including Nishitani, may have been somewhat oblivious to, or have accepted uncritically, the mythical content and narrative structure of its writings. Consequently, it can be argued that Zen must come to recognize and justify its own sense of narrative history before it can be utilized by Nishitani as a means of refuting the view of history typical of the West.

There are several important implications of the first two aporetics for an understanding of traditional Zen theory and practice as seen from the standpoint of contemporary intellectual history. One implication concerns the role of the kōan as a concrete, specific form of religious practice for monks in training in the context of the Zen monastic institution. The essential quality and rationale for the Ma-tsu style dialogue is to escape from and avoid any ceremonialization in terms of a completely spontaneous, experientially based, boundary-free form of communication. In most of the recorded conversations the participants use rhetoric and wordplay to defeat and embarrass the conceptual fixations and expectations of their dialogical partner. The Zen masters are particularly celebrated for their irreverent, superindividualistic spirit defying all conventions. "Thus, Lin-chi's 'ordinary man with nothing to do' is someone who does not care about ritual and pays only lip service, inasmuch as it may legitmate his predication, to the doctrine of transmigration. Rites are denounced for their empty formalism."[26] But in contrast to the supposed idealistic goal, "the so-called wordless transmission of mind by mind (*ishin-denshin*) represents only the idealized religious aspect of the Dharma transmission process. Zen master and disciple may evoke this mystical paradigm through ritual ceremony in the master's room (*shitsunai*), but other, more mundane institutional concerns can govern the actual succession and promotion of the Dharma 'heirs.'"[27] For example, if a disciple of a famous abbot left his original temple after the master's death, he would likely seek to automatically receive lineage certification from his new temple based merely on prior status even before meeting the abbot there. Furthermore, beyond the impact of ritualization and partisan concerns in the transmission process, it appears that the masters after death were often idolized, iconized, and even mummified to preserve them in an "eternal" state. This appears to violate or even to make a mockery of the kind of spiritual, here-and-now (rather than materialistic or immortal in any literal sense) transcendence the masters in the dialogues are supposed to embody.[28] Thus, *the third aporetic is that in Zen, perhaps like many another bureaucratic or religious institution, there is a basic gap between the ideal aims and actual methods in the selection of successors and transmission of truths.* Although Dōgen himself seems to have been clear, consistent, and conscientious in internalizing and spiritualizing the meaning of rituals and symbols,[29] later developments in the Sōtō sect beginning with Keizan were more eager to incorporate and syncretize elements of local, mythico-ritualistic religiosity into the selection of successors and the transmission process.[30]

Another implication in the aporetics of traditional Zen involves the way Zen history has been presented in contemporary scholarship deriving from nineteenth century, teleological models of history. The teleological model is problematic in that it betrays a modern tendency, as exposed by Nietzsche and Foucault,[31] among others, to expect history to follow recognizable patterns leading to clearly designated goals. The teleological approach reconstructs the life of a Zen master by piecing together references to his exploits scattered throughout the various chronicles, and this is a very challenging and demanding scholarly, hermeneutical task. However, an historical reconstruction done in this fashion tends to rely exclusively on internal sources within the Zen tradition that have something at stake ideologically in presenting an orderly view of their own history. The result is that some modern historians of Zen, who do an otherwise first-rate job of working with original texts, take their hermeneutic cue somewhat uncritically from sectarian sources. This may lead to an unfortunate and often counterproductive coincidence between the expectations of contemporary scholars and the sectarian rhetoric of traditional texts.[32] For example, it seems likely that the Sung authors eulogized the T'ang masters in accord with the traditional Chinese emphasis on glorifying a "golden age," and debates among contemporary scholars discussed in chapter 1 on identifiying the Zen "classical period" perhaps reflect and are somewhat bound by this tendency. Furthermore, the teleological model seems to betray the concept of transhistorical time that Nishitani advocates based on a refution of theocentrism and anthropocentrism. In accepting the conflation of myth and history offered by Zen, teleological historians echo and perpetuate what McRae labels the "string of pearls" approach to the lineage of masters. This, McRae writes, "create[s] a sequence of vivid snapshots of the patriarchs, each with his own biography and set of teaching, much like a beautiful necklace of identical pearls. Alas, from the standpoint of history we find that the pearls are illusory and the necklace only a convenient fiction. There is virtually nothing that is known about [Zen] during the seventh century that does not come down to us filtered through the perspective of the eighth century or later periods."[33] Therefore, *the fourth aporetic of Zen studies is that the teleological model of history is directly at odds with the philosophical ideal of here-and-now experiential time and history expressed in the dialogues.*

Another key problem with conventional studies has been a tendency to repeat unreflectively some of the polemically generated stereotypical images of key thinkers and schools in terms of all too neat opposing factions, including subitism vs. gradualism, silent illumination vs. kōan introspection, as well as the Northern vs. Southern, and Rinzai vs. Sōtō schools. This is in spite of the fact that the professed aim of Zen awakening is an uncompromising nonduality without partiality, exception, or any subtle bifurcation. For example, although it is crucial to his philosophical strategy to deny the existence of a sovereign Zen sect and to speak on behalf of Buddhism as a whole, some of Dōgen's text is "ablaze with a sectarian fervor so intense that it would seemingly lay sole claim to the true teaching of the Buddha and, by implication at least, relegate the competing schools of Japanese Buddhism to heterodoxy."[34] Indeed, ideological differences between competing Zen factions did exist, but the issues involved in these debates were not necessarily played out in their original context in the sedimented and often excessively polarized manner that is sometimes presented and interpreted in today's scholarship. Much of the polarization and polemic within the Zen sect is traceable to trends in Chinese Mahayana Buddhism,

such as the *hankyō* (C. *pan-chiao*) system used in Hua-yen of the classification and ranking of doctrines in a way that clearly judges and prioritizes
philosophical standpoints in support of one's own position. Tsung-mi, who
partially for lack of other sources is a major historian of T'ang Zen, presents
the history of Zen schools in *hankyō*-like fashion by offsetting and drawing
judgments concerning opposing ideologies. Furthermore, Zen polarization
is a product of Tokugawa era religious and social issues. It is likely that prior
to Tokugawa there was little sense of strong sectarian identification or
definition within Japanese Zen. The lines between Rinzai and Sōtō came
to be drawn for two main reasons. First, the Buddhist parish system (*danka*)
enforced by the shogunate compelled all denominations to compete with
one another for recruitment purposes, and this trend was later supported
by Shinto/Buddhist separation during the Meiji period. Also, the advent
of the Ōbaku Zen sect during Tokugawa was an instigation for Rinzai and
Sōtō to shore up their respective apologetical arguments.

There have been at least four times in the history of Zen when the
question of polarization has become particularly pronounced: (1) the
formative period when the sudden enlightenment vs. gradual enlightenment debate was framed by Shen-hui in the *Platform Sūtra* around the
rhetoric of Hui-neng's Southern vs. Shen-hsiu's Northern schools; (2) the
Sung era, when the central controversy, which greatly influenced Dōgen's
discourse, between Hung-chih's doctrine of *mokushō-zen* and Ta-hui's
kanna-zen first took on the proportions of a Sōtō vs. Rinzai schism; (3) the
revival of the latter debate, played out in Tokugawa Japan with Hakuin as
the primary Rinzai advocate and critic of Sōtō, which was still identified
with the *mokushō* position, and Menzan Zuihō was among the leading Sōtō
apologists; (4) and the twentieth-century version of this debate, with D.
T. Suzuki playing the main Rinzai role and the Sōtō forces somewhat
fragmented and delayed in responding.[35]

The subtext underlying these controversies—especially the debates
concerning sudden vs. gradual enlightenment, and *mokushō-zen* vs. *kanna-
zen*—is the issue of defining meditation in terms of dynamism over and
against quietism. For rhetorical purposes this issue then gets posited in
strictly sectarian terms, so that sect and doctrine are conflated: if someone
takes one position he must be embracing all of the tenets associated with
that sect while opposing in principle the tenets of the other sect. In fact,
nearly all Zen masters and schools of thought seem to concur in supporting
the priority of contemplation dynamically actualized in spatio-temporal
reality and the deficiency of a quietist approach that may represent a

withdrawal from concrete affairs. This seems to be the message of many of the kōans, including MMK case no. 7 in which Chao-chou instructs a monk who appears overly eager to attain an enlightenment that would be cut off from the world of actuality, "go wash your breakfast bowls"; and another saying which asserts that "carrying water and chopping wood is the wonderful Tao." Some of the points of disagreement among Zen thinkers concerning which view of practice truly represents the correct approach to dynamism give rise to cogent philosophical arguments. But at the same time each sect tends to set up its polarized rival as a straw man. This is the game of apologetics, or of rallying the troops in support of one's own perspective by denigrating what is portrayed, or what must be misportrayed for the sake of partisan rhetoric, as its opposite. The problematic becomes particularly acute when the subsequent debates greatly affect or even determine the way the earlier stages are understood. For example, an understanding of Dōgen's participation in stage (2), which is itself read back into defining stage (1), to a large extent represents a composite of stages (3) and (4) applied retrospectively. This indicates just how sedimented the self-knowledge of the tradition has become. Therefore, even if Zen philosophy has a transcendental or self-surpassing dimension in a metaphysical sense of overcoming the one-sided views in earlier Buddhist as well as other religious and philosophical systems in the manner claimed by Nishitani and others, this is not necessarily a sufficient rationale to obviate the need for an archaeology of knowledge to sift through the layers of conventionality concerning the stages of historical development.

Therefore, many modern accounts are one-sided because they are based largely on sectarian rhetoric misleadingly projected as historiographical evidence, as well as discrepancies in the contemporary religious practices of Zen sects retrospectively ascribed to the historical background and doctrinal development of the works in question. The traditional tendency to conflate polemics with historical actuality is compounded by the equally problematic modern tendency to view religions in somewhat oversimplified monolithic and/or polarized terms. That is, if a thinker is known to be in favor of one idea (i.e., pro-position A), it is expected that he or she must be opposed to its antithesis (anti-position not-A). Since kōan and zazen are seen as opposed, if Dōgen is pro-zazen he must be anti-kōan. Thus, *the fifth aporetic is the contradiction between the philosophical ideal of nonduality and the apparent obsession with sectarian, polemical rhetoric that falls into an exclusivistic "us vs. them" mentality.* As Thomas Cleary points out, "Japanese polemic and Western historians have elevated [differences in method of teaching] to the status of a controversy or even a schism, but this exaggeration has no basis in the actual Chinese records of the original activity."[36]

The Function of Literary Criticism

What, then, is to be made of these apparent contradictions between Zen's mythical history riddled by hagiography and polemics and its philosophical ideal of transhistorical time, and how can discourse analysis contribute to a clarification of the relation between these opposing trends? Generally, there have been two responses to the aporetics of Zen, and discourse analysis seeks a middle path between the extremes they represent. The first response is that of the modern, Western-influenced Zen apologist, such as D. T. Suzuki, who, in his well-known public debate with Zen historian Hu Shih, argued that too much attention to the question of historicality misses the essence of the Zen experience.[37] Suzuki is certainly not insensitive to historical or literary issues. However, he often supports a psychological perspective that succumbs to the "string of pearls" view that enlightenment experience is uniform and identical across generations. This view also seems to stress the timeless, ahistorical quality of religious fulfillment construed to transcend historical conditioning and to be impervious to historical investigation. The approach at the other extreme is an unbridled skepticism, which was initiated as early as the Sung era by rival Buddhist sects, some of whom launched "direct attacks" on Zen. In works such as *Stop the Lies* (*Chih-ngo*), for example, T'ien-t'ai school critics claimed that Zen chronicles were "a wrong presentation of history mainly depending on sources of the Ch'an sect. The aim of this false genealogy is to mislead the people of the country to a confusion."[38] This skeptical view is extended by modern scholars such as Takayuki Nagashima, who argues that he has proven the "nonexistence" of Hui-neng as an outright "fabrication," though he accepts the status of the sixth patriarch as "symbol." [39]

Although Nagashima is extremely critical of Zen's sense of history, the contrast he sets up between fabrication and symbolism points to the need for an approach that reaches a compromise between and takes priority over apologetics or refutation. An alternative method emphasizing the theme of the symbolic significance of the chronicles relative to their historiographical inadequacy is suggested by Bernard Faure, who uses a structuralist analysis of the legends surrounding the personality of Bodhidharma to refer to the first patriarch as a "religious paradigm"[40] rather than a historical figure. If Bodhidharma functions as a paradigm, then Zen's deficient history would become secondary to its symbolic value. Faure also applies a literary critical method to studies of Dōgen in the context of the development of Kamakura Zen, and to the relation between the embryonic Sōtō school and the more established but vulnerable Daruma-shū sect. In an essay arguing from the standpoint of intertextuality, Faure points out that even the authorship of the KS is not certain, for "the final version is the result of a collective enterprise," and "the very concept of authorship may prove inadequate here." He then adds a somewhat skeptical and fatalistic comment by suggesting that the fascicles of the KS "become part of the same field of discourse [as other texts of Kamakura Buddhism], *squares on a chessboard that had to be filled by one pawn or another . . .* [T]hey are all hierarchically interrelated, and no pawn should be considered independent."[41] Therefore, according to one current perspective found in both Bielefeldt (arguing from a positivist perspective, as mentioned above) and Faure (deconstructionist), the aporetics of Zen studies *throw into question not only the identity of Dōgen as author but the creativity and value of the writings attributed to that name.*

However, too much skepticism also neglects the key issues of discourse analysis: what is the literary structure and function of the legends themselves which contain the dialogues with which the Zen writings are preoccupied, and how does this influence Dōgen in relation to other kōan collections and interpreters, including Ta-hui? One way out of the impasse between fact and fabrication, myth and historiography, apologetics and skepticism is to continue to extend the suggestions of Faure and Nagashima concerning intertextuality and symbolism in order to analyze Zen not in terms of factual history but literary history. A literary historical approach, according to John C. Maraldo, "would focus on the evolution of literary forms but avoid claims about their internal representation or misrepresentation of historical reality. . . . In factual history, texts are the given measure for deciding the facts about the life of some person or school. . . . In literary history, on the other hand, language patterns serve as the measure for determining the identity of linguistic forms . . . across time, to establish the existence of particular if fluid motifs, stories, and genres."[42] For Maraldo, a literary approach has several advantages. First, it focuses on the symbolism of personages whether they are strictly factual or not, and thus offers a compromise between historiographical skepticism and uncritical, unhistorical apologetics. Also, it catalogues and analyzes the rhetorical topoi of storytelling and recording, the repetition and transformation of motifs and episodes, the textual usage of other texts, such as quoting, "plagiarizing" in the sense of putting words into the mouth of another and embedding texts within texts, or layering commentary and source. Further, it assesses the differences between colloquial and refined expressions, as well as the use of metaphor and figurative speech.[43]

It is important to recognize that to a large extent the studies of Suzuki and Nishitani use a literary methodology, although their work is not identified as such and is sometimes criticized for lacking this dimension.[44] It is also significant that in recent years literary criticism has been applied at an accelerated pace to studies of other scriptural traditions, particularly in the area of biblical criticism and Talmudic studies. For example, modern Christian theology has to some extent been guided by the Vatican injunction to carry out "form criticism" of the New Testament so as "to make judicious inquiry as to how far the form of expression or the type of literature adopted by the sacred writer may help towards the true and genuine interpretation."[45] In a similar vein, Meir Sternberg makes a very interesting and fruitful fundamental distinction in biblical scholarship that may also be applicable to Zen studies between historically based "source-oriented" analysis and literary based "discourse-oriented" analysis. According to Sternberg, "source-oriented inquiry addresses itself to the biblical world as it really was, usually to some specific dimension thereof . . . [like] the real-life processes that generated and shaped the biblical text . . . [so] interest focuses on some object behind the text—on a state of affairs or development which operated at the time as a source (material, antecedent, enabling condition) of biblical writing and which biblical writing now reflects in turn." He goes on to argue that

> Discourse-oriented analysis, on the other hand, sets out to understand not the realities behind the text but the text itself as a pattern of meaning and effect. What does this piece of language—metaphor, epigram, dialogue, tale, cycle, book—signify in context? What are the rules governing the transaction between storyteller or poet and reader? . . . What is the part played by the omissions, redundancies, ambiguities, alternations between scene and summary or elevated and colloquial language?[46]

The Relation Between Literary and Historical Issues

The suggestions of Maraldo and Sternberg concerning literary criticism and discourse-oriented analysis are quite innovative and thought-provoking in highlighting the complementary and overlapping concerns of historical and literary studies. However, to some extent both scholars may be construed as suggesting an older pattern of bifurcating history and literature, or context and text, and as giving priority somewhat to literature rather than attaining a genuine methodological compromise. In his study on *Intertextuality and the Reading of Midrash*, Daniel Boyarin points out the need to be sensitive to the notion that "the relation between 'textuality' and 'history' has often been presented as if they were mutually exclusive ways of understanding the literary text."[47] Boyarin recommends avoiding one extreme of seeing literature as "occupying an autonomous ontological realm, divorced from and 'above' the material and social conditions of its production," as well as the other extreme of understanding "the text to be wholly determined by and to be a reflection of its historical circumstances." Intertextuality for Boyarin helps provide a middle ground by illustrating that "Meaning is produced in the creative interaction between text being read, reader, and other texts. . . . [so that] There is a certain erasure of difference between the text being interpreted and the interpreting text."[48] It is also helpful to heed the argument made by Hayden White that while historical texts are not necessarily reducible to narration, they must at least be recognized as containing a narrative foundation aimed at promoting a vision of symbols, heroes, and icons. On the relation between narrative and heroism White writes, "a historical narrative is not only a *reproduction* of the events reported in it, but also a *complex of symbols* which gives us directions for finding an *icon* of the structure of those events in our literary tradition."[49]

From the standpoint of intertextuality, the questions (of fact or fiction, historicity or mythology) become rather secondary, if not altogether irrelevant, in that the emphasis shifts from examining the intentionality of independent authors to appreciating the tapestry of quotations which comprise all texts. According to Roland Barthes, the "writerly" (author) and "readerly" (reader) dimensions of a text are so intertwined that "'I' is not an innocent subject, anterior to the text. . . . This 'I' which approaches the text is already itself a plurality of other texts, of codes which are infinite, or more precisely, lost (whose origin is lost)."[50] Foucault similarly argues, "the author's name manifests the appearance of a certain discursive set and indicates the status of this discourse within a society and a culture . . . [I]t is located in the break that founds a certain discursive construct and its very particular mode of being."[51] This author-less view of intertextuality, in which there is an "erasure of difference" between the interconnected interpreting-text and interpreted-texts, as well as between author and reader, seems parallel to the Buddhist notion of the egoless, insubstantial, and thus interdependent nature of reality. It points to the need to examine the semiotic, discursive field encompassing text in relation to context as well as untext.

Furthermore, according to postmodern views of intellectual history, one way of dealing with a text's apparent historiographical deficiencies and inconsistencies is to transmute the issue by regarding historical writing as a literary form with a fundamentally narrative structure. Intellectual historians and philosophers of history such as Barthes, Foucault, Lyotard, Ricoeur, and White, responding especially to the Nietzschean view of the multiple perspectives of truth, no longer see the matter of history merely as an objective (or external) and linear (or sequential) process, which is the typical nineteenth-century model. Rather, history is considered a tropological form of discourse, or an unfolding self-critical literary structure that "contain(s) an irreducible and inexpungeable element of interpretation."[52] That is, history is not the cataloguing of a chronological sequence of facts but the dynamic reordering of time in the telling of a narrative, which represents "the syntagmatic dispersion of events across a temporal series presented as a prose discourse."[53] Narrative theorist Robert Scholes maintains, for example, "there is no recording, only constructing reality"— that is, there is no objective reality but an open-ended "text" which simultaneously engages author and reader, narrator and interpreter. Dramatist Eugene Ionesco suggests: "Realism does not exist. Everything is invention. Even realism is invented. Reality is not realistic."[54] Also, Barthes, who has considered the significance of Buddhist contemplation in relation to textuality, maintains that "the writerly text is *ourselves writing*, before the infinite play of the world (the world as function) is traversed, intersected, stopped, plasticized by some singular system . . . which reduces the plurality of entrances, the opening of networks, the infinity of languages."[55] Therefore, postmodernist criticism considers the formation of textuality and issues in historicality not to be antithetical but inseparable, overlapping, and often indistinguishable concerns in the discourse of a tradition. The notion of intertextuality also does not exclude a consideration of extratextual matters, such as the impact of politics and economics on the formation of texts (including the 845 suppression of Buddhism), but it is primarily involved with examining how signs and symbols encode messages in interconnected oral and transcribed genres.

In this light, a number of recent commentators on Zen, including Buswell, Faure, Maraldo, and Nagashima seem to agree that the question for the historian becomes one of looking beyond the issue of verifying or disproving the historicality of Zen legends in order to discover the "spiritual ideal" or "religious paradigm" underlying Zen's elaborate mythicization.[56] As Yanagida strongly suggests in his major work on the formation of the transmission of the lamp literature, the most mythical-hagiographical of the Sung genres, studies of this material that are aimed merely at discrediting its historical claims are unsatisfactory unless researchers are sympathetic and able to penetrate to the level of "sacred narrative" (*shūkyō-setsuwateki*) as the basis of the chronicles' function. Because the chronicles were created for that purpose, Yanagida writes: "One who knows only how to repudiate or to dismiss the stories as factually unhistorical is not qualified to read the lamp histories. For it is an obvious premise that they do not transmit solely historical fact."[57]

In evaluating the relation between dialogues and chronicles from a literary standpoint, the issue is not one of defining classical and post-classical epochs, or of arguing for or against the verifiability of the historical claims of the texts. Rather, the aim of literary criticism or discourse analysis is to show that the apparent contradiction between truth and method in the dialogues and chronicles is resolvable by analyzing the diverse ways these genres have captured and/or deliberately misplaced the underlying dialogical unit within the context of the religious symbolism of a larger literary structure. It highlights and explores the narrative structure or "creative historiography" in Zen chronicles in the sense that they choose to misrepresent historical facts for symbolic purposes. This is seen not as a deficient means of writing history but as a way of legitimizing the sect through the deliberate selection of a form of discourse that is compatible with the demythological aim of the kōan collections' philosophical approach to "creative philology" through manipulation and displacement of tropes.[58] Discourse analysis suggests that the genres represent complementary and interdependent approaches to organizing common material: the chronicles use mythical themes of pilgrimage, prophecy, and predestined meetings to create romanticized narratives of the lives of eminent masters and thereby establish the continuity of generation-to-generation lineage; and the kōan collections, a genre that can include Dōgen's KS *Shōbōgenzō*, stress the tropological structure inherent in the kind of radical demythologizing the masters undertake so as to penetrate all discursive, symbol-generating thinking. From this perspective, Zen literature appears consistent rather than plagued by aporetics, with the issue of literary symbolism and narrative structure providing at once the lock and key for critical interpretation.

The Kōan as Religious Symbol

At this point it is important to distinguish the ways that postmodern categories are used in regard to two kinds of texts: literary and/or historical texts that are created in a basically secular setting, and the writings of Zen, which is essentially a religious tradition, that is, an institutionalized or socially and historically conditioned philosophy of soteriological attainment, or enlightenment, reached through the appropriate use of edifying symbols. The aim of discourse analysis is not to reduce the kōan to a literary form with historical implications, but to see how literary as well as historical features expressed in narratological and tropological structures contribute to the construction of the kōan as Zen's main religious symbol. In purely literary arts, signs and symbols are contingent upon the literary value of the piece, whereas in religion, literary signs come to function as symbols of transcendence. That is, in a religious or spiritual quest, the edifying symbol ec-statically stands out from or transcends the entire field of discourse, and it takes priority over other signs in that its signification of a sacred, transformative experience holistically rises above the sum of its semiotic components. According to Ricoeur, the transcendental function of religious symbols derives from their ability to utilize for the purpose of psychological instruction the inexhaustible resources of a cosmic source of truth. Therefore, the cosmic and psychological origins of symbol precede subsequent interpretations: "Cosmos and Psyche are the two poles of the same expressivity; I express myself in expressing the world; I explore my own sacrality in deciphering that of this world."[59] Accomplishing this, for G. Bachelard, also calls upon a profound and unifying poetic imagination, which "puts us at the origin of the speaking being; it becomes a new being of our language, it expresses us in making us that which it expresses."[60] In religious discourse, therefore, it is the profoundly subjective response that transforms the ordinary sign into an active symbol, which according to Paul Tillich is an indicator that allows participation in what it symbolizes.[61]

On Psychological Interpretations

Because of the emphasis in religions in general, and in Zen in particular, on the priority of subjective participation in symbols and personal change as a key to soteriology, it could be argued that a psychotherapeutic model of interpretation aimed at depicting the process, or the "psychodynamics,"[62] of self-transformation is more suitable than a discourse (literary) model for kōan studies. Furthermore, Zen Buddhism appears different than many religions in which symbols clearly refer to the Sacred, or a numinous, transcendent source from which they spring as metaphorical discourse. Buddhism has been referred to as a "religion of (psycho)analysis" because of the focus in Pali and Abhidharma literature on dissecting the multiple causes and conditions of suffering not in reference to a divine force but solely in terms of the defilements (kleśa) and ignorance (avidyā) of human awareness and the possibilities for enlightenment generated by wisdom (prañjā) and compassion (karuṇā). It is often said that Buddhism "is not a religion" at all due to its emphasis on this-worldly, humanistic enlightenment, as in the Buddha's saying (cited by Dōgen), "Right here there is no second person,"[63] or in Dōgen's KS "Genjōkōan" passage, "To study the Buddha Dharma is to study the self. To study the self is to forget the self . . . and to cast off body-mind of self and others."[64] Zen in particular seems to stress an anti-authoritarian iconoclasm, represented by Lin-chi's famous utterance, "If you see the buddha, kill the buddha," that attempts to defeat as obstructive of satori all symbol-making that refers to some transcendental power standing in contrast to concrete, here-and-now reality. The basis of Zen realization is what Kyoto school thinkers call "absolute nothingness" (zettai mu) or Bodhidharma's "Just emptiness, nothing sacred." Zen is the path of self-power (jiriki), in which the ultimate truth is known as no-thought (munen) or no-mind (mushin) because it is not a concept beyond the concrete world but is attained through one's own exertion of nonconceptualizable meditative awareness. Zen realization has been referred to as a "radical humanism" that is based on the kind of individualism found in modern psychology, including Jungian or Morita psychotherapy.[65] The Zen master's relation with his disciples has also been compared to the role of the therapist in relation to his patients.

Part of the argument for supporting a psychological rather than a literary interpretation of Zen is that kōans are intended to function as provisional, pedagogical tools rather than as propositional truth-claims. That is, kōans are not used to explain or to argue for or against a particular understanding of reality, or to posit what Heidegger calls an onto-theological (metaphysical, or ontological, and/or theological) truth-claim. Instead, the aim of kōans, as of some earlier forms of Buddhist discourse, such as the Buddha's silence, Prajñāpāramita Sūtras' paradox, and Mādhyamika dialectical negation, is liberation from the tendency to assume the verifiability of innately relativistic positions. As the Chinese Mādhyamika philosopher, Chi-tsang, has suggested, "the right view is the refutation of all one-sided views." In that vein, kōans are *instructive*, or heuristic, in that they are activated only relative to a fixation and delusion, and *provisional*, or catalytic, in that they cease to function and leave no trace of hypostatization once liberation has been attained. Kōans need to be situationally appropriate, and they may become misleading or irrelevant if evoked either too much before or after the specific delusion for which they are appropriate. Several noted dialogues highlight the catalytic quality of Zen discourse, which is dependent upon and yet also self-extricating from traditional Buddhist doctrines. For example, Ma-tsu tells his disciple Ta-chu,

> I have here not a thing to give you. . . . What Buddha Dharma
> can you expect to learn from me?[66]

And when another disciple inquires why he has suggested that "this very mind is buddha" (*sokushin-zebutsu*, a phrase also often used by Dōgen) if that term is not intended to represent an absolute truth, Ma-tsu responds: "In order to stop the crying of little children." When then asked what he teaches once the crying has stopped, Ma-tsu goes on to say that the only truth is to "*embody* the Great Tao,"[67] thereby indicating the psychological-existential rather than onto-theological significance of Zen discourse.

Lin-chi similarly highlights the fundamentally therapeutic nature of Zen dialogues when he refers to his teaching as medicine:

> This mountain monk has not one Dharma to give to people; [I]
> just cure illness and untie knots (release bonds).[68]

That is, there is no substantive content behind or beyond the teaching, which, once it becomes effective in capturing (or recapturing) the primordial state of enlightenment, is no longer useful or needed. (In problematic fashion, however, Lin-chi also asserts in the same passage that his transmission and lineage are the "correct" ones.) Another example of Zen pedagogy occurs in Hui-hai's sayings on sudden enlightenment. When Hui-hai discusses the relativity and ultimate emptiness of the terms *mu* (no, negation, nonbeing, or nothingness) and *u* (yes, affirmation, being, or manifestation), he is asked by a disciple, "[If] even *u* and *mu* cannot be sought, on what ground can the true body [of buddha] be established?" Hui-hai responds:

> It is because you ask such a question [that the true body of buddha
> is established]. If no such question is asked, then the name "the
> true body" will not be set up. Why so? This is just like the case

of a bright mirror: when it confronts something, it shows the image of the object; when it confronts nothing, it shows no image at all.[69]

Therefore, the Zen dialogue has no set, fixed, or single possible response. The responses it uses are flexibly and provisionally based on situational context and level of discourse, with affirmation freely giving way to or overturning negation, and vice versa. Negation, silence, paradox, and abbreviation may be in a particular instance—but are not inherently or necessarily—preferable to their opposite; the only constant is the decentric play of tropes displacing one another.

Furthermore, it is important to recognize that the connection between modern psychology and Zen is multifaceted and complex. There are at least four ways that psychologists, Buddhologists, and related scholars and thinkers have connected psychology to Zen experience. First, Suzuki, among others, has extracted basic Freudian categories from out of their context in psychoanalysis—including the unconscious, or the distinction between conscious and unconscious, anxiety, and transference—to employ them as a means of interpreting for the contemporary Western reader the dynamics of Zen awakening, especially the qualities of spontaneity and suddenness characteristic of the state of mindlessness. In particular, Suzuki has associated some of the Zen terms for ultimacy, such as Buddha-nature or One Mind, with the unconscious, which acts as a fulcrum for stimulating realization. A second approach is evident in works by Jung, Fromm, Horney, and other post-Freudian psychologists comparing—or highlighting parallels as well as disparities between—Zen and various forms of psychotherapy from a contemporary vantage point. A third perspective is the development of several hybrid forms of therapy, most notably Morita therapy, which integrate some aspects of Zen understanding of the limitations and potentials of human awareness with conventional forms of psychology.[70]

A fourth approach, which in many ways is an extension of the second approach into the arena of social criticism, emerges in the context of discussions that examine various alternative forms of religiosity and/or secularized spirituality in modern society. Some of these discussions have considered to what extent psychotherapy, which is an outgrowth of a scientific worldview, or Zen, an imported form of mysticism, can function in the West as a surrogate for traditional forms of worship. Zen supporters have argued that for those interested in a thoroughgoing existential-ontological liberation that is free from the impediments of traditional theology, despite affinities to Zen praxis, psychotherapy does not provide a sufficiently radical paradigm for an extrication from conceptual limitations. Zen, on the other hand, is able to root out the cause of all delusions at their source. For example, in comparing Zen and Victor Frankl's logotherapy, Sandra Wawrytko argues that "many parallels are to be found . . . including glimmerings of enlightenmental insight into the key role of suffering. Yet, Frankl is never fully able to liberate either himself or Logotherapy from Samsara, as reflected in his view of death as a necessary guarantee of life's meaning. Only Zen is able to transcend both self (ego) and Samsara, by means of the resources inherent in Original Nature. Its attitude of detachment toward death, without succumbing to denial, epitomizes its overarching efficacy."[71] In a similar vein comparing Zen and Jung, Abe Masao maintains, "according to Jung it is the collective unconscious or the unknown self which is responsible for hindering us psychically. Instead of analyzing psychic diseases one by one, Zen tries to dig out and cut away the very root of the human consciousness beyond consciousness, including the Jungian or any other hypothesized realm of an unconscious. Zen insists that only then can complete emancipation from human suffering be achieved and the true Self be awakened."[72]

Therefore, the psychotherapeutic model for interpreting kōans is by no means a monolithic, systematic approach, but consists of affinities drawn with depth and humanistic psychology as proposed by D. T. Suzuki and other leading figures in both Zen studies (Abe, DeMartino, Dumoulin, Kasulis, Sekida) and psychotherapy (Benoit, Fromm, Horney, Jung, Konda).[73] The first two of the four approaches to Zen and psychology described above are primarily descriptive and comparative, and the latter two are primarily prescriptive and normative. The concern here is to consider the implications of the descriptive methodology for understanding the significance of discourse analysis. The descriptive psychological model seems to have certain advantages over mystical and philosophical interpretations because it emphasizes the concrete experiential transformation realized in Zen through the dispossession of the ego, the abandonment of illusion, and the attainment of the fundamental nature of selfhood—the "original face" (honrai no memmoku), "seeing into [one's own-]nature" (kenshō), or state of "no-thought" (munen)—which Suzuki generally refers to as the "unconscious" (without necessarily keeping in mind differences with the notions of unconscious in Freud and Jung).[74] This approach highlights the view that the kōan is aimed at creating a tension or conflict between two levels of awareness—the logical and irrational, discursive and intuitive, conscious and unconscious—resulting in an impasse or barrier to understanding and consequent sudden breakthrough to enlightenment. According to Stanley Tambiah, the psychotherapeutic approach sees the kōan as a performative "trigger mechanism" that opens the door to awakened insight: "Whether literally meaningful or not . . . the prime value of these repeated sayings is their therapeutic value as 'focusing' mechanisms. . . . The repeated formulae as 'supports of contemplation' or transporters into a trance state do so, not by a direct assault on the actor's senses and inflicting an immense psychic toll on him or her, but by a more indirect conventional illocutionary employment of them as instruments of passage and as triggering mechanisms."[75]

The kōan is seen as deliberately causing a "double-bind" or psychological impasse based on three stages, according to Suzuki: First, the accumulation of theories or conceptual vantage points; second, an eventual saturation of the intellect creating the conditions for an imminent release of spiritual energy forcing, third, a penultimate psychic explosion leading up to the entrance into transcendental awareness.[76] The psychological situation created by the kōan can be compared to a cup filled to the brim with liquid which needs only one more tiny drop (i.e., the *watō*) till it spills over (an explosive effect symbolizing awakening). Examples of kōans that create a fundamental psychic barrier, or "gateless gate" (*mumonkan*), leading to the transition from the second to the third stage that Suzuki depicts include: dialogues demanding that a disciple describe enlightenment without using either words or no-words; commanding a disciple to be struck whether or not an appropriate response is given; ordering a disciple to find a goal without being allowed to pursue or look for it; or forcing a disciple to bring water without moving the cup that contains it. This process of fostering what Hakuin refers to as the great doubt as a necessary stage for *satori*—in the sense that "the greater the doubt (or death), the greater the *satori*"—seems parallel to Rollo May's psychological account of the role of profound anxiety and doubt in the act of creativity.[77]

However, there appear to be several limitations in the use of psychotherapy as a methodology for Zen studies. First, it is generally not fully sensitive enough to the complex evolution of the conceptual and literary forms of the kōan tradition.[78] It often sees Zen thinkers as part of a uniform ideological continuum (i.e., "string of pearls") without sufficient regard for the problematics of historical context. Furthermore, the psychological approach tends to presuppose the kind of bifurcation between a hopelessly futile rationality and a transcendental, unutterable illogicality that kōan practice in Dōgen's view, at least, seeks to overcome. On the other hand, in some of his writings Suzuki points to the need for a text-driven rather than self-oriented approach. For example, he often comments on the difficulty in comprehending Zen utterances that reflect the attainment of a higher or transcendental level (Skt. *lokottara*, J. *kōjō*) of awareness, in which language "becomes warped and assumes all kinds of crookedness: oxymora, paradoxes, contradictions, contortions, absurdities, oddities, ambiguities, and irrationalities."[79] Here Suzuki indicates that the key to deciphering the awakening experience is not so much the psychological processes as the role of language, which is never straightforward in Zen but always indirect and decentric. This seems to be a good explanation of why the KD refers to Zen teachings as "strange words and extaordinary gestures," and it may accurately portray the Rinzai approach to sudden enlightenment through an instruction fully "outside the scriptures" as well as Dōgen's continuing hermeneutics.

Symbolism and the Sacred

As indicated above, one major implication of the psychotherapeutic view is the argument that Zen is founded on an iconoclasm that is anti-authoritarian and thoroughly humanistic, and therefore antisacred and antisymbol as well. But it would be misleading and perhaps a violation of the spirit of the kōan to take iconoclasm too literally as representing a one-sided opposition to sacrality. Thus, the central objection to discourse analysis raised by the psychological model can be overcome by clarifying the relation between Zen and notions of the sacred and the function of symbols. First, as Ricoeur and others point out, the term sacred does not necessarily imply a vertical transcendence cut off from mundane existence. It can also suggest a horizontal experience of transcendence, or a *realizational* truth,[80] that sacralizes concrete reality so that "within the sacred universe there are not living creatures here and there, but life is everywhere as a sacrality, which permeates everything."[81] For Ricoeur, the sacred generates an overabundance of meanings that have a nonlinguistic dimension, and its symbolic articulations exemplify a polysemous quality that encompasses nonsemantic as well as metaphorical modes of expression. In this vein, Zen's understanding of nothingness is not an arbitrarily pessimistic or nihilistic negation, but should be considered a universalist and utopian view of the sacred whereby the absolute is manifest through each and every concrete

spatiotemporal phenomenon, and discourse and silence profoundly inter-
act as modes of symbolic disclosure.[82] For Zen, "Either nothing and nowhere is sacred, or everything and everywhere is . . . [for all things are]
capable of teaching and manifesting the Dharma, an extremely dynamic
quality."[83]

The second point concerning Zen's relation to the sacred is that it
must be recognized that there are numerous kinds of religious symbols
beyond the overtly visible and tangible material symbols Zen typically
repudiates in its discourse, such as objects of worship (though it uses
portraits of masters [chinsō] for example, ceremonially in the course of its
rituals). The broad range of religious symbols can be divided into the categories of the external (i.e., statues, icons) and the internal (visualizations,
ideas), the visual (paintings, calligraphy) and the aural (song, chants), and
the oral (dialogues, sermons) and the written (scriptures, commentaries).[84]
In addition, each of these categories can be seen as functioning in terms of
eliciting a conceptual or a nonconceptual response from the participant.
Kōans are not the only kind of religious expression that has an element of
vagueness and mystery based on nonconceptuality. Nearly all religious
symbols, to some extent, cultivate opacity, ambiguity, elusiveness, and
enigma in order to create an indirect communication triggering a subjective realization of truth.

If the soteriological aspect of Zen has priority over the psychotherapeutic and philosophical, then the kōan could be analyzed as an example
of religious symbolism with significant parallels to the enigmatic and
paradoxical passages of scriptures and mystical texts. For instance, Martin
Buber and Gershom Scholem, despite discrepancies in their approaches to
Jewish mysticism, stress the uniqueness of the kōan in the context of world
religions while pointing out affinities with Hasidic tales.[85] Both Zen and
Hasidism are based on awakening through a living encounter with the
concrete reality of truth embodied by the master; that is, truth is a state of
being that is transmitted through the whole person and not necessarily
words. Also Hasidic legends often highlight fanciful and otherworldly
features of the masters' lives[86] in a way that is in accord with Zen's
mythologization to popularize the tradition.

On the other hand, it does appear to be the case that Zen naturalism
and puritanism, and Buddhist thought in general, is particularly clear and
adept in recognizing the need to subvert deliberately any attachment to or
fixation with the symbol-making process. The aim of the saying attributed
to Lin-chi on "killing the buddha" is to expose the partiality and relativity

of all symbols, including even the most subtle internal symbol reflecting gnoseological awareness. As Sōiku Shigematsu writes, the Zen standpoint is like an empty mirror which "maintains not only impartiality and discrimination simultaneously but also mindlessness and nonattachment; nothing at all is left on its surface, though it actually has reflected the image."[87] Thus, there is a creative tension within Buddhism as a whole that is particularly reflected in the Zen kōan between constructing and deconstructing symbols, which is parallel to the issues involved in the juxtaposition of textuality and untextuality, as discussed above. According to William LaFleur, Buddhism "pursued, on the one hand, the elaboration of an extensive system of Buddhist symbols and, on the other, the subjection of the entire symbolization process to a radical critique that was itself grounded in Mahayana Buddhist thought. The seeming paradox is that the Buddhist symbolic system was forced to undergo analysis on bases that were themselves Buddhist."[88]

Therefore, it does not seem appropriate to argue that the position of Zen is antisymbol or devoid of the use of symbolism. Even on the external level, Zen has a rich variety of visual symbols, including painting, calligraphy, and gardening, as well as oral and aural symbols, such as poetry, teisho (sermons) and the chanting of sūtras, though the ideal aim of these Zen arts is to disclose simplicity rather than to create an elaborate ceremonialism. But the key development in the history of Zen occurs when the main Zen symbol is transformed from the transfer from master to disciple of Bodhidharma's robe or begging bowl, which still function as external, ritualized symbols, to the Ma-tsu-style satori dialogical exchange, a truly nonconceptualizable and internal, oral symbol rooted in meditative awareness.[89] Dōgen's frequent comments on the spiritual meaning of the first patriarch's robe as well as of Mahākāśyapa's receiving a flower from Śākyamuni demonstrate his commitment to internalizing, existentializing, and equalizing external symbols that reflect a state of mind taking place not in the past or the future but right here-and-now in a comprehensive present moment encompassing the dimensions of "already" and "not yet." With the development of the dialogue genre the transmission of the Dharma is henceforth determined experientially by the result of the spontaneous encounter and verbal exchange, instead of being signified ceremonially by the passing on of the robe or bowl. Once the dialogues are firmly established as the symbol of lineage, they are also open-ended enough to support further transmutation into at least three main symbolic models: the iconoclasm of the watō, and the hagiography of the chronicles, in addition to

Dōgen's hermeneutic approach. The differences between these three and other approaches are based on the respective understandings and utilizations of the tropology that goes into creating the spontaneous, transformative dialogical encounter. For example, Chao-chou's *Mu* and Te-shan's "refreshing the mind" can function differently in various commentatorial texts depending on whether the ironic, metaphoric, or metonymic quality of the words is highlighted.

Discourse Analysis in Dōgen and Kōan Studies

When discourse analysis is applied to the topic of "Dōgen and the Kōan Tradition," the goal is to situate Dōgen's text within the horizon of the development of kōans as well as the ramifications and reverberations of intertextualized Sung genres in their appropriate historical context. To accomplish this, there must be an encounter not only with the aporetics of Zen studies as a whole, but also with the central aporetic underlying Dōgen's relation to kōans: *Dōgen appears in some works, especially the SZ, to be one of the harshest critics of kōans, and yet in most other writings he cites dialogues and kōan cases frequently as the primary source and authority of truth.* This issue can be resolved only by recognizing in the writings of Dōgen and others the multiform nature of the expressions of their religious traditions. That is, discourse analysis separates, and then reexamines from the standpoint of intertextuality, the relation between polemics and philosophy, and mythology and demythology. It assumes that there are some times when a tradition is making a bid for power in a sectarian setting, or in a concrete socio-political context, and other times when it expresses a truth claim that it sets above historical conditioning—not that these levels always can or should be completely distinguished and segregated from one another. Thus, a corrrective for polarization within a tradition is to explore how polemics contributes to, rather than conflicts with, the overall discourse of the religious movement.

In addition, discourse analysis discusses recent approaches to intellectual history that stress the importance of an archaeology of knowledge to reconstruct the attitudes of Zen thinkers such as Dōgen from their own historical vantage point rather than from the sedimented way they have been portrayed in later stages of the tradition. Thus, history is seen as complex, multifaceted, and disunified rather than singular, uniform, and linear. It is just when a tradition insists upon a consistent and uniform self-presentation that the postmodernist scholar tries to uncover substrata representing areas of diversity and plurality, or "the diffusive, rupturing, disseminating, differential, deconstructing play of differences in their own discourse."[90] This helps create a decentric vantage point that may not necessarily reflect the way the tradition chooses to remember its own history, but that can perhaps be more faithful to the tradition in some essential respects than the tradition is to itself. The aim is to show the tradition's history not in terms of its own retrospective lens but as it was probably actually happening in its time. What traditionalist historians leave out of their accounts may have actually been among the most crucial factors, and what they highlight may not have been so important. Discourse analysis is not concerned with verifying the truth or falsity of historical claims, but with analyzing the use of literary forms including narratives to set up icons, symbols, or paradigms that function relative to the transmission of what the tradition considers truth, which may by definition defy verifiability.

Therefore, the advantages of discourse analysis as a methodology for kōan studies are:

1. It looks holistically at Zen writings as intertextual and interdependent genres rather than as isolated, independent, and often conflicting works of autonomous authors, thereby reorienting the polarization and hagiography of the tradition by recognizing its multiple levels of discourse;

2. It does not delve exclusively into literary critical issues while ignoring questions of history and historiography, but rather tries to clarify historical matters by looking at the narrative quality of both historical and pseudohistorical works in order to reconcile the aporetics of Zen discourse concerning the relation between text and untext, and mythology and demythology;

3. Nor does it focus on literature and history alone, but rather seeks to highlight the symbolism of religious fulfillment underlying literary forms, so that each genre is understood in its formation and development in terms of the way it reflects and portrays a particular view of spiritual attainment;

4. And it also includes, without methodological conflict, key aspects of psychoanalysis and psychotherapy as applied to literary criticism and an analysis of the creative process of Zen thinkers, who are known for struggling with and/or against the greatness of their mentors and rivals.

Directions for Part II

The main aspects of discourse analysis that will be applied to Dōgen and kōan studies in Part II include intertextuality and genre criticism, which deal with the formation and organization of Sung/Kamakura Zen texts, especially the KS *Shōbōgenzō*, and narratology and tropology, which refer to the texts' underlying structure and meaning. These categories will be used to discuss historical, literary, philosophical, and psychological issues in assessing Dōgen's relation to the kōan tradition by situating Dōgen's text in the intertextual, discursive field of the kōan collection genre. The next chapter begins a deconstruction of the conventional, polarized view of Zen history by examining Dōgen in the terms of the discourse of Chinese and Japanese Buddhism of his era. It assesses how Dōgen and Ta-hui each inherited and responded to the kōan tradition in order to clarify the different cultural and linguistic influences Dōgen absorbed from both Chinese and Japanese religiosity and culture. Chapter 3 also discusses, in light of recent Japanese textual studies of the dating and authenticity of Dōgen's kōan collection compiled in Chinese, how the two *Shōbōgenzō* texts were created in relation to one another as well as in connection to Dōgen's Chinese predecessors, including Ju-ching and Hung-chih, and to his rivals, especially Ta-hui and the Japanese Zen monks he influenced.

While Dōgen often critiques and even opposes what has come to be the mainstream Rinzai interpretation of many of the kōan cases, it is clear that he is working within the rhetorical and conceptual context of the kōan tradition by rethinking the ideas and refashioning the language of kōan texts. A close reading of Dōgen's text shows that he often cites favorably the sayings of his supposed opponents, and criticizes the teachings of his supporters. Dōgen generally honors the same "heroes" that are favored by kōan proponents by commenting extensively on well-known cases appearing in Zen records, histories, and kōan collections. In order to drive home a point he is trying to make to his disciples, he often evokes a celebrated character in the sayings of the prominent patriarchs as a final source or arbiter of authority. Therefore, differences of opinion between Dōgen and other interpreters of kōans can be treated not so much as hard and fast ideological conflicts, but as examples of divergent literary genres or alternative styles for handling the source material.

In other words, discourse analysis is not primarily concerned with looking at Dōgen, or at any Zen master or author, as an independent, autonomously intentional subject. In Chapter 3, which deals with the relation between Dōgen, Ta-hui, and other Sung masters as well as with the connection between the MS and KS texts, the notion of intertextuality helps break down barriers between bodies of writing and emphasizes the interdependence and mutuality of various texts that share a common pool of source materials. In Zen, the anecdotes, legends, and dialogues on which kōans are based continually appear and reappear, and they are interpreted and reinterpreted in numerous kinds of texts so that the boundary lines between these works or genres is easily blurred. The KS and HR both use the same sources though in different styles and for different reasons. Furthermore, discourse analysis highlights the role of the configuration of styles or genres in relation to other forms of discourse within the tradition. As David Tracy suggests, "when we say [names of authors], we refer only secondarily to the historical persons whose names we utter. We refer rather to a style, that is, to some individuating way of envisioning the world that is produced in the distinctive style of X. . . . Criticism of style, rather, is a method, a theory, an explanation of how individual meanings are produced through peculiar strategies of stylistic refiguration."[91]

Therefore, setting up the contrasts between the texts of Dōgen and Ta-hui may be less fruitful than highlighting the affinities between Dōgen's text and other kōan collections. By regarding the two *Shōbōgenzō* texts as "open intertexts" involved with the tradition rather than as isolated "autotexts" only critiquing it, the next chapter sets the stage for drawing out the connections between the roots and branches of the tradition. Once it is established historically that Dōgen's main philosophical text is integral to the kōan tradition, the fourth chapter analyzes the literary use of symbols in various Zen genres. It examines the full range of the history of kōans, especially the transition from T'ang source dialogues to recorded, formal cases as reflected in the Sung texts. The literary form of *satori* dialogue is the symbol which paradoxically expresses a refutation of all forms of symbol-making. However, the dialogues as the roots of the tradition are open-ended and flexible, and should not be identified or equated with paradox alone, which is but one aspect of their overall function. Paradox can be subsumed under the broader category of irony, one of the four master tropes. Yet the key to the dialogues is not the use of one particular rhetorical figure of speech or another, but the continual movement back-and-forth between tropes which are alternately selected to undermine or displace one another.

Chapter 4 develops a tropological interpretation of the root or source dialogues based on the notion of parallactic (rather than paradoxical) displacement of and by the tropes of discourse. On that basis, it critically interprets in the tradition's branches the relation between the narrative mythology that is used to establish heroic leaders and lineage in the chronicles and the demythological tropology that is used as a vehicle for self-awakening in kōan collections, including the KS. These rhetorical trends that are evident in the Bodhidharma legend and dialogue, when taken together, constitute a "seamless narrative" interweaving mythical and demythical elements. The final sections of the chapter examine the differences in the ways that Dōgen and other kōan collections and com- mentaries interpret the Bodhidharma, the Mu, and other cases. This discussion focuses on how Dōgen fashions the tropes in a way that is essentially different than the interpretation of kōans found in the HR and in Ta-hui's commentaries, and yet remains fully compatible with and supported by the innate flexibility of the source dialogues.

PART II

Interpretive Studies

THREE

Inter- and Intra-Textuality

A Tale of Two *Shōbōgenzō* Texts

On Contextualizing Dōgen's Texts

This chapter examines textual and historical issues in establishing Dōgen's relation to the kōan tradition by demonstrating that Dōgen's main philosophical text, the Japanese KS *Shōbōgenzō*, functions in the field of discourse of Sung era kōans and kōan collections in a way that is very much compatible and complementary with mainstream kōan texts such as the HR and others. While the KS has its own distinctive approach, it may well stand closer in religious function and literary style to some of the kōan collections than does the shortcut method of Yüan-wu's main disciple, Ta-hui, although Ta-hui's overall approach to Zen itself is quite complex and should not be reduced to a single element. Thus, the significance of the KS can be clarified by highlighting the points of convergence and contrast between these and other modes of Zen discourse. As discussed in the previous chapter, Dōgen studies, and indeed Zen studies as a whole, is haunted by a number of aporetics that tend to bifurcate the tradition into all-too-neat categories of opposing ideologies. The aim here is to correct conventional scholarship based on partisan polemics and sectarian polarization culminating in the Rinzai vs. Sōtō, and zazen vs. kōan debates that have tended to dominate many of the modern understandings of the styles of discourse in the era of Dōgen's Zen. The key to accomplishing this is to clarify issues in intellectual history which help show that the KS does play an integral role in—because it is fundamentally intertextually connected with the texts representing—the transition from T'ang source dialogues to the formalized Sung kōan cases. This, in turn, compels a rethinking of the underlying aims of the Zen dialogues as reflected in the literary genres that emerged in the Sung era. The next chapter will use literary critical models of discourse analysis concerned with narrative and tropical theory to examine the different ways the dialogues function in the various genres leading up to the formation of the KS text.

Therefore, two main issues must be investigated in order to free an understanding of Dōgen's text from stereotypical polarization. The first issue concerns the formation of Dōgen's text in the ideological context of his reactions to his Rinzai rivals and Sōtō predecessors in Sung China and his attempt to initiate a new genre for the transmission of Zen to Kamakura Japan. The question of how Dōgen came to write the KS in the Japanese vernacular—as one of the first such major Buddhist works in Japan, where the custom at the time was to write in the more prestigious Chinese language—has long been a central concern of Dōgen studies. Part of the answer to this lies in examining Dōgen's extensive citations of *satori* dialogues accompanied by his novel, unorthodox interpretations, despite his sometimes strident criticism of the kōan as a method for attaining enlightenment. The key is to understand Dōgen's relation to a constella-tion of prominent figures in Sung Zen who greatly influenced his thinking and writing: Ju-ching, his Chinese Sōtō mentor whom he considered the only genuine master left in China; Hung-chih, a Dharma predecessor of Ju-ching's at T'ien-t'ung monastery and a compiler of several noted kōan collections who was also known for his advocacy of *mokushō-zen* (silent illumination); Rinzai priest Ta-hui, proponent of the *watō* method who is said to have burned the HR, and who also became a frequent target of Dōgen's criticism; and Ta-hui's teacher Yüan-wu, compiler of the HR, a commentary on an earlier kōan collection by Unmon school monk Hsüeh-tou. It is also important to clarify the relations among the Sung Zen leaders, particularly the connections between Hung-chih and Ta-hui, who, though apparently close personal and professional associates, were also harsh critics of each other's approaches to meditation. It will be shown that Dōgen was affected by all four figures—the teachers as well as the opponents—in both positive and negative ways, and that the entire complex of interrelations between the Zen masters of this period defies superficial analysis. Based on a nonpolarizing examination, a strict bifurcation along sectarian lines that is characteristic of conventional studies tends to be broken down. Never-theless, Dōgen's own position on kōans has unique features, and is thus neither wholly independent nor dependent on the views of those who influenced him. Harold Bloom's psychoanalytic literary criticism of the role of creative misreading in the intertextualized formation of texts is a useful way of explaining where Dōgen's interpretations stand in relation to his teachers and rivals.

Another topic in analyzing the formation of the KS in relation to the kōan tradition is to bring to light recent studies by Japanese scholars that have made it clear that a textual analysis of Dōgen's MS collection of three hundred paradigmatic cases, the *Sanbyakusoku* compiled in 1235, is crucial for an understanding of the KS *Shōbōgenzō* and its levels of discourse. The KS is a collection of philosophical essays on Mahayana and Zen topics which in most editions contains from sixty to ninety-five fascicles, though the Sōtō tradition based on the remarks of Ejō, Dōgen's first disciple, maintains that Dōgen hoped to complete one hundred fascicles (perhaps to emulate the one hundred case HR text). The MS appears to be the less interesting and less important text because it is a listing of cases without original commentary. Long considered apocryphal, new studies based on recently discovered manuscripts of early versions of the text now demonstrate that the MS was authentic. These findings support the view that Dōgen was working within the kōan tradition, and they lend credence to the legend, if appropriately (i.e., symbolically) interpreted, that Dōgen copied the entire HR text in a single evening before leaving China to return to Japan. These recent studies thus help offer a different picture of what Dōgen probably had in mind in developing the distinctive style of writing exemplified in the KS. This is especially important for understanding the middle years of Dōgen's career beginning in the late 1230s, when he was completing the MS and also began working seriously on the KS, and culminating in the early to mid 1240s when his KS production reached its creative peak as he was leaving the Kyoto area to settle in the Echizen mountains. This was the period when Dōgen was struggling with quarreling factions in Kyoto several years before he established the independent Eiheiji temple far from the capital.

However, from the standpoint of discourse analysis, attempting to discuss issues of biographical intentionality is less effective than the effort to locate stylistically the MS and KS texts in connection to two other key works: the SZ, a collection of Dōgen's sermons, sayings, and anecdotes compiled around the same time as the MS also includes some of Dōgen's criticisms of kōans; and the EK-9 collection, which contains poetic commentaries on about ninety paradigmatic cases, many of which are also cited in the MS and the KS. That is, in addition to the KS, which includes commentary on numerous kōan cases, and the SZ, which cites several kōans, Dōgen is responsible for three kōan collections, the MS, EK-9, and IH (although the last is of course rather questionable). The relation between these five texts as well as additional writings of Dōgen—which often refer back to the same source material, generally the *satori* dialogues in addition to citations from Mahayana *sūtras*, but for different purposes— can be considered a matter of "*intra*-textuality." This complements the *inter*-textuality linking Dōgen's writings as a whole with the Sung chronicles and kōan collections from which he draws the majority of his citations.

Conventional View of Dōgen and the Kōan Tradition

Sources

The next step is to begin clarifying and correcting the conventional view of Dōgen's relation to the leaders of Sung Zen who influenced his approach to kōans. But first it is necessary to consider more precisely what is meant by referring to the conventional view. The term "conventional" here indicates the typical, or even standard, accounts of Zen history that derive from a combination of mutually reinforcing factors. Modern studies that rely almost exclusively on traditional sources, whether autobiographical or biographical, or primary or secondary, are working with material that is internal to the tradition and therefore nonverifiable, or apparently beyond verifiability. The modern, teleological perspective of history generally seeks to maintain objectivity by analyzing and comparing the various traditional accounts, but it often ends up tacitly accepting and thus unable to stand back from the sources it must rely on, which are frequently romanticized, exaggerated hagiographies. On the other hand, strict, skeptical historiography may go too far in rejecting the traditional sources, thereby throwing out, so to speak, the baby with the bathwater. There is a level on which the "facts" of Zen history are and will probably always remain unknowable to us by virtue of the temporal distance involved in interpreting them. While there is little that can be established with factual certainty, the conventional sources are often all there is to work with so that there is no genuinely objective frame of reference by which to judge the truth or falsity of historical claims. Thus historiographical refutation, which itself cannot escape from relying on the traditional materials, is not necessarily more valid than what it repudiates. It also tends to lose sight of the narrative and tropical structure of its sources. The aim of discourse analysis, on the other hand, is neither to echo nor to cast aside traditional sources, but to allow the tradition to self-reflectively assess how its conventional truths have come to be so taken, and to understand the relation between the mythical and demythical elements in its sacred accounts. At the same time, discourse analysis seeks to reconstruct how things probably stood during the period in question without the distorting lens of sectarian dichotomization.

In the case of Dōgen studies, the conventional view is based on two kinds of sources. The first includes autobiographical references in works such as the *Hōkyōki*, a posthumously discovered record of Dōgen's conversations based on the personal instructions and guidance he received during his training under Ju-ching while in China, in addition to anecdotal passages in the KS, EK, and SZ texts. The second type of source includes numerous sectarian biographies, the most important of which is the *Kenzeiki*, compiled over two hundred years after Dōgen's death. This work was extensively annotated in the *Teiho Kenzeiki* by noted Sōtō scholastic Menzan Zuihō during a Tokugawa revival of sectarian studies while the Sōtō sect was in competition with Hakuin-inspired Rinzai Zen in addition to the developing Ōbaku sect as Buddhism was struggling for its survival against tremendous social and political difficulties. Both kinds of sources are problematical and unreliable. The autobiographical references are frequently connected to sectarian polemic, especially a glorification of Ju-ching as the only authentic teacher of the Dharma in Sung China and an accompanying denigration of Ta-hui as an unworthy Dharma-heir. The sectarian biographies contain much of the mythology and hagiography reminiscent of the Sung era Zen chronicles. Menzan's text, which on one level has the advantage of utilizing and combining materials from a variety of sources, only seems to exacerbate the problems. Menzan was an outspoken critic of kōans, and he was the Sōtō apologist largely responsible for the retrospective presentation of Dōgen's approach as standing consistently and uniformly in support of *shikantaza*. This image, to a large extent, is a projection of the *Teiho*'s Tokugawa era polemic against Hakuin. It is also clear that the *Teiho*, when compared to earlier versions of the *Kenzeiki*, deliberately exaggerates key events in Dōgen's life that are already romanticized in the original text, ranging from his aristocratic background to his meetings with Japanese Buddhist luminaries, such as Eisai. Many of the claims in both the *Kenzeiki* and *Teiho Kenzeiki* as well as other traditional biographies now appear exceedingly unlikely from an historiographical standpoint. Thus, some of the leading modern biographical studies of Dōgen in both Japanese and English that have relied uncritically on the

Kenzeiki-based material end up contributing to a perpetuation of the conventional view.

The conventional view that derives largely from Menzan's text paints a picture combining biographical and doctrinal elements that complement one another in support of Dōgen's pro-zazen and anti-kōan stance. The conventional account begins when Dōgen traveled to China during the period 1223–1227 because he had a profound doubt concerning the Japanese Tendai doctrine of original enlightenment (*hongaku shisō*). Like other reformers of the Kamakura period, including Hōnen, Shinran, and Nichiren, Dōgen grew dissatisfied with the Tendai church that had long dominated Japanese Buddhism. Tendai worship, the reformers apparently felt, engaged in a variety of esoteric practices, somewhat corrupted by a preoccupation with gaining imperial patronage, in a way that overlooked the need for a simple, sustained access to realization for diligent individual seekers. Dōgen's doubt is expressed in the opening lines of *Fukanzazengi*: "Originally the Way is complete and all-pervasive. How does it depend on practice and realization?"[1] When Dōgen experienced his profound uncertainty, he was already exposed to Zen, which had recently been introduced to Japan by Eisai. He went on to accompany Myōzen, one of Eisai's main disciples, to the continent in pursuit of the true Dharma (*shōbō*) of patriarchal Zen that was unavailable in his native country. According to the SZ, Dōgen felt that

> while studying the teachings, my foremost concern at first was to become the equal of the ancient wise men of my country or those who were known as "great teacher" (*daishi*). But, on reading the traditional [Buddhist monk] biographies in such texts as the *Kōsōden*, or its sequel *Zoku Kōsōden*, about the life and teachings of the great teachers and practitioners of the Buddha Dharma [in China], it was clear that their approach was not the same as that of the teachers today. . . . I realized that the teachers of this country are no better than worthless rubbish. My body and mind were transformed accordingly.[2]

The Quest for an Authentic Teacher

During his travels, Dōgen visited several of the leading Five Mountains Zen monastic centers in eastern China on T'ien-t'ung and Ayüwang mountains. He was particularly interested in the Ching-te-ssu temple on Mt.

T'ien-t'ung, whose abbot was Wu-chi Liao-p'ai, since this was where Eisai had trained and was also Myōzen's destination. Ching-te-ssu temple had a long history and excellent reputation as a major training center, with both Hung-chih and Ta-hui having served as abbots in the twelfth century. However, as Dōgen began his first-hand observation of Chinese Buddhism in action there, he quickly became somewhat disillusioned by the laxity in behavior and in the power of concentration on the part of many of the practitioners he encountered. His disappointment led him to wonder if the true Dharma could indeed be found in China. He later wrote, for example, "although there are many in Sung China who consider themselves the legitimate heirs of the buddhas and patriarchs, actually very few study the true path and therefore very few can teach the true path. . . . Now, even those who have almost no understanding of the great way of the buddhas and patriarchs become the masters of monks in training (unsui, literally '[floating like] clouds and [flowing] like water')."[3]

The main exception to the sense of dismay Dōgen felt during the early part of his stay in China, as recorded in the Tenzokyōkun, was the chief cook at Mt. Ayüwang, who Dōgen encountered on two highly illuminating occasions that greatly influenced his view of language and kōans in relation to zazen. When they first met while he was still on board ship due to illness just after landing in China, the cook impressed Dōgen with his dedication to the "practice of the Way" (bendō). The cook maintained a genuinely meditative stance in pursuing the fine details of everyday activities, and he regarded even the act of purchasing mushrooms needed to prepare the monastery's daily meals as a form of religious praxis. This gave Dōgen a sense that sitting meditation does not refer merely to a specific discipline or posture, but represents the continuous process of spiritual training (gyōji) applied to all affairs. Second, while Dōgen later was on a visit to Mt. Ayüwang, the cook instructed him that the mystery of "words and letters" (monji) is nothing other than "one, two, three, four, five," such that "nothing is concealed throughout the entire universe" (henkai fuzōzō). From this conversation Dōgen deeply realized that language not only is efficacious but expresses the very essence of nondual awareness of humans and nature. As Dōgen writes in KS "Nyorai zenshin," "Bukkyō," and other fascicles, sūtras are not only words but are conveyed throughout the entire realm of the universe, or as the "whole body of Tathāgata."

Thus, Dōgen's encounters with the cook, who vividly acted out the Zen dictums "everyday mind is the Way" and "a day without work is a day without food"—especially when compared to what he saw in the typical monastic situation—helped set up in his mind a contrast and conflict between two fundamentally distinct approaches to Zen realization. One perspective stressed the creative use of language perpetually applied to and reflecting each and every facet of existence (*kyōzen itchi*, oneness of Zen realization and *sūtras*) right here-and-now. But the other, less acceptable perspective overemphasized the sparsity of expression based on silence (*kyōge betsuden*), and thus seemed to neglect the necessity for renewed and enhanced practice by anticipating enlightenment as a futural event beyond description. While not identifying himself with the former position, Dōgen was increasingly critical of those monks who were lulled into the inadequate view indicated in the second perspective that it was somehow sufficient to learn to recite a handful of phrases, taken out of context, from the records of the great T'ang patriarchs without a thorough study of the entire Buddhist canon. As he later argues in the KS "Kenbutsu" fascicle:

> Nevertheless, in Sung China lately there are those who would call themselves Zen masters. However, they neither understand nor have experienced first-hand the profundity of the Buddha Dharma. Instead they merely recite a few choice words of Lin-chi or Yün-men, and mistake that for the complete way of the Buddha Dharma. If the way of the Buddha Dharma could be reduced to a handful of words of Lin-chi or Yün-men, it would not have survived to the present day. We should not refer even to Lin-chi and Yün-men as exalted masters of the Buddha Dharma, and today's practitioners are inferior to both of them, and hardly worth mentioning. These worthless fools cannot awaken to the essence of the *sūtras*, but instead slander the *sūtras* without justification while at the same time neglecting to study them. They should really be considered non-Buddhists [or heretics] who are unworthy of the teachings of the buddhas and patriarchs, or even of the teachings of Lao-Tzu or Confucius.[4]

At this stage, Dōgen clearly had mixed feelings concerning the best way to appropriate the true Dharma. On the one hand, he was committed to the ideal that the essence of Buddhism—not to be confused with the heretical notion supported by Ta-hui and others that the three teachings including Buddhism, Taoism, and Confucianism are of equal value—was beyond sectarian divisions, and therefore did not abide the labels of "Zen" or "Sōtō Zen." Yet Dōgen was also keenly aware of the decline of Buddhism since its golden age in T'ang China. He felt that during the period subsequent to the severe persecutions of Buddhism in 845 that Zen alone represented the most direct and complete access to the Dharma, and he also recognized the current strength of the Rinzai sect, particularly the Yang-chi line represented by Ta-hui and his followers. But he was critical of contemporary Rinzai masters, and at times even of the eminent founder of the sect, Lin-chi, for an attitude that obviated the need for sustained practice through the expression of the universal *sūtras*, and he would later assert that it was "only the followers of Tung-shan" who kept the Buddhist way alive.

Dōgen was undergoing a prolonged turning point in his quest as he began to realize that his main concern was that he was unable to find an authentic, charismatic teacher who could help him bring out his innate potential for enlightenment. He describes the ideal master in "Gakudōyōjinshū": "A true master is he who, regardless of old age or prestige, comprehends the right Dharma clearly and has received the certification of a true master. He gives no priority to words and letters or to intellectual understanding. . . . He is the person in whom living and understanding fully correspond to each other."[5] In basic accord with the notion of patriarchal Zen, Dōgen considered that an authenticated personality integrating experiential and intellectual dimensions surpasses any particular use of words needed to express the Dharma. Then, while on a trip away from T'ien-t'ung mountain, and on the verge of returning to Japan in despair after two largely unsuccessful years in China, Dōgen learned of the death of Wu-chi, which saddened him at first. But he was also advised of the genuinely strong character of the new abbot of Ching-te-ssu temple, Ju-ching, who was a Sōtō master following in the path of Hung-chih. A century earlier, while Ta-hui was leading the Rinzai Yang-chi line to a peak period as a popular religious movement, Hung-chih had stimulated a Sōtō revival after generations of dormancy. Now Sōtō was coming into a position of authority at the temple once again after a long period, since the time of Hung-chih, of Rinzai leadership there.

Dōgen reports that he had prophetic dreams that helped guide his journey through China,[6] and according to tradition Ju-ching also dreamt the night before meeting Dōgen that a present-day Tung-shan would soon arrive. When Dōgen returned to T'ien-t'ung, he immediately found upon his face-to-face meeting with Ju-ching that the new abbot was the only master he had ever met who was truly committed to perfecting zazen without compromise. It is recorded in the opening passages of the EK, "as soon as I saw Ju-ching, I realized clearly that my eyes are horizontal and that my nose is vertical. Having conquered all delusions [after training with Ju-ching], I returned to Japan empty-handed [that is, without needing copies of *sūtras*, relics, artifacts, etc].["][7] The vast majority of masters in Sung China paled in comparison, for they functioned under the "pretext" of practicing zazen and made a mockery of the memory of Bodhidharma.[8] Dōgen's encounter and discipleship with Ju-ching marked the complete shift from his interest in Rinzai and kōan studies, initiated while still in Japan, to his wholehearted conviction in Sōtō and zazen practice, the only authentic form of the Dharma left in China. When Dōgen returned to Japan, however, at first he would not necessarily be interested in founding a new sect there known as "Sōtō Zen" because of his great respect for the universality of Buddhist truth that knows no labels. But perhaps somewhat in the vein of Martin Luther, who proclaimed "Here I stand, I can do no other" when persecuted by church authorities in late medieval Europe, Dōgen's sense of integrity in the face of mounting sectarian opposition and political intrigue in Japan propelled just this turn of events, forcing in particular his move in 1243 to remote Echizen province, where he established Eiheiji as a new temple fully independent from Kyoto-based Tendai and Rinzai sects.

For two years Dōgen trained diligently under the guidance and instruction of Ju-ching, until he eventually attained enlightenment through the spontaneous yet complete liberation experience of the "casting off of body-mind" (*shinjin datsuraku*). According to the major biographical sources, including *Kenzeiki*, this experience took place during a prolonged and intensive meditation session when Ju-ching chided the monk who had fallen asleep while sitting next to Dōgen: "To study Zen is to cast off body-mind. Why are you engaged in singleminded sitting (*za*) slumber rather than singleminded sitting meditation (*zazen*)?"[9] Upon hearing this reprimand, Dōgen attained a "great awakening" (*daigo*) from his previous doubts concerning the relation between meditation and enlightenment. He later entered Ju-ching's quarters and burned incense, reporting, "I have come because body-mind is cast off." Ju-ching responded approvingly: "Body-mind is cast off (*shinjin datsuraku*); cast off body-mind (*datsuraku shinjin*)." When Dōgen cautioned, "Do not grant the seal [of transmission] indiscriminately," Ju-ching replied, "Cast off casting off (*datsuraku datsuraku*)!" Thus, *shinjin datsuraku* marks not only Dōgen's personal awakening, but constitutes the basis and substance of the transmission of the Dharma between Chinese mentor and Japanese disciple. The phrase is particularly noteworthy in this exchange because it is manipulated by

Ju-ching through inversion and tautology to represent command and foreshadowing, description and inquiry, evaluation and challenge.

When Dōgen left China in 1227, he became a major spokesman for the philosophy of Ju-ching, who died one year later. Dōgen's personal record of his conversations with his mentor in China, the *Hōkyōki*, as well as his frequent citations of Ju-ching's sayings and poems throughout his collected writings, still stand, along with Ju-ching's *goroku* text, as a major source of the Chinese master's teachings.[10] While Dōgen is often critical of such Zen luminaries as Hui-neng and Lin-chi, he never fails to lavishly praise Ju-ching as the one true teacher of Sung China. He repeatedly refers to Ju-ching with a term of respect and affection, *kobutsu* (lit. "old or ancient buddha or master"), which he also uses occasionally in reference to Hung-chih as well as Chao-chou and other T'ang masters. Apparently, Dōgen felt that Ju-ching's teaching offered much more than the usual rhetoric about meditation and eloquent poetic utterances, for he lived out fully his understanding of the Dharma. Or, to paraphrase a key passage in the KS "Busshō" fascicle, he exemplified the simultaneity (*dōji*) of buddha-realization and Buddha-nature, or of potential and actual enlightenment. For Ju-ching, all aspects of existence must reflect a commitment to zazen. Therefore, Ju-ching as a vigorous and exacting role model supports Dōgen's doctrine of *shushō ittō*, the oneness of practice and attainment experienced as a continuing temporal process, which contrasts with the Rinzai emphasis on *satori* as a once-and-for-all goal to be reached in the future.

Furthermore, Dōgen and Ju-ching underwent with—or, rather, through—each other the unique experience of *kannō dōkō*, a sense of spiritual attunement or cosmic resonance between teacher and disciple that is essential for the appropriate transmission of the Dharma. Citing an important passage from the *Lotus Sūtra* Dōgen argues that the patriarchal transmission can take place "only between a buddha and a buddha" (*yuibutsu yobutsu*), in that the buddha-to-be or potential buddha must already be at least partially awakened to the innate ground of Buddha-nature. *Kannō dōkō* functions on two levels at the same time. On the level of relative truth, a basic Confucian-oriented hierarchical distinction always remains between the seniority and superiority of Ju-ching as master and the deferential attitude of Dōgen, the disciple. However, on the level of the absolute Buddha-nature, the difference between Dōgen and Ju-ching disappears, and the two become equal partners in a mutually illuminating and perpetually renewable co-experience of full involvement in the realization of buddhahood. Thus, in granting Dōgen the seal of transmission,

Ju-ching emphasized the Dharma's transcendence of temporal and spatial limitations. Yet, the buddhas and patriarchs who inherited the Dharma from each other were not to be construed simply in their transhistorical and universal context. The document of succession which Dōgen received from Ju-ching was not meant to be a chronology of the buddhas and patriarchs who inherited the Dharma within temporal and spatial confines, but a crystallization of the universal continuity and the transcendent vitality of the Dharma concretely embodied by the buddhas and patriarchs.[11]

This understanding seems to be more authentic and appropriate than the traditional Rinzai patriarchal transmission, which in some cases by the Sung era had degenerated into the selection of an ambitious heir by a powerful master based primarily on partisan or political concerns.

Silent Illumination (Mokushō-zen) *vs.* Kōan *Introspection* (Kanna-zen)

In addition to Ju-ching, Dōgen's approach to zazen and kōans was greatly influenced by three other Chinese masters who were prominent nearly a century before his journey, including the Sōtō priest Hung-chih, who was abbot at T'ien-t'ung two generations before Ju-ching, and the Rinzai priests, Yüan-wu and his disciple Ta-hui, also a T'ien-t'ung abbot. Another important figure in the Sung/Kamakura constellation is Dainichi Nōnin, founder of the Daruma-shū sect in Japan who never traveled to China himself but who sent two surrogate priests in 1189 to receive certification in Ta-hui's lineage. Figures 3.1 and 3.2 illustrate in abbreviated form the conventional Sōtō and Rinzai lineages.

To see clearly how the lines get sharply drawn separating Dōgen's pro-zazen Sōtō perspective from Ta-hui's pro-*watō* Rinzai viewpoint, it is crucial to understand the interactions and relations between Dōgen's forerunners. Of particular significance is the fundamental controversy between Hung-chih's advocacy of *mokushō-ʐen* and Ta-hui's doctrine of *kanna-ʐen*. In this debate, most of the vituperative comments come from Ta-hui, who repeatedly accuses the *mokushō* position of supporting a static, uneventful, and endless procession toward enlightenment resulting in a state of mind that is passive and quietist. Ta-hui charges that *mokushō* leads to "sitting wordlessly with eyes shut beneath the black mountain, inside the ghost cave," which amounts to the same frustration and spiritual

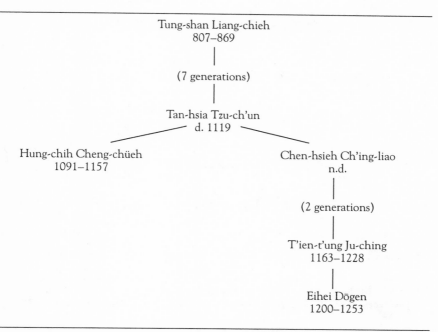

Figure 3.1 *Sōtō Lineage. Dōgen's lineal relation to Hung-chih and Ju-ching.*

impasse as "sitting on a mountain of knives or in a forest of swords, in a boiling cauldron or in the coals of a furnace."[12] Ta-hui warns that those who are preoccupied with "keeping the mind still," but who lack the experience of "smashing the mind of birth and death," will "inevitably be dividing emptiness into two,"[13] thereby wasting the opportunity to gain enlightenment.

Hung-chih responds in the short poetic manifesto, "Mokushōmei," not so much with a direct counterattack, but by clarifying the distinctively objectless and timeless nondualistic experience of silent illumination. He argues that silent illumination does not lead to vacancy and detachment, but culminates in total participation in the world so that "The ten thousand forms majestically glisten and expound the Dharma,/All objects certify it, every one in dialogue/Dialoguing and certifying,/They respond appropriately to each other."[14] Also, in the poem "Zazenshin," which is greatly admired though significantly rewritten by Dōgen in the KS fascicle of the same title, Hung-chih identifies *mokushō*, which "knows without touching things" and "illumines without encountering objects," with singleminded zazen practice.[15] Hung-chih's *mokushō-zen* approach implicitly accuses

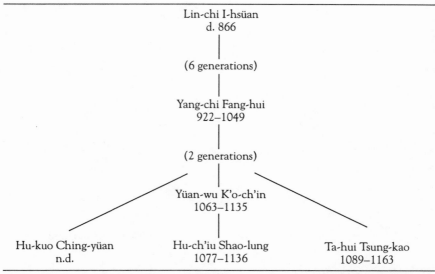

Figure 3.2 *Rinzai Lineage. Ta-hui's lineal relation to Yüan-wu. [Also, Dainichi Nōnin's disciples received certification from Ta-hui's disciple, Fo-chao Te-kuang (1121–1203).]*

Ta-hui's *kanna-zen* of irrationalism, and the latter retorts that Hung-chih advocates a state of consciousness of "cold ashes and dead wood." This debate was continued long past Dōgen's time and was echoed in Hakuin's Tokugawa era polemics against the silent illumination school. That is, the "dispute [in China] was carried over to Japan, where to this day it remains—albeit in somewhat altered forms—the primary ideological rationale for the separation of the two major Japanese schools of Rinzai and Sōtō."[16]

In other words, each side accuses the other of misplacing or misusing the source dialogues, and of lapsing into a state that escapes from rather than remains fully involved in nondualistic reality. Thus, according to the conventional account, based on his personal experiences with his master as well as his awareness of the contradictions and deficiencies in Rinzai, Dōgen stresses the priority of the pure, continuous activity of zazen-only or just-sitting (*shikantaza*) as coeval with enlightenment, since this activity (*gyōji*) is consistent with the practice of all buddhas from time immemorial. At the same time, Dōgen refutes the efficacy of the kōan as a method of realization because it results in a false goal of terminating thought. Influenced by the two Chinese Sōtō teachers he refers to affectionately as "old buddha," Ju-ching and his predecessor at T'ien-t'ung monastery, Hung-chih, Dōgen mistrusts the kōan because of its irrational procedure of stressing incomprehensibility and absurdity rather than the capacity of language to disclose ultimate truth. Dōgen's view is considered the opposite of the Rinzai approach, which favors the use of the kōan as the focal point of meditative practice. Rinzai Zen in Sung China and Kamakura Japan sees itself as the continuation of T'ang Chinese Southern school masters, including Ma-tsu, Chao-chou, Te-shan and Lin-chi, who are known for using a pithy, anecdotal style of pedagogy, often with abrupt commands or nonverbal reprimands such as "sticks and shouts." Following the interpretation of Sung master Ta-hui, Hung-chih's close personal associate but main ideological opponent, Rinzai Zen emphasizes the technique of the *watō*, which involves an introspection (*kanna-zen*) or rumination on the indecipherability of terse phrases that compress the source dialogue or kōan so that it functions as an abbreviated catalyst for enlightenment. This polarization seems to be reflected in the way that Dōgen's Zen replaces the kōan seen in terms of studying paradigmatic cases or precedents (*kosoku-kōan*) as embodied by the two famous collections, HR and MMK, with the doctrine of the kōan realized in everyday life (*genjōkōan*) through the total dynamic functioning (*zenki*) of birth-and-death (*shōji*). According to the conventional view, the KS as a form of Zen writing appears to be an anti-kōan tract, or at least a non-kōan-oriented approach to Zen thought in contrast to the major kōan collections. Therefore, Dōgen decries the kōan used as a teleological means to the end of reaching enlightenment in a way that violates his basic principle of the oneness of practice and attainment (*shushō ittō*), while Ta-hui charges that silent illumination lapses into a counterproductive quietism.

Table 3.1 outlines the conventional polarities dividing Dōgen's Sōtō and Ta-hui's Rinzai concerning kōans, zazen, practice, transmission, and enlightenment.

Dōgen's Refutation of Kōans

It is important to point out that there are several key passages in Dōgen's collected works that do seem to support the notion that he was a harsh critic of the kōan, and of Ta-hui in particular, as well as a staunch supporter of zazen-only. However, these passages must be interpreted in their appropriate context and in terms of the level of discourse they represent. For example, in the SZ Dōgen explicitly links the priority of just-sitting with a refutation of the efficacy of kōan studies in response to a question from Ejō, his first disciple, which echoes a similar question Dōgen had once asked

Table 3.1. *Dōgen vs. Ta-hui. The conventional points of contast between Dōgen's Sōtō and Ta-hui's Rinzai doctrines.*

Dōgen/Sōtō	Ta-hui/Rinzai
shikantaza (just-sitting)	kōan (catechistic riddle)
mokushō-zen (silent illumination)	kanna-zen (introspecting the kōan)
genjō-kōan (spontaneous realization of kōan)	kosoku-kōan (paradigmatic cases)
kyōzen itchi (oneness of Zen and sūtras)	kyōge betsuden (special transmission outside the scriptures)
henkai fuzōzō (nothing concealed throughout the entire universe)	furyū monji (no reliance on words and letters)
gyōji (sustained practice)	watō (head-word technique)
shushō ittō (oneness of practice-attainment)	satori (sudden enlightenment)
kannō dōkō (cosmic resonance between buddhas)	soshi-zen (patriarchal lineage)

Ju-ching, as recorded in the *Hōkyōki*. Ejō asks, "When we combine zazen with studies of recorded sayings and kōans, we can understand only one point in a hundred or a thousand in grasping the meaning of the sayings and kōans, but in zazen even this much eludes us. So why must we devote ourselves to zazen?" Dōgen responds,

> Although the *kōan-watō* seems to improve one's understanding slightly, it actually leads further and further from the way of the buddhas and patriarchs. If you devote yourself exclusively to zazen without regard to any attainment, even to the attainment of enlightenment, this itself is the way of the patriarchs. Even though the ancient masters stressed the value of both introspecting the kōan (*kanna-zen*) and just-sitting in zazen (*shikantaza*), they clearly emphasized zazen. While some have claimed to gain enlightenment through the *watō*, the real cause of enlightenment is the function of zazen.[17]

But two points must be kept in mind in interpreting this passage. First, the SZ is not necessarily a reliable source because, unlike the KS, it is not claimed by the Sōtō tradition to have been written by Dōgen but was recorded by Ejō from Dōgen's talks and sermons. More significantly, the terms Dōgen refers to as the object of his critique are kōan-watō in connection with kosoku-kōan, which suggests that he specifically refutes the watō technique of interpreting kōans, and not necessarily the kōan in and of itself.

Similarly, in the KS "Sansuikyō" fascicle, when Dōgen labels as "pseudo-Buddhists" and "scatterbrains" those who understand the kōans only as "incomprehensible utterances," he is really attacking the shortcut method which he feels misappropriates the source dialogues:

> In great Sung China today, there is a group of scatterbrained people who are so numerous that they cannot possibly be over-come by the minority of authentic practitioners. They maintain: "Phrases such as 'The east mountain walks on the water' and 'Nan-chüan's sickle' are incomprehensible utterances. The idea is that a word or phrase involving thought could not be one of the Zen sayings of the buddhas and patriarchs, for only incom-prehensible utterances are the sayings of the buddhas and patri-archs. Therefore, Huang-po's training stick and Lin-chi's thundering shout exceed comprehension, and are beyond dis-criminating thought. This is known as great enlightenment prior to any sign of the universe's sprouting itself. In the past, masters often employed as skillful means certain phrases in order to cut off entangling vines (kattō) because they are beyond comprehen-sion."

> Those who utter such nonsense have not yet met a true master, and lack the "eye" (or insight) of proper study. They are fools not worthy of mention. . . . What these pseudo-Buddhists regard as "incomprehensible utterances" are incomprehensible only to them, not to the buddhas and patriarchs. . . . If [these utterances] are nothing more than incomprehensible, then whatever appears to be comprehensible must not be. Such people are all over Sung China, and I have met any number of them. It is a pity that they do not know that thought is discourse, or that discourse releases [or breaks through] thought (aware beshi, karare nenryo no goku naru koto o shirazu, goku no nenryo o tōdatsu suru koto o shirazu).[18]

Here Dōgen forcefully argues that the problematic approach is the one based on extracting main phrases from the source dialogues, such as "The east mountain walks on water," which are then considered to epitomize an innately baffling irrationality and incomprehensibility. The phrase itself is not troublesome to the intellect if interpreted in light of the full context of the dialogue. Dōgen's citing this particular phrase, initially attributed to Yün-men, seems to be a veiled reference to the general deficiencies of the *watō* technique of Ta-hui. According to his traditional biographies, Ta-hui is said to have had great difficulty in solving the enigma of this phrase during his quest for enlightenment, and Dōgen here and elsewhere implies that perhaps he was never successful (though the story of Ta-hui's certification is confirmed by his biographies). Furthermore, whereas Ta-hui reduces the source dialogue to a mere phrase in order to cut off discourse completely, Dōgen goes on in the fascicle to offer an extended discussion with interlinear commentary—resembling the interpretive method of the HR and other kōan collections—of the multiple meanings of Yün-men's saying in relation to other Zen sayings he cites that deal with the phantasm of "the flowing (or moving) mountains and the nonflowing (or stationary) waters." From Dōgen's standpoint, Ta-hui's illogical approach sees discourse as a skillful means used to cut off and defeat the "entangling vines" (*kattō*) of conceptual thought. Dōgen's implication, also emphasized in the SZ "Kattō" fascicle, is that such a view fails to understand how language itself can effectively disentangle the vines of discrimination through the use of those very vines of word-tangles.

For Dōgen, this process involving the use of self-deconstructing/reconstructing entanglements is exactly what the source dialogues, when guided by zazen meditation, can accomplish for genuinely attained buddhas and patriarchs. By stressing the need to "study how to cut off entanglements by using entanglements . . . in order to transmit entanglements in terms of entanglements . . . [for] the transmission of the Dharma is itself an entanglement," Dōgen seems to go beyond Lin-chi's view that he "releases or unties knots." In the crucial final sentence of the "Sansuikyō" passage above, the inversion of the phrases, *nenryo no goku* and *goku no nenryo*, suggests a bivalent element that is reinforced by the two meanings, or at least the double-edged meaning, of "thought" (*nenryo*) in relation to speech. Thought has both a positive meaning in creating insight and clarification and a negative implication in causing bondage and attachment. Also, the verb *tōdatsu suru* (literally "to penetrate or permeate" plus "to expel or escape") indicates a twofold significance of overcoming and exploiting in relation to thought. Thus, language is the self-extricating potential of thought itself. That is, language at once transcends or is emancipated *from* thought and *allows* thought to transcend or break through itself through the disentangling vines of entanglement. Dōgen's view contrasts with what can be referred to as an "instrumentalist" view of the kōan, embraced by Ta-hui and most subsequent Rinzai masters including D. T. Suzuki, as a strategic spiritual device designed to create a psychological impasse followed by a dramatic breakthrough to a realm beyond rationality. Dōgen sees language not as inherently illogical or potentially exhaustible, but as the continuously liberating and transformative unfolding of thought through reflection on the inner dynamism of the realization-kōan (*genjōkōan*).

The crucial role of language in the ongoing, dynamic interplay of absolute and relative is expressed in a waka from Dōgen's Japanese poetry collection entitled, "A special transmission outside the teachings." Here, Dōgen cites a traditional Zen motto associated with the position on language attributed to Chinese masters Te-shan and Ta-hui that he elsewhere refutes. According to Dōgen's critique, the Ta-hui approach sees enlightenment as outside the world of conceptual discourse and it uses absurd utterances in kōan cases to create an impasse with language and thought that requires a breakthrough to a nonconceptual and nondiscursive understanding. Ta-hui's standpoint fosters subtle dichotomies between language and Dharma, thought and attainment, and thus the absolute and relative. Dōgen's verse uses a variety of wordplay—such as a pun on the word *nori*, which means both "seaweed" and "Dharma," and on the phrase *kaki mo tsukubeki*, which can mean either "oysters must reach" or "writing must exhaust"—to reinterpret the motto so that it suggests not a duality but a profound and paradoxical inseparability or creative tension between these realms:[19]

Kyōge betsuden	A special transmission outside the teachings
Araiso	The Dharma, like an oyster
Nami mo eyosenu	Washed atop a high cliff:
Takayowa ni	Even waves crashing against
Kaki mo tsukubeki	The reefy coast, like words,
Nori naraba koso.	May reach but cannot wash it away.

For Dōgen, the key to understanding the efficacy of the source dialogues is to see Zen masters as alchemists who turn the raw material of ordinary words, the enriched possibilities of which usually remain unrecognized, into magically alive, metaphorical and metonymic manifestations of enlightened awareness. It is in this sense that the creative expressions of Zen sayings develop rich textures of verbal communication that support the injunction to "*not rely* on words and letters."

In KS "Sesshin sesshō" and "Ōsakusendaba," however, Dōgen attacks Ta-hui himself more directly and explicitly as the epitome of what has gone wrong in Sung Buddhism, and he casts doubt on whether Ta-hui is a true follower certified by the patriarchs. He writes:

> When my former teacher [Ju-ching of Mt. T'ien-t'ung], an old master, entered the lecture hall he frequently referred to "old master Hung-chih." However, my former teacher was the only one who referred to Hung-chih as an old master. In Hung-chih's time there was another monk named Ta-hui Tsung-kao of Mt. Ching, who is said to have been in the lineage of Nan-yüeh. Most people during the Sung era thought Ta-hui the equal of Hung-chih. Some even considered Ta-hui to be superior. This error was due to the fact that monks and laypersons alike in Sung China studied superficially, did not possess an insight into the way, and had not yet acquired knowledge of self or others.

In "Jishō-zammai" Dōgen goes so far as to question the legitimacy of the certification of Ta-hui's enlightenment, although probably this was done primarily for partisan reasons in order to win some of his main followers away from a rival Zen sect, the Daruma-shū of Dainichi Nōnin, that adhered to Ta-hui's teaching.[20] Dōgen maintains, "Those who are not aware [of Ta-hui's deficiencies] rank him the equal of the ancient masters, but those who are aware consider him to have failed. His words do not illumine the great Dharma but are nothing more than childish gibberish."[21] The "Jishō-zammai" fascicle begins in typical KS fashion by reinterpreting the traditional Zen doctrine of "self-fulfilling *samādhi*" as expressing not a one-sided or dualistic enlightenment based on a single person, but a realization beyond the distinction of self and other, individuality and multiplicity. But perhaps more than any other piece in Dōgen's collected writings, this fascicle turns into unconcealed polemic against a sectarian opponent, and seems to go astray from the primary philosophical issues it raises.

Rethinking the Conventional View

In recent years, a number of works have begun to challenge the conventional polarities, and to point out issues of continuity and consistency linking Dōgen to the kōan tradition. As scholars have increasingly been coming to grips with the aporetics of Zen studies, particularly in dealing with the formative stages of the tradition, it becomes clear that there are chinks in the armor surrounding the conventional view of the Sung/Kamakura era. At least it is evident that the apparent bifurcations of *kanna-zen* and *mokushō-zen*, *kosoku-kōan* and *genjōkōan*, and Rinzai and Sōtō, are complicated and to some extent vitiated by several textual, historical, and ideological factors. These factors are highlighted by the irony that according to traditional accounts it was Ta-hui, the popularizer of the kōan, who burned the printing blocks of the HR compiled by his own teacher, Yüan-wu, whereas Dōgen, the opponent, copied the same text in a single night just before returning from China to Japan.[22] Below, a discussion of the philosophical significance of the legends concerning Ta-hui and Dōgen in relation to the HR will suggest that neither figure strictly supported or rejected the use of kōans; this polarity is primarily based on later debates. But in reconstructing how each thinker viewed the role of the kōan in his own time, it is evident that both were critical of what they saw as abuses in its application and sought to restore its genuine significance as a symbol of religious transformation. Both contributed to the effort in the Sung/Kamakura era, a time of nostalgia and self-reflection for Zen, to reassess the strengths and weaknesses of a tradition that could never be recreated in the way that it was pictured to have existed in the T'ang. Therefore, the difference between Dōgen and Ta-hui is not merely a matter of antithetical kōan vs. zazen standpoints, but of two alternative visions of what most makes kōan practice effective as a form of meditation. The result, explored more fully in Chapter 4, is Ta-hui's shortcut method based on the trope of irony in contrast to Dōgen's scenic route approach based on metonymy.

Dōgen's Relation to Sung Chinese Masters

The conventional view is buttressed by two main features: first, Dōgen's strong opinions about his personal and ideological relations to the Sung masters, as well as the lineal loyalties and conflicts among his predecessors; and second, apparently fundamental discrepancies in the structure and style of his main text, the KS, in comparison with kōan collections as well as the transmission of the lamp and recorded sayings genres. However, a closer look at either of these issues from any one of a variety of angles raises key questions about the validity of the conventional view. First of all, it now appears that Dōgen's attitude toward his Sung Sōtō predecessors (Hung-chih and Ju-ching) and Rinzai rivals (Yüan-wu and Ta-hui), in addition tö their relations to each other, is multifaceted and rather ambivalent or double-edged. For example, in a key passage in KS "Jinshin-inga" Dōgen delivers a rather stinging critique, minus Ta-hui's vitriolic polemic, of "old buddha" Hung-chih, whose poetry he reinterprets and rewrites in the KS "Zazenshin" fascicle.[23] Here Dōgen seems to be praising (or damning with faint praise) Hung-chih's verse on the "Precepts of Zazen Practice," which he maintains is the only expression of the meaning of zazen among the numerous available ones that truly reflects the teachings of the buddhas and patriarchs. Then Dōgen provides interlinear comments on Hung-chih's verse that steer it into a new direction, and finally he offers an original verse justified by arguing that "the problem is not that Zen master Hung-chih failed to express the matter correctly, but that it can also be expressed as I have done so."

In rewriting the verse, Dōgen offers what could be considered a subtle but devastating criticism of Hung-chih's quietism that is somewhat along the lines of Ta-hui's refutation of his Chinese Sōtō rival.[24] The two verses begin in identical fashion with the lines, "Dynamic functioning of all buddhas/Functioning dynamism of all patriarchs," thus indicating that the primary aim is to reveal the dynamic quality (ki) of meditation. But Dōgen immediately and significantly departs from Hung-chih in the next two lines, which provide the structural foundation for most of the rest of the poem. Hung-chih writes:

> Knowing without handling things
> Illuminating without encountering objects.

Dōgen changes it:

> Spontaneously disclosed (gen) without thinking
> Fully manifest (jō) without obstruction.

In this way, Dōgen shifts the emphasis from silent illumination, which appears to be detached from and uninvolved with the realm of things and objects, to one of his favorite doctrines, genjōkōan, or the spontaneous disclosure or manifestation of the kōan here-and-now. Whereas Hung-chih's view may be seen, as Ta-hui charges though for different reasons, as being aloof from the concrete world and lacking dynamism, Dōgen advocates full participation in and through all phenomena.

This theme is carried out in the way Dōgen rewrites the next several lines which build on the previous passage. According to Hung-chih: "Knowing without handling things/Its knowledge is in and of itself mysterious/Illuminating without encountering objects/Its illumination is in and of itself wondrous." Dōgen's version reads: "Spontaneously disclosed without thinking/Its spontaneous disclosure is in and of itself revealed/Fully manifest without obstruction/Its full manifestation is in and of itself realized (shō)." By altering a handful of words and phrases in appropriate places, Dōgen transforms Hung-chih's verse in order to eliminate any subtle gap between consciousness and reality that may be implied by the original terms "mystery" and "wondrous," and he stresses the complete and unimpeded here-and-now *realization* of enlightened awareness. Dōgen also changes the final lines from "Fish swim slowly . . . Birds fly past the horizon" to the tautological or trans-mimetic passage, "Fish swim like fish . . . Birds fly like birds," to accentuate reality just as it is without a sense of pursuing a goal or destination in the far-off distance.

Thus, Dōgen's critique of Hung-chih seems parallel to Ta-hui's refutation without necessarily supporting Ta-hui's conclusions. At least it reinforces the Rinzai thinker's analysis of the limitations of silent illumination, and attempts to dissociate *shikantaza* from the *mokushō* approach. For Dōgen, zazen is directly linked to the eminently active experiences of *genjōkōan* and *shinjin datsuraku*. Therefore, it is important to recognize that while Hung-chih's "silent" method is not as reticent as it appears, it is also not appropriate to link Dōgen with Hung-chih's approach to meditation or with Hung-chih's countercritique of Ta-hui. Dōgen criticizes the *watō* method not because it avoids the silence for which it attacks Hung-chih, but precisely for its absence of expressiveness. In other words, Dōgen's critique of Ta-hui is based on grounds nearly opposite to those used by Hung-chih's critique of Ta-hui, and actually seems to echo the way Ta-hui attacked his Chinese Sōtō counterpart. As indicated above, Dōgen's emphasis on the need for a continuing hermeneutic clarification of the *sūtras* seems to place him closer to the *kyōzen itchi* view (oneness of scriptures and Zen) than to the *kyōge betsuden* approach (Zen as a special transmission outside the scriptures). The latter perspective was first attributed in the transmission of the lamp literature to Bodhidharma and was also apparently also embraced by Ta-hui and most Rinzai masters. But in a *Hōkyōki* passage based on a teaching attributed to Ju-ching, Dōgen declines to affiliate himself with either view because the Dharma transcends any distinction of "inside" or "outside" in relation to words and scriptures. Furthermore, in the KS "Kattō" fascicle, Dōgen argues against the conventional interpretation of the Bodhidharma "skin, flesh, bones, marrow" dialogue, which suggests that the marrow is the inner dimension and the skin the outer dimension, by arguing that both skin and marrow as well as flesh and bones represent relative and provisionally established degrees of understanding. "What Bodhidharma said to the four disciples," he writes, "is fundamentally the selfsame expression. Although it is fundamentally the selfsame expression, since there are necessarily four ways of understanding it, he did not express it in one way alone. But even though each of the four ways of understanding is partial or one-sided, the way of the patriarchs ever remains the way of the patriarchs."[25] Thus, Dōgen is neither strictly for nor against the use of language to express the Dharma, but is primarily concerned with highlighting the unique dynamism of *shikantaza* as a matter of continuing effort or activity (*gyōji*).

The issue is complicated by the question of where Hung-chih really stood in relation to his critic and friend Ta-hui, who he apparently recommended as his successor for the T'ien-t'ung abbacy. For example, according to Korean Rinzai Zen tradition, which is very much dependent on the theoretical framework provided by Ta-hui's thought, it was Hung-chih who formally systematized Ta-hui's important list of "ten defects" or imperfect ways of observing the *Mu watō*.[26] The list of defects emphasizes the need to overcome any subtle lingering attachment to a conceptual, discriminative mode of thinking, and by stressing a self-reflective quietude it may point to an ideological convergence between *watō* and silent illumination. Since Hung-chih never responded in kind to Ta-hui's more abrasive comments, which echoed Zen Southern school polemic dating back to the T'ang, it may be the case that he considered the Rinzai attack to be pitted against misinterpretations of the *mokushō* approach in the practice of his Sōtō contemporary, Chen-hsieh, who was a direct lineal predecessor of Ju-ching (see fig. 3.1 above).[27]

In any case, Dōgen did not simply perpetuate the stereotypical Hung-chih vs. Ta-hui debate. He participated on another level in a game of ideological oneupmanship the Zen masters were playing concerning whose approach could best overcome a static view of realization in favor of dynamism. However, in discussing Dōgen's philosophical argument for dynamism in contrast to staticism, it is important to recognize that all three Sung forerunners—Hung-chih, Yüan-wu, and Ta-hui—used extensively some of the expressions featured in Dōgen's writings, including the key terms genjō and zenki, that reflect the vitalist rather than quietist nature of realization. Yet in a crucial passage in the KS "Jinshin-inga" fascicle, Dōgen critically comments on the verses by the three thinkers concerning Pai-chang's famous "fox" kōan, and he takes each to task for their lack of a genuinely dynamic approach to the Buddhist doctrine of causality.[28] The fox kōan, which is included as the second case in the MMK, is notable for the way it uniquely combines a typical Buddhist moral tale involving karmic retribution with folk legends of trance possession by animal spirits to disclose subitaneous, unimpeded Zen enlightenment. According to the paradigmatic case, a monk who appears to be human but is really a fox turns out to be suffering five hundred animal rebirths as a karmic punishment for having misunderstood the meaning of causality long before, in a previous lifetime, when he was a head monk. At that time he had insisted, in response to a disciple's inquiry, that an enlightened person is unaffected by or does not fall into causality (furaku-inga). Now, many lifetimes later, he beseeches Pai-chang for a "turning word" (tengo) to release him from his suffering. When Pai-chang says, "There is no one who does not obscure causality (fumai-inga)," the man-fox dies and attains full enlightenment (Skt. parinirvāṇa) as the fox body is buried by the current monks. Hearing this story, Pai-chang's disciple Huang-po asks what would have happened to the monk if he had answered correctly the first time. When challenged by the master to step forward, Huang-po slaps Pai-chang, who claps and amusedly exclaims these words of approval, "I thought the barbarian had a red beard [symbolic of Bodhidharma], but here is another red-bearded barbarian!", that is, another master enlightened in the manner of the first patriarch.

The case is thus divided into two parts: first the moral tale, followed by the demonstrative dialogical exchange. Yet both parts highlight the fundamental irony that by verbally negating causality one must suffer from its effects, but by verbally affirming causality one is released from it. The dialogue that concludes the case appears to heighten this paradoxical view of causality, and implies that there is no relevant conceptual understanding of the issue, and therefore no language appropriate to expressing it. The standard Rinzai interpretation is suggested in Shibayama's modern commentary, "When 'not falling' and 'not ignoring' [or not obscuring] are both transcended and wiped away, you can for the first time yourself . . . get hold of the real significance of this kōan. . . . What I want you to know is that Zen is alive and active in quite another sphere where it makes free use of both 'not falling' and 'not ignoring.'"[29] Psychotherapist Carl Jung echoes the Rinzai interpretation when he argues that kōans are "of such paradoxy, that even an expert is completely in the dark as to what may emerge as a suitable solution. Moreover, the descriptions of the experiences are so obscure that in no single case could one perceive any unobjectionable rational connection between the kōan and the experience."[30]

However, according to Dōgen's interpretation this paradoxical, anti-conceptual view is not satisfactory, for by tending to deny causality in the name of transcending it, it not only violates basic Buddhist moral precepts but reverts to a dualistic contrast between the pure and impure, flux and serenity, and freedom from and subjection to causation. Dōgen charges that all three of his Sung predecessors lapse into the misguided view and betray a misunderstanding of causality. Hung-chih's verse, "To talk about not falling into or not obscuring causality/Is to remain captive to the discriminating mind," overemphasizes the relativity of freedom from and subjection to causation. Yüan-wu's verse, "For nothing can escape from the perfect mirror of causality/Which is as vast and universal as the sky," seems better in emphasizing that "nothing can escape . . . ," but even this has traces of denying cause-effect in identifying causality with the emptiness of "sky." Ta-hui's verse, "Not falling into and not obscuring causality/Are as closely related as stone to earth," according to Dōgen, clearly remains trapped by the duality it claims to have surpassed. In a sermon for a bereaved lay follower and in other writings, Ta-hui ponders the relation between two views of death: one based on karmic causation and retribution, for which merit accrued during this lifetime may lead to a Pure Land rebirth; and the other, its seeming philosophical opposite, in which there is a genuine Zen realization that "Since there is no birth and extinction, and no cycle of rebirth,/There is neither changing nor destroying of the diamond body."[31] Ta-hui did not attempt to reconcile the two perspectives or explain the sequence of merit and emptiness, but left the issue of their relation to one another open for further meditative questioning—an attitude Dōgen might also find problematic.

Dōgen's own approach to the issues of karma and causality is complex and may be seen as also somewhat contradictory, especially according to recent interpretations.[32] In the KS fascicle, "Daishugyō," which also deals exclusively with the fox kōan, Dōgen seems to express a view supporting freedom from or not falling into causality in a way that resembles the MMK approach, and can be seen as going against the grain of the "Jinshin-inga." According to the commentary in "Daishugyō," Dōgen characteristically argues for the enlightened status of all parties involved at all stages of their interaction, and thus asserts that the man-fox spoke the truth in his original denial of causality and that these words are of equal value to Pai-chang's maintaining the importance of not obscuring causality. However, in EK-9 no. 77 Dōgen writes the following *juko*: "When an old man said, 'A person of great cultivation does not fall into causality'/He negated the law of causality but was not an ordinary fox/When he asked Pai-chang for an appropriate turning word/Mountains and rivers spontaneously transformed themselves into foxes in order to clarify the way."

In the "Jinshin-inga" fascicle, the not-falling view seems to be misguided, and the correct view is to see that "the law of causality is clear and selfless (*watakushi nashi*)." That is, causality functions continuously and consistently in an impersonal manner regardless of whether it is accepted or rejected, affirmed or denied by particular persons. This view is also referred to in KS "Immo" as the effortlessly (or nonactively) natural (*mui-jinen*), which is beyond the polarities of causation and noncausation or conditioned and unconditioned but can never depart from the impersonal law of causality. Selfless causality thus stands in contrast to the inherently limited view of the conditioned (or actively) natural (*ui-jinen*), which sees causality as a matter of linear sequence thereby presupposing enlightenment as freedom from the barrier of karma.[33] The effortlessly natural view recognizes the value of not obscuring causality (*fumai-inga*), while the actively natural view mistakes not falling into causality (*furaku-inga*) for transcendence. From the standpoint of not obscuring causality, Shibayama's argument about the "free use" of subjection to and independence from causality misrepresents enlightenment, which must be based on a wholehearted acceptance of selfless causality. Furthermore, Ta-hui's approach is all too willing to let a dichotomy stand between bondage to and freedom from causality. Dōgen's approach to causation expressed in "Jinshin-inga" and other fascicles has sometimes been characterized as a conservative, puritanical reaction against antinomian elements in Buddhism and in support of strict Sōtō monasticism. But his critique of both the Rinzai and Sōtō approaches to this issue indicates that his argument lies mainly on philosophical and literary rather than purely ethical or ritualistic grounds in emphasizing the dynamism of conditioned reality.

Dōgen and the Sōtō Tradition

In addition to the complexity and ambiguity involved in interpreting Dōgen's relations with the three twelfth-century masters, recent studies have made it clear that Dōgen's admiration for Ju-ching, which for the most part seems genuine and unconditional, may be compromised by two factors. First, Dōgen's accelerated eulogizing of Ju-ching seems to occur in the writings of his later years in direct proportion to his increasingly shrill criticism of Ta-hui in "Jishō-zammai." In that sense, he does contribute to the polarization of Zen while at the same time protesting against it. In the KS "Bendōwa" fascicle and elsewhere Dōgen argues that all the Zen schools reflect the "single, continuous lineage" of the "essence of the Buddha-mind seal." Yet his praise for his mentor, like his attacks on Ta-hui, were probably based more on sectarian concerns in establishing a new, independent Zen sect in Kamakura Japan than on sheer respect for Ju-ching's Sung Chinese teachings. The other factor involves the nature of the realization of the Dharma directly transmitted from Ju-ching to Dōgen. Although Dōgen's traditional biographies all maintain that his enlightenment experience of *shinjin datsuraku* was transmitted and certified by Ju-ching, there is strong evidence that this crucial doctrine was not actually originated by Ju-ching but instead reflected Dōgen's own mishearing or creative and deliberate misrepresentation of his Chinese mentor's teaching.[34] While the term *datsuraku* (like *genjōkōan*) was commonly used by Sung Zen masters (for example, Hung-chih used this term), the phrase *shinjin datsuraku* is a novel construction.[35] *Shinjin datsuraku* does not actually appear in Ju-ching's recorded sayings, though Dōgen repeatedly asserts in his writings that his mentor frequently uttered the injunction, cast off "body-mind" (*shinjin*, or in Chinese, *shen-hsin*). Ju-ching's record, however, does include in one instance a similar phrase, cast off the "dust from the mind" (Ch., *hsin-ch'en*), which also appeared in other Zen texts of the period.[36] Takasaki Jikidō has argued that *hsin-ch'en* has dualistic implications, indicating a subtle separation of the purity of mind and the defilement of dust, and that Dōgen must have had a "tremendous misconception" in substituting "body" for "dust," homophones in Japanese (*jin*)—a deliberate mishearing in order to remove latent duality.

According to Takasaki, Dōgen may have either misheard the term due to a lack of a full comprehension of Chinese, intuitively misrepresented it, or purposefully changed it. But Kurebayashi Kōdō has pointed out flaws in Takasaki's judgment because Dōgen's appropriation and application of

Ju-ching's Chinese utterance into Japanese could not possibly be based on such a simple misunderstanding; the homophonic correspondence on which Takasaki's analysis depends does not function in the same way in Chinese as it does in the Japanese language.[37] Nevertheless, it is evident that Dōgen developed a new idea beyond Ju-ching's thinking, and he may have tried to offer a constructive and meaningful criticism of a latent dualism in Ju-ching's approach to Zen training, in a way that is parallel to his rewriting of Hung-chih's verse on zazen.

At the same time that it becomes clear that Dōgen was not as close to the position of Hung-chih or as fully aligned with Ju-ching as the conventional view may assume, it is equally apparent that his approach was not so distant from the views of some of the Rinzai leaders other than Ta-hui. While Dōgen at times does refute Lin-chi's own doctrines, these comments generally do not include the ad hominem remarks found in his attacks on Ta-hui's credibility, and it must be noted that he also dared at times to critique Hui-neng.[38] On the other hand, Dōgen never directly criticized Yüan-wu, and he wrote the important KS "Zenki" fascicle entirely as a commentary on Ta-hui's teacher's verses concerning the doctrine of "total activity" (*zenki*), which indicates that he did not view the dynamism vs. quietism controversy strictly along sectarian lines. Dōgen even praised Ta-hui in the SZ, an early work, for his total commitment to meditation. In one passage, Ta-hui is depicted as a paragon of dedication to zazen when Dōgen retells the tale that Ta-hui persisted in his meditative exercise despite a life-threatening sore on his buttocks because he felt that this ailment only increased the urgency and need for religious practice.[39] As indicated in Chapter 1, Dōgen also apparently borrowed the title "Shōbōgenzō" ("Treasury of the True Dharma-eye") from Ta-hui's collection of over six hundred cases (though this term had been used as the title of other Zen texts as well).[40] This term, which Miura and Sasaki suggest Dōgen understood to refer to a compilation of kōans,[41] appears in the title of three of his works: the *Shōbōgenzō Zuimonki* and the *Shōbōgenzō Sanbyakusoku* in addition to Japanese vernacular *Shōbōgenzō*.

In addition, on several occasions Dōgen appears to approve of using a training method that is comparable to Ta-hui's *watō* approach in that it tends to extract an abbreviated kernel from traditional paradigmatic cases. In the SZ he comments on the kōan in which Nan-ch'üan cuts in half the cat that his monks had been quarreling over, while Chao-chou puts his shoes on his head in a deliberately absurd protest apparently against both the fighting and the killing (MMK case no. 14, HR nos. 63–4, MS no. 181).

Dōgen suggests that the phrase "cutting the cat" is an example of a "turning word" (*tengo*), which is a kind of shortcut technique—also mentioned in Pai-chang's fox kōan—that is supposed to have an immediate, decisive, and complete transformative effect on the listener/participant in the dialogue. "Were it not a turning word," he says, "the mountains, rivers, and great earth could not be identified with the wondrously pure and clear mind, and we could not explain that 'this very mind itself is buddha' (*sokushin-zebutsu*)."[42] Also, at the conclusion of the lengthy two-part KS "Gyōji" fascicle Dōgen supports a distilled form of learning about Zen recorded sayings when he writes, "You must quietly reflect on how fleeting life is, and realize that expressing even just two or three words of the buddhas and patriarchs is fully expressing the [teachings of the] buddhas and patriarchs. What is the reason for this? It is because the buddhas and patriarchs all realize the oneness of body-mind, and each and every one of the words they express reflects the compassionate body-mind of all buddhas and patriarchs."[43] According to this passage, a single word or phrase appropriately spoken can capture the entirety of truth.

All of these examples suggest once again that Dōgen's disparaging remarks about Ta-hui, like the increased pace of his eulogies of Ju-ching, were based more on partisan concerns in establishing his monastic order in Japan than strict ideological discrepancies. That is, it appears that in many of his comments Dōgen was not really preoccupied with the pros and cons of the Sung Chinese thinkers. Rather, his main concern was with the founder of the powerful Daruma-shū Zen sect, Dainichi Nōnin, whose followers included Ejō and many others who were to become the mainstays of Dōgen's Kōshōji and Eiheiji temples and the leaders of the Sōtō movement after Dōgen's death.[44] Unlike so many Japanese monks of the era, Nōnin never traveled to China to receive certification, but instead sent two of his followers who were given ordination by Te-kuang, Ta-hui's foremost disciple who Dōgen accuses in the KS "Gyōji" fascicle of being lax in meditation, ignorant of the Dharma, and greedily ambitious. Therefore, by attacking Ta-hui, whose certification of enlightenment he also questioned, and Te-kuang, Dōgen was perhaps indirectly besmirching the leader of the group of potential followers he was trying to win over. At the same time, Dōgen's praise for Ju-ching was necessitated to some extent by his need to hold up a single patriarchal role model, even if somewhat fictive or exaggerated (which is nothing new in the Zen tradition), in contrast to the flaws in the Ta-hui/Nōnin faction. Dainichi Nōnin's style of instruction, one of the earliest examples of Zen training in Japan, was actually much closer to

Japanese Tendai *hongaku* thought which Dōgen also criticized than to the *watō* method.[45] But it is likely that some of Dōgen's doctrines were specifi- cally designed as a critique of Nōnin's failure to be legitimately certified— for example, the notion of *kannō dōkō*, which emphasizes the need for continuing interpersonal spiritual communion between master and disicple, such as Dōgen had experienced first as a student in China under Ju-ching and then years later in Japan in the converse role with Ejō.

Furthermore, an examination of some of the most important Sōtō sect writings prior to and succeeding Dōgen does not indicate that its leading thinkers were trying to throw down the gauntlet against all kōan practice. For example, Hung-chih was not only firmly involved in the mainstream, but was a leader at the forefront of the kōan tradition. Despite his advocacy of the *mokushō* style of meditation in some writings, the T'ien-t'ung abbot compiled two kōan collections, one with prose (*nenko*) and the other with poetic (*juko*) comments, each of which was expanded significantly by Wan-sung's prose commentaries. Hung-chih's verse collection became the basis for the highly regarded SH text that Wan-sung edited into a six-tiered literary form integrating verse and prose exegesis of paradigmatic cases that is structurally nearly identical to the HR. Thus, Hung-chih played a role in relation to Wan-sung and the SH that is parallel to the role of Hsüeh-tou in relation to Yüan-wu and the HR. Although it is probably a lesser known text, the *Shōyōroku* is used widely in Japanese Zen training today along with the MMK, which was compiled by a Sung Rinzai priest.

In addition, a study of the recorded sayings of Ju-ching, by whose authority Dōgen's criticisms are supposedly voiced and whom he is careful only to praise, indicates that Dōgen's mentor was not a major player in sectarian controversies in Sung China and that his views on kōan inter- pretation and practice often do not diverge significantly from those of his contemporary Rinzai masters.[46] Apparently disappointed in his teacher's *goroku* collection when it was completed and brought to Japan in 1242, nearly fifteen years after Ju-ching's death, because it did not contain the level of insight and challenging instruction he remembered, Dōgen blamed the lack of creativity and originality in the text on the Chinese disciples who edited it. Although there is much of interest in Ju-ching's *goroku* text, including his prose and verse comments on kōans, it probably does not stand out as a leading representative of the Sung era recorded sayings genre. Dōgen's own kōan collections, the three hundred case MS and the ninety case EK-9, were probably patterned on the collections of Hung-chih and Yüan-wu rather than on Ju-ching's writings or sayings. The MS includes several kōans also cited in the HR, though the main sources are the recorded sayings of Yüan-wu, as well as of Ta-hui and Hung-chih, in addition to the earlier chronicles or transmission of the lamp histories, including the KD and ST texts from which the Sung masters drew the material for their kōan collections.[47] Also, the EK-9 contains Dōgen's *juko* on many of the cases also cited in the MS.

The other main works in early Japanese Sōtō Zen, Keizan's *Denkōroku* and "Zazenyōjinki," are for the most part supportive of kōans. Keizan was the fourth generational patriarch in the lineage, but he came to be looked on as the second leading figure due to his influence in solidifying and expanding the Sōtō institutional structure.[48] Keizan spent time during his early training studying Tendai thought as well as the esoteric traditions in Japan, but his enlightenment experience was attained through contemplating a kōan case under Gikai, to whom the Dharma had been directly transmitted by Ejō. Keizan went on to develop an eclectic approach to teaching monks, and he was also greatly successful in popularizing the Sōtō sect in the northern countryside. The *Denkōroku*, his most influential work which has a chapter for each of fifty-three patriarchs beginning with Śākyamuni and culminating in Dōgen and Ejō, seems to be a hybrid of the Sung transmission of the lamp histories and the kōan collections, as it includes the use of verse commentary at the conclusion of each chapter. The title, which means "Transmission of the Light," as well as its structure of tracing the generational succession of Zen masters, is a takeoff on the name and style of the most famous of the Sung Zen chronicles, the KD, or "Transmission of the Lamp written in the Keitoku period," which is one of the primary sources of kōan cases. Even in the "Zazenyōjinki" ("Admonition for zazen practice"), Keizan indicates that two kōans from the MMK, case no. 1 on Chao-chou's *Mu* and case no. 37 on the "oak tree in the garden," are particularly useful in steadying the mind during meditation. In addition, some contemporary Zen teachers rate the *Denkōroku* as one of five seminal kōan texts used in monastic training, along with the HR, MMK, SH, and MS.[49] Thus the *Denkōroku* could be considered closer in style to Rinzai literature than to Dōgen's KS philosophical writings, which no one in the Sōtō tradition ever seriously attempted to match.[50] In this founder-centered sect, most medieval studies were either biographies of Dōgen or commentaries on the KS, but Sōtō did not really become identified with an anti-kōan stance until the Tokugawa era debate between Hakuin and Sōtō apologists such as Menzan, who edited and commented on the KS and other works.

Contrasting Dōgen and Ta-hui

At this point, it is useful to reconsider the nature of the strands of continuity and discontinuity between Dōgen and Ta-hui concerning the value of kōans. On the one hand, it is clear that Dōgen was never really fully locked into one specific view with an axe to grind against kōans. Rather, he strongly asserts, especially in early writings such as the KS "Bendōwa" fascicle, that it is important to seek the essence of Buddhism regardless of sectarian labels or doctrinal divisions. According to Dōgen, all forms of essential Buddhism that authentically promote the Dharma first and foremost are fundamentally the same. Despite the polemical pro-zazen and anti-kōan injunctions appearing in the SZ, Dōgen also makes a key point concerning spirituality in the same work with which all Zen masters, and to some extent perhaps all Buddhist teachers, could probably agree. He argues that it is a personal sense of dedication and determination that leads to the attainment of enlightenment and underlies the efficacy of any particular form of practice, including both zazen meditation and studies of paradigmatic kōan cases formulated by former great masters: "Even if you practice zazen for just a single instant," he says, "or study just a single phrase of instruction in the Dharma, genuine Buddhism will prosper. . . . If you pursue the Way with intensity, whether you practice zazen-only, study kōans of the ancient masters, seek intellectual understanding, or exercise sincere devotion, then you will reach the heights and fathom the depths."[51]

In that light, it is possible to suggest a reorganizing of the conventional lineage charts to reflect the multiple influences Dōgen absorbed from both Sōtō and Rinzai masters. Figure 3.3a below shows that Dōgen's thought is a product of four predecessors who interacted with one another, rather than one or two, and indicates their primary doctrines that influenced Dōgen, while Figure 3.3b simply highlights the combined impact on Dōgen of Hung-chih, Ta-hui, and Ju-ching, who all served as T'ien-t'ung abbots.

On Bloomian "Misreading"

However, the key question that now must be raised reflects a concern that is converse to the concern of the conventional view: that is, if Dōgen does have some historical and ideological affinity with Ta-hui after all, then why does he seem compelled to author considerable, even excessive, polemic directed against him? And, more significantly, if Dōgen's message is in basic accord with that of all Buddhists, or at least all Zen Buddhists, why must

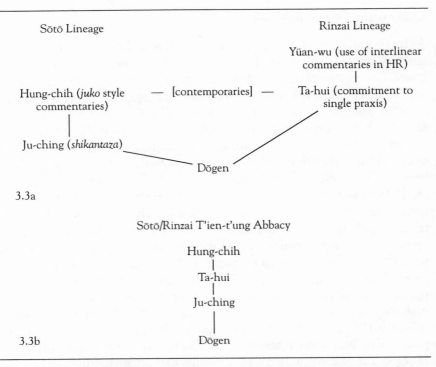

Figures 3.3a and 3.3b *Alternative Lineage.*   *Alternative lineage charts, reflecting combined influences of Sōtō and Rinzai masters on Dōgen's approach to kōans.*

he also revise and rewrite the sayings of even the "old buddhas" in his direct Sōtō lineage? Part of the answer to these questions lies in the Zen patriarchal tradition itself, which demands that disciples eventually surpass the masters who may have had to scold or humiliate them with "sticks and shouts" (e.g., in the sense that "you have to be cruel to be kind") in the earlier stages of their spiritual quest. One way of clarifying the significance for Dōgen studies of Zen's insistence that disciples criticize and surpass their teachers is to evoke Harold Bloom's psychoanalytically rooted literary criticism. According to Bloom, the most genuinely creative acts in poetry take place when a junior poet either deliberately or unconsciously—but invariably in response to the underlying "anxiety of influence" exerted by a sense of competition with the mentoring senior poet—misreads the works of his or her mentor. Thus, intertextuality for Bloom is not just an impersonal process in the formation of texts, but it must have a subjective or willful motivating component. The following remark, which deals exclusively with the creative process in poetry composition and transmission, could apply to Zen patriarchy if the word "Zen" is substituted for "Poetic" and "masters" for "poets": "Poetic Influence—when it involves two strong, authentic poets— always proceeds by a misreading of the prior poet, an act of creative correction that is actually and necessarily a misinterpretation."[52] Furthermore, for Bloom, "misprision (meaning mistaking, misreading, and misinterpreting), both necessary and inescapable, occurs between one poet and another and between a critic and a text because, essentially, exact repetition or identification is impossible and because, quintessentially, identity is slavery and death; difference is freedom and vitality."[53] Therefore, Dōgen *must creatively misread* and alter the words of Hung-chih and Ju-ching in addition to Ta-hui, even if he fundamentally agrees with the teachings of all Zen masters, in order to "clear imaginative space"[54] for himself, or carve his own philosophical niche, and thereby to ensure the integrity, independence, and individuality of his religious vision.

The Bloomian process of creative misprision is complex and multifaceted. Bloom analyzes six levels of interaction in the anxiety of influence, all of which have oedipal overtones, ranging from a rather severe or violent overthrow of the senior poet by the junior poet to a more subtle, understated form of sublimated protest or revision. For example, Dōgen's attacks on Ta-hui could be considered an example of Bloomian "kenosis," which is a breaking device or a movement towards discontinuity. His rewriting of Hung-chih seems to represent "clinamen," which is a corrective movement implying that the precursor poem was accurate to a certain point but then should swerve in the direction the new poem takes, and his subtle critique of Ju-ching's approach to *shinjin datsuraku* is "daemonization," whereby the later poet uncovers a power that is implicit in but yet just beyond the reach of the parent poem. Also, Ta-hui's burning of his teacher Yüan-wu's text could be considered an example of "askesis," or a movement of self-purgation in which the later poet establishes his solitude separate from all others, including the much admired precursor.[55]

The application of Bloom's argument in terms of Zen patriarchy highlights the point that the uniqueness of Dōgen's manner of expressing the Dharma in no way violates—even if it involves criticism or repudiation—but actually supports, sustains, and perpetuates the teaching of the "old masters" according to the irreverent, anti-authoritarian spirit of the seminal patriarchs. If Dōgen were not so strong and authentic in his expression, then he would have become a mere echo of his predecessors, and this would represent a loss or diminishment in the line of transmission that they themselves need to extend to him to legitimate their role in the lineage. According to Dōgen's philosophy of being-time, the future and past are inseparable and equalizable from the standpoint of the holistic moment encompassing existential continuity or passage. Therefore, the greatness of a thinker like Dōgen, as of Bodhidharma, Hui-neng, Lin-chi, and Hakuin, among others, is that their form of instruction transcends, while being fully in accord with and extending and fulfilling, the orginality and creativity of precursors and successors alike.

Nevertheless, Dōgen and Ta-hui certainly reached different conclusions concerning the relation between kōans and meditation, and it is clear that the discontinuity between them is rooted in a number of social, political, and philosophical factors in addition to the aforementioned literary-psychological aspects. Thus Bloom's psychoanalytic approach, which may imply that creative rewriting is a willful, arbitrary process, needs to be complemented by a historically based archaeology of knowledge. It is important to remember that Dōgen and Ta-hui were neither contemporaries nor compatriots, but lived a century and a country apart. They had different concerns at disparate junctures in history, and the diverging influences they absorbed and audiences they addressed helped shape their respective views of language. While both thinkers are consistent with the fundamental aims of Zen, each had to deal with an array of political pressures and ideological twists and turns in the secular and ecclesial levels of society. For example, problems in attaining state patronage, competition with other Buddhist sects and non-Buddhist religious movements, and appeals to popular and elite levels of religiosity—all of these factors helped condition their understanding of the kōan as a form of spiritual practice.

Cultural Influences

Both Dōgen and Ta-hui were notable for responding rather aggressively to bewildering political upheavals that challenged the validity and vitality of the religious institutions of their day, and both must receive credit for establishing reforms that helped promote and sustain the Zen sect. There is little doubt that East Asian Zen—Rinzai and Sōtō in China, Japan, and Korea—would not be as stable or genuine a religious institution today without their commitment to authenticity and innovation at crucial turning points in the history of the tradition. Both thinkers are also known for formulating a single, simple method of praxis that is comprehensive in that it is portrayed as the only technique necessary to capture completely the essence of Zen enlightenment. However, the conventional black-and-white opposition between *shikantaza* and *watō* is somewhat misleading because these doctrines represent but one level of discourse in the complex teachings of Dōgen and Ta-hui. That is, the Zen masters at times boil down their instruction to a simple formula not because that is all they have to offer, but as a skillful means to appeal to a particular sector of their audience that was probably only ready to receive a single, clear idea. The overall teachings of both thinkers contain multiple dimensions of discourse and cannot be limited to one specific notion. Therefore, it is important to clarify the background and different levels of meaning out of which the better-known doctrines emerged.

Ta-hui's response to his personal suffering resulting from turbulent political circumstances was to continue to affirm throughout his career the value of secular society or laypersons, primarily the scholar-officials of Sung bureaucracy who constituted a "small elite group of educated men from whom administrators, judges, policy-makers and teachers of the Chinese empire were drawn."[56] The scholar-officials were primarily guided by the morality of emerging Neo-Confucianism, but Ta-hui was convinced that they should still seek Zen enlightenment. In insisting on the integrity of non-monks and eliminating the traditional distinction between monastic and lay practice, Ta-hui tried to be especially sensitive to the emotional needs of his secular bureaucrat followers. The shortcut method was perhaps developed primarily for this group,[57] or at least they were a crucial sector of the audience targeted by Ta-hui. The *watō* was influenced by the ideal in the thought of Mādhyamika Buddhism and philosophical Taoism of using paradoxical forms of expression to highlight the priority of silence—for example, Chuang Tzu's view that words function like a fishnet that can be discarded after catching fish, symbolizing the meaning that the words are intended to convey. It was conceived by Ta-hui as a corrective for Neo-Confucian metaphysical speculation that had been influenced, perhaps inappropriately, by Hua-yen and T'ien-t'ai holistic philosophy, which Zen had already absorbed and transmuted in terms of the kōan tradition. The *watō* also probably tried to capture some of the appeal of the emerging *nembutsu* (C. *nien-fo*) method, which was designed by devotional Pure Land Buddhism to represent a single, simple but complete form of other-power (*tariki*) meditative praxis.

In addition, during the course of his career Ta-hui showed an increasing concern for developing a creative response to the Zen lay constituency emerging in the Sung era due to social and political circumstances by perfecting the genres of sermons (*fusetsu*, lit. "general preaching") and letters. While not turning at all from a profound interest in the spiritual progress of his monk disciples, he had a twofold attitude toward the lay followers. First, they could be instructed in ways that would demonstrate the connection between absolute and relative truth, so that they could apply the meaning and relevance of the former into the world of the latter with which they were preoccupied. Second, beyond the interweaving of two levels of truth, Ta-hui was committed to the notion that laypersons should be able to attain enlightenment within their daily lives, that is, the Dharma could prevail without requiring the kind of personal sacrifices normally required for the sake of religious discipline.

Dōgen's reaction to political insecurity stemming from verbal and even physical attacks on his temple by the mainstream but declining Tendai church was to create a monastic utopia at Eiheiji temple, secluded in the pristine natural splendor of the Echizen mountains. Earlier in his career, while still in the Kyoto area shortly after returning from China, Dōgen asserted the unity of laypersons and monks, and of men and woman, as he tried to appeal to aristocratic literati in the capital. It has been reported that at this time Dōgen may have participated in secular literary activities such as poetry contests (*renga*), and befriended the famed poet Fujiwara Teika. But after suffering repeated persecutions at the hands of rival sects from Mt. Hiei located just north of Kyoto, Dōgen first moved to the village of Fukakusa and then to Kōshōji temple in Uji to the south of the capital. Dōgen's eventual withdrawal to Eiheiji was coterminous with an exclusive focus on monastic discipline, for which he at times has been criticized for embracing a puritanical elitism inconsistent with his earlier liberalism.

In early Kamakura Japan, mainstream and reform religious move-ments alike were equally under the sway of Tendai *hongaku* thought. The hegemonic Tendai church has sometimes been portrayed as a mother-figure giving birth to rebellious yet somehow affectionate children, including Dōgen, Hōnen, Shinran, and Nichiren. In the case of Dōgen, there has been considerable recent scholarly debate concerning the impact of Tendai in relation to Zen thought on his philosophical development.[58] This is a complex issue because it involves taking into account the connections concerning philosophy, styles of scriptural commentary, and techniques of meditation between T'ien-t'ai/Tendai and Ch'an/Zen in Sung China as the background for understanding the interaction between established Tendai and various formative aspects of Zen in Kamakura Japan. Dōgen seems to be critical of non-Buddhistic or heretical "naturalistic" tendencies (*jinengedō*) in *hongaku* thought, which absolutizes all of the phenomenal world as being one with the original (*hon*) reality without the need for spiritual purification. Dōgen was probably aware that this type of criticism had already been leveled from within Tendai by *hongaku* thinkers, such as Shōshin, and he never directly repudiated the Tendai teaching. He sometimes used the word *hon* (original) in other, related compound terms, such as *honshō myōshū* (original realization-wondrous practice). Dōgen's approach to Zen is distinctive in the way it draws out implications in the doctrine of original enlightenment concerning the oneness of practice and attainment, language and reality, and contemplative and conceptual thinking based on the polysemy and multidimensional wordplay of kōans when rigorously applied through zazen. Dōgen's standpoint was also largely influenced by the literary traditions of T'ang Chinese Zen and of early Japanese religion as well as the sacramentalism of Japanese esoteric Buddhism (*mikkyō*), all of which tend to stress the efficacy of poetic metaphor or scriptural recitation in disclosing spiritual attainment.

That is, Dōgen's understanding of the kōan is based on an approach to philosophy of language supported by a combination of elements in Chinese Zen and Japanese religiosity that view literary symbols as the essential means of conveying spiritual truth. First, Dōgen seeks to be sensitive and to recapture the poetic creativity and ingenuity of early Zen masters, for whom "ultimate reality [is] revealed to the mind's eye in concrete phenomena. Metaphor and poetry are ideally suited to function in this way,"[59] so that "it had become commonplace to discuss poetry in terms of [Zen], to say that poetry . . . 'is like' [Zen]."[60] Rather than negate the poetic and metaphoric as a hindrance to awakening, Dōgen sees these and other tropes of discourse as an inexhaustible reservoir from which awakened consciousness draws its inspiration. Dōgen's approach also reflects his initial training in Japanese Tendai Buddhism on Mt. Hiei, which is of course a different ideological context than what was experienced by Ta-hui. In the early Kamakura period, Tendai was an eclectic sacramentalism that seemed to draw upon the emphasis in early Japanese mythology and poetry on direct participation in the reality that is being symbolized in the sense that the mountain, for example, neither represents nor houses but *is* the *kami* or divine potency. Joseph Kitagawa refers to this view as a "nonsymbolic understanding of symbols" because the ontological identification of symbol and sacred is prior to yet establishes the epistemic ground for a sense of distance that is presupposed for a symbol to re-present the sacral object.[61] Tendai affirmed the efficacy of *sūtra* study and recitation as a locus of religious truth, particularly the *Lotus Sūtra*, which is cited by Dōgen more than fifty times in his collected writings.[62] It also integrated the use of sacred syllables, or *dhāraṇī*, and circular designs, or *maṇḍala*, which are techniques connecting the subjective psychophysical universe with the limitless potentialities of cosmic awareness "penetrating every sphere of phenomenal existence."[63] Tendai, in turn, had absorbed Kūkai's Shingon esoteric notion of the oneness of sound, meaning, and reality: "From the Shingon standpoint, each and every thing in the universe is an 'expressive symbol' (*monji*) of the dharmakāya. In fact, the universe as a whole is the 'symbolic embodiment' (*sammayashin*) of the dharmakāya as the Buddha, Dainichi."[64] In addition, Dōgen was familiar with the Tendai exegetical approach, deriving from Chih-yi's Chinese commentaries, particularly the four levels of interpretation or commentary (*shaku*) based on: (1) linguistic context and conditions for attainment (*innen*), (2) classification or ranking of doctrines (*hankyō*), (3) evaluation of the fundamental standpoint or essence (*honjaku*), and (4) contemplation of mind (*kanjin*).[65] According to Dōgen's understanding the fourth level, *kanjin-shaku*, gives the interpreter license to go beyond the source material in the text and to creatively offer original philosophical perspectives and insights supported by meditative awareness. The effort to surpass while in the process of commenting on Zen dialogues and anecdotes is the method often used by Dōgen in his discussions of *kosoku-kōan*.

In addition, Dōgen is influenced by classical Japanese literature which conventionalizes complex wordplay involving puns, homophones, and grammatical restructuring to accentuate the polysemous quality of words in devices such as "relational words" (engo) and "allusive variation" (*honka-dori*). The latter technique, in which a poem is created by using an older poem and providing subtle variations of wording that evoke new feelings playing off those expressed in the source poem, might anachronistically be considered an early literary technique that valorizes intertextuality.[66] As indicated in Chapter 1, many of these features of language and poetics are also prevalent in Chinese language and literature. On the other hand, when Chinese and Japanese are contrasted, it appears that of the two the latter has greater fluidity and flexibility in regard to the possibilities for wordplay. According to David Pollack, Japanese appears to function in a metonymic, diachronic, and horizontal mode whereas Chinese is metaphorical, synchronic, and vertical. Pollack argues that Chinese can be compared to a "black hole," which has a gravitational force so powerful that meaning collapses upon itself centripetally, but that Japanese is like a "supernova," which has a central core radiating meaning outward with such force it can scarcely be contained. Furthermore, "Chinese and Japanese can be, and often have been, characterized as, respectively, monosyllabic as opposed to polysyllabic, isolating as opposed to agglutinating, and un-inflected as opposed to highly inflected . . . [I]n other words, meaning in Chinese is located primarily in the creation of formal structures. . . . Meaning in the case of Japanese is created of extreme polysemy by syntagmatic codes of linking that, by limiting the direction of radiation [from the supernova], serve to polarize and give coherence."[67]

One way to consider the nature of Japanese and its impact on Dōgen is to discuss the link between language (*kotoba*) and mind (*kokoro*) in the creative process, stemming to a large extent from the relation of word and thing in early Japanese religiosity. The original meaning of language in Japanese culture is probably connected to agrarian animistic/shamanistic practices involving *kotodama*, or the belief in the soul or spirit (*tamashii*) of words (*koto*). According to Roy Miller, the Old Japanese *koto* (words, speech, language) is related to the verb *katar* (tell, relate) in the same way that the English "tale" is related to "tell." This also seems comparable to the connection Martin Heidegger draws between Saying and the traditional term "saga" as a mythopoeic mode of discourse prior to the distinction between *mythos* and *logos*. Like many ancient religions, from biblical to tribal cultures, the Japanese people affirmed the power of the word or name to provide mastery over things (the same is probably true for China). Miller shows that in the practice of early Japanese homeopathic magic there was a strong connection between the term *koto* meaning words and another homophonous term *koto* meaning affair, matter, or thing. According to Miller, "the idea that the 'thing' referred to by a given word is coeval as well as coextensive with the 'word' that refers to it is at the heart of the whole matter."[68] *Kotodama* is also connected to *kotoāge* (literally "lifting up words"), a ritualistic, liturgical practice based on the metaphoric transference of the identification of word and thing from the terrestrial to the supernatural plane. Thus, it was believed that naming or calling upon a thing desired would cause the "thing" so "named" to materialize.

While animistic sources establish the affinity of word and thing in Japanese language and thought, one of the earliest classical literary references to *kotoba* demonstrates the inseparability of language and the mind as the perceptive organ for things. In his famous preface to the *Kokinshū* imperial poetry collection, Ki no Tsurayuki depicts mind (*kokoro*) as an undeniable impulse toward poetic creativity that inevitably flourishes like a natural force in response to the stimuli of the seasons and elements:

> The poetry of Japan takes hold in the mind of man and springs forth in the innumerable petals of words. Because of humans' intense involvement in the world [it is poetry] that expresses the inner attitude of the mind upon viewing [the sights of the world] and hearing [its sounds].[69]

According to Tsurayuki, the mind represents the potential of consciousness to perceive phenomena and creatively describe them. When activated by some impressions generated by external stimuli like the sights and sounds of nature, the *kokoro* responds by expressing *kotoba* that directly record its feelings about the event. Thus, *kotoba* is part of a constellation of thing-word-mind, whereby the mind is continually perceiving and responding to things (*koto*) through poetic speech. Nishitani Keiji comments on this connection: "In Japanese, the 'meaning' of a given *koto* (a term signifying either 'matter' or 'affair,' as well as 'word') can also be called 'mind,' or *kokoro* . . . [thus] the mind of the matter at hand (or the very reality become manifest in the *koto*) reflects into the mind of man, and the mind of man reflects itself onto the mind of the *koto*. This living transmission of minds being projected onto one another as they are, and the obtaining of mind that this effects, is the elemental mode of the understanding of meaning."[70] Therefore, Dōgen inherited and helped culminate a tradition in which the intimate connection between language and phenomena is sustained by the human capacity to express the true nature of things as they are in both their profound mystery (*yūgen*) and utter simplicity. His composition of the KS in Japanese reflects these influences. While the MS collection is of course a Chinese work, the fact that the Kanazawa manuscript contains *katakana* (Japanese syllabary used for pronunciation and grammatical changes of foreign languages) appearing in the margins next to Chinese terms may indicate the transitional quality of this work as Dōgen began to introduce and develop the new Japanese style of writing.

Table 3.2 summarizes the main points of ideological impact, including social/historical/political background as well as philosophical and literary influences, leading to the different views of language in relation to kōans in Dōgen and Ta-hui.

Table 3.2. *Influences on Dōgen and Ta-hui. Comparison of primary concerns of and historical and cultural influences on Dōgen and Ta-hui.*

	Dōgen	Ta-hui
a. Historical Period	13th-century Japan (early Kamakura)	12th-century China (early Southern Sung)
b. Social Background	Aristocratic literati	Scholar-officials
c. Reaction to Political Turmoil	Withdraws to nature	Affirms secular society
d. Projected Audience	Monks exclusively—use of *jishu* style	Laypersons—develops *fusetsu* and *tegami*
e. Main Ideological Rival	Tendai *hongaku* thought	Neo-Confucian morality and metaphysics
f. Syncretistic Tendencies	Literary techniques (e.g., *honkadori*)	Popular Buddhism (e.g., *nembutsu* chant)
g. Language Influenced by	Shinto and Shingon power of word—Japanese "supernova"	Taoist and Mādhyamika paradox and silence—Chinese "black hole"
	resulting in	
h. Philosophy of Language	Polysemous wordplay—Expansive and comprehensive continuing hermeneutics	Monosyllabic silence—Simplification and radical reduction of bounds of discourse
i. Simple but Complete Praxis	*Shikantaza*	*Watō*

On the Burning and the Copying of the HR Text

Some of the main differences between seminal Zen thinkers, Dōgen and Ta-hui, are highlighted by the ironic juxtaposition of legends concerning Ta-hui's burning and Dōgen's copying of the text of Yüan-wu's HR text. According to traditional accounts, which are only first mentioned in the preface to a Yüan era edition of his *goroku* text, Ta-hui destroyed the xylographs of the text so that it could not be distributed in China for nearly two hundred years. Even if the account of Ta-hui's burning the text is true, it is highly unlikely that the HR was totally suppressed for such a long period. The HR probably was read by Chinese Zen practitioners, yet its prominence was apparently diminished until a manuscript was prepared in

1317 by a layman, Chang. This version did not arrive in Japan until 1332, a century after Dōgen's IH version of the HR as well as the MS collection. The Ta-hui legend is no doubt at least greatly exaggerated. But it does have a mythical significance in indicating his resistance to an unwitting hypostatization of traditional cases by his Sung era disciples, who may have lost the initial sense of the spontaneity and irreverence with which the kōans were supposedly created by earlier generations of T'ang era masters. Burning the HR, like Te-shan's destroying his copies and commentaries on the *Diamond Sūtra*, becomes an ideal symbol for Ta-hui's skepticism about language and emphasis on direct, personal experience of reality. Ta-hui was not a one-sided, uncritical advocate of kōans, and his *watō* method offered two distinct but inseparable messages. First, he was aware of problems inherent in the kōan as a form of spiritual training, especially for the new Confucian elite of scholar-officials who needed a simplified interpretation that could be integrated with their secular lifestyle, and the *watō* was aimed at offsetting their somewhat naive intellectual aspirations and philosophical preoccupations. It undercut their tendency to asssume that they could reason their way toward truth. At the same time, the scholar-officials were not familiar with the references and citations from Zen chronicles evoked by kōans, and the *watō* method suggested that it was not necessary to learn this voluminous material in order to progress toward enlightenment. For his monk disciples, however, Ta-hui sought not to diminish but rather to perfect the kōan by developing the *watō* method as a step beyond conventional studies of paradigmatic cases and catechistic memorization of a set curriculum, and as a way of focusing intensively one's power of meditation on a single, deliberately disturbing and doubt-provoking topic, as Ta-hui himself experienced prior to his attainment.

Therefore, what Ta-hui prescribed for laypersons may have been somewhat different than his instructions for monks, and when he indicates that the *watō* is the only method needed, this probably meant something quite different for the disparate audiences. But in either instance, he backed up the shortcut technique that is intended to capture the essence of the kōan with a list of ten defects of conceptualization. The ten defects, supposedly systematized by Hung-chih and then extensively commented on by Korean monk Chinul, stress the need to negate all distractions involved in treating the Mu *watō* and other cases as a matter of intellectual endeavor. By forcing the disciple, whether lay or monastic, into a position in which he or she has no recourse to conventional thinking, the *watō* generates a doubt that is a necessary transformative turning point leading to realization. According to Ta-hui, "the clever are actually obstructed by their cleverness, and can't gain a sudden breakthrough"[71] unless they are first overwhelmed—to undermine their cleverness—and then eventually able to overcome profound inner doubt.

The legend about Dōgen's "one night *Hekiganroku*" is surrounded by myth, superstition, and secrecy in a way that involves syncretistic tendencies connected with influences from popular Buddhism, Shinto, and Japanese folk religions. In some versions a bodhisattva guides his hand to speed up the copying process, or he is protected by the assimilated deity of Mt. Hakusan, a *yamabushi* center north of Eiheiji temple that also became an important pilgrimage site for Sōtō trainees. In other versions the uninitiated are forbidden from viewing the text lest they go blind. It was long reported that a manuscript was housed at Daijōji temple that was apparently made available only to high priests within the Sōtō order. In 1931 D. T. Suzuki received permission to inspect and publish the IH manuscript, and since that time other scholars, including one of the foremost modern Sōtō scholars, Etō Sokuō, have studied the text.[72] Although questions have been raised about the authenticity of the calligraphy in the Daijōji version of the IH, it is not implausible to think that Dōgen brought a version, perhaps even the first version, of the HR to Japan, although Dōgen surely did not copy it in a single night. This might indicate that the text was important in China in the thirteenth century despite the legend about Ta-hui's burning it. Therefore, the IH text is probably not apocryphal, though it is significantly different than the standard edition of the HR kōan collection in several ways.[73] Dōgen's version also contains one hundred cases but only eighty of these are the same as the full list of standard HR cases, and they follow a somewhat different sequence. Also, while the IH cases are recognizable as a version of the HR, the wording ranges from slightly to very different in Dōgen's version, and the commentaries are considerably shorter. It is also important to note that there are no kōan cases from the HR cited in Dōgen's MS, and only a handful are cited in the KS.[74] Therefore, it is not at all clear that the HR was an important, direct influence on Dōgen. On the other hand, Dōgen's commentatorial style, as will be explained in Chapter 4, does resemble the HR in key ways. Thus, while the legends about Dōgen's text have often been seen as obscuring and mystifying his connection to the HR, in light of recent studies they may also be interpreted as enhancing a sense of the mystery and importance of his version of the main collection of kōans. The legendary quality surrounding the IH text, when seen in relation to Dōgen's writings, highlights the point that, whether or not he specifically admired or cited the HR, Dōgen became one of the primary disseminators of Chinese Zen

dialogues, sermons, and epistles—the raw material of all kōan collections—
to an audience of thirteenth-century Japanese Buddhists newly interested
in Zen.

Apparently, prior to the Kamakura period, when Tendai *hongaku*
thought was dominant, Japanese Buddhists were exposed primarily to the
early T'ang Zen texts of Bodhidharma and Hui-neng (corresponding to the
materials found at Tun Huang in the twentieth century), though these
works had never really become popular in Japan. However, as previously
discussed, what came to be known as "kōans" in the Sung developed out
of a literary tradition in China that was formed subsequent to the sixth
patriarch. The origin of kōans was the records of *satori* dialogues, or
spontaneous encounters between masters and disciples, first used by Ma-tsu
and then associated with subsequent masters in Ma-tsu's Hung-chou lineage. It seems that these records (which were not included in the Tun Huang
materials) were probably already available in Japan in the KD and related
texts that were studied by members of the Daruma-shū. However, the
Hung-chou lineage dialogues may have been considered "too original and
too Chinese" to gain wide acceptance by the Japanese audience—that is,
until Dōgen helped introduce and legitimize them, just at the time when
the HR may have temporarily disappeared, or at least was diminished in
importance in China because Ta-hui had burned the xylographs.[75] The
reform-minded, "new" Kamakura Buddhism was apparently a fortuitous
time for Japan to receive the message of Zen emphasizing individuality,
spontaneity, and independence from formal institutions. Just as Zen's
antistructural, iconoclastic attitudes were suited to post-845 Sung China
after the persecution of Buddhism, so too—though for somewhat different
reasons—were they appropriate for the period in Japan following the
Tendai-dominated Heian era as part of a rebelliousness against Court-sup-
ported Buddhism.

Even though Ma-tsu was the forerunner of Lin-chi and thus of Dōgen's
main rival sect, it was Dōgen's KS that was largely responsible for bringing
and spreading Ma-tsu's Hung-chou school texts, through Sung recensions,
into his native land. And just as Ma-tsu had contributed to the sinitization
of Buddhism in the T'ang, Dōgen was largely responsible for the Japanization of Zen by incorporating elements of symbolism in Japanese religiosity
and literary styles to his presentation and interpretation of Zen dialogues.
The symbolic theme of HR being copied in "one night" indicates that
Dōgen had to act quickly and decisively in developing a style that would
allow him to at once transcribe/disseminate and comment/critique the

Sung chronicles and records. Therefore, when Dōgen argues for the position of zazen-only, the English term "only" should not be understood in the
sense of excluding any other approach or technique. Rather, it means "just
zazen" or "just sitting," and it implies a *single-mindedness* of purpose and
dedication to the quest for enlightenment, so that it is only or just on the
basis of zazen and the experience of the sublime liberation of *kaiin-zammai*
(ocean-reflection *samādhi*) that the dialogues and kōans can be understood
and conceptually processed.

The Two *Shōbōgenzō* Texts

The above discussion diffuses the conventional sense of polarity and
conflict and points to common roots shared by Dōgen and the kōan
traditon. It shows that Dōgen, as well as Sōtō masters Hung-chih and
Ju-ching before him, were not uniformly hypercritical of Rinzai Zen,
Ta-hui, or the use of kōans, although at times a refutation of this lineage
and doctrine emerged as an important level of discourse in Dōgen's writings. At the same time, Ta-hui was not one-sidedly opposed to Dōgen or
to the Sōtō sect, and there is a strong sense for both thinkers of the need
to be critical of what had gone wrong in Sung Chinese Zen regardless of
sectarian affiliation. The argument concerning the connection between
Dōgen and the kōan tradition has thus far taken a somewhat "negative
angle" in the sense that it has shown some of the inconsistencies and
contradictions in the conventional view. This makes it clear that Dōgen
had no objection to dialogues or kōans, and did not abhor the kōan
collection genre in principle. However, the case can be demonstrated more
positively by taking a closer look at the formation and structure of Dōgen's
kōan collections, especially the compilation of three hundred cases in the
MS collection and also the verse commentary on ninety cases in the EK-9
collection, and in particular at how the MS contributed to the formation
of the KS text. The intratextual connections between these works establish
the MS as a link to the kōan tradition and sets the stage for an intertextual
comparison in Chapter 4 of Dōgen, not just with Ta-hui and the *watō*
method, but also with the full range of Sung genres.

History of the Text

As the major studies of the MS acknowledge, there have been many
difficulties in verifying the authenticity of the MS text, which for most of

its history was either unknown or considered apocryphal. Until the twentieth century, the only version of the MS that was known was a Tokugawa
era commentary, the *Nenpyō Shōbōgenzō Funogo* by Shigetsu Ein, which
was released by his disciple Honkō Katsudō in 1766 during a period of
revival of Sōtō sectarian studies. However, this text was considered by many
to be spurious because of Dōgen's reputation as an opponent of kōans and
the fact that there was no original version available to support the contention that Ein's rather late commentary dealt with a book actually composed
by Dōgen. Kawamura Kōdō comments on the difficulty many Sōtō followers had in accepting the status of the MS, especially during the Tokugawa
period. Kawamura points out that a sense of uncertainty often went beyond
ordinary suspicion or misgiving in that many resisted or even refused to
investigate the MS because doing so would upset their assumptions concerning the priority of zazen. Then, a portion of an MS manuscript dating
from 1287—the middle of three sections which contain one hundred cases
each—was discovered in 1934 by the Kanazawa Bunko library. However,
the Kanazawa manuscript was inconsistent in some ways with the version
in Ein's commentary, so this discovery did not necessarily confirm the
authentic status of the MS as Dōgen's own work. Some scholars, particularly Yanagida, speculated that even if the MS existed, it was put together
not by Dōgen himself but by his followers including Ejō, the compiler of
the SZ, who were former members of Dainichi Nōnin's Daruma-shū sect.[76]

Kawamura's discovery in Sōtō temples of two Muromachi manuscripts
of the MS text, the Shinpōji and the Eishōin manuscripts, plus an undated
manuscript (the Jōkōji manuscript, perhaps from Muromachi but probably
as late as 1715), occurred while he was conducting research on the
formation of the sixty-fascicle version of the KS. In *Shōbōgenzō no Seiritsu
Shiteki Kenkyū* (Historical Studies in the Formation of the *Shōbōgenzō*),
Kawamura provides a critical edition of the various versions of the MS text;
there are six in all, including the Kanazawa mansucript and the three
manuscripts Kawamura discovered in addition to the NS and an original
handwritten copy of the NS text Kawamura also found. Also, Kawamura's
book offers a modern Japanese translation of the entire MS text. Since the
publication of his work in 1986, Kawamura has discovered another
Muromachi MS manuscript. All the MS versions, along with all available
KS versions, are published by the Sōtō sect in a continuously updated
multivolume edition (nearly thirty volumes are currently available) of
Shōbōgenzō (MS and KS) texts, the *Shōbōgenzō Shūsho Taisei*. In addition,
the forty-one volume photo-fascimile edition, the *Ei-in-bon Shōbōgenzō*,

contains reproductions of the MS Kanazawa, Shinpō, and Eishōin manu-scripts along with several KS manuscripts.

Kawamura maintains that the authenticity of the MS text is now certain although there are quite a few minor discrepancies, which he carefully documents, between the Kanazawa and NS versions and the three Muromachi manuscripts he discovered. However, it must be pointed out that there still remain several unresolved questions concerning the dating and content of the manuscripts as well as the purpose and function of the MS. First, there are several important and hard-to-explain gaps of time that must be considered in evaluating the authenticity of the text. The first gap is between Dōgen's life and the earliest manuscript in 1287, which is not unique among Dōgen's works that are for the most part known from posthumous editions. Although some extant KS fascicles, in addition to other manuscripts, especially the *Fukanzazengi*, are generally considered to be in Dōgen's own calligraphy, it may be impossible to authenticate any of these. The next gap is between 1287 and the time of the recently discovered Muromachi manuscripts, which is about a century, and then between the Muromachi versions and Shigetsu's NS commentary during the Tokugawa, which is about three hundred years. The main reason for this lengthy time gap is the fragmentation and divisiveness within the Sōtō order during the late medieval period. The sect was not unified at that time, and it was broken down into numerous subdivisions of branch houses (*bunke*) and streams (*ryū*) led by masters at particular temples, some of them competing with one another and others simply not in communication. It is likely that studies of the MS were kept alive in some streams and not in others, and additional discoveries of medieval manuscripts may give a clearer picture of which of these groups valued the text most highly. The third time-gap is between Ein's Tokugawa commentary and the twentieth-century Kanazawa discovery, which is probably due to a lack of interest by the Sōtō orthodoxy in kōan studies.

Another question concerning the authenticity of the MS involves the primary Sung Zen textual influences on the construction of Dōgen's work. According to Ishii Shūdō, the single main influence on the MS is the ST, from which Dōgen selected 129 paradigmatic cases. By Ishii's counting, the other important influences were the *Wanshi Goroku* (43 cases), the KD (42 cases), and the *Engo Goroku* (38 cases).[77] The ST is a rather obscure text primarily known as a precursor of the more prominent SR. It does not appear to have been a major factor in Sung Zen and, more importantly, it is not a primary influence on the KS. This could feed speculation that the

MS is an apocryphal work. However, Kagamishima Genryū argues that questions about the ST influence do not invalidate the authenticity of the MS. He points out that there are a number of problems (most of which are also discussed at length by Ishii) in making an accurate count of the sources of the MS because the same cases often appear in several Sung works and it is sometimes difficult to determine from which one Dōgen was selecting. Kawamura believes that further research may well turn up additional Sung texts that influenced the formation of the MS. The main point is that while Dōgen was in China he was reading a wide range of Sung texts and was as fully immersed in the kōan tradition literature as any master of the time.

Although questions remain in need of further investigation, all the main Zen scholars including Yanagida now concede the authenticity of the MS. Furthermore, it can well be argued that an analysis of the relation between Dōgen and the kōan tradition does not depend on a verification of the status of the MS. Rather, the argument is based primarily on the role of kōans in the KS, which cites 319 cases (at least 64 are also cited in the MS), and in the EK-9, which cites 298 cases (92 are cited in the MS).[78] The main debate among scholars at this point is not about the authenticity of the MS text but about its purpose and function in connection to the KS. Much of the debate revolves around the role of the preface (jobun), which is not included in the Kanazawa text's middle section but does appear in the Muromachi manuscripts as well as in the NS text. The brief preface evokes the legacy and lineage of patriarchal transmission from Śākyamuni through Bodhidharma and beyond, and it concludes by asserting that "the three hundred cases represent the fundamental insight originally transmitted from patriarch to patriarch. Now the pure expression of the ancient masters is our own." If the preface is authentic, as Kawamura believes, this supports Dōgen's own sense of the importance and value of the MS for his collected writings. But if it was added on by later editors, as Ishii suggests, then Dōgen's attitude toward the MS remains unclear.

Kawamura maintains that the composition of the KS grew out of the MS both historically and conceptually, and therefore it must have been intimately connected with the Sung Zen chronicles and dialogues on which the MS, as a collection of kōans modeled to some extent after the HR, was based.[79] Kawamura's thesis about the connection between the MS and the KS assumes that Dōgen was involved in kōan studies during his stay in China and that he tried to develop a new approach to Zen transmission in composing the Japanese KS in relation to kōans extracted from Sung chronicles. According to Kawamura, after his return to Japan from China Dōgen began compiling the MS as a listing of his favorite cases, and while in the midst of this project he started to create the KS in Japanese as its commentary. Ishii points out that the *kana* notations in the margins of the Kanazawa text suggest that there was a two stage process of transition in Dōgen's writing style. First, Dōgen collected paradigmatic cases in Chinese using the vernacular syllabary for his disciples who could not read the original. But Dōgen's thinking and writing continued to evolve until the new work—the KS in *kana* (Chinese *kanji* combined with Japanese syllabary) rather than in *kanbun* (only Chinese characters)—eventually overshadowed and replaced the MS as the main expression of his religious convictions, reflecting his new vision. This reversal in the roles of the two works, with the KS ascending in priority and the MS becoming its "foot-note" rather than vice versa, marked the most critical turning point in Dōgen's career leading to his creative peak that has caused many modern Japanese thinkers to label him the greatest philosopher in the history of their country. Thus Kawamura and Ishii see the MS as preparatory (*jun-biteki*) yet containing the same essential truth that is expressed in a somewhat fuller and more genuinely expressive way in the KS. Mizuno Kōgen looks on the MS as personal notes or memos Dōgen kept for himself while in the course of beginning to prepare the KS, and Yanagida stresses the role of the MS as a textbook used for the training of Sōtō acolytes who were not yet ready to study the KS.[80] These three interpretations are not inconsistent in that they all stress the function of the MS as secondary to and supportive of the KS. An interesting issue for further research is to determine how significant the textbook function was for the sect in the post-Dōgen, early to late medieval era, when Sōtō practice seemed to rely on other kinds of kōan collections.

Intra/Intertextuality: Implications for Categorizing Zen Kōan Texts

The independent but very much interrelated studies by Kawamura and Ishii for the first time have examined in great detail the historical formation and philosophical implications of Dōgen's MS collection in connection both to the more prominent interpretive essays in the KS and to the Zen chronicles and recorded sayings on which both *Shōbōgenzō* texts rely for their source material. One of the main contributions of Kawamura's study is to provide a list cross-referencing the three hundred cases cited by Dōgen in the MS with their sources from Sung texts as well as the fascicles of the KS in which they are interpreted. The list also includes cases cited in the

EK-9. Prior to the works of Kawamura and Ishii that appeared in the mid-to late-1980s, Kagamishima Genryū's 1965 book, Dōgen Zenji to In'yō Kyōten-Goroku no Kenkyū (Studies in Zen Master Dōgen's Citations of Sūtras and Recorded Sayings), was the first main work analyzing the way Dōgen's writings, especially the KS, reflect his knowledge and interest in the material from the Zen recorded sayings texts also used as sources for the major Sung kōan collections, especially the HR and MMK.

Kagamishima's study makes two important contributions. In the main text it reconstructs the hermeneutic principles Dōgen uses in his creative rereading and rewriting of traditional Zen sources. Kagamishima analyzes several examples illustrating how Dōgen transforms Zen expressions that seem to imply an attainment of enlightenment in the future into an emphasis on full realization in the holistic present moment, or turns sayings that unwittingly convey a subtle distinction of absolute and relative into an evocation of nondualistic unity. For example, in KS "Tajintsū" Dōgen reinterprets and remythologizes the notion of supernormal powers (tajintsū, lit. "penetrating or reading other's minds"), gained as a by-product of meditation, as an evocation of the fundamental inseparability of beings and Buddha-nature.[81] In the second part of the book Kagamishima provides a comprehensive list of all of the Chinese masters whose sayings and poems Dōgen cites and comments on in his collected writings along with the original source and location of each of these citations. Kagamishima's early book focused on the influence that Zen goroku and Mahayana sūtras (kyōten) exerted on Dōgen, but he did not deal with Zen dentōroku chronicle texts. However, in response to the studies on the MS by Kawamura and Ishii, Kagamishima published a short but intensive reflection on the implications of Dōgen's kōan collection for understanding his citation of Sung Zen sources by stressing the importance of the chronicles rather than the sūtras. The title of the essay indicates Kagamishima's change of direction: "Dōgen Zenji no In'yō Tōshi-Goroku nitsuite: Mana Shōbōgenzō o Shiten toshite" ("Zen Master Dōgen's Citations of Transmission of the Lamp Histories and Recorded Sayings: Perspectives on the Mana Shōbō-genzō").

Appearing shortly after Kawamura's work on Dōgen's kōan collection, Ishii's 1988 book, Chūgoku Zenshūshi Wa: Mana Shōbōgenzō ni Manabu (Discussions on the History of Chinese Zen: Studying the 'Chinese' Shōbōgenzō), was conceived as a follow-up to his major study, Sōdai Zenshūshi no Kenkyū (Studies in the History of Sung Era Zen), which examines the role of the KD written in 1004 in establishing the historical framework of Zen lineage and transmission. Ishii's work on the Chinese *Shōbōgenzō* includes his own listing of the sources for Dōgen's citation of cases, emphasizing the influential role of the ST *dentōroku* text. It also discusses Dōgen's interpretations in the KS of themes from paradigmatic cases, most of which are also included in the MS and the EK-9, in comparison with alternative Zen perspectives. Ishii thus complements Kawamura's historical account of the formation of the MS in relation to the KS by giving a more philosophical treatment of several dozen cases in connection to the full range of ideological issues involved in Sung Zen theory and practice. For example, Ishii discusses the multiple textual and hermeneutic concerns in examining Dōgen's handling of the famous kōan in which Chao-chou answer's "*Mu*" (literally "no" but also conveying "nonbeing" or "nothingness") in response to the disciple's query, "Does a dog have Buddha-nature?" This case is included as no. 114 of the MS (14th case of the middle section). It was apparently taken by Dōgen directly from Hung-chih's collection (no. 18), and it also appears as the first case in the MMK. Since the dialogue is attributed to Chao-chou, one of the most aggressively irreverent T'ang masters, it is important to get a sense of his overall religious outlook as expressed in his many other notable anecdotes and conversations. But doing this drives home the point that the teachings of Chao-chou, like those of most other T'ang masters, are known primarily through his recorded sayings and the transmission of the lamp histories which were compiled during the Sung era. Referencing the sources for a particular kōan as well as the variations involved in a particular kōan interpretation takes part in a kaleidoscopic process involving fluid textual boundaries and ideological paradigms. Thus, prior to examining Dōgen's interpretation of a kōan case, it is necessary to consider different versions of the dialogue in the various Sung chronicles as well as the commentaries on Chao-chou by Hung-chih, Ju-ching, Ta-hui and others. Then, it is important to take into account that Dōgen's writings include several references to the dialogue: it plays a crucial role in his highly original discussion of no-Buddha-nature (*mu-busshō*) in KS "Busshō," and it is also cited in a EK-9 poem and in "Gakudōyōjinshū."

The lists provided in these Japanese studies, particularly in the works of Kawamura and Ishii which are translated in Appendix II, catalogue and cross-reference the connections between Dōgen's writings and T'ang and Sung masters and texts, and they disclose the sense of mutual influences and often unrecognized borrowing involving the various genres of Zen literature, including transmission of the lamp histories, recorded sayings of the masters, and kōan collections in relation to Dōgen's KS, MS, EK-9, and SZ texts. All of these texts are working within the same matrix of signs and signifiers. The KS is not an autonomous and self-contained work of an independent, intentional subjectivity but "an intertextual construct, comprehensible only in terms of other texts which it prolongs, completes, transforms, or sublimates." Julia Kristeva argues that "every text takes shape as a mosaic of citations, every text is the absorption and transformation of other texts." Furthermore, intertextuality suggests "a text's dependence on and infiltration by prior codes, concepts, conventions, unconscious practices, and texts . . . [that function] as an abysmal ground."[82] This is not a matter of the way a texts makes allusions to former works in the conventional sense, which presupposes the separateness and unity of the works in question, but the profound thematic and stylistic intertwining of various genres in a tradition. The intertextual connections between Dōgen and the kōan collections are sufficiently strong to suggest that the rhetoric of polarization is limited to a particular level of discourse which, if taken out of context, gives a misleading picture of the overall development of the tradition. Far from being anti-kōan the *Shōbōgenzō* consists of novel interpretations, sometimes in several different versions, of dozens of kōans. Thus the impact of the lists in Kawamura and Ishii is to show that it is necessary to interpret Dōgen not in terms of his opposition to the kōans, even though that appears to occupy one level of discourse in his writings—the one primarily motivated by partisan concern—but the interaction between the multiple texts and doctrines formulated during the Sung and Kamakura periods.

Highlighting the inseparability of intra- and inter-textuality indicates that Dōgen's writings are not isolated from or antagonistic toward, but stand textually and ideologically very much integrated with the kōan tradition in several respects. Yet, while Dōgen is not necessarily pro-kōan, the philosophical essays comprising the KS *Shōbōgenzō*, nearly every one of which contemplatively free associates through glossing several sayings of the partriarchs, can be understood as a "kōan-text" with a different literary structure than the major kōan collections (including Chinese Sōtō ones) reflecting a divergent vision of the symbolic function of the kōan in connection to language, meditation, and religious fulfillment. Dōgen's kōan collection, the MS, cannot be compared to the classic collections because it is just a listing of cases without commentary. But even though the KS itself has a different structure than the kōan collections of the period, it is intratextually related to two Dōgen works that are constituted in the more standard kōan text fashion, the MS and the EK-9, in addition to the IH. As Isshū Miura and Ruth Fuller Sasaki suggest, the KS "is now considered to be a collection of Dōgen's explanatory discourses on the kōans of his original collection. . . ."[83] It would also seem that the term 'Shōbōgenzō' was used by Dōgen with the meaning of 'kōan collection.'" The KS can be interpreted as part of the mainstream of the kōan tradition and of Sung Zen literature, as well as of Japanese religiosity.

This emphasis on Dōgen's contribution to the intertextual main-stream of the tradition, however, does not diminish but rather highlights the unique creative impulses of the KS, the seeds of which are already evident in the MS. For example, Dōgen's interpretation of the Ma-tsu "polishing the tile" kōan in several KS fascicles argues that Ma-tsu was enlightened not after, as in the traditional account, but before the conver-sation with his master actually began.[84] Even without commentary, the MS reports the case in just this way, indicating that Dōgen was already involved in making creative emendations of the source material at this early stage in his career. Furthermore, while the KS draws material from the dialogues contained in many of the texts in all three Sung genres, it is clear that (when compared with the way that other texts utilize many of the same source dialogues) the HR and the KS often make the most similar, yet still distinct, stylistic and thematic choices in handling common material. Peter Gregory comments that Suzuki's one-sided Rinzai portrayal of the kōan tradition "represents only one of the possibilities that could have developed out of the various alternatives that were available in eighth- and ninth-century China."[85] Intertextuality makes us aware of the multiple possibili-ties, or branches, deriving from the tradition's roots. The MS, when seen in connection to the KS and the IH, becomes "a window," though some-what darkened, opening up a view from the standpoint of Dōgen's approach into Sung Zen, thereby relativizing each of the various Chinese genres. Since Dōgen began his writing by mimicking the HR, the fact that he did not continue this way and that the KS does not make the same choices as the kōan collections, but rather forges a new direction based on common roots, brings into fresh perspective the possibilities for utilizing and inter-preting the source dialogues.

There are at least five main options within the tradition: (1) an emphasis on the creator of the dialogues, or an author-centered approach as in the dentōroku chronicles stressing narrative emplotment; (2) an emphasis on the individual interpreter of the dialogues, or a master-cen-tered approach as in the goroku records stressing personal selection and instruction of cases; (3) an emphasis on distilling the dialogues and anecdotes, or a case-centered approach as in the kōan collections stressing intensive philosophical commentary; (4) an emphasis on decocting the distillation even further, or a *watō*-centered approach as in the DR stressing the shortcut method; and (5) an emphasis on doctrinal hermeneutics, or a topic-centered approach as in the KS, which is not so much about or on but rather creates commentary that strives to be like or to actually become a new form of kōan. In addition, there are a number of variations by modern scholars, such as cross-referencing patriarch and text,[86] or kōan and text as in the SSK. A critical comparison of the tropological structure of each of these paradigms will be explored more fully in the following chapter.

FOUR

Narratology and Tropology

Skin, Flesh, Bones, Marrow/
Marrow, Bones, Flesh, Skin

On Resolving the Aporetics of Kōan Studies

Part I examined three main aporetics in studies of Dōgen's relation to the kōan tradition: the paradoxical relation between the voluminous, sophisticated textuality of Zen writings on history and philosophy and the defiantly untextual orality of the source dialogues; the seemingly disturbing contradiction between the mythological, hagiographical style of Zen pseudohistorical documents and the aggresively demythological message of the lives and teachings of the masters portrayed therein; and the tension in works of Dōgen and in sectarian commentaries between a sometimes strong critique and at the same time a generous use of paradigmatic cases. The arising of the conventional bifurcated view of Dōgen and kōans was also discussed in terms of the interlocking problematics of traditional polarization and polemicized rhetoric, as well as in connection to deficiencies in modern teleological approaches to history. The previous chapter was primarily concerned with overcoming the conventional view in relation to the third aporetic by reevaluating the network of relations between Dōgen and the Sung masters he criticized and admired, and by demonstrating the intertextual connections between the KS and various Sung genres. Chapter 3 showed that the MS is not only a bridge linking Dōgen to kōan texts, but a window offering insight into the tremendous diversity in terms of how Sung texts handle source dialogues. This chapter deals with the first two aporetics by using a genre criticism based on the arborescent metaphor to show that apparent inconsistencies—between textuality and untextuality, and mythology and demythology—are part of a seamless narrative reflecting the way the roots of the tradition lead to multiple branches in thematic and stylistic approaches to presenting and interpreting the dialogues. The chapter depicts the fundamental flexibility and open-endedness of the roots or the Ur-genre, the source dialogues, that are based on a decentric use of tropical discourse, as well as the ways the branches, or the various Sung genres, capture and/or deliberately displace these roots within their literary structures.

First, the chapter explains why genre criticism is useful in clarifying the formation of Dōgen's KS text in relation to the variety of Sung styles and intentions in handling the source dialogues. It demonstrates how the KS arose in the midst of a veritable explosion of Zen texts in the eleventh through thirteenth centuries, including numerous examples of the three genres of the *dentōroku* (transmission of the lamp histories), *goroku* (recorded sayings), and kōan collections. Genre criticism further breaks down the multifarious uses of the dialogues into two main categories: the mythological *tōshi-roku*, or narrative chronicles which legitimate lineages within the sect, and the demythological *kōan-roku*, or philosophical commentaries on kōan cases. In this context, the KS can perhaps best be interpreted by grouping it in the *kōan-roku* category of kōan collections and kōan commentaries that use the source dialogues for a common purpose. The continuity linking the *kōan-roku* works is their shared focus on creating philosophical commentary on specific dialogues as tools for instruction, rather than on using the dialogues to create a narrative history as in the chronicles. This compatability occurs despite significant points of discontinuity or differences in the texts' conclusions about the use of kōans in relation to other forms of religious practice, such as zazen or scriptural studies.

However, this categorization, which groups texts together from the general perspective of surveying the full range of possibilities of the tradition's discourse, is not intended to obfuscate the distinctive style of each of the *kōan-roku* texts. It highlights the multifaceted and complex rather than monolithic nature of the category, and thus allows for an analysis of the unique features of the KS by determining where it stands in relation to the texts to which, relatively speaking, it bears the greatest affinities. A genre approach opens up a critical comparison of the interpretive method and philosophy of language of the KS in comparison with several of the *kōan-roku* texts it closely resembles in offering interlinear commentary on paradigmatic cases, including the HR and the MMK in addition to the records of Hung-chih, Ju-ching, Ta-hui, Yüan-wu, and others. There are three main interpretive models within the *kōan-roku* category: Ta-hui's one-word or one-phrase shortcut *watō* method, the HR's "wraparound" interlinear commentary, and Dōgen's scenic-route hermeneutic approach. The differences between these approaches revolve around the role of abbreviation and brevity in relation to commentary and textuality. To some extent all three approaches emphasize a kind of abbreviation. The HR, which both zeroes in on key terms and expands its commentary, and the *watō* method, which absolutizes abbreviation and negates exegesis, are not necessarily in accord with each other although they were formulated by teacher and disciple respectively. In emphasizing extensive commentary and wordplay, and in using abbreviation only in the sense of glossing particular words and phrases, the KS appears closer to the HR than the HR is to the DR. Yet literary structural and semiotic differences in the arranging of the relation between the citation of *kosoku-kōan* and the placement of the interlinear commentary announce that each of these texts has its own ideological priorities: the HR prioritizes precedent cases, and the KS prioritizes innovative commentary. At the same time, the KS and DR are somewhat similar in warning against the reification of kōan cases in collections such as the HR. However, the KS's stress on the polysemy and efficacy of language beyond abbreviation stands apart from the iconoclastic implications based on the priority of silence in both of the other two approaches.

Understanding the KS as a *kōan-roku* text that contributes to the transition from T'ang *satori* dialogues to Sung kōan collections helps redraw the lines of continuity and discontinuity in the tradition as a whole. Therefore, a key element of genre criticism involves rethinking the conventional view of the kōan tradition by retracing the steps in the establishment of the T'ang sources and their transformation to Sung paradigmatic cases. The development of the tradition has conventionally been portrayed in teleological fashion. According to the conventional view, what came to be referred to as "public cases" originated in Ma-tsu's sparse, dialogical form of communication that was based on a profound use of brevity harboring silence. The dialogues necessarily and inevitably evolved into an ever more terse literary form that resulted in a process of distillation and abbreviation culminating in the *watō* method, which extracts from out of the dialogue key maieutic phrases, such as "the east mountain walks on water" and "three bundles of flax," which in some cases contain just a single word or single syllable, such as Chao-chou's Mu. The dialogues are seen not for their rhetorical value but exclusively as psycholinguistic trigger mechanisms that deliberately create a powerful doubtblock or the impasse of a psychological double-bind. The following characterization by John Wu seems to reflect the way that the psychological dimension of the watō approach has at times been read back into accounts of the original function of kōans: "For, once you mistake the kung-an for a puzzle to be solved by intellectual acumen, you will be glued to it as a fly to the fly-paper. The great masters of Ch'an have invariably used the kung-an to drive you to the wall, so that in your intense agony you may open your inner eye and see that the hopeless labyrinthine maze you are in is nothing but a nightmare, which disappears as soon as you awake."[1]

The watō-oriented reading of the history of kōans, which presumes that the shortcut method represents the pinnacle of the tradition and then retrospectively interprets the entire history to justify and support this particular view of the function of kōans, tends to exclude Dōgen's approach from any serious consideration. When this attitude is coupled with Dōgen's own frequent critique of kōans, it is little wonder that Dōgen and his method of interpretation are rarely mentioned in the history of the tradition. But if kōan and watō are no longer identified, and if some of the teleological implications in the conventional account are broken through by dealing with the fact that the majority of Zen writings in various genres were created subsequent, and perhaps in response, to the 845 suppression of Buddhism, then the conventional history begins to unravel. The key to challenging the conventional view is to reinterpret the meaning of the source dialogues in terms of their open-ended parallactic rather than paradoxical function. This sets the stage for interpreting Dōgen's hermeneutic approach to traditional cases, such as Chao-chou's Mu and Bodhidharma's "skin, flesh, bones, marrow," as an alternative interpretation that can be considered just as consistent with the aims of the source dialogues as the iconoclastic perspective stressed in other Sung kōan commentaries. It becomes possible to retrace the historical stages so that the dialogues as the basic literary unit are seen as leading not necessarily to the iconoclasm and irony of the watō, but to a variety of genres expressing differing viewpoints, including the continuing hermeneutics and use of metonymy in Dōgen's perspective. Therefore, a genre criticism of Sung texts underscores the deficiencies in the conventional emphasis on paradox and silence as an exclusive interpretation of the meaning of kōans that is supposedly reflected in the teachings of the main kōan collections. The point, however, is not simply to reverse the tide and to proclaim the superiority of Dōgen's approach, but to reflect open-endedly on the tropological significance of diverse interpretations of the dialogues, as well as on alternative implications in the role of abbreviation in *kōan-roku* commentaries.

This chapter is divided into two sections. Each section clarifies one of the two aporetics in kōan studies that have been discussed above in order to explain the thematic and stylistic factors influencing the formation of the KS text. Part A focuses on the multiple styles for treating source dialogues in terms of the relation between mythology and demythology in the Sung genres, and part B examines the tropical basis of the alternative interpretive methods concerning textuality and untextuality within the *kōan-roku* category. The aim of genre criticism is to move back and forth in discussing the roots and the branches of the tradition according to a tropological model, emphasizing the variety of rhetorical structures of significant words and phrases, rather than a teleological model of inevitable, linear progression toward silence.

Section A. "Skin, Flesh, Bones, Marrow"

Rethinking the Conventional View

This section reexamines the sources for and the conception of historical stages in the *watō*-based interpretation of kōans. The conventional, teleological view of the dialogue tradition tends to see the Sung Zen genres as "stepping-stones" leading inevitably to a culmination in the abbreviated shortcut *watō* method. This approach tends to identify a certain view of the ideological continuity in the tradition with an inevitability driven by historical imperative, and it is based on two interlocking conflations. One is the conflation of the original dialogues with the subsequently formulated *watō* method, whereby it is assumed that the abbreviation and silence of the *watō* must have been the intention of the creators of the dialogues all along. The other is the conflation of certain thematic and stylistic affinities between texts dealing with kōans with a pattern of historical evolution, as if history unfolded out of necessity to culminate in the *watō*. The aim of discourse analysis is to avoid a fixed, unarguable conclusion based on polarization, but rather to show the multidimensionality and flexibility of the original Zen sayings and dialogues that led to a variety of styles and methods of interpretation. This involves deconstructing the misguided sense of continuity by showing points of diffusion, rupture, and discontinuity within the tradition in order to reconstruct or reestablish the lines of continuity around the two main categories of mythical, narratological *tōshi-roku* chronicles and demythical, tropological *kōan-roku* collections.

Sources

The key to correcting the conventional view's conflation of certain strains of ideological continuity with historical inevitability is first to dislodge it from and then to rethink the significance of its primary sources. As already indicated, one of the main problems in historical studies of Zen is the lack of reliable, objective sources external to the tradition and the consequent near total dependency on internal, unverifiable sources. As in the case of studies of Dōgen's life and thought, the internal, traditional sources for Zen history in China are especially unreliable as factual history because of their sectarian bias and mythical, hagiographic tendencies. Furthermore, methodological problems are compounded in that the very genres of Zen texts that fail to be accurate from an historiographical standpoint can also not be considered ahistorical in the sense that they ignore and remain oblivious to, or seek to rise above, historical concerns altogether in the name of expressing an eternalist ideal. A difficulty in dealing with Zen texts is their pseudohistorical quality in feigning an objective historical account of patriarchal transmission while presenting primarily a mythical version guided by lineage orthodoxy.

The voluminous *dentōroku* literature is the genre that is the most significant source for the conventional view of Zen history in two senses: it establishes and executes the pseudohistorical theory of transmission, and it serves as the storehouse of dialogical anecdotes that are presented and interpreted in *goroku* and kōan collection texts as demythological kōans. The aporetic concerning the seemingly contradictory juxtaposition of mythical and demythical elements of discourse is located at the discursive juncture at which the original oral spontaneity of the dialogues is camouflaged or displaced, or perhaps misplaced or even manufactured within the literary structure of the chronicles. There are several distinctive features in the *dentōroku* portrayals of masters and lineage. The keystone is the theory of direct, person-to-person patriarchal transmission beginning with the seven primordial buddhas culminating in Śākyamuni, whereby standard mythical buddhological figures are reinterpreted as transmitters of the Zen lamp.[2] The process continues through the twenty-eight Indian patriarchs—the first twenty-seven are standard non-Zen Buddhist teachers—leading up to Bodhidharma, who travels east and becomes the first patriarch in China. The transmission further unfolds with the next five Chinese patriarchs leading up to sixth patriarch Hui-neng, and it goes on to include over a dozen subsequent patriarchs of various lineages; the exact number varies in different versions. In the *dentōroku* texts, patriarchal transmission transpires not through liturgy, scriptural exegesis, or—despite the emphasis on sacred personages—sacerdotal performance. It only occurs through the transference of understanding from one enlightened mind to another enlightened mind, using the term mind (*shin* or *kokoro*) here in the holistic sense of "heart-mind" encompassing intellectual and emotional, and spiritual and sensory dimensions. The transmission is passed on from one generation to the next in that there is only one preeminent master at one time who selects only one disciple who, in turn, as the anointed successor inherits the right to choose his single main follower. The selection process is accompanied by a sense of profound affinity and predetermination that is often dramatized by mythical anecdotes including premonitory dreams and other portents. Key transitional events are often attended by heavenly signs or natural signatures to highlight the "reenactment of archetypal drama between each patriarch and his successor,"[3] which in some cases is symbolized physically in myths by an exchange of skeletons or a physiological transposition from outgoing to incoming master.

The development of the association of patriarchal selection and transmission with a specific lineage and genealogy evolved in a number of T'ang era texts, according to the studies of Yanagida.[4] In the T'ang transmission of the lamp texts the selection process after Hui-neng is often identified with only one orthodox lineage; just as there is one lineage culminating in the sixth patriarch, so there is only one following from him. But the Sung texts, especially the *Sodōshū* and the KD, generally take a multibranched approach that allows several lineages, referred to as dynastic "houses" or "families" (*ke*), to co-exist at the same time so long as each in its own way follows the basic rules of generation-to-generation, mind-to-mind selection and transmission.[5] (An exception to this rule is the Sung era *Tenshō Kōtōroku*, which has a decidedly Rinzai lineage orientation.) Each of the five houses has a different style of instruction and sense of ceremony, but all are intertextually connected and contribute to the overall Zen outlook. Furthermore, there is an underlying level of "interpersonality" concerns in that Lin-chi and Te-shan, for example, despite coming from different lineages (though they may have shared some students), exhibit remarkably similar methods of ruthless "sticks and shouts" teaching.[6] Most Zen masters are known for the qualities of fierce independence and unmitigated integrity that is exemplary for all disciples.

The formulation of the theory of patriarchal transmission in relation to genealogy was influenced by several elements in Buddhist and Chinese religiosity. To a large extent the *dentōroku* accounts of Zen masters' lives and teachings grew out of another voluminous genre of early Chinese Buddhist literature containing monk biographies. But the monk biographies, which cover a host of Buddhist saints, priests, meditation and *vinaya* masters, and other luminaries in addition to the Zen patriarchs, tend to be less mythical and more straightforward in treating biographical materials. For example, "The biographies [of patriarchs appearing] in the [*Den Hōbōki*] are, generally, uncomplicated; their subjects are still shadowy figures, unadorned, for the most part, with the fanciful stories and pseudofactual detail added later to bring both emotional appeal and authenticity to their characters."[7] On the other hand, monk biographies do contain mythical, supernatural elements that filter into *dentōroku* accounts that are perhaps taken over from Taoist tales of immortal saints as well as from legends of the advent of Maitreya (J. Miroku), the future buddha. The theory of transmission was also influenced by several meditative traditions. These include the listing in Indian Buddhism (and in Hinduism) of the lines of teaching traditions, the T'ien-t'ai distinction between transmission through *sūtra* or words and through *shikan* meditation as experientially embodied by an authentic master, and the sense of patriarchy that Kashmiri meditation masters brought to China.

However, the key to the transmission paradigm was the incorporation of a Confucian sense of ancestralization emphasizing the honoring of the past accomplishments of senior family members that was combined with motifs taken over from the pattern of imperial succession. In the eighth century Shen-hui's Southern school ideology subdued the Northern school by developing a Confucianized "pedigree" family tree based on imperial models of selection and succession to power that greatly appealed to both monks and literati. Shen-hui stressed that there can only be one true emperor (and therefore one patriarch) in each generation. Thus, "Shen-hui's success is due on large part to his skillful manipulation of the symbols of ritual politics . . . [or] the literati ideal of the orthodox lineage, or rather the idea of the legitimate imperial clan lineage, to try to convince his audience that his was the legitimate line of succession."[8] By the Sung era, Zen was able to appeal for patronage by following a familial model that mirrored the Confucian extended family social structure and the imperial ideal of genealogical succession, with leaders of each family (*ke*) and its lineage (*shū*) referred to as *sō* (grandfather or patriarch) and the followers referred to as *deshi* (pupils or disciples).

Studies of Zen historical issues, particularly involving individual masters, are complicated by the multiplicity of the sources containing legends, anecdotes, and dialogues in the *dentōroku*, the *goroku*, and to a lesser extent even in the kōan collection texts. As Yanagida Seizan indicates in his biographical study of Lin-chi, the accounts of the patriarch's life are scattered in anecdotes throughout many sources, including the *Sodōshū*, KD, *Sō Kōsōden, Tenshō Kōtōroku, Den Bohōshōjū*, and *Gotō Egen*, in addition to several versions of the *Rinzai Roku*, which appear both independently and as part of larger *goroku* editions. Yanagida notes that

> with the possible exception of the account in the *Sōkōsōden*, which, though a biography in the true sense [it is classified here as part of the monk biography genre], is disappointingly terse, all these accounts are less concerned with the facts of Lin-chi's life than with his sermons and mondos, anecdotes associated with him, the lineage of the Lin-chi School, and the transmission of its teachings and practices. . . . If we could construct a chronology of the Master's life, it must be a tentative chronology only, based for the most part upon traditional material, rather than upon facts that can be substantiated with historical accuracy.[9]

Because of the overlapping and competing versions of the life and teachings of each master and of each house, with some versions more or less embellished in comparison with alternate versions, several options are available to the modern historian: historical reconstruction, skeptical criticism, and symbolic interpretation. Most modern apologists and/or historians do not accept uncritically the mythical treatment in the *dentōroku* accounts, but they have no choice but to reconstruct on the basis of this material. When historians conflate traditional, partisan hagiography with historiographical biography, the result is problematic in two ways: it becomes deficient as an historical study, and it is not necessarily faithful to or able to capture fully the concerns and aims in the mythology of the original texts. Therefore, in exercising the first option historians are forced to confront the necessity of the second or third option. However, according to Yanagida, a skeptical critical view is misdirected if, while working exclusively from within traditional pseudohistorical sources, it tries to dismiss the validity of these materials altogether and fails to evaluate their symbolic or mythical meaning and function.

The second level of significance of the *dentōroku* genre for the conventional view is that these texts are considered to constitute the third of five stages of the kōan tradition. The *dentōroku* texts function as a storehouse and reference work for kōans. An interesting example of the importance of this feature concerns the Bodhidharma "skin, flesh, bones, marrow" dialogue analyzed in the KS "Kattō" fascicle. Ishii traces the historical development from the earliest mention of the anecdote in T'ang texts to the full flourishing of the tale in Sung era *dentōroku* texts, especially the KD.[10] In the first reference in the *Rekidai Hōbōki* (779), the passage only refers to three disciples who express Bodhidharma's marrow, bones, and flesh (the sequence is reversed from later versions), and there is no dialogue, that is, no mention of what it is the disciples say or do not say to be so rewarded. While the second version, in the *Hōrinden*, refers to four disciples, the next three versions recorded in 819, 841, and 952 revert to three disciples, and the famous dialogue involving the four disciples does not appear until the KD version. However, while the KD does play a crucial role as a storehouse in the development of the kōan tradition, the frequently cited number of seventeen hundred kōans, which is actually based on a fanciful counting of the number of masters portrayed in the text, is an imaginative figure that has itself become part of Zen lore. The *dentōroku* genre, therefore, seems to represent a crucial point of transition between the second stage of creating spontaneous dialogues and the fourth and fifth stages of kōan collections and *watō* method, respectively, that both seek to recapture the spontaneity that was somewhat lost during the third stage. In other words, in the conventional view the *dentōroku* genre is at once praised for storing and criticized for losing the spirit of the dialogues. While the *dentōroku* texts are crucial as storehouses, they are also seen as stepping stones, that is, as necessary though ultimately bypassable obstacles on the way to salvaging the essential, abbreviated shortcut approach.

Five Stages

The teleological implications in the conventional view, which is not so much untrue as it is one-sidedly biased, indicates that there are five stages in the history of dialogues and kōans. The first stage refers to the seminal figures, Bodhidharma and Hui-neng. While the writings attributed to the first and sixth patriarchs appear in a more or less straightforwardly discursive form, and are thus *pre-dialogue*, the early leaders are also known for their spontaneous encounters and skill in transforming disciples through wit and wile. Both demonstrate a flair for ingenious wordplay and provocative, paradoxical utterances, with Bodhidharma cited in two kōans in the HR and MMK, including his famous retort to Emperor Wu that good deeds will gain "no merit" and his offering his disciple Hui-k'o "peace of mind," and with Hui-neng cited in three cases in these collections, including his telling his disciples that it is neither the flag nor the wind that is blowing but the "mind." However, the early patriarchs are primarily noted in the Zen tradition for their personalities and their tales of transformation which seem to perfectly complement one another: Bodhidharma, the Indian brahmin, sacrificing a life of power for singleminded pursuit of the Dharma, and Hui-neng, a rural illiterate attaining the position of highest authority in the sect. The dialogues in the HR and MMK are known both as anecdotes contributing to sacred narrative and as *kosoku-kōan*.

The next stage covers the lineages of Ma-tsu and Shih-t'ou, including such towering figures as Lin-chi and Chao-chou in the eighth and ninth centuries, as well as lines stemming from Te-shan and Yün-men. This is the period, particularly in the Hung-chou school, of mind-boggling *spontaneous encounters and the deliberate use of disturbing and even rough tactics* that created what many have referred to as the golden age of Zen. According to their unsystematic, collected sayings, which, with the possible exception of Huang-po, were not recorded until the Sung era or even later, these T'ang masters sought to capture the living word of Buddhism through spontaneous and situational didactics to liberate "someone who has become paralyzed and religiously impotent by his dependence on some pre-determined religious position."[11] Here the generally anecdotal and aphoristic, enigmatic and epigrammatic function of the oral dialogue is in its freshest and most vital subitist state.

The third stage is the eleventh-century appearance of the *dentōroku* style narrative chronicles, biographies, and other *records which gather, collect, and store the dialogues* not so much to create spiritual transformation as to establish genealogy and the style of the five Zen houses. This stage represents a critical turning point in that in storing the dialogues it tends to surround them with an excess of textual structure and material. Thus

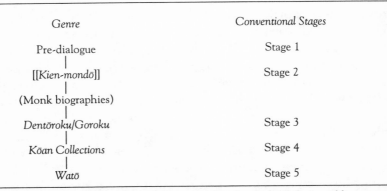

Genre	Conventional Stages
Pre-dialogue	Stage 1
|	
[[Kien-mondō]]	Stage 2
|	
(Monk biographies)	
|	
Dentōroku/Goroku	Stage 3
|	
Kōan Collections	Stage 4
|	
Watō	Stage 5

Figure 4.1. *Five Stages. A flowchart of the conventional, teleological view of five stages of the dialogue tradition culminating in the* watō *method but excluding reference to Dōgen's KS.*

the dialogues created in the second stage are at once lost and found in the third stage. Their essence is to some extent saved in the fourth stage but these texts bear a carryover of too much writing from the previous stage, so that it is only the fifth stage that gets to the heart of the intentions in the second stage. The fourth stage is the twelfth- and thirteenth-century *kōan collections which rediscovered and commented extensively* on the essential role of dialogue. The final stage is the *use of the main phrase technique* in the thirteenth-century and later that highlights the iconoclasm and brevity of the dialogues by eliminating any residual tendency to reify the kōans through the building up of an extensive body of commentaries. Dōgen's texts are generally not mentioned in the conventional history. Or, if the MS is taken into account it may be seen only as an appendage to the fourth stage, while the KS is often interpreted as a text isolated from, if not necessary antithetical to the tradition.

Figure 4.1 provides an all-too-simple flowchart of the five stages in the conventional view. The dialogues are not a genre in and of themselves, for even in the teleological approach the dialogues are seen not as merely coming first in the chronological sense but as an Ur-genre, or the roots at the basis of the next three genres. The continuing connections and influences of the roots on each of these stages should ideally not be depicted in two-dimensional fashion, and this is indicated here by placing the term *kien-mondō* in double brackets. Also, the monk biographies are included in this list in parantheses because of their influence on the *dentōroku* texts.

A Genre-Critical Approach to the Stages

There are several important problems concerning the beginning, the middle, and the concluding stages of the conventional view's account of the development of the kōan tradition. First, recent studies have shown that Zen dialogues were probably first developed by Northern school thinkers prior to the post–Hui-neng Ma-tsu period.[12] It is difficult to determine when or why the dialogue approach first began, but it is undoubtedly not the exclusive property of the Hung-chou school. A more significant problem for understanding the relation between the Sung genres involves the dating of the texts in each genre. The teleological view suggests a line of progression from one genre to the next, and this may at first seem to be substantiated in that the *dentōroku* began to appear in the late tenth and early eleventh centuries and the most prominent kōan collection, the HR, appeared in the twelfth century, over a hundred years later. However, the earliest kōan collections, including the *Setchō Juko Hyakusoku* on which the HR is based, were actually composed around the same time as the *dentōroku* texts in the eleventh century, and both genres continued to be written and to coexist for several centuries thereafter. Furthermore, and this point is crucial, the *goroku* texts were also being written at the same time as both *dentōroku* texts and the kōan collections, often by the same Zen thinkers. The *goroku* genre is quite complex and cannot be neatly identified with or collapsed into one of the other genres, and when this is taken into account the teleological view is further undermined. For example, the *dentōroku* texts have a formal, almost baroque quality, whereas the *goroku* texts are written in a colloquial, rustic language. Some of the *goroku* texts, especially those dealing with T'ang masters, emphasize lineage (*shike*-style) in a way that appears closer to the *dentōroku* genre. But *goroku* texts dealing with Sung masters stress individual instruction (*kojin*-style) in a way that resembles the kōan collections. The lists in table 4.1 demonstrate the simultaneous composition of the range of Sung texts.[13] A third problem with the conventional view is the presumption that the tradition has—and had to have—culminated in one and only one conclusion—the *watō*—to the exclusion of other alternatives, including the KS. This exclusivity could well be seen as a "a drastic narrowing in the scope of the tradition"[14] that was once rich in multiple possibilities.

In light of the questions raised about the conventional view by the dating of the Sung texts and the complexity of the *goroku* genre, it is necessary to reconsider the connection between the roots and branches of

Table 4.1 Dating of Main Zen Texts in Four Genres

Monk Biographies	Transmission of the Lamp Histories	Recorded Sayings	Kōan Collections
Kōsōden, 519	Den Hōbōki, early 8th c.	Huang-po (Ōbaku) Denshin Hōyō, 858	Fen-yang (Fun'yō) Roku, by 1024 (1101?)
Zoku Kōsōden, 645–667	Rekidai Hōbōki, 779	Shike Goroku, late 900s?	
Sō Kōsōden, 988	Hōrinden, 801	Lin-chi (Rinzai) Roku, 1046	Hsüeh-tou (Setchō) Juko Hyaku-soku, 1026
	Sodōshū, 952	Yün-men (Unmon) Goroku, 1076	Hekiganroku, 1128
	Keitoku Dentōroku, 1004	Yang-chi (Yōgi) Goroku, 1088	Ta-hui (Daie) Shōbōgenzō, 1147
	Tenshō Kōtōroku, 1036	Kosonshuku Goroku, 1100s	Hung-chih (Wanshi) Juko and Nenko Hyakusoku, 1166
	Kenchū Seikoku Zokutōroku, 1101	Yüan-wu (Engo) Goroku, 1136	
	Shūmon Tōyōshū, 1133	Chao-chou (Jōshū) Roku, 1144	Shōyōroku, 1224
	Shūmon Rentōeyō, 1183	Ta-hui (Daie) Roku, 1172	Mumonkan, 1228
	Katai Futōroku, 1201	Hung-chih (Wanshi) Kōroku, 1201	MS Shōbōgenzō, 1235
	Gotō Egen, 1253	Ju-ching (Nyojō) Goroku, 1238	KS Shōbōgenzō, 1231–53
	Zoku Dentōroku, 1372		

Note: A partial listing of the titles and dates of composition of many of the main Zen texts in each of the main genres. The aim of this chart is to highlight the Sung era composition of the main texts of the kōan tradition. However, some of the dates are undetermined, approximate, contested (for example, the Chao-chou record may have appeared two centuries earlier). In some cases, the dating represents a time gap in that the earliest appearance of a text now available is probably much later than the original composition, unless the original date is a fabrication.

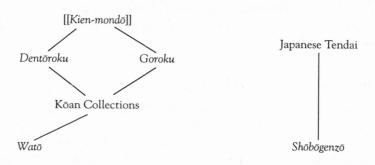

Figure 4.2. *Modified View. A modification of the conventional view with the* dentōroku *and* goroku *recognized as coterminous developments, and the KS* Shōbōgenzō *representing a separate stream primarily influenced by Japanese Tendai thought, yet somehow contained within the context of the dialogue-kōan tradition.*

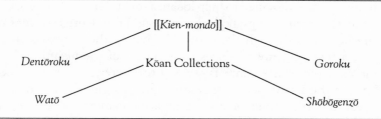

Figure 4.3. *Beyond the Conventional View. Attempting to go beyond the teleological view, with the* dentōroku, goroku, *and* kōan-roku *all seen as coterminous, and the KS recognized as part of, though in some ways still distinct from, the kōan collection genre; the* watō *seen as another variation or offshoot of the kōans rather than as their necessary fulfillment.*

the kōan tradition. Figures 4.2 and 4.3 show alternative ways of systematizing the development of the tradition in order to clarify the relation between Sung genres and to relativize the importance of the *watō* method by integrating Dōgen's KS into the historical process. The first figure highlights the simultaneous composition of the *dentōroku* and *goroku* texts, and begins to suggest that both the *watō* and the KS models of interpretation are possible outcomes of the kōan collection genre. However, there are two limitations in Figure 4.2: it still separates kōan collections from the *dentōroku* and *goroku* genres, and it also views the KS as a separate stream.

Figure 4.3 tries to go beyond the conventional view more fully by putting the three genres on an equal footing and situating the KS in the mainstream of the kōan tradition.

On the Formation of Zen Genres

The next step in formulating a genre critical approach to the development of the roots and branches of the tradition is to discuss a theory for reconstructing lines of continuity by analyzing the literary affinities and divergences among the genres. The goal of genre criticism is not to generate a cluster of unrelated or even antithetical texts out of methodological convenience or in a way that blurs meaningful distinctions. Nor does it seek to highlight rhetorical similarities based on a superficial sense of style. Rather, genre criticism maintains that the form of the text itself has a significant discursive quality that signals reader and critic alike about where the text stands on key issues. As David Tracy argues, "genres are not merely taxonomic devices designed to help locate a text ('This is a novel'). Genres are productive of meanings: both the sense and the figured referent of the text are produced through the genre."[15] That is, the very existence and status of a textual genre produces many levels of the meaning that any specific example of the genre is seeking to reference. For instance, the hallmark of the kōan collection genre is the placing of the paradigmatic case near the beginning of a chapter accompanied by a wraparound commentary, or prose and poetic comments prefacing and following the case. One of the reasons that the KS appears disparate from the other kōan-roku texts is that it highlights a topic in Buddhist thought and practice so that cases are used as part of, rather than as the source that is separated from commentary. But in evoking kōan cases in its commentary on the topic, the KS does seem to value kōans as a source and authority of truth in a way that is closely linked to the kōan-roku texts, which similarly justify an interpretation of one case by one master by citing a similar case of a different master.

Thus, genres are not taxonomic but discursive classifications which, according to Tzvetan Todorov, generate "horizons of expectation" for the audience seeking to appreciate them and "models of writing" for authors who try to contribute and to further their cause. That is, genres at once mirror the needs and influence the aspirations of the community engaged in discourse, which seeks the institutionalization and codification of its own norms and rules of form and meaning. Todorov writes that "a society chooses and codifies the acts that correspond most closely to its ideology; that is why the existence of certain genres in one society, their absence in another, are revelatory of that ideology and allow us to establish it more or less confidently."[16] The arising of a genre does not represent an abstract, theoretical decision by an author, or group of authors, to set up a new form of writing. Rather, genres are historical constructs that evolve due to a combination of conditioning factors that are both textual and extratextual, and they articulate an obligatory form to which author and audience subscribe in a way that delimits the possibilities for a tradition's discourse. The existence of a genre marks the recognition and acceptance by a community of its own literary needs that have been carried out in a particular time and place.

However, genres are by no means fixed and closed systems. Rather, they are open-ended and fluid constellations of intertextual writings that are continuously developing, breaking down, and giving rise to new genres. Thus, the notion of genre criticism extends the category of intertextuality to encompass the coming into and going out of existence of the interrelationship between texts, or of shifting alliances between texts or between thematic or stylistic sectors of texts. When one genre representing hegemonic attitudes and ideals, images and syntax, starts to devolve, a new genre is likely to emerge constituting a shift in the nature of discourse, or a textual paradigm-shift that leaves some elements of the former genre in tact but also alters and revises others as a matter of the reinterpretation and transformation of previous works. Generally speaking, genres come forth out of other genres due to a need to express some new level of a tradition's self-understanding. This takes place as "a genre evolve[s] into a new genre through a process of inversion, displacement, or combination of elements according to new rules. Likewise a new discourse does not emerge as a whole from out of nowhere but reinterprets, transforms, or overturns the rules of previous discourse."[17] Once a genre has addressed a new need and has gained acceptance, it comes to exist in varying degrees of connection to the eclipsed genre, ranging from an intense dependency and even parasitic relationship to a fiercely independent status marking a radical break from the earlier kinds of texts. In the birth-death evolutionary process, there is naturally an attrition rate engulfing many of the newly formed as well as the older genres, as the striving for dominance can only be determined with events taking their course over time. One strategy for the success of a new genre is to disguise itself, either knowingly or unwittingly, in some of the forms of the older genre in order to share some of its lustre.

Genres and Religious Truth

In the history of religious traditions, genres are intimately related to spiritual visions and sources of truth, so that the emergence of a new genre is likely to be coterminous with the arising of a novel vision of what constitutes truth. As new genres come to the fore, they tend to preserve many of the levels of reasoning and the stages of commentatorial history from older texts. But in bringing to the forefront a particular form—whether it is allegorical or legalistic, syncretistic or simplistic—there lies an implicit decision concerning the nature of the spiritual state. Most religions establish a hierarchy of genres based on their power to convey the deepest and most genuine meanings of the sacred. Scriptures, which may be considered to constitute expressions of divine intervention or the words of a venerated holy man or founder of the tradition, have the greatest prestige and authority and thus set the standard of authenticity by which other genres are judged. Usually, a new genre emerges in a religion not in direct competition with scripture itself, which is beyond reproach or the need for justification, but as a vehicle for commentary that rivals other interpretations of the scripture's true meaning and significance. Often, the earliest genres that develop in a tradition after the establishment of scripture, even though it may take them many years to evolve fully, take on a special status based on their proximity to the founding vision, and they thereby become fixed as canonical. More recent genres sometimes have a difficult time gaining acceptance or legitimacy, although their originality or uniqueness may help serve as the basis for the formation of a new sect or movement within the tradition.

Thus, most religions have two main genres in coexistence: one is the ultimate authority of scripture, and the other is the main arbiter of its meaning in an entrenched commentatorial genre, including for example "text and midrash [or Torah and Talmud], sutra and shastra, classic and commentary, Qur'an and Sunna."[18] Scriptures have a timeless quality, but commentaries change over the course of time, although some of them may become canonized and thereby immortalized. To stay open to the need for new developments and change, many religions also encompass alternative or antistructural, esoteric traditions that set up their own genres that stand in a dual relationship to the mainstream structure, at once inverting and even flouting while emulating and incorporating the forms and ideals of the dominant texts. When an antistructural movement has a gnoseological orientation, such as Kabbalah, Sufism, Gnosticism, and Neo-Platonism, it develops genres that stress the value of a contemplative, interior vision rather than the priority of an external source of truth such as revelation, and it often features poetry and other forms of indirect communication. It frequently happens that there is a mutually beneficial give-and-take rather than exclusivity between structure and antistructure so that, for example, Talmud contains a level of "secret" meaning and Kabbalah uses midrashic discourse resembling Talmudic commentary on Torah. Each religion develops its own criteria and methods for either embracing the antistructure as a branching or spinning off from the mainstream or rejecting it as heretical and unworthy of regard. For its part, the antistructure, though it seeks to diffuse and disrupt the mainstream, also often tries to borrow some of the authority and power of the dominant genres.

In Asian religions as a whole, and in Buddhism in particular, the gnoseological tradition is often very closely linked to the mainstream, which seeks justification for its vision of truth in terms of meditative techniques without recourse to divine intervention and with a profound distrust of words for referring to absolute reality. For example, the *Upanishads* ("neti, neti"), Pali *Nikāyas* ("silence on unedifying questions"), and the texts of philosophical Taoism ("he who speaks does not know") are humanly-created instructional guides to spiritual attainment through contemplation. In these cases, the text itself, rather than taking on the role of arbiter of authority, becomes somewhat secondary to an inner truth, and therefore untextuality or the de-canonizing, self-deconstructing nature of the text is an important factor in evaluating the role of scripture. Nevertheless, even in the gnoseological, contemplative traditions, there may be a tension concerning the most appropriate means of providing an explanation of transcendental truth, that is, a debate between rational and antirational, textual and antitextual, exoteric and esoteric, and communal and individualistic modes of discourse. Although inner truth may be beyond rationality, there is also a need to explicate and transmit it in a way that has its own logic, even if it is indirectly expressed.

Antistructure and Zen Categories

Furthermore, in the history of Buddhist texts, particularly Mahayana, there is an increasing tendency to deify the Buddha through buddhological speculation, and a concomitant rise in claims for supernatural powers of revelation and salvation attributed to buddhas. The advent of Zen to a large extent functions as an antistructural, antitextual movement protesting against, inverting, and overthrowing many of these trends in the larger tradition. But the transition from T'ang to Sung Zen also demonstrates what happens when what began as a fundamentally antistructural inversion of the mainstream finds itself turning into an establishment structure. Or perhaps it reflects the new establishment inventing antistructural origins to conceal or camouflage its real status. The Zen dialogues, which are said to originally epitomize an antitextual attitude and style with an emphasis on orality and spontaneity, become reified in a catechistic framework and then placed at the forefront of the *kōan-roku* texts. The tension that remains in the growing cult with its ever expanding sets of intertextually connected genres explains in part the aporetics of Sung Zen, which creates *tōshi-roku* chronicles that are designed to legitimate and justify the existence of the movement through myth and hagiography and at the same time creates *kōan-roku* texts that seek to retain the irreverent, iconoclastic standpoint on which the arising of the cult depends. The aporetics of textuality and untextuality is located at this discursive juncture, and the question the KS confronts— a key question also confronted by the HR and DR *kōan-roku* texts—is, What is the best strategy for preserving the appropriate balance?

Zen texts evolve out and play off of, and yet also often attempt to undermine or subvert, many of the earlier Buddhist genres, which are similarly concerned with methods of teaching and transmitting the Dharma. As Judith Berling has shown, the early genres that seem to have had the greatest impact on Zen include Pali *sūttas*, or records of the words and deeds of the Buddha, and *jātakas*, or birth tales of the Buddha usually expressing the moral implications of karmic retribution. In both genres there is a strong element of supernaturalism, perhaps borrowed in part from popular, hagiocentric religious movements, in depicting the ways that buddhas and bodhisattvas preach, convert, and transform the world. Many of the Mahayana *sūtras* and monk biographical writings continue to expand upon and enhance the supernatural, otherworldly atmosphere of Dharma instruction by evoking celestial realms, magical effects, the saving power of myriad bodhisattvas, and personal transformations and transmutations of messianic deities through different lifetimes or into other kinds of living beings. In some interpretations, especially of the *Lotus Sūtra*, the text itself is also considered to have efficacious power when recited, chanted, or copied.

According to Berling, the antistructural tide leading up to Zen moves away from the supernaturalism, folk elements, and liturgical practices of

early and Mahayana Buddhist genres toward an emphasis on the internali-
zation, personalization, and concretization of subitaneous enlightenment
expressed through logic-defying verbal and nonverbal utterances. The
inversion of the dominant genres begins with the *Prajñāpāramitā Sūtras'*
antilogical, paradoxical discourse based on the refutation of all metaphysical assertions from the epistemologically nonconceptualizable and onto-
logically nonsubstantive standpoint of emptiness (*śūnyatā*). It continues
with the *Vimalakīrti Sūtra's* emphasis on the wisdom of a layman, which
"undercuts the distinctions between buddhas, bodhisattvas, and laymen,
even those of gender, arguing that all such distinctions are illusions that
obscure true understanding." However, the *Prajñāpāramitā* texts retain a
straightforward, didactic format, while the character of Vimalakīrti takes
on an otherworldly aspect in emulating the Buddha's capacity for "ex-
pounding Dharma, quelling doubts, correcting errors, using supernatural
powers, converting or significantly advancing the understanding of the
audience."[19] The *Platform Sūtra* combines elements from both of these
works, especially paradoxical, iconoclastic expressions with an emphasis
on the role of a humble, uneducated, nonelitist teacher. In the *Platform
Sūtra*, a contemporaneous patriarch replaces the supernatural view of
buddha, and there are no celestial realms or bodhisattvas. Furthermore, the
trikāya (three bodies of buddha) system of buddhology is radically reversed
so that the historical body (*nirmāṇakāya*), or actual embodiment of buddha,
is viewed as the most, rather than the least, significant level of realization
in the sense that all three levels are considered to be internalized and
incorporated into a seeing into [one's own-] nature (*kenshō*).[20] On the other
hand, the *Platform Sūtra's* dramatic tale of Hui-neng's advency is couched
in a new mythicization of generation-to-generation patriarchal transmission that offers an account that appears to be altogether lacking in historicity. Furthermore, the inversion from supernaturalism to naturalism itself
takes on supernatural proportions, so that there are descriptions in somewhat mythical, hagiographic terms of just how down to earth and human
is the personality of Hui-neng.

The early Zen writings, such as the *Platform Sūtra* as well as accounts
of the life and teaching of Bodhidharma and other patriarchs, appear to be
reacting to and yet they also still somewhat reflect the models of the older
Mahayana genres. The breakthrough to a distinctively Zen discourse based
on a new religious vision is initiated with the *satori* dialogues attributed to
Ma-tsu that represent a dynamic process of change in literary structure
influenced in part by Taoist, Confucian, and folk styles of dialogical

discourse. The dialogues take the antistructural, antilogical, and antitextual attitudes of earlier works to a new dimension in overthrowing all one-sided assertions and biased leanings by means of a self-deconstructing provisionality. The baffling, quixotic style of the Ma-tsu dialogues is evident as early as eighth- and ninth-century records of Huang-po, Pai-chang, and Layman P'ang, as well as precursory transmission of the lamp texts such as the *Hōrinden*. But, since many of the records are of later vintage, the dialogues did not gain prominence or priority until they were housed in the three Sung genres, the *dentōroku*, *goroku*, and *kōan-roku*. At that point, the originally oral utterances became written texts. "As a result," according to Yanagida, "the records of those words and actions assumed the status of scripture. Or, rather, there occurred a change in the very conception of the scriptures themselves. Rather than the recorded sayings texts of Chinese teachers being granted a status equal to that of the translation of Indian *sūtras*, the *sūtras* came to be regarded as the Buddha's 'recorded sayings.'"[21] From this perspective, it is not the case that dialogues substituted for *sūtras*, but that the *sūtras* themselves had come to be looked on as examples and extensions of the dialogues. In that sense, Zen discourse inverts the very meaning of scripture, so that scripture is not an independent textual authority standing over and above the commentaries created parasitically around it, but scripture is an offshoot of oral commentaries (or antitextual noncommentaries) which actually take on the status of scriptures when they are put in a written form. The relation between texts is thus reversed from the standard hierarchy of scripture–commentary (written)–commentary (oral) to the new Zen decentric discourse of orality-*as*-(anti)scripture (or de-canonized scripture).

Nevertheless, as the Sung texts or records containing dialogues became *sūtra*-like textual entities taking on some key aspects of the role of scripture in terms of exerting authority and power over the intellectual life of the tradition, another level of commentary inevitably began to spring up around them. That is, although the dialogues as oral commentaries (or noncommentaries) originated, according to the tradition's rhetoric, as the antithesis of written scripture, once they came into scripturalized form there was a need for them to be presented and interpreted in an appropriate commentatorial style that helped dissolve an artificial separation of scriptural vs. commentatorial textual traditions. The aim of the development of the Sung genres beginning in the latter part of the tenth century is twofold: to find a literary setting or context that is consistent with the function of the dialogues, and to try to eliminate the gap between scriptural and commentatorial textuality. Each of the genres came to terms with these issues in a distinctive way. Of course, as genres are in the process of being formed the new texts being written are not necessarily intended to be identified with one or another genre for these categorizations largely derive from subsequent analysis. Furthermore, the lines of distinction between the genres are somewhat blurred because of their overlapping, intertextually related concerns. For example, the *dentōroku* texts growing out of monk biographies and reflecting the interface of Zen writings and folk Buddhist miraculous tales take a position on the borderline between the kind of mythology and hagiography contained in earlier Mahayana *sūtras* and in the biographies, that are used to generate a sense of lineage to help legitimate the Zen sect, and the emphasis on personalization and humanism in the *goroku* texts. While most of the main *dentōroku* texts stress transmission genealogy (*tō*-style, or transmission-style), especially the KD, others like the *Kenchū Seikoku Zokutōroku*, the SR, and the ST, which is so influential on Dōgen's MS collection, present the transmission theory at the beginning and then go on to offer a listing of *kosoku-kōan* (*yō*-style, or essential principle-style). The *goroku* genre—particularly those records of T'ang masters dealing extensively with pilgrimage in a biographical section that stresses genealogy—function on the borderline between the pseudohistorical *dentōroku* chronicles and the philosophical commentary of the kōan collections. The T'ang master lineage-oriented (*shike*) *goroku* are closer to the *dentōroku* style, while the Sung master individual-style (*kojin*) *goroku* are closer to the kōan collections. Because of the intertexually connected and crossover status of the texts in the various genres, particularly in the *goroku* genre, it seems preferable to refer to two main categories utilizing the source dialogues, as reflected in Figure 4.4.

In the *tōshi-roku* genre category the dialogues tend to get submerged in serving the purpose of larger themes, including genealogy and personal biography. In the *kōan-roku* texts the kōan cases are clearly identified and highlighted as the centerpiece of the text. In that sense, the latter texts may appear to be truer to the roots of the tradition than the former, but at the same time narrative elements do not disappear altogether in the *kōan-roku* texts. The chronicle quality is submerged, but not necessarily totally subverted. The mythology-demythology aporetic is not only a matter of the relation between the *tōshi-roku* and *kōan-roku* texts, but is located within the boundaries of the discourse of the latter category as well. The *kōan-roku* collections, especially the HR, preserve within their overall structure the process of the selecting of *kosoku-kōan* from earlier texts, as

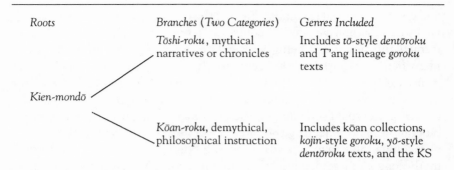

Figure 4.4. *Roots and Branches. This figure shows the relation between the roots and branches of the kōan tradition with the dialogues generating two categories of texts, and the genres aligned with each category.*

well as several levels of commentary on these cases. The HR also undertakes an abbreviation process in zeroing in on key words and phrases for interlinear commentary. Both the KS and the DR enter into the discourse in order to moderate the tendency in HR-style collections to create a reification and catechization of paradigmatic cases. The KS again submerges the dialogues but in a different sense than both the *tōshi-roku* KD or the *kōan-roku* HR texts in order to forge a more consistent and continuing unity of oral case-as-(noncanonized)-scripture-as-commentary. Whereas many examples of the *kōan-roku* genre may end up reinstituting scripturality and thereby losing touch with the antitextuality of the source dialogues, and while Ta-hui's *watō* approach may go to another extreme of eliminating textuality altogether, Dōgen seems to be trying to hold onto the antitextual ideal of spontaneous but continuing creativity while composing a literary form in which the antagonism between orality and writing, scripture and commentary is at once captured and diffused.

Roots and Branches

The aim of this section is to take a closer look at the styles of the *tōshi-roku* and *kōan-roku* categories in relation to the source dialogues in order to clarify the influences from the Sung genres on the formation of the KS. This section focuses on the the aporetic of mythology-demythology, which sets the stage for treatment of the rhetorical structure underlying the relation between textuality and untextuality in Part B.

Ur-Genre: Defining Kien-Mondō

The next step is to discuss the meaning of Zen dialogue and its role in training, teaching, and transmission. Regardless of whether the dialogues were spontaneously created in the T'ang and precariously preserved in the Sung, or were a rhetorical invention formulated in the Sung that was projected back into the T'ang for the sake of legitimating genealogy, it is clear that dialogues based on *kien* function as the literary basis of the various genres. In the teleological view of the tradition, the dialogues are considered to represent incipient *watō*, and the Sung genres are seen as stepping-stones leading with a stage by stage inevitability to the foregone conclusion of the priority of the *watō* based on the understanding that ineffability and silence represent the essence of the tradition. In a nonteleological, decentric view, the dialogues are not destined to progress inexorably toward the *watō*, but are seen as underlying a number of alternative approaches.

The term *kien-mondō* has been translated here as "*satori* dialogue" or "transmission dialogue," but the standard English translation that was apparently approved of by Yanagida is a rather less ambitious term, "encounter dialogue." *Kien-mondō* contains four Chinese characters grouped into two words of two characters each. The difference in translations primarily concerns the first word, *kien*, and is not so much a difference of kind or interpretive principle but of degree of emphasis on certain implications of the characters. In the word *kien*, both characters are filled with meanings reflecting the history of Buddhist thought concerning causality and karma as well as key aspects of East Asian (particularly Japanese) social relations, and the compound also has a distinctive flavor pertaining to the master-disciple relation in Zen that is beyond the sum of its semiotic components. First, *ki* has a twofold dictionary meaning of opportunity, occasion, or moment in time, as well as of loom, machine, or airplane. The first set of definitions implies a sense of chance or luck in terms of right timing, fateful occurrence, or an idea or event whose "time has come." The second set suggests the operation of a mechanism—either an antique, pretechnological hand-driven or an electrically generated device—although in some usages *ki* can also refer to a living organism. The link between these two sets of meanings seems to be the notion of a temporal occasion for a dynamic happening or process of functioning. In folk literature, the imagery of a loom may take on supernatural proportions implying a celestial weaver of the strands and webs of karmic fate.

In Zen thought, *ki* is used by Dōgen, who is influenced by Yüan-wu's teaching on this point, in the sense of the active or dynamic nature of meditation, as in the term *zen-ki* or "total activity," which refers to the inseparability of life-and-death realized each and every moment: "Life is not coming or going. Life is not presence or appearance. However, life is the manifestation of total activity (*zenki*), and death is the manifestation of total activity. You must realize that birth and death exist in the limitless Dharma realized by one's self."[22] In some Zen writings, *ki* also conveys a "mind" or a level of mentality that is capable of responding to a particular level of discourse, such as a Hinayana-mind (*shōjō-ki*) or a Mahayana-mind (*daijō-ki*).[23] It therefore suggests a mind ripe for the opportunity to receive instruction and, by extension, it means the process of seeking and establishing a relationship with the right master.

The second character, *en*, means connection, relation, or affinity, sometimes referring to family relations or the bonding of a social group, and also implying karma, fate, or destiny. It seems to have three inseparable implications: a sense of chance, of good or bad fortune, in being "thrown" (in the Heideggerian sense) into a network of social relations; a presumption about the ensnarement and inescapability of said network, or of being trapped by circumstances and obligations; and, somewhat paradoxically, the vehicle through meeting the appropriate people and fulfilling responsibilities to become free from such social bondage, so that a marriage may be consummated or a religious encounter and relation completed by virtue of *en*. The latter implication suggests Dōgen's interpretation of *kattō* as complications or entanglements that release entanglements. In Buddhism, *en* is the translation for the Sanskrit *pratyaya*, or condition, as in the term *in-nen* (Skt. *hetu-pratyaya*), or the primary causes and secondary conditions which constitute the factors of production of conditioned reality. *En* also is used in an important compound, *en-gi* (Skt. *pratītya-samutpāda*), signifying the dependence or relationality aspect of the concept of dependent or relational origination (*gi* is arising or origination). In popular religion, *engi* implies omen, luck, or portent. The term is also used to refer to a legend (*densetsu*), such as a temple's "foundation legend" (*tera no engi*) that depicts in mythical, animistic terms the origins and history of a temple and the sources of its divine protection. *Engi* thus acts "as a vital factor in transmitting to others the impression that a particular site was special."[24] Therefore, *en* is very much involved in the fundamental Buddhist worldview of cause and effect, encompassing the concept of karma in both philosophical and popular senses, as well as the notion of interdependent co-arising on metaphysical and social-ethical levels.

The compound *kien* implies an opportune moment that is not necessarily predetermined by karma or fate, but is a consequence of a multiplicity of causal and conditioning factors, and perhaps more than mere happenstance or coincidence. It suggests that all the forces at work have come together in an appropriate mixture setting the stage for an event to take place. *Kien* refers to the building up of the complex temporal ingredients necessary for an occurrence, and it represents an understanding of events that takes a middle way between the view that there is a sudden and unpredictable appearance of something from out of nowhere and the view of predetermination. It also conveys an existential dynamism in that there needs to be an exchange, encounter, or interchange, an intense and most likely foreshadowed meeting or rendezvous between master and disciple, who are meant by the intertwining of their potentialities and fates to come together in a mutually beneficial way. It refers to an encounter between two parties that is necessary for each one, including the teacher just as much as the student, to transcend to the next level of self-realization. The term *kien* has been used in Zen tradition to refer to a master's particular style of teaching, as well as the lineage deriving from him. In that sense *kien-mondō* becomes the vehicle in Zen for the transmission ceremony (*kanjō*, Skt. *abhiṣeka*). In many Buddhist sects the transmission ceremony involves the baptism of a disciple marking his ritual passage through a watershed mark in training. In Zen, however, although the kōan came to be catechistically ritualized in the Sung, the T'ang source dialogues were supposed to represent an antiritualistic form of ceremonial transmission. Furthermore, the translation of *kien* as "transmission" or "*satori*" is supported by Kawamura's suggestion that Zen dialogues as commented on by Dōgen and others are exemplary of the process of *shōden no buppō*, or "rightly transmitted Buddha Dharma."[25] Yet, because transmission or *satori* is not necessarily guaranteed to take place in every dialogical situation, there is no question that "encounter" must also be considered an appropriate rendering. On the other hand, from Dōgen's standpoint as expressed, for example, in his interpretation of the Ma-tsu "polishing the tile" kōan, both master and disciple at the beginning as well as at the end of their meeting are considered fully enlightened.

If *kien* refers to a karmically influenced and temporally realized master-disciple transmission, the second word, *mondō*, means at once something more and less than "dialogue." The two characters literally mean question (*mon*) and answer (*tō* or *dō*), inquiry and response, problem and solution, and the compound can mean debate, dispute, or catechism.

Mondō suggests a sudden process of coming to a breakthrough under-standing or insight in a way that is perhaps more sophisticated philosophi-cally than ordinary dialogue. That is because mondō functions in the Socratic sense of an oral exchange that is genuinely undogmatic in seeking to expose the deficiencies and delusions in a participant's or disciple's approach. However, due to their fundamental pedagogical provisionality, Zen dialogues are somewhat different and perhaps far less conversational than ordinary as well as Western-style philosophical dialogues. If dialogue often implies an open-ended conversation in which both parties are committed to reaching a higher truth by pushing each other up to and beyond the limits of their understanding, Zen dialogues often try to defeat any reliance on the ordinary question-answer process by demonstrating the foolishness of questions with absurd, incongruous replies. Unlike the sustained, intricate, and dialectically progressive nature of Socratic dia-logues that seek to persuade a partner in conversation about the virtue of reasoning one's way toward truth, Zen dialogues are brief, allusive, and epiphanous, and they are based on personal transformation.[26] Therefore, it may be more appropriate to refer to them as "dialogic exchanges or encounters," and to kien-mondō as a "transmission dialogic encounter." One of the main differences between Sung genres is that the tōshi-roku texts provide reports about the context of the dialogues in order to validate lineage, whereas the kōan-roku texts record the dialogues to try to capture some of the electric spirit of the spontaneous exchanges. The chronicles are engaged in creative historiography and the kōan texts are engaged in creative philology. Kien-mondō serves as the "creative" base out of which both categories of texts develop.

Tōshi-roku: *Narrative Emplotment*

As discussed above, the conventional, teleological view of Zen literature sees the tōshi-roku chronicles—encompassing tō-style dentōroku and T'ang master shike-style goroku texts—serving the dialogues by acting as a kind of "looseleaf" storehouse or stepping-stone from which the essential material can be picked at will while the remaining mythical passages are overlooked or discarded. The conventional view at once accepts the pseudohistorical accounts in the chronicles and then turns from them in favor of the demythical kōans. However, since the dialogues are contained in the elabo-rate, systematic chronicles, and also since mythical elements often find their way even into the concrete, anecdotal kosoku-kōan, it is necessary to find a compromise between uncritical, apologetical acceptance and skeptical positivist historiography concerning the chronicles; that is, a middle ground between Nishitani's overemphatic affirmation of the superiority of the Zen view of history and the overstated criticism of the Zen chronicles by some historians. The suggestion here is that the dialogues serve the chronicles by functioning as the basic literary unit that is carefully crafted and selected to promote and advance the narrative texture. Demonstrating this involves analyzing how dialogues operate on two inseparable levels. One is to see the way they contribute to the macro or extensional level of the larger narratological structure. The second level, which is explored more fully in Part B, is to break down the figures of speech in the actual exchange of words in terms of the micro or intensional level of tropological structure.

As Dale Wright argues, narrative is selected as a form of expression in Zen chronicles not out of ignorance of a better approach to recording history, but due to a deliberate decision to find the most appropriate manner of communicating the meaning of patriarchal lineage and inheritance.[27] Narrative is useful because, as Jean-François Lyotard notes, it is a form of discourse which in the right setting communicates more persuasively and pervasively with its audience than a scientific explication of knowledge. Narrative has an inner logic or means of organizing and systematizing its material that is *instructional* by transmitting wisdom to insiders of a lineage through figures of speech and wordplay related to tropology. It is also *transactional* in engaging the reader as participant in the events depicted by setting up an alternative rhythm of time.[28] Roland Barthes further stresses the transactional element by describing the evocative mutuality and intimacy of author (which he refers to as the "writerly" dimension of a text) and the reader (or "readerly" dimension), who partakes of the "pleasure of the text" through joyous or ec-static reading.[29] In addition, Todorov makes a distinction between two kinds of narrative genres: "mythological" narratives, which might include the monk biography texts, and which have a relatively simple logic of succession; and "gnoseological" (also called "epistemical") narratives, which seem to cover the *tōshi-roku* texts, "in which the logic of succession is supported by [a more complex] transformation, narratives in which the event itself is less important than our perception of, and the degree of knowledge we have of it."[30] Zen chronicles can also be referred to as "normative" narratives that function in response to the need for spiritual transformation.

A survey of recent theories of narration indicates that there are several main factors generating the narrative structure: there is a basic literary unit or "kernel" of composition that is synthesized after considerable thematic conflict into at least two higher, more complex levels: one consisting of character development, and the other of overall plot or theme. This narrative synthesis occurs by virtue of a restructuring of time to attain an inseparability and translinearity of past, present, and future revolving around pivotal, epiphanous moments.[31] In Zen chronicles, the *satori* dialogue—dialogue can be considered the "preeminent enactment" in narrative for it involves showing rather than mere telling[32]—is the basic unit or nucleus that acts as a catalyzer for the complexity of narration. Furthermore, the synthetic levels operate on two dimensions simultaneously: first, the remarkable transformational experiences of individual Zen masters, as portrayed in the *shike*-style recorded sayings; and, second, the uniform process of transmission from master-to-master dating from time immemorial till the present day, as depicted primarily in the lamp histories.

The chronicles thus use the dialogues to mythologize and hagiologize the line of succession of masters whose lives fit into a common pattern, which recalls the analysis of liminality in the rite of passage of heroic missions as suggested by van Gennep, Turner, and Campbell.[33] The first stage is the agonizing doubt and sense of hopelessness by someone of impassioned hope concerning the proper interpretation of traditional doctrine, often involving the meaning of a perplexing line from the *sūtras*, as when Hui-neng hears of and Te-shan studies the *Diamond Sūtra*, or when Dōgen questions the Tendai sect's interpretation of the *Awakening of Faith* or *The Lotus Sūtra*. The next stage is the consequent prolonged impasse to enlightenment leading to a seemingly endless search for the right teacher, a process that can lead to years of frustration and false starts.[34] Part of the torment and perplexity is due to the contention that there are so very few authentic teachers left (which was the reason Dōgen departed Japan for China). On the other hand, for disciples there can be only one right teacher who responds to the needs of a particular student and, at the same time, for masters there must be a period of waiting and/or seeking for one prized disciple. Then after years of special training comes the sudden, dramatic breakthrough experience of *satori*, usually occurring after the disciple has been shamed or humiliated to a point beyond hope and hopelessness, will and no-will, by an almost brashly self-confident yet incorruptible master. The master understands just how to extricate the disciple from his conceptual fixations, often by using an absurd gesture such as shouting, stamping, or hitting with a stick, or by some form of outrageous humor.[35] The final stage is the continuing quest of the newly anointed successor to determine or receive the appropriate heir to the lineage. Approval of the master-to-be in the next generation, who will eventually prove capable of surpassing the master who chose him, requires initiatory testing through another series of verbal and/or nonverbal dialogical exchanges.

The function of the dialogue as the basic unit on the lower synthetic level is to create a concrete and vitally human situational context through which *satori* spontaneously occurs. The dialogue captures the moment of liberation, so that temporality is experienced in terms of peaks and valleys relative to the time before and after the event of attainment or modes of realization. Since the two participants in the conversation represent the timeless paradigms of enlightenment and delusion, the already-attained and the yet-to-be, the reader is transactionally engaged to place him or herself into the scene; that is, to playfully imagine how to respond to a strict, uncompromising master's query or to size up a stubbornly deluded disciple. On the higher synthetic level, the aim of the chronicles is to fashion a narrative discourse that tells "history" in the sense of depicting the origins, continuity-in-change, and intermittent periods of closure of the distinctive way the Zen sect has been transmitting the Dharma. The dialogue becomes a window to the "fusion of [temporal] horizons,"[36] in that all enlightenments, despite different methods of attainment, represent experiences of the timeless Dharma and are therefore the selfsame. That is, dialogues on the lower level are appropriately linked to a temporal situational context, and on the higher level are transtemporal and unbound by particular temporal occasions. Dialogues are also significant in serving as an internal, gnoseological symbol of authentic transmission from teacher to disciple that becomes more powerful than the visible, tangible symbol of the Bodhidharma's begging bowl that was used in earlier times.[37] Therefore, the chronicles disavow factual historiography because their philosophy dictates that the main characters of the narrative—the attained masters— are not substantive entities but represent interchangeable and transpositional possibilities for self-discovery. Thus, intertextuality leads into what can be called the "interpersonality" concerns of the text for which the hero, as Faure writes, "should be interpreted as a textual and religious paradigm and not be reconstructed as a historical figure or a psychological essence."[38]

Kōan-roku: *The Eclipse of Narrative*

The *kōan-roku* category primarily includes the *kojin*-style *goroku* texts, especially records of Sung era masters, the formal kōan collections, such as the HR, SH, and MMK, Dōgen's KS text, and the yō-style *dentōroku* texts. The transition from the styles and themes of the *tōshi-roku* to the *kōan-roku* category, especially in the case of *goroku* texts, is a movement from a classical to a colloquial style, from collective to individual themes, and from a genealogical to a pedagogical method. The *kōan-roku* texts use an informal, even rustic literary style emphasizing the personal selection of *kosoku-kōan*, and at times the creation of new cases based on the master's sense of his disciples' needs as well as his own skill in philosophical interpretation and instruction. In this category, the source dialogues are no longer submerged for narrative purposes, but are now highlighted for the sake of philosophical exploration and clarification. One of the main concerns of the *kōan-roku* texts seems to be to call attention to the point that the classical style and formal, uniform structure of the *dentōroku* texts contrasts sharply with the rustic, colloquial style of the dialogues for the reason that "(c)hanging T'ang vernacular into Sung literary language might be compared to translating New York City street slang into Oxford English."[39] Because of the stylistic requirements of the *dentōroku* genre, the texts tend not to read like a record of authentic discourse, so that the polishing and so-called improvements they provided for the source dialogues probably had the effect of altering or even lessening the *kien-mondō* style. The *kōan-roku* texts strive for a calculated roughness, which may end up getting lost in the flowery language and the revisionist, though equally formal structure of the HR. The DR and the KS both seek in different ways to go beyond the HR by returning once again to the colloquial, spontaneous spirit of the dialogues.

As William Powell notes, the *kojin*-style *goroku* texts "focus attention on individual masters rather than on the collective heritage." That is, rather than conveying the entire transmission process in a way in which individual personalities tend to get blurred, the *goroku* bring together in a single text relevant material about a particular, individual master otherwise scattered throughout various works or even within a single large *dentōroku* work. For example, "in the lamp records the anecdotes involving a particular figure are usually found not just in his own section, but also in that of his master, the various other masters he may have visited, and his students." However, the aim of the *goroku* texts is not just to condense biographical material into a single work but to steer in a different direction by creating "word portraits" of the patriarchs that are comparable to the actual portraits that were made of a master by his designated successor. The records do not offer a systematic teaching, but are an attempt "to preserve and transmit through the characters of individual masters . . . the [pedagogical] style of particular houses."[40] Berling notes that "[m]any of the collections of the period are divided among discourses (shang-t'ang, jōdō), examinations (k'an-pien, kanben), travels (yu-fang, ryōhō or hsing-lu, gyōroku), formal examination of students (hsiao-ts'an, shō-san), poems, and comments." She goes on to conclude that "[d]espite these various categories, however, the collections favor the enigmatic, paradoxical exhanges of Ch'an dialogue over more discursive, doctrinal statements."[41] That is, the enigmatic dialogues are highlighted as the ends of the discourse rather than the means. Yet the role that the dialogues play in an individual master's narrative history is by no means lost altogether. Rather, it is played upon in developing an allusive quality, or a semiotic field of pseudohistorical allusions, in referring to past deeds or utterances of famous masters that is useful for the instructional goals of the dialogues. Therefore, it can be said of the kojin-style goroku texts that "[t]raditional narrative strategies are not so much abandoned as transformed . . . "[42]

When the goroku texts are read as a whole story of the master rather than as discrete incidents, or are read as contributing primarily to the overall narrative of patriarchal transmission, even the kojin-style texts can sometimes seem to closely resemble the tō-style dentōroku genre. But when the discrete literary unit of the dialogue was lifted out of the narrative context, the goroku texts began to evolve into the kōan collection genre. The kōan collections beginning in the early eleventh century grew out of and branched off from, but were also subsequently at least partially and implicitly critiqued by, goroku texts compiled by Ta-hui, Dōgen, and others in the latter part of the twelfth century and later. The Sung era kōan collections attempt a formalization in using kōans as a method of religious practice by organizing and interpreting the dialogues, utterances, sermons, and anecdotes culled from recorded sayings, transmission of the lamp histories, biographies, and poetry collections without regard for personality. While it is unclear exactly how kōan collections were used during this formative period, McRae suggests a catechistic interpretation by arguing that these collections were apparently intended to function as courses of study or "teacher manuals." "The public case anthologies were, in a word, pedagogic tools of the most basic order,"[43] whereby the structure of the texts does not provide any sense of lineage, house style, individual masters, or collective historical Ch'an experience.

On the other hand, it may be somewhat misleading to suggest that there is no trace of lineage in the collections because in citing or culling material from the KD, for example, the commentaries in these texts do not just refer to a decontextualized dialogue. Rather, the dialogue they cite carries an atmosphere of personality, house style, and genealogy that gives it a necessary aura of authority. For instance, in HR case no. 20, Yüan-wu comments on the fact that both Ts'ui Wei and Lin-chi, who are of different lineages, give the identical answer (hitting the questioner, Lung-ya, with his zazen cushion) to the question of the meaning of Bodhidharma's coming from the west. In fact, what happens in the kōan collections is that while personality and lineage are generally not dealt with directly, they still help form a meaningful literary backdrop that is constantly alluded to in passing references. Names of masters and brief passages of their sayings become succinct semiotic trigger mechanisms calling to mind a vast storehouse of records of their works and their standing in the Zen genealogy. For example, MMK case no. 3 concerning Chu-ti's cutting off a young disciple's finger is effective in the literary tradition because his "one-finger teaching" technique is already well known from HR case no. 19 and other chronicle sources. Also, Yün-men's "upside-down statement" in HR case no. 15 in response to the question, "When it's not the present intellect and it's not the present phenomena, what is it?", has an impact because it plays off of HR case no. 14 and other sources in which Yün-men maintains that "the teachings of a whole lifetime" are nothing other than "an appropriate statement."

The notion of collecting and commenting on the kōan as a public (kō) record (an) or testimony of the spontaneous and therapeutic insight expressed by a Zen master in transmitting the Dharma probably began to develop in the late T'ang era and was systematized primarily by the Yang-chi line of the Rinzai sect. It appears that Nan-yüan in the second generation after master Lin-chi was among the first to use the words, blows, and gestures associated with traditional anecdotes and parables in instructing and illuminating disciples. The earliest kōan collection is attributed to Fen-yang, several generations later, consisting of three portions of one hundred kōans each. These include traditional cases that are selected and recorded as well as new queries developed by Fen-yang and alternative answers he created to older riddles. Both of the latter two categories indicate the importance of an individual master's originality and creativity in contributing to this new genre. Wu-tsu, following Yang-chi, also created his own cases and helped establish the kōan as a regular part of Zen training. His main disciple, Yüan-wu, used the one hundred case collection of Yün-men school master Hsüeh-tou as the basis of the HR. Yün-men, the founder of the school, in addition to being known for his emphasis on "one-word barrier" expressions, was one of most popular masters and creators of kōans cited in various collections, including the MS.

Of the major collections, the formation of the SH text, which is sometimes looked upon as the Sōtō sect's version of the HR, has a similar history and literary structure when compared to the earlier Rinzai text. In the HR, Yüan-wu contributed the introduction to each paradigmatic case as well as notes and commentary on both the cases and Hsüeh-tou's poems so that each chapter contains six sections. The HR has (1) a pointer or introduction by Yüan-wu (this section is not always included), (2) the case initially selected with (3) Hsüeh-tou's verse commentary, and Yüan-wu's (4) notes on the case and (5 and 6) his interlinear prose commentary on the case and the verse. The SH, in which Wan-sung's commentaries are based on cases and poetic commentaries taken from Hung-chih's *Juko Hyakusoku*, has (1) a pointer by Wan-sung, (2) the case initially selected by Hung-chih, (3) Wan-sung's prose commentary on the case, (4) Hung-chih's verse commentary, (5) Wan-sung's prose commentary on the verse, and (6) Wan-sung's interlinear remarks and additional sayings. The structure of the MMK is much more streamlined and contains only three sections: case, brief prose commentary, and single verse poetic commentary (although this leaves the door open for modern commentaries on traditional interpretations). As an indication that some aspects of the rivalry between Rinzai and Sōtō that came to the fore in Japan were not necessarily prevalent in Sung China, the HR and other collections have a multibranched attitude toward Zen genealogy and generally cite representatives from all the Zen schools as well as pre-Zen Mahayana thinkers like Seng-chao.

Each of the kōan collections has a distinct pedagogical style. Dōgen's KS may at first appear to be closely related to the MMK collection, with which it shares many common citations of *kosoku-kōan*. The KS uses more kōans that are also found in the MMK than found in the HR or in the SH collection, even though the latter is based on the writings of his Sōtō ancestor, Hung-chih. However, since the MMK was not introduced into Japan until after Dōgen's death and the SH was modeled on the HR, it seems clear that the HR collection, which was probably still very popular in China during Dōgen's visit there despite Ta-hui's criticisms (and burning) of it, was the primary influence on the formation of the KS' interpretive style. On the other hand, the problem that was perceived in the HR style by both Ta-hui and Dōgen was the tendency to reify kōan cases, or to turn them into cliché-ridden stereotypes, so that the antimyth of icono-

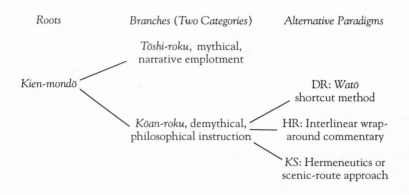

Figure 4.5. *Alternative Paradigms. This figure expands figure 4.4, which shows the relation between the roots and branches of the kōan tradition, by indicating that the kōan-roku category leads in turn to three alternative interpretative models, including the HR wraparound and, following from yet also critiquing that, the DR shortcut and the KS scenic-route approaches.*

clastic dialogue became part of a new mythology. As Figure 4.5 indicates, both thinkers responded to this problematic by using "poison to counteract poison": for Ta-hui this meant seeing the kōan as self-negating, or using the kōan to negate the need to use kōans through the *watō* method (while he continued to comment on kōans in his sermons and lectures); and for Dōgen this meant seeing the kōan as self-transcending, or turning the commentary on kōans recharged with polysemous wordplay into new kōans. Kōan collections emphasize cases, but these are invariably still identified with masters. The same emphasis is found in the MS collection, but the KS shifts the focus to Dōgen's presentation and interpretation of topics, and suppresses the interpretation of master-centered *kosoku-kōan*. The records of Dōgen and Ta-hui could be considered "post-kōan collection" texts, not really in a chronological sense because kōan collections continued to be compiled, but in the sense that they were reacting to and seeking to correct the kōan collection style.

It is important to note that the compilers of most of the prominent kōan collections, including the HR, SH, MS, and Ta-hui's *Shōbōgenzō* (the MMK is the main exception to this), were also authors of significant *goroku* records. While it is difficult to determine what motives prompted the Sung

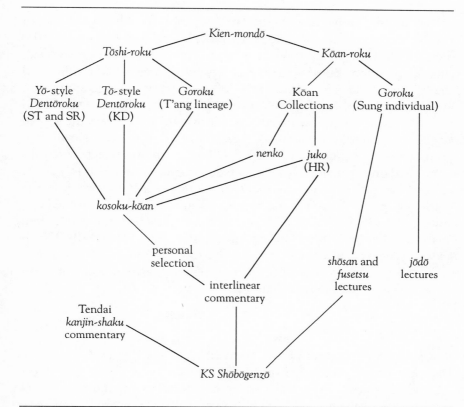

Figure 4.6. *Interpretive Influences on the KS. This figure shows how Dōgen's KS interpretive style was influenced by the selection of* kosoku-kōan *in dentōroku texts, the interlinear commentary in kōan collections, and* shōsan *and* fusetsu *lectures in goroku texts, in addition to Tendai mind-contemplation commentary.*

masters to use one genre or another, the key point is that the post-kōan collection texts tended to reduce or even to eliminate the temporal as well as the literary structural gap between saying and recording, or case and commentary. At this juncture in the development of Zen discourse, the contemporaneous master/philosopher—for the most part in a demythologized, nonheroic context—began to supersede the *kosoku-kōan* tradition as the expression of the living embodiment and authority of truth, and his lectures, sermons, letters, and other forms of expression gave his followers an opportunity to participate in the living word (*wa*) in a new era of originality and creativity that has been referred to as a (second) golden age of Zen. In the *kojin*-style *goroku* genre, both the formal, brief *jōdō* lectures and the more informal but lengthier *shōsan* discourses were delivered in a prescribed, ritualized fashion. But the latter category, which particularly influenced the KS style, tended to restore a sense of spontaneity and ingenuity to the analysis of *kosoku-kōan*. Figure 4.6 shows the stylistic influences on the KS from Sung genres, and also includes reference to the influence of the Tendai *kanjin-shaku* interpretive method. According to this figure, there are four primary stylistic influences on the KS: (1) the method of selecting *kosoku-kōan* based on personal preference suited to instructional needs in *yō*-style *dentōroku* as well as other genres; (2) the interlinear commentary, or the glossing of particular words and phrases taken from dialogues in the kōan collections; (3) the *shōsan*, or *jishu*, and *fusetsu* style lectures which often analyzed kōan cases in original and innovative ways; (4) and the Tendai *kanjin-shaku* style of commentary, which took license to alter or recast source material during the writing of commentary based on contemplative awareness attained through meditation.

Impact: Seamless Narrative

Before analyzing more fully the relation between the KS and the alternative *kōan-roku* paradigms from a tropological perspective, it is helpful to reflect on and summarize the relation between the mythical and demythical tendencies in Zen discourse. Are they in conflict or compatible, and if the latter, is this generated by design or accident? What are the implications for clarifying the issue of textuality and untextuality that will shed light on the formation of the KS text in its genre classification? The impact of the compatibility of mythology and demythology in Zen discourse was the delivery of a message especially pertinent to the post-845 era of Chinese religion and culture through an appeal to both intellectual/elite (or "great") and popular/folk (or "little") traditions. After the suppression of Buddhism which left its sophisticated scholastic tradition discredited and largely abandoned, the Zen masters as described in the dialogical chronicles laid claim to representing the personal embodiment of the Dharma without the need for recourse to a higher authority or source of truth, such as scripture or scriptural exegesis.[44] Yet Zen's ideal of lineal precedent, transmission, and succession gained credence in evoking the guru-disciple relationship typical of Indian traditions.[45] This enabled the Zen sect to compete with several rival forms of Chinese religiosity. On the level of great tradition, the Zen emphasis on personal cultivation and attainment underlying doctrinal learning appealed to the humanistic attitude of the dominant class of Neo-Confucian scholar-officials[46] and the emulation of imperial ceremonialism in the ordination process was probably aimed at winning state patronage. Also, the Zen therapeutic view of religious language as being suitable to particular spiritual ailments had an appeal comparable to philosophical Taoism, particularly Chuang Tzu's extraordinary facility with "goblet words," while the give-and-take structure of the dialogues resembled neo-Taoist colloquies. Furthermore, the Zen emphasis on personalization and subitization may have had a greater appeal than the exegetical and more gradual approach to meditation in the T'ien-t'ai school. On the level of little tradition, the oracular and shamanistic qualities in the legends of deified masters like Bodhidharma made them the rival of the immortal saints of the leading hagiocentric folk religion, popular Taoism, while at the same time the down-to-earth, concrete quality of enlightened patriarchs offered an immediate here-and-now hope to believers in the advent of the future buddha, Maitreya.[47] In addition, the formulaic-repetitive quality of the highly condensed dialogues that were easy to memorize and recite offered a spiritual technique comparable to the *nembutsu* chant of Pure Land Buddhism.

The uniqueness of Zen in this religio-cultural setting pertains to the way the dialogues and kōans seek to demythologize transhistorically the myths concerning the sect's heroes, or to the profound interaction between the building up and the deconstructing of mythical discourse. The quintessential example of this twofold tendency is the account of Bodhidharma, referred to in the *Hōrinden* and later chronicles as the twenty-eighth Zen patriarch and the first on Chinese soil. Bodhidharma is depicted in the chronicles as the third son of a king who crossed the Yangtze on a single reed, meditated for nine years facing the wall of a cave till his legs withered away before gaining enlightenment, and commanded his foremost disciple to cut off his arm during a snowstorm as proof of his dedication. In some versions of the legend Bodhidharma is deified in that he performs supernatural feats, including conquering illness, poison, and death. Tea is said to grow from the eyebrows he ripped off his face and discarded in disgust at himself for having dozed off during meditation. In contemporary Japanese culture, limbless Daruma dolls (symbolizing that arms and legs have been cast off after years of sitting meditation) are used as a sign of good fortune and divine protection. Most of the later Zen masters are depicted not as miracle workers but in more down-to-earth fashion, yet supernatural occurrences like prophetic dreams, preordained encounters, and natural signatures for human affairs (such as flowers blooming or snow falling at appropriate moments) frequently accompany each stage of their path.

But the process of demythologization that the masters' personal example and doctrinal instruction represents is also reflected in all aspects of the myth. Some of the more radically iconoclastic examples of this are Te-shan's burning of the *sūtras* out of disdain for textual studies and Lin-chi's proclaiming "If you see the buddha, kill the buddha" in refutation of iconographic and hagiographic worship. For Bodhidharma, demythologization is epitomized by his legendary iconoclastic interview with Emperor Wu, which was perhaps introduced into the traditional account by Shen-hui in 732 and by the time of the KD in 1004 had become the "most popular and enduring of [Zen] legends."[48] According to this tale, Bodhidharma instructed the emperor that copying *sūtras* and building temples will gain him "No merit" for, indeed, there is only "Just emptiness, nothing sacred," such that "I [Bodhidharma, which means "law of wisdom"] do not even know [my own name]." Furthermore, the legend of Bodhidharma's arrival in China is itself demythologized by several kōans concerning the question, "What is the meaning of the first patriarch's coming from the west?" In case no. 37 of the MMK Chao-chou responds with the non sequitur, "The oak tree in the front garden," and in case no. 20 of the HR both Ts'ui Wei and Lin-chi retort by the negation, "There is no meaning." Also, Ma-tsu's response to the query is to kick the disciple/inquirer who is subitaneously awakened as a result,[49] and in yet another encounter dialogue a master when asked this question stands on one leg and then hits his uncomprehending student.

Section B. "Marrow, Bones, Flesh, Skin"

However, this seamless narrative is not without rifts and rends, many of which are deliberately created by the demythologizing, untextualizing tendencies that are generated within and yet are continually testing the limits of Zen discourse. Two centuries after the initial Sung explosion of Zen *kien-mondō* texts, demythologization was continuing to take place on several interlocking levels of critiquing, decanonizing, decontextualizing, and personalizing the buildup of Zen patriarchal myths, so that it is necessary to take a closer look at points of discontinuity, discord, and diversity to appreciate the KS's relation to other *kōan-roku* texts. Furthermore, evoking the image of a seamless narrative may suggest an uncritical valorization that violates the tradition's own self-critical stance. The limitation in using the image of seamlessness as a means of portraying the tradition is highlighted in HR case no. 18 (comparable to MS no. 60), in which master Hui-chung playfully answers the emperor's question about what he will need after death by saying "Build a seamless monument for me." When the perplexed emperor asks what the monument would look like, Hui-chung remains silent.

The post-kōan collection era that was dominated by creative individual commentary on kōans generated a problematic based on a potential revived reification of patriarchalism, which is addressed in HR case no. 11 and MS no. 202: Huang-po, calling his disciples in disgust "gobblers of dregs," argues "that there are no teachers of Ch'an in all of China." When a monk asks about the leaders of numerous monastic communities, Huang-po responds, "I do not say that there is no Ch'an; it's just that there are no teachers."[50] Once patriarchy is demythologized or re-demythologized, however, what is the next step for a tradition that has no recourse to return to an orality that was perhaps invented in the first place? One way of avoiding the risk of an overemphasis on the patriarch is to continue to submerge personality into interpretive text in a way that at once preserves and subverts the ideal of untextuality. Then, the remaining myth to be broken through becomes the antimyth of untextuality, which is approached by the HR, KS, and DR texts through developing strategies of abbreviation that involve zeroing in to interpret the key components of the rhetorical structure of the source dialogues.

Therefore, demythologization, marking a transformation of myth to antimyth, canon to anticanon, patriarchy to textuality, and then textuality to untextuality, is not an end but rather the beginning of a new level of discourse, and not the solution in the sense of constituting a fixed position that is firmly established but the continual opening of a hermeneutic door to several possibilities of interpretation. Hee-Jin Kim characterizes Dōgen's creative project as "a radical demythologizing and, in turn, remythologizing of the whole Buddhist symbol-complex of original enlightenment, the Buddha-nature, emptiness, and other related ideas and practices."[51] While this suggestion is useful, it is also necessary to clarify the point that "remythology" does not indicate the creating of a new myth in the sense of the chronicles, but represents a return to the creative wellspring of the source dialogues. The dialogues are flexible and open-ended roots that are nonreliant on and yet are provisionally supportive of a variety of branches.

For example, mythology or demythology, as well as silence or polysemy, are neither required nor excluded by the tropological foundation of *kien-mondō*.

The Elements of a Tropological Interpretation

This section develops a tropological methodology to examine how Dōgen's emphasis on a polysemous, hermeneutical interpretation contributes to the multivalent dialogue tradition. This analysis will first explicate the fundamental parallactic rather than paradoxical structure of the dialogues, as seen from a rhetorical rather than a psychological standpoint. This method provides an overview and a means for categorizing the basic differences in the ways the genres and subgenres handle the dialogues in order to clarify Dōgen's interpretive stance in comparison with other main *kōan-roku* texts.

Paradoxical and Parallactical Interpretations

Because Zen dialogic encounters often mark or even demand the end of dialoguing in the customary sense of an ongoing conversation, they have generally been interpreted as a tentative form of expression based on the priority of ineffability. As cited in Chapter 1, for example, John McRae argues that "Ch'an is more emphatic than any other Buddhist School in its position that the ultimate goal of religious practice cannot be understood with words." This interpretation seems to be supported by a theme common to many of the dialogues, for example MMK case no. 32, which suggests that neither words nor no-words, neither speech nor silence can disclose the Dharma. In a similar vein, Te-shan proclaims that whether or not the truth is explained by his disciple he will deal out thirty blows of his stick. According to the psychological interpretation, kōans are paradoxical expressions that strive to generate a double-bind situation based on the (1) accumulation of theoretical knowledge; the (2) eventual saturation of the confounded intellect leading to a labyrinthine impasse of self-doubt; and (3) an explosion of ordinary consciousness that finally allows entrance through the gateless gate into true reality.

However, even though the dialogues often deliberately lead language to the point of an immovable barrier or unbreakable impasse, it is also the case that language functions in the dialogues as the necessary vehicle for overcoming the very obstacles that verbal expressions create. That is, the barriers to enlightenment that arise from language can only be broken through by means of language, which is at once the lock and key to authentic understanding. For example, the *Rinzai Roku* highlights the crucial role in Lin-chi's dialogues of the turning word (*tengo*), or the appropriate turn of a phrase or illuminative, tropological wordplay.[52] Also, Tung-shan Shou-chou of the Yün-men school (two generations before Hsüeh-tou) distinguishes between "living words," which are apropos of the moment and ideally suited to an encounter situation because they reflect the interpenetration of universality and particularity and the inseparability of subjectivity and objectivity, and "dead words," which fall back on predictably and ineffectively logical responses to dynamic, translogical inquiries. Ta-hui in his polemic against silent illumination identifies living words with the *watō* method and dead words with other forms of discourse that depend on language, including explanations of *mokushō-zen* (which ironically refers to "silent" illumination). But, it is possible to reverse Ta-hui's interpretation somewhat by seeing the notion of living words as stressing that language is an inexhaustible source of meanings, a reservoir of possibilities of symbolic expression, or a window that opens up to the potential for authentic discourse. This view of the tradition marks a shift in interpretation that helps establish a direct link between the multidimensional and multiperspectival nature of Zen dialogical encounters and Dōgen's hermeneutic method of commentary. The question then becomes one of clarifying the contrast between the multidimensionality of language functioning in the positive, illuminative sense of living words and the deluded, deficient use of dead words which "master trivia and lose sight of the essential."[53]

One way of establishing a transition from a psychological-paradoxical approach to kōans that sees language as an obstacle to a tropological-parallactic approach that sees language as a vehicle is to critically examine a philosophical explanation of paradox presented by Chung-ying Cheng. Cheng argues that paradoxicality is the key to the efficacy in the way language is used in Zen discourse as a philosophical mode of attaining and expressing spiritual realization. Some of the salient examples of Zen paradox include the sayings "the east mountain walks on water" and "while studying Zen mountains are no longer mountains," as well as the coexistence of "yes" and "no" in Chao-chou's responses to the question of whether the dog has Buddha-nature. However, paradox in Zen, according to Cheng, is not only based on the conjunction of two contradictory ideas or phrases, such as affirmation and negation in the second and third examples, but reflects the relation of an utterance to a broader and more basic discursive

context. Paradox refers to an even more fundamental incongruity between
the semantic or surface structure of the actual words used in the dialogues
and the deep ontological structure conveyed by the implications and
connotations that are beyond and yet embedded within the verbal dimension. Cheng argues that paradox

> is intended to have the force to bring out a deeper meaningful-
> ness for the Zen question or the Zen statement without changing
> or rejecting the surface form of the semantic structure or state-
> ment . . . [and this] can be regarded as a dialectical process for
> revealing a very deep ontological structure by means of or in
> virtue of the incongruity of the surface semantic structure of the
> paradoxes in reference to a standard framework of reference.[54]

An example of deep ontological paradoxicality is MMK case no. 37 (and
MS no. 119), cited above, in which Chao-chou responds with the phrase
"The oak tree in the garden" to a monk's query, "What is the meaning of
Bodhidharma's coming from the west?" In this instance, the paradox exists
only in the *dialogic relation between question and answer* even though the
question in and of itself and the answer in and of itself do not contain
paradoxes. The answer could be considered very straightforward, and not
at all paradoxical or quixotic, if it were provided in the context of a different
kind of inquiry. Another example illustrating this point is the entire saying
attributed to Ching-ying Hung-hsin, "Before studying Zen mountains are
mountains, while studying Zen mountains are no longer mountains, and
after completing the study of Zen mountains are mountains." In this case,
the concluding assertion that mountains are mountains is anything but
paradoxical if taken out of the context of the preceding lines. Decontextualized, "mountains are mountains," like "oak tree in the garden," is not
enigmatic but is striking because it is such a straightforward, simplistic
assertion. But in the context of the whole saying, the third line, in addition
to the second line, becomes highly paradoxical.

Cheng further argues that there is a double level of meaning of the
kōan's function: one for the unenlightened who are in the process of
seeking *nirvāṇa*, and the other for the enlightened who have already
attained it. Rather than distinguishing between two levels of selfhood, such
as conscious and unconscious as in psychological models of interpretation,
he makes a distinction between two levels of understanding. According to
Cheng, the puzzles and paradoxes of Zen dialogic exchanges achieve a
liberation from ontic commitment on the basis of the freedom of the deep

ontological structure of emptiness and nonattachment. They are instructive for those who remain fixated and thus need to receive but can only partially understand the message of ontological freedom. Upon the attainment of enlightenment, however, the paradoxicality of the kōans disappears for those who knowledgeably express them, because "Zen paradoxes are paradoxical to those who are not enlightened in Zen. Once a person has Enlightenment, the paradoxes are no longer paradoxical to him even though they remain the same in their linguistic appearance."[55] Thus, while stressing paradoxicality Cheng's conclusions seem to concur with Isshū Miura and Ruth Fuller Sasaki, who argue that the kōan is not "ever a paradoxical statement except to those who view it from outside. When the kōan is resolved it is realized to be a simple and clear statement made from the state of consciousness which it has helped to awaken."[56]

Cheng's emphasis on paradox captures to a large extent the meaning and function of the *watō* method, which calls attention to the inner contradiction of all forms of speech, and it thereby deepens the psychological view that kōans lead to the great doubt-block. But the main strength of his approach is his analysis of how enigmatic language—in the sense that "the more enigmatic the form of expression, the more effective the discourse"— is used efficaciously in the dialogues. This stands in contrast to other interpretations that seem to overemphasize the importance of wordlessness based on a conflation of iconoclasm and irreverence with the necessity for ineffability and silence. However, there appear to be several problems in Cheng's methodology that point to the need for a more flexible and comprehensive analysis of the philosophy of language in the Zen dialogues. One problem concerns his distinction between two levels of understanding. The first level of paradoxicality, depicted as the unenlightened pursuit of liberation, seems appropriate for evaluating the iconoclastic view as reflected by the MMK warning that any interpretation of Chao-chou's Mu is "like having bolted a red hot iron ball. You try to vomit it but cannot."[57] In the *watō* tradition, however, the aim of kōan practice is not to solve the paradox but to realize the hopelessness of any attempt to find solutions. It seems that much of the kōan's effectiveness rests on its defiance of common or refined logical sense. Thus, the idea of the second level that Cheng and others suggest, that for the enlightened the kōan is a "simple and clear statement," may be self-contradictory for his methodology, unfaithful to the *watō* approach, and yet not able to capture fully Dōgen's hermeneutic view either. For example, this second level may work for interpreting "mountains are mountains" and "the oak tree in the garden," but it would not be effective in interpreting "the east mountain walks on water," which is neither simple nor clear. Furthermore, Cheng's distinction between two levels of understanding (the unenlightened and enlightened) points to a more fundamental problem concerning his notion of paradoxicality, which again rests on a distinction between the semantic content of words and phrases and the ontological structure or background frame of reference. One aspect of this problem is that the tendency to dichotomize may be at odds with the emphasis in Zen discourse on holism and nonduality. For example, in his commentary in the KS "Sansuikyō" fascicle on the "mountains are mountains" saying, Dōgen characteristically ascribes enlightened status to the standpoints expressed in all three lines, including the first, thereby overcoming any opposition between enlightened and unenlightened, or consciousness and unconsciousness. But the key issue for Cheng's approach is that the discourse in the dialogues is even more complex than the incongruous juxtaposition of two levels or two structures (or three stages in the psychological view), and probably contains multiple levels of meaning functioning in simultaneous and overlapping fashion.

Rather ironically it is Suzuki, the leader of the psychological approach to paradoxicality, who points the way out of the problems in Cheng's method. In a passage cited in Chapter 2 that marks somewhat of a departure from his psychotherapeutic interpretation, Suzuki argues that on the higher or transcendental level of awareness, the understanding is not simple and clear for language "becomes warped and assumes all kinds of crookedness: oxymora, paradoxes, contradictions, contortions, absurdities, oddities, ambiguities, and irrationalities." Suzuki's comment indicates that paradox, or semantic-ontological incongruity, is but one aspect of a multifunctional discourse that encompasses various kinds of expression on the boundary between words and wordlessness. These include brevity, reticence, withholding information, pauses, ambivalence, backtracking, and repetition, many of which contribute to the narrative quality in the chronicles, in addition to disturbing questions, such as rhetorical questions, inconsequential or vague and unanswerable questions, and questions that cut off answers or cannot be answered, as well as inconclusive, deliberately naive, or absurd answers. All of these examples can be grouped under the category of the trope of irony in that they function as modes of negation designed to undermine an attachment to literal or metaphorical forms of expression. Zen paradoxes and ironies are somewhat parallel in function to the Buddha's silence or to Mādhyamika dialectical negation.

But Zen dialogues and sayings also extensively use other kinds of tropes expressing an emphatic or affirmative standpoint involving tautology, redundancy, and simple descriptions as well as elaborate symbolism and rhetoric. For instance, the sayings "mountains are mountains" and "the white bird by the silver vase under moonlight"—which perhaps originate in a paradoxical context but also can be subsequently decontextualized— are unique descriptive expressions with tautological overtones conveying the richness of natural simplicity. The "oak tree in the garden" is another kind of literal utterance that functions as a metaphor for enlightenment, and the old woman's punning in Te-shan's "rice cake" anecdote is an example of metonymic wordplay. These examples are not paradoxical, and they defy being grouped into one category of meaning. Furthermore, Chao-chou's *Mu* seems to function either as irony or as synechdoche depending on whether it is taken to mean "no" in the sense of negation or "nothingness" in the sense of the universality of Buddha-nature.

Therefore, rather than focus on the paradoxical, it may be more appropriate to emphasize the parallactical nature of Zen discourse in which various contexts are seen differently as perspectives are undermined, displaced, shifted, or reinvested with meaning. In parallactical discourse there is a continuing process of displacement of tropical perspectives by other tropical perspectives, or a deliberately extended shifting of the modes of signification as soon as they appear to be hardened in order to uproot hypostatizations and confound expectations.[58] According to Cleary, "Certain features of authentic Chan commentary, such as overturning previous formulations, switching points of view, alternating support and opposition . . . are reflections of the diagnosis and treatment of sclerotic tendencies in the transmission of Chan lore . . . [W]hen the external vehicles of the expression of the teaching—such as symbols and terminology—become routinized or dogmatized and lose their original impact."[59] A tropological analysis of the dialogues helps locate Zen as a decentric or pedagogically flexible and provisional discourse without reference to a particular standpoint or truth in which the movement between tropes, rather than the end of or the contradictions within language, is crucial to the dynamics of liberation. A prominent example of expressions that are multivalent and self-corrective, and constantly aimed at overturning stagnant perspectives, occurs in a Ma-tsu dialogue concerning his former disciple, Ta-mei, who had been trained in Ma-tsu's early view that "this very mind itself is buddha." Ta-mei then learned that his master had changed his view, because too many followers were growing blindly attached to it as a naive affirmation, to the negation "neither mind nor buddha." Hearing the new expression, Ta-mei declares that he will stick to the original view and leave Ma-tsu to promote the change. When informed of this, Ma-tsu remarks, "The plum is ripe," a pun on the disciple's name that literally means "big plum." Ma-tsu's pun represents a metonymy in drawing out through word-play an accidental association between name and enlightened state of mind: authentic awareness can be symbolically disclosed through particular, seemingly arbitrary, verbal connections. The master praises his disciple for criticizing the teacher, but if Ta-mei "had been shaken by the new teaching and adopted it blindly simply because the master had changed his teaching, Ma-tsu would have said that the plum was far from ripe."[60]

In Zen discourse if literalness, as in the first saying "mountains are mountains," is at the root of a disciple's problematic understanding then it must be offset by the figure of speech appropriate in that context for overturning this problem, such as irony as in "mountains are not mountains." One of the main instances of this use of irony occurs in HR case no. 18, cited above, in which Hui-chung in responding to a question tells Emperor Su Tsung that after he dies he will need a "seamless monument." When the emperor takes this answer literally and asks what the monument will look like, Hui-chung's lengthy silence undermines the attachment to the literal. But if the negative implications of irony become self-limiting, then it is certainly possible and perhaps preferable for literalness to be evoked again, on a new, revised level, to function as the necessary corrective, as in the final "mountains are mountains." Many Zen sayings that appear primarily paradoxical are really concerned with pointing out that all possibilities for expression and nonexpression have a context for which they are suitable. Everything and therefore nothing is problematic, so any trope can be utilized effectively in dialogue as long as there is no fixation or dependency on it. The key to the successful use of tropical expressions seems to derive from the *effortless*—nonreliant, provisional, flexible, and self-undermining—quality in the questions and answers in the sense that the rhetoric is not contrived or forced but is a direct and immediate though at times still enigmatic effusion of an awakened mind.

Applying Tropology

Zen dialogues seem to specialize in evoking irony by exploiting the opacity, elusiveness, and enigmatic quality of language through omission, ambiguity, oxymoron, paradox, and reticence, as in the oft-repeated paradoxical refrain, "Explain the Dharma without speaking and without remaining silent, or by using neither words nor no-words."[61] In Biblical religion, *nomen* (naming) is the basis of *numen* (sacrality), but for Zen *numen* is often the absence, negation, or withholding of *nomen*. However, Zen discourse also displays the flexibility to return from the depths of irony to a seemingly simple "surface" affirmation of the concrete particulars of everyday reality, as in "oak tree in the garden."[62] For example, Nishitani stresses the importance of letting the thing (*koto*) speak for itself, as in his emphasis on Bashō's verse "From the pine tree learn (the *koto*) of the pine tree/And from the bamboo (the *koto*) of the bamboo."[63] Between the surface affirmations and descriptions on the one hand and examples of negation and silence on the other hand there are also many examples of metaphors and other figures of speech. For instance, Zen dialogues often use expressions that are deliberately nonsensical or absurd, such as Chao-chou's putting his shoes on his head when told how Nan-ch'üan cut in half a cat that two sets of monks were fighting over. But the case in which Chao-chou's tells a monk who is overly eager to attain enlightenment to "wash his bowls" after breakfast (MMK case no. 7, MS no. 67) is more complex because the command appears to be absurd in the context of the dialogue and yet is very concrete and pragmatic when decontextualized. Parallactic shifting also helps explain two key aspects of Zen discourse, subitization and humor, which are very much related. The frequently drastic, uncompromising movement between tropes creates the conceptual atmosphere for the suddenness of awakening that is often triggered by a humourous response, which is due to radical shifts in perspectives that undercut expectations by giving literal responses to figurative queries or vice versa.[64] Therefore, to depict Zen discourse only in terms of irony and silence, or in terms of any single rhetorical structure, is one-sided and misleading. Rather, Zen surface affirmations, absurd utterances, and ironic negations display "a boundless openness devoid of all fixed metaphysical centers . . . [with] a radically disruptive freeplay of textual signifiers."[65]

One way of explaining the diversity as well as the self-corrective outlook in Zen dialogues is to refer to the analysis of the tropics of discourse in Western literary criticism and intellectual history. The analysis of the tropes has been a central focus for a wide range of critics beginning with Giambattista Vico and Benedetto Croce and including in recent times Stephen Ullman, Roman Jakobsen, Paul de Man, Umberto Eco, and Hayden White, among others. Nearly all theorists deal with the four master

tropes: metaphor, metonymy, synechdoche, and irony. The debates primarily concern defining the relation between the four tropes: which of the
tropes has priority as the key to understanding rhetorical language, and
what is the underlying connection, whether logical, sequential, or otherwise, between all four? Despite the existence of four tropes, most of the
discussions have revolved around the contrasts between pairs of concepts:
the literal and figurative, metaphor and metonymy, and the metaphorical
and ironic. First, the four tropes as figures of speech are generally contrasted
with literal speech, or the mimetic verbal representation of objects. Literal
or mimetic speech seeks to be verifiably and objectively faithful to phenomena and to present things as they are without distortion, whereas the
figures of speech, despite differences between them, are fundamentally the
same in that they knowingly alter or modify external reality for the sake of
presenting a rational argument, emotional impression, or poetic imagery.
However, from the Zen standpoint, as expressed by "mountains are mountains" and "carrying water and chopping wood is the Tao" in addition to
other sayings, it is also crucial to include in the discussion another level of
expression which can be referred to as the "transmimetic." The transmimetic trope includes Zen surface affirmations and descriptions which
appear to be examples of mimesis but are imbued with a profundity and
richness of implication that qualifies them as examples of a fifth trope.
These expressions deliberately try to mimic mimetic expressions, but they
are really located at the other end of the rhetorical spectrum and can only
be appreciated if understood in relation to migrating through the other four
tropes. Transmimetic expressions convey the suchness (Skt. *tathātā, nyo-
nyo*) or as-it-isness of reality, free of reference to subjective consciousness
that might appear to taint the unencumbered moment of perception, and
they closely resemble the Japanese poetic ideal of profound mystery (*yūgen*)
conveyed through the suggestive overtones of meaning (*yojō*) stemming
from an awakened, transcendental awareness.

The second contrast that is often discussed in analyses of tropology
concerns the debate about whether metaphor or metonymy is the essential
trope or the main rhetorical category that is the basis of the other figures
of speech. Ullman and Jakobsen support metaphors, which are based on
portraying similarities between objects of experience and thus have a true
originality and expressive power. These critics consider metonymies, which
are based on accidental associations, to be interesting only to the extent
that in their being derivative of metaphors they often approximate a
metaphorical function. However, de Man and Eco reverse this under-

standing, and they consider metonymy to be the basis of the metaphor's figurality that "can be traced back to a subjacent chain of metonymic connexions which constitute the framework of the code and upon which is based the constitution of any semantic field, whether partial or (in theory) global."[66] For these critics, metonymy generates a comprehensive and creative network of verbal associations on which metaphors depend and derive, so that the second trope is the authentic basis of the first.

In the debate as explained thus far, there has not been much reference to the other two tropes, synechdoche and irony, for by implication they are dependent on the main trope, whether it is metaphor or metonymy. To take all four tropes more fully into account, White reframes the issue as a contrast not between two tropes, but between the first three of the tropes—metaphor, metonymy, synecdoche—which establish identity through comparison and association, and the fourth trope—irony—which calls into question and undercuts any fixation with the analogies contrived therein. White describes the "plot" of the dynamic movement of discourse in terms of what he calls the erratic "diatactical" shifting—rather than the logical dialectical progression—between tropes as follows:

> The archetypal plot of discursive formations appears to require that the narrative 'I' of the discourse move from an original metaphorical characterization of a domain of experience, through metonymic deconstructions of its elements, to synecdochic representations of the relations between its superficial attributes and its presumed essence, to, finally, a representation of whatever contrast or oppositions can legitimately be discerned in the totalities identified in the third phase of discursive representations.[67]

White points out that metaphor discloses similarities in differences, and that both metonymy and synechdoche reveal similarity in terms of the relation between whole and parts: metonymy reflects the whole in all its parts, and synechdoche does the reverse, moving from particularity to wholeness. Irony, on the other hand, reflects a self-critical perspective undermining the associations in the first three tropes. White refers to the discursive process as an archetypal plot because he argues that history is a narrative emplotment with an underlying element of interpretation projected onto the "objective" source material. He analyzes how Vico and Croce directly, and Foucault indirectly, characterize major historical trends as tropical shifts, such as the development of human and natural sciences

or the transition from aristocratic to democratic government in the seven-
teenth through nineteenth centuries.

Although White's emphasis on the priority of irony, as well as on the
sequence for realizing it, seems to be applicable to the *watō* method, it is
not appropriate for understanding Dōgen's decentric, nonhierarchical view
of tropes. On the other hand, White's interpretation of metonymy is particularly significant for understanding Dōgen's standpoint because of the way
the second trope successfully straddles the border between the metaphorical, in suggesting similarities, and the ironic, since it is also deconstructive
of metaphorical characterizations. To take this point a step further, seen in
light of Dōgen's emphasis on polysemous wordplay as well as the Eco/de
Man analysis of tropology, White's thesis about the contrast between the
metaphorical quality of the first three tropes and the undercutting agency
of irony could perhaps be restated. This would now refer to a contrast
between metaphor, which asserts the validity of associations, and the
metonymic quality of the last three tropes, which are all involved in undercutting and yet also in reexploring and rewriting from varying angles the
metaphorical associations that any of the other tropes seems to be making.

One way of assessing the significance of White's approach for illuminating the role of tropes in Zen discourse is to consider an extraordinary
parallel between his view of "diatactical" movement and Bodhidharma's
dialogue with four disciples who are vying to become the anointed Dharma-
heir, which was discussed in Chapter 1 in connection to the notion of *kattō*
as a prime illustration of Dōgen's critique of the conventional view of
kōans. The movement between tropes is played out in the original dialogue
very close to the way White describes it as Bodhidharma asks his disciples
to display their knowledge by succinctly summing up the essence of the
Dharma. The first disciple says, "Neither cling to words and letters, nor
abandon them altogether, but use them as an instrument of the Tao." This
answer suggests an understanding of the metaphoric or instrumental quality of language, as when Buddhism compares the Buddha-nature to the sun
or moon light, to an ocean and its waves, or to the roots and branches of a
tree. Bodhidharma responds to the disciple, "You express my skin,"[68] which
implies that metaphorical analogy, though valuable as a pedagogical tool,
reflects a relatively superficial level of insight. Or as Ma-tsu answers when
asked why he asserts "mind itself is buddha," "It is in order to stop the baby's
crying."[69]

However, the second disciple's answer, which expresses Bodhidharma's "flesh," is more profound: "It is like Ananda's viewing the Buddha-land

of Akshobhya, seeing it once and never seeing it again." This represents a metonymic or indirect, contiguous association of the Buddha-land and the unmentioned Dharma that at once reinforces and begins to undercut the role of metaphor by the final phrase suggesting the fleetingness of the analogy.[70] Zen dialogues frequently rely upon metonymy through wordplay, punning, and homophones to cut off an attachment to metaphorical comparison based on resemblance. For instance, in MMK case no. 41 Bodhidharma makes a liberating wordplay when he tells the struggling and restless Hui-k'o, who is thus made to realize that he cannot literally bring forth his mind to be pacified, "I have thoroughly set it at rest." Then, the third disciple indicates another level of identity beyond metaphor by saying, "The four elements are emptiness, and the five *skandhas* are non-being. But in my view, there is not a single dharma to be expressed." This synecdochic equalization of the elements and *skandhas* as microcosm with ultimate reality or macrocosm, or of the parts with the whole, which expresses the first patriarch's "bones," is especially emphasized in Hua-yen and T'ien-t'ai holistic doctrines such as "three thousand [dharma-realms] in a single thought" (*ichinen sanzen*). But when the fourth disciple, Hui-k'o, simply bows reverently without even opening his mouth—an ironic undermining of the limitations and contradictions in the first three answers—Bodhidharma's approval is indicated by "You express my marrow."

In the KS "Kattō" and "Ōsakusendaba" fascicles based to a large extent on a Chao-chou dialogue concerning the Bodhidharma anecdote, Dōgen strongly criticizes the conventional view of the kōan which emphasizes that silence is the deepest level of understanding beyond language. Dōgen's interpretation can also be considered a critique of White's approach, if White's view of the tropes is associated with each of Bodhidharma's disciples, by demonstrating the priority of a parallactic rather than diatactical movement between tropes based on the priority of metonymy instead of irony. Yanagida has traced the historical and ideological background underlying Dōgen's criticisms, which are largely connected to the differing roles of T'ien-t'ai/Tendai thought in China and Japan.[71] In China, Zen discourse on the priority of silence was somewhat influenced by Buddhist esotericism and was also a reaction against—that was in turn criticized by—the T'ien-t'ai emphasis on scriptural exegesis. In Japan, however, where Dōgen and other Kamakura thinkers were initially trained in Tendai *hongaku* thought which had already absorbed much of the esoteric traditions, silence was seen as a problematic standpoint connected with the non-Buddhist monistic principle Dōgen refers to as the Senika heresy.[72] Dōgen was positively influenced by Tendai methods of manipulating verbal expressions to draw out their underlying philosophical significance, and while in China he was probably also sympathetic to T'ien-t'ai refutations of Zen polemics.

Dōgen's interpretation of the Bodhidharma dialogue is based on four main points. First, he maintains that all of the disciples, not the fourth or any other single one, have completely and simultaneously expressed and realized Bodhidharma's expression, so that "All four disciples heard and realized [skin, flesh, bones, marrow] all at once . . . [as] a complete manifestation without partiality." Second, because each of the disciple's answers as well as each of Bodhidharma's responses are the selfsame, there can be no sense of hierarchy or sequence separating them, nor any distinction whatsoever between superficiality and depth. To defeat the notion that the first disciple who expresses the skin is more superficial and inferior to the profound, superior fourth disciple who expresses the marrow, Dōgen cites Chao-chou's assertion (in the *Jōshū Roku*) that "The old teacher has no reliance (*furyū*) on marrow." Chao-chou chides his disciple, who is fixated with marrow alone as the deepest level, for "slandering Hui-k'o." He points out that marrow and skin are inseparable, so that one cannot be expressed without the other, and if the disciple speaks only about marrow it is clear that he has not even realized the skin. Dōgen also explains the equalization and interchangeability of the four responses (and by application of the four tropes) by relating the Bodhidharma dialogue to a legend originally found in the *Mahābhārata* and also cited in the HR (case no. 92) of the king of a land called Saindhava who asks his retainers for four items, all of which came to be known as "saindhava" (J. *sendaba*): salt, a chalice, water, and a horse. Dōgen cites Hsüeh-tou's comment (which is not included in the HR chapter), "When salt is requested, I will offer a horse." He further maintains that "When Bodhidharma requested saindhava, his four disciples offered him a horse, salt, water, and a chalice. We must study why it was that when a horse, salt, water, and a chalice were requested as saindhava, [any one of] the disciples [may have] offered [only] a horse or [only] water."[73]

Extending from the "Ōsakusendaba" passage, Dōgen's third point pertains to the pedagogical significance and relativity of each response. Since all the expressions are "fundamentally the selfsame expression," each one is correct for each of the four disciples in question and furthermore the possibilities are limitless. If there had been six disciples, Bodhidharma would have spontaneously made additional responses, for example, by telling his disciples that they express his "eyeball" or "body." And if there were hundreds or thousands of disciples, each one with his own unique expression would have found a suitable response from the first patriarch. The fourth point in Dōgen's interpretation refers to the interpenetration of each and every answer and response, which are equally all-pervasive and are permeating the entire being of master and disciples, speaker and listener, as well as writer and reader. "You should realize," he maintains, "that when you express me, then I express you, expression expresses both me and you, and expression expresses both you and me."[74] Furthermore, there is a profound sense of mutuality between questioner and respondant so that each of the latter's expressions is fully compatible and conducive to the former's own spiritual path, just as the retainer knows which saindhava to bring the king, who, for his part, has already requested the saindhava appropriate for the retainer to bring.

Based on the interpenetration of all forms of tropical discourse, Dōgen emphasizes that the inherent polysemy of language overflowing with multiple meanings is the vehicle for the liberating function of *kattō* as disentangling entanglements or the self-unraveling complications of language. In contrast to White, Dōgen sees the tropes not as sequentially related, even in the erratic diatactical sense, but as interchangeable rhetorical modes without any sense of progression or teleological implication. The trope of metonymy operates as the fulcrum enabling continual parallactic shifting because it encompasses the back-and-forth movement from metaphor to irony, from wordplay to deconstruction, and from part to whole. It is helpful to note here that the compound term *hiniku*, which literally means "skin-flesh" (and by implication metaphor-metonymy) in the Bodhidharma kōan's first two responses, has come to mean "irony" in modern Japanese. From Dōgen's standpoint, metonymy is the fundamental trope because of its simultaneously synthetic and deconstructivist capability, encompassing the full range and mutuality of tropes extending from metaphor through irony.

The merits of a decentric, parallactic view of tropological interpretation can further be demonstrated by considering three dialogues that deal with the topic of "mind" (*shin* or *kokoro*). In Mahayana Buddhism, as Dōgen stresses in the KS "Sokushin-zebutsu" fascicle, the concept of mind is inherently paradoxical because it can suggest either the state of deluded, defiled individual mentality or the universal, all-embracing reality beyond yet realized through the distinctions of subject and object, human and natural. Zen discussions about mind are often related to the notion of "no-mind" (*mu-shin*), and Ma-tsu is said to have paradoxically proclaimed that "mind is buddha" (an affirmative stance in MMK case no. 30) and that there is "no mind, no buddha" (an ironic negation in case no. 33). In the first dialogue also cited above, Bodhidharma tells his disciple Hui-k'o, who in another dialogue has already cut off his arm as a show of determination and resolve but who in this anecdote remains unable to pacify his disturbed mind, to bring him the mind so it can be put at rest. Hui-k'o replies, "I have searched for the mind, and it is finally ungraspable (*fukatoku*)"—"ungraspable," the term highlighted in the *Diamond Sūtra* that is also used in the Te-shan rice cake dialogue, is an unwitting wordplay in this dialogue. Bodhidharma seizes upon the response as an indication that his efforts at pacification have been successful, and he responds, "I have thoroughly set [the mind] at rest for you."[75] In another MMK dialogue (no. 29, MS no. 146), Hui-neng tells two monks who are arguing while watching a flag blowing in the breeze whether it is the flag or the wind that is actually moving: "'It is neither the wind nor the flag that is moving. It is your mind that is moving.' The monks were struck with awe."[76] In a third dialogue, a monk, who dogmatically maintains upon questioning that a stone must be contained in his mind since from the Buddhist viewpoint everything is an objectification of mind, is told "your head must feel very heavy in carrying a stone like that in your mind."[77]

There is a paradox operating in each of the dialogues based on a contradiction between the literal and figurative, physical and mental, material and spiritual, or real and ideal levels of understanding. In the Bodhidharma dialogue, for example, Hui-k'o's awakening occurs when he exhausts his search for his mind understood as if it were a literal object and he realizes the metaphorical basis of the term "mind." Furthermore, there are paradoxes in the relationships among the dialogues. For instance, while the Hui-neng dialogue has an idealistic implication in suggesting that there is no world of objects apart from mind, the first and third dialogues represent a corrective to this view by disclosing the problems inherent in viewing the mind either as a unity containing all of the objects of this world or as an entity that is explicitly identified with one particular object. However, an exclusively paradoxical interpretation, though preferable to an emphasis on ineffability, is reductionistic. It sees the dialogues functioning in a uniform way and thus does not sufficiently explain their far-reaching, multiple implications. Paradox is a particular kind of expression that is relative to the parallactic shifting and displacement of tropes based on a self-deconstructing, self-correcting pedagogical provisionality.

In the Bodhidharma dialogue, the term mind functions as a metaphor for the disciple's restless and disturbed "state of mind," which gets liberated through a metonymic displacement. That is, the mind becomes free when the metaphor is displaced as metaphor and is replaced by metonymy, which straddles the fence between metaphor and irony. This occurs not so much in terms of the paradox of not finding the mind, but through a semiotic shift to metonymy tinged with irony that undercuts an attachment to the metaphor taken literally. This discloses to the disciple an understanding of the polysemous implications of the term *fu* (non or un) in *fu-katoku* (ungraspable), which has many of the same levels of meaning as *Mu* in the Chao-chou "Does the dog have Buddha-nature?" dialogue: it can mean no as absence or nonexistence, or suggest the nonreferentiality of the question, or convey ontological nothingness. In the Hui-neng dialogue, however, mind functions as a synechdoche reflecting totality in order to overcome the debate concerning the movement of the flag that is operating on the level of metaphor. The basis of this dialogue is to demonstrate a profound coincidence between the mind as a synechdochic sign and the totality as signified. But in the third dialogue, that kind of synechdoche is undercut by a metonymy now related to the metaphorical sense, which at once plays off of and partially contradicts the idealistic implications in the Hui-neng anecdote.

Dōgen's commentary on the Hui-neng dialogue in the KS "Immo" fascicle highlights the crucial role of tropical hermeneutics in the discourse of Zen dialogues. He first expands the scope of the synechdoche by writing that if "your mind is moving," then it must be the case that "*you* are moving," that is, the entire person, and not just the mind if understood in the sense of intellect or mentality. Then Dōgen both justifies and undermines the enhanced synechdoche through a transmimetic, tautological expression: "because 'movement is moving,' 'you are you.'" Dōgen reinforces the function of transmimesis when he comments on a related source dialogue concerning the sound of a ringing bell that there is the "ringing of the breeze, the ringing of the bell, the ringing of the air, and the *ringing of the ringing*."[78] The result of the multiple levels of sound is not cacophony, but the "unsurpassable storehouse of the true Dharma-eye (*shōbōgenzō*), supreme quiescence, nonaction, or *samādhi*." Furthermore, Dōgen's commentary also implies the ironical view that "no one is moving."

Another example of tropological methodology is found by considering again Dōgen's interpretation of a dialogue he frequently cites in which Ma-tsu, while practicing zazen, discusses the role of meditation with his master, Nan-yüeh. Both the source dialogue and Dōgen's commentary revolve around the reference to a mirror as a metaphor for the enlightened mind, and both seek to subvert and overthrow the metaphor when it is taken too literally, but they do this for different purposes and with nearly opposite conclusions. In the source dialogue Nan-yüeh uses the metaphor of polishing a tile to create a mirror to show the futility in his disciple Ma-tsu's practicing of zazen in order to become a buddha. This dialogue appears paradoxical because it highlights the contradiction between practice and attainment. From a tropological standpoint, however, Nan-yüeh's strategy is to play off the mirror-as-original enlightenment metaphor by metonymically displacing it with the irony of polishing the tile. This recalls Hui-neng's transmission *gāthā* in which he denies the image of a mirror that represents primordial wisdom and needs to be wiped free of secular dust. Nan-yüeh's shifting of tropes highlights his view of religious practice. Just as a tile is not likely to yield a mirror no matter how much effort one applies, zazen will not result in creating a mirror—the displaced, initial metaphor—symbolic of enlightenment because original mirror-enlightenment must already be present without needing cultivation or training to realize it. In his commentaries on the dialogue in the KS "Kokyō" and "Zazenshin" fascicles, Dōgen subverts the original subversion through a tropical hermeneutics that can be referred to as "atomization"[79] because it zeroes in on and then develops and rhetorically refines the smallest verbal units in the dialogue. His argument is based on the assertion that polishing a tile does make a mirror. This may be considered a realistic application of metaphor in that some tiles will have a reflective surface after being polished or a nonsensical, ironic twist on Nan-yüeh's irony that further decenters a metaphor that has been introduced into the discourse for subversive purposes. Dōgen also creates a metonymic displacement by building up a series of transmimetic expressions—"Ma-tsu becomes Ma-tsu" and "zazen becomes zazen"—in order to use the dialogue to legitmate his view of zazen as the method of "practice in realization" (*shōjō no shu*) and thereby refute a Ta-hui *kanna-zen* interpretation.

Dōgen's KS Text in Comparison with *Kōan-roku* Texts

Tropological methodology functions on two levels. In addition to helping analyze the rhetorical structure of the dialogues, it can also support genre criticism by highlighting the different literary approaches in each genre with the Ur-genre of the *kien-mondō* serving as an open-ended template of

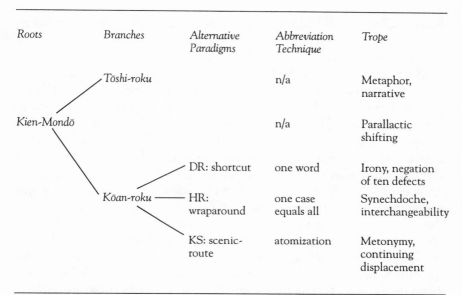

Roots	Branches	Alternative Paradigms	Abbreviation Technique	Trope
	Tōshi-roku		n/a	Metaphor, narrative
Kien-Mondō			n/a	Parallactic shifting
		DR: shortcut	one word	Irony, negation of ten defects
	Kōan-roku	HR: wraparound	one case equals all	Synechdoche, interchangeability
		KS: scenic-route	atomization	Metonymy, continuing displacement

Figure 4.7. *Role of Abbreviation. This figure builds on figures 4.4 and 4.5 by showing the role of tropical discourse and abbreviated expression in the various genres and alternative paradigms of the* kōan-roku *category in relation to the parallactic shifting generated in the source dialogues.*

parallactic shifting. As indicated in Figure 4.7, the *tōshi-roku* narratives stress the role of metaphor, which fosters the projection of an idealized sense of correspondence between historical events and the heroic, transmissional motifs of the patriarchs. The *kōan-roku* category texts, which stress philosophical ideas over narrative, still rely on the chronicles' view of history though not in a literal or even allegorical sense but as the allusive semiotic background for understanding demythical utterances. While these texts may use the mythical historical accounts if it suits their antitextual aims, all express an indirect, ironic edge associated with one of the other three tropes that undermines an attachment to direct correspondence.

The key to discerning the tropological orientation in the alternative paradigms in the *kōan-roku* category is the self-liberating role of abbreviated expression. A feature that is shared by the KS and the kōan collections, though they would appear to accuse each other of perpetrating the problems, is their emphasis on admonishing disciples against the traps and pitfalls of misinterpreting kōans through a faulty appropriation of ineffability leading to either too much or too little interpretive language. Abbreviation as used in the *kōan-roku* texts zeroes in on the essential linguistic unit as "a poison to counteract poison" in order to master language: (1) for Ta-hui the *watō* method absolutizes abbreviation in order to overcome the ten defects of conceptualization or intellectual errors; (2) in the HR the penetration of a single kōan is considered to be identical with breaking through all kōans; (3) and for Dōgen atomization glosses particular words and phrases that disclose the undivided truth. From a tropological perspective, for Ta-hui the truth is ironically found in no kōans, for the HR any kōan can function as a synechdoche for all others, and for Dōgen the uniqueness of each and every part of the kōan has a metonymic quality expressing yet subverting totality. Thus the KS and the HR share an holistic rhetorical perspective that stands in contrast to the DR, but the HR and DR ultimately agree on ineffability and silence that contrasts with the KS's emphasis on polysemy. It should also be stressed that these three are not the only possibilities or branches to derive from the roots or dialogues. For example the later Kamakura era Japanese master, Daitō Kokushi, emphasized the role of capping phrases (*jakugo*), which when "applied to live situations as well as written texts . . . is supposed to be able to make a comment, resolve a specific conundrum, convey a Zen insight, transform another's awareness, resonate like a line of poetry, or perform several of these functions simultaneously."[80] In Daitō's commentaries on the HR and other sources, there are several varieties of capping phrases including the use of a single word, playful words, incomplete sayings, and deliberately contradictory or confusing sayings. Unlike Ta-hui, however, Daitō does not absolutize abbreviation, but develops a notion of the interaction of complex, intensive commentary and brevity; for example, he constructs a list of twenty capping phrases ranging from a single sentence with a single capping phrase to two separate dialogues involving two different masters containing several capping phrases embedded within them.

The KS and the HR Texts

Despite obvious and important differences in the literary structures and philosophical aims of the texts, as well as the fact that they do not often cite the same paradigmatic cases, Dōgen's KS is thematically and stylistically remarkably similar to the HR. The following depiction of the HR text (in contrasting it with the SH's "warmer and more subtle" style) would seem to apply to the KS as well: "[it creates] Dharma combat—challenging, dynamic, full of put-downs and penetrating insightful wit."[81] In fact, although further studies of the KS in relation to Sung *kōan-roku* texts need to be carried out, it seems that the HR is perhaps the one text in all of Buddhism that comes closest to Dōgen's text. The symbolism of the IH legend is quite significant in highlighting this relationship. Just as the MS is a bridge between the KS and the Sung genres based on intertextuality, from the opposite direction the HR is one of the main links between the kōan tradition and Dōgen because of a shared focus on the method of interlinear commentary known as "turning upside down" to disclose a multiperspectival viewpoint, such as using "surface or forward words" (*omote no go*) which comment from a conventional standpoint and "deep or backward words" (*ura no go*) which comment through perplexity and disturbance. The HR is the necessary piece of the puzzle in which the KS and the DR stand as opposites stemming from a single main, shared source. The differences between the texts reflect their diverging tropological orientations. Although both emphasize the unity of part and whole, the KS stresses the particularity of situational context through metonymy and polysemy whereas the HR stresses universality and timelessness through synechdoche and ineffability.

The similarities and differences between the texts can be explained with reference to some of the examples of common citations of *kosoku-kōan*. These include the KS "Ōsakusendaba" fascicle and HR case no. 92, which both deal with the case of "Mañjuśrī striking a gavel" (also cited in MS no. 141 and SH no. 1); the KS "Kokyō" and HR no. 68, which comment on San-sheng's "it is nameless from time immemorial" (also in MS no. 294, SR vol. 10, and *Wanshi Kōroku* no. 53); and the KS "Kattō" and HR no. 1, which discuss different cases attributed to Bodhidharma. The comparison of "Ōsakusendaba" and HR 92, both of which also cite kōans attributed to Chao-chou and Hsiang-yen concerning the meaning of saindhava, is especially interesting because of the striking similarity in the texts and the apparent influence of the latter on the former. The content of these texts is over fifty percent identical, so that the differences in handling common material are particularly instructive.

The main similarities in the KS and the HR seem based on the fact that both texts are responding to a sense of failure, or even counterproductivity, in the ordinary discourse of the tradition. They seek to revitalize the tradition through the process of selecting and offering detailed commentary on *kosoku-kōan* that thereby becomes identified with a highly personal and for the most part thoroughly consistent philosophical viewpoint. While both texts neither repudiate Zen mythical history nor avoid lineage polemics—for example, the KS "Kattō" begins and ends by evoking the standard Zen genealogy based on the twenty-eight patriarchs—these themes are generally suppressed in favor of philosophical cogency. However, it is important to clarify the significance of philosophical consistency or cogency in terms of how the texts try to be faithful to the ideals of demythologization and untextuality. For both, the primary aim is to support pragmatically and provisionally the religious praxis of disciples rather than to construct philosophy in an abstract intellectual sense. According to HR no. 1, the goal is "to melt the sticking points, untie the bonds, pull out the nails and draw out the pegs, to cut down brambles for people."[82] While the KS and HR rely on the dialogues as sources of authority and truth, their interlinear commentaries often involve playing off of, contradicting, or turning topsy turvy kōan cases as part of a strategy of "'presenting sideways and using upside down.' This is the practice of using a story, saying, term, or symbol in a way that departs from the obvious or the stereotyped, traditional view. This practice is exercised, according to Zen writing on the subject, to help break up the 'nest of cliche' which Zen teaching often cites as both a symptom and a cause of mental stagnation."[83] For example, both texts are known for their scathing critiques of what they consider deficient viewpoints, and they even risk committing sacrilege against the hallmark Zen tenets, as when the HR refers to the Mahākāśyapa anecdote as "the messy scene of passing the flower,"[84] or when Dōgen criticizes Hui-neng's doctrine of kenshō (seeing into [one's own-] nature) and repudiates many T'ang and Sung Zen figures. Furthermore, their ideas are expressed through multiple levels of wordplay that achieve an eloquence by combining prose and poetry rather than by logical argument. The aim of wordplay is to disclose a deep structure of consciousness that promotes the shifting and integration of multiple perspectives, or a free thematic association reflecting samadhic awareness that unifies part and whole.

The main differences between the KS and HR involve the way their literary structures reflect their understanding of the relationship between enlightenment and language. The structure of the KS is unique in a tradition that was exploding with new genres and paradigms, and it is quite distinct from the major kōan collections as well as Zen recorded sayings and transmission of the lamp histories. While the tōshi-roku genres—the lamp histories and shike-style recorded sayings—focus on the nonconceptual truth embodied by the charismatic personality of a great master who carefully initiates a chosen successor, the HR, MMK, and other compilations are centered on the traditional case still associated with one of the patriarchs that is usually extracted from an encounter dialogue in the previous works reflecting a mind-to-mind transmission; their commentaries cite other anecdotes, parables and interpretations to amplify concentration on themes established by the case. The KS, on the other hand, revolves around doctrine. Each fascicle sets up a key Mahayana or Zen notion of philosophy or practice and uses various cases and *sūtra* passages (generally overlooked by the collections which see themselves as "separate from the teachings") as sources for elaborating on the meaning and significance of the doctrine. Thus, the dialogue of the traditional case is subsidiary to Dōgen's novel and creative philosophical perspective: *it becomes illustrative rather than paradigmatic.* Also the KS, which not only cites poetry but is often composed in elegant language, integrates prose and poetry commentary more fully than the HR, which clearly separates *juko* and *nenko* styles of commentary into independent sections of each chapter of the work. Yet in addition to its poetic quality, the KS also reflects some degree of influence from Abhidharma or *śāstra* literature by way of Tendai *kanjinshaku* commentary in its use of line-by-line analysis exploring the metaphysical and psychological implications of doctrine.

The priority given to doctrinal theme in the KS is illustrated by comparing the KS "Ōsakusendaba" and HR no. 92, which focus on the same kōans. The main case in the HR chapter is the following kōan, for which Hsüeh-tou gives a *juko* commentary that mentions the notion of saindhava:

> One time when the World-honored one sat on a dais [to preach the Dharma, before uttering even a word] Mañjuśrī struck the gavel [to signal the end of the discourse] and said, "When seen clearly the teaching of the king of Dharma is just like this: this is the teaching of the king of Dharma."[85]

Dōgen also makes this kōan one of several centerpieces in the fascicle. In addition, both texts cite the same cases in which masters respond to being questioned about the meaning of saindhava: Chao-chou folds his hands silently and bows, and Hsiang-yen tells his inquiring disciple to "come over here," and then when he does so, hits him. The HR no. 92 contains the following structural elements: introduction of the case (by Yüan-wu) that evokes the universal meaning of all kōans; the citation of the main case (by Hsüeh-tou) on "Mañjuśrī's gavel"; a *nenko* commentary (by Yüan-wu) equating the kōan to other similar ones, such as Hui-chung's "seamless monument"; a juko commentary (by Hsüeh-tou) that asks, "If only one of [the monks] had realized the value of saindhava/Would Mañjuśri have needed to strike the gavel?"; and interlinear commentary (by Yüan-wu) on the *juko* that quotes a passage from the *Nirvāṇa Sūtra* explaining saindhava and that also cites the aforementioned cases of Chao-chou and Hsiang-yen.

The KS text, using many of the same kōan and commentary elements, changes their order and meaning quite significantly. The KS opens with a *gāthā* evoking the notion of *kattō* by comparing the relation of words and wordlessness to that of tangled vines and a tree. *Kattō* is never discussed directly in the main body of the fascicle, but it is alluded to again in a brief reference identifying Bodhidharma's questioning of his four disciples with the four saindhavas. The fascicle continues by quoting the same *Nirvāṇa Sūtra* passage that is cited in the HR and by commenting on the importance of understanding saindhava. This is followed by the Chao-chou kōan and the Hsüeh-tou kōan ("When salt is requested, I will offer a horse") on saindhava, along with a mention of Hung-chih's discussion (including a defense of Hung-chih's lineal pedigree) on the fundamental compatibility of the seemingly contradictory dialogues. After the allusion to Bodhi-dharma and a brief discussion of a Nan-ch'üan kōan, the KS continues with interlinear commentary on the Hsiang-yen kōan, which is followed by the Mañjuśrī kōan and the Hsüeh-tou verse from the HR that mentions saindhava plus additional commentary. Therefore, the texts are nearly identical in citing the Mañjuśrī, Chao-chou, and Hsiang-yen cases in addition to the *Nirvāṇa Sūtra*.

Yet several key differences between the texts are apparent. First, the HR comments and cites cases on saindhava rather in passing because it was briefly referred to in a *juko* on a main case that does not even mention saindhava, whereas the KS transforms saindhava into a doctrine of consid-erable significance and uses the cases to illuminate its meaning. For the KS, saindhava represents the profound mutuality and reciprocity between king and retainer symbolizing master and disciple, as well as the pedagogical interchangeability of questions and answers in accord with other doctrines such as *kattō* and *kannō dōkō*, but with its own flavor. Second, the HR does not see either the Mañjuśrī case or the saindhava cases it cites as unique or distinctive, but repeatedly equates them to other cases. The KS, on the other hand, seeks to reconcile contradictory responses to questions about the meaning of saindhava by stressing the pedagogical provisionality and continuing hermeneutics involved in the processes of making requests as well as receiving responses that philosophically elaborates on—using an interpretive method that coincides with the theme of—the four "sain-dhava." According to Dōgen, "All activity and expression throughout twenty-four hours is nothing other than *requesting* saindhava. All activity and expression throughout twenty-four hours is nothing other than *offering* saindhava."[86] Thus, the HR, by not attempting to define or explain the meaning of the cases it cites, suggests the priority of ineffability and concludes with an emphasis on enigma as an end in itself. For example, the Hsüeh-tou verse implies that Mañjuśrī used the gavel to end the lecture because there was no one in the audience who could understand saindhava. In the KS, however, the doctrine of saindhava becomes part of an argument for an erasure of the distinction between enlightened and unenlightened understanding, such that "[Mañjuśrī's] gavel is itself saindhava" for which request and offer are inseparable and interchangeable. In commenting on the Hsiang-yen dialogue, Dōgen rhetorically asks whether it was a matter of "requesting saindhava, [or of] receiving saindhava being offered."

In this KS fascicle, as with his commentaries on cases such as Ma-tsu's "tile" and "mountains are mountains," as previously discussed, Dōgen elimi-nates any distinction between or judgment concerning right and wrong, or enlightened and unenlightened interpretations. Furthermore, instead of setting up an opposition of untruth and truth represented by the dialogue taking place between a deluded disciple and enlightened master, Dōgen tries to show that the expressions of both parties if properly interpreted—for example, Hsiang-yen's disciple who is being struck as well as the teacher who is striking him—constitute the truth of the Dharma. The KS is a less "conservative" text than kōan collections like the HR in that it allows for or even demands taking license with tradition in accord with the spirit and intention of the T'ang masters' spontaneous utterances. In many instances, the highly critical tone of the KS is directed toward perfecting what could or should have been said to establish or demonstrate full enlightenment throughout the dialogues from the standpoint of *kanjin-shaku* commentary.

One of the main illustrations of how this approach contrasts with the HR concerns the following case known as San-sheng's "it is nameless" that is cited in the KS "Kokyō" and in HR no. 68:

Hsüeh-feng: Each of the monkeys bears a primordial mirror.

San-sheng: Since time immemorial it has been nameless. Why do you refer to it as a "primordial mirror"?

Hsüeh-feng: This is a flaw.

San-sheng: Why do you panic so? You do not even understand the head-word (or topic, *watō*).

Hsüeh-feng: It is my fault [for I have been busy with everyday tasks (as abbot)].[87]

The HR gives this case a brief mention, without analysis, as part of its commentary that includes biographical anecdotes on another case involving San-sheng's dialogue with his teacher, Yang-shan; that is, this case is brought up, somewhat in *tōshi-roku* historiographical/biographical style, because it is one more aspect of the legend of how San-sheng came to study with the right master. The KS, however, delves into a lengthy interpretation, or reinterpretation, of the case as one of many examples that illustrate the doctrine of the primordial mirror (*kokyō*). According to the conventional interpretation, the case supports the priority of ineffability by criticizing Hsüeh-feng, who admits that he is really to blame, for trying to name the unnameable or to label what is beyond words. San-sheng forcefully points out the inherent limitation of any use of language. But the main feature of the KS commentary is to argue that Hsüeh-feng is fully enlightened in his responses, although he probably could have answered San-sheng differently at the turning point in the middle of the dialogue. Dōgen maintains that after San-sheng's first question, "Why do you refer to it as 'primordial mirror'?", Hsüeh-feng should have answered simply but directly, "[It is] the primordial mirror, [it is] the primordial mirror!" Nevertheless, his expressions admitting that there is a "flaw" and that he is at "fault" should not be taken to indicate that he is to blame or even that a mistake has been made, for his daily temple activities transcend the dichotomy between correct and incorrect standpoints and therefore fully justify any expression he may have uttered. Hsüeh-feng and his utterances, which in this instance can be seen as sardonically self-deprecating, reflect complete enlightenment without partiality or hesitation.

Therefore, abbreviation for the HR involves the synechdochic use of one word, phrase, or kōan that "sum[s] up all spoken words into a single phrase, gathering the universe into a single atom." The HR further maintains that one kōan equals all kōans, such that "[if you] penetrate one place, and [then] you penetrate ten thousand places all at once."[88] At the same time, however, the HR in the final analysis denies the efficacy of kōans and asserts ineffability and iconoclasm in a manner that sets the stage for

Ta-hui's more decisive assault on the ability of language to disclose truth. According to Yüan-wu's commentary, although Hsüeh-tou generally "shatters [everything] with one hammer blow . . . of a single phrase," the formal style of some of his *juko* indicates that even he at times has "fallen into the weeds . . . [by] produc[ing] words on top of words, phrases on top of phrases, ideas on top of ideas."[89] For Dōgen, on the other hand, the technique of atomization captures and glosses the way a single word or phrase polysemously overflowing with an abundance of multivalent meanings "cut[s] off entanglements by using entanglements [and thereby] transmit[s] entanglements in terms of entanglements." In commenting on a line from the San-sheng kōan, Dōgen maintains that "the word" (*wa*) of "You do not even understand the head-word (*wa-tō*)" refers to

> the word that is being spoken, the word about to be spoken, and the word already spoken. The head-word is itself the realization of truth, that is, it reflects a complete, unimpeded realization that is simultaneous with the realization of the great earth and all sentient beings. [90]

For the HR, therefore, the signified, or the universal equality of kōans, stands behind and supports the utility of signs, or particular examples of kōan cases, but it also lies beyond the reach of even the most subtle, indirect language of the dialogues which is in the end incapable of expressing truth; there is a transcendental signified which signs do not attain. For Dōgen, each sign, that is, each word or phrase in a kōan that is atomized and glossed, dislodges and dehypostatizes any fixation with a signified by manifesting the dynamically shifting, decentric truth that is inseparable and necessarily linked to any and every particular sign.

The KS and the DR Texts

Dōgen and Ta-hui each cast himself in the role of the preserver of the post-kōan collection dialogue tradition and deliberately overstated his attack on his rival (Hung-chih for Ta-hui, and Ta-hui for Dōgen) as corrupting the authentic lineage for partisan polemical reasons. It seems clear that there are many affinities in the aims of the two thinkers. Both stress the dehypostatization of kōans so that they are understood as experientially based expressions reflecting a thoroughly subjective awareness of original enlightenment rather than propositional truths about an objectifiable ultimate reality. They maintain, however, that the practitioner who seeks to overcome conceptual fixations must transmute rather than simply negate discursive consciousness in examining the kōan. Also, Dōgen and Ta-hui strongly caution against awaiting or anticipating enlightenment as a final goal in a way that loses sight of the dynamism of spontaneous realization fully integrated with life-and-death.

Like Dōgen, Ta-hui reacts against the hypostatization and reification of kōan cases as pointers to a transcendental signified. His method of dislodging this fixation is to use signs, or *watō*, as self-deconstructive yet discrete semiotic units that highlight and capture the psychodynamics of the moment of transformation from unenlightenment to enlightenment. For Dōgen, the semiotic unit is continually expanded and extended in multiple directions simultaneously. In the KS "Kokyō" fascicle cited above, Dōgen refers to the metonymic quality of *watō* (used in this context in a generic sense of topic or theme) to convey "the complete, unimpeded realization of truth" that allows for shifting to other metaphorical and ironic modes of tropical discourse. Ta-hui did not invent the term *watō* but he emphatically gave it a specialized meaning exclusively focusing on irony which seeks to expose the inadequacy of all discourse. For Dōgen a trope is a *discursive vehicle* that leads to the exploration of other tropes, but for Ta-hui the ironic *watō* represents the "trope to end all tropes."

One of the difficulties in interpreting the kōan is that the iconoclastic view tends to define it negatively in terms of the pitfalls inherent in coming to terms with the practice. Ta-hui, stressing the shortcut method, refers to the *Mu* kōan (and other pithy, maieutic examples, such as "three pieces of flax," "the cypress tree in the garden," or "the east mountain walks on water") as "a knife cutting through the doubting mind," "a snowflake falling on a hot stove," "an iron rod that cannot be swallowed," or "a mortar and pestle used to smash misconceptions."[91] He admonishes, "As the inquiry goes on steadily and uninterruptedly you come to see that there is no intellectual clue in the kōan, that it is altogether devoid of sense as you ordinarily understand that word, that it is entirely flat, devoid of taste, has nothing appetizing about it . . . [and] you will become aware that you have pushed yourself like the old rat into a blind alley."[92] Following the lead of Tung-shan Shou-chou, Ta-hui distinguishes between the "live word," which is tasteless in providing no clues to be fathomed as to a rational interpretation of meaning but puts an end to the functioning of discriminative awareness, and the "dead word," which is given logical or philosophical analysis that only leads to the snare of intellectualism. The term *Mu* can function either way depending on the approach of the practitioner.

If seen as a "live word" it becomes a devastating weapon smashing through the causes and consequences of the ten defects, discussed below, that pinpoint all of the possible deceptions and delusions of conceptual think-ing; the Mu liberates the mind from any concern with yes and no, having and not having, being and nothingness. But as a "dead word" it perpetuates the vicious cycle of partial views, leading to the extremes of nihilism or realism. Thus, the Mu watō, according to Ta-hui, highlights and extends to the furthest possible extent the unbridgeable gap between symbol and reality, or language and truth, creating an anguishing sense of the utter futility of all ideas and discourse that is a necessary psycholinguistic impasse setting the stage for a breakthrough to satori.

Dōgen, however, advocates continually exploring and expanding the meanings of words; for example, Mu may be interpreted in terms of privation, absence, negation, or as a paradoxical affirmation in negation. Dōgen does not establish a formal set of rules for discourse that parallels the ten defects, but it is possible to observe a number of rhetorical patterns he uses consistently, such as (among other examples that could be cited) transposing lexical elements, making syntactic changes to alter the seman-tic meaning, reinterpreting expressions referring to illusion as referring to enlightened reality, drawing out the philosophical implications in everyday talk through puns and other forms of wordplay, all of which are based on the method of abbreviated, atomized glossing.[93] In commenting on the phrase muchū-setsumu ("disclosing a dream within a dream"), for example, Dōgen rearranges the sequence of the four kanji—mu (dream), chū (within), setsu (disclosing), mu (dream)—in several ways to highlight the multiplicity of possible meanings:

> It is a dream disclosing a dream within (chūmu ari, musetsu ari);
> or within a dream disclosing a dream (setsumu ari, muchū ari). If
> there is no within a dream, there is no disclosing a dream. If there
> is no disclosing a dream, there is no within a dream.[94]

For Dōgen, all words are potentially "living" if creatively interpreted, and it is only those which are left uninterpreted that are allowed to remain in a "dead" state.

One way of assessing the connection between the thinkers whose seemingly opposite approaches derive from a common source of demy-thologization and untextuality in interpreting irreverent satori dialogues is to consider the distinction John Dominic Crossan sets up between myth, which "establishes world," and parable, which demythologizes or "subverts [that very] world." Parable, he argues, in showing the limitations of myth and deliberately shattering world is neither antimyth nor a replacement of myth. It must be self-critical and self-subverting, so that "(e)ach time the Parable is in danger of becoming fossilized and turned into a myth, it subverts its own domestication and breaks the very structures that would contain it."[95] In Crossan's terms, the kōan is an eminent example of parabolic religion "that continually and deliberately subverts final words about 'reality' and thereby introduces the possibility of transcendence" in contrast to mythical religion "that gives one the final word about 'reality' and thereby excludes the authentic experience of mystery."[96] However, Ta-hui and Dōgen differ significantly on the aim and outcome of the subversion process. For the former subversion is an end in itself leading to a state of no-words beyond myth and antimyth, but Dōgen seeks to collapse the distinction between myth and parable so that the symbol-making of mythic awareness itself is continuously self-subverting.

The contrast between Ta-hui's iconoclastic shortcut method and Dōgen's polysemous scenic-route can be further illustrated by considering the following Soren Kierkegaard anecdote, which in offering an existentialist critique of systematic philosophy highlights the need for an "indirect communication" to convey the profound subjectivity of religious truth:

> What the philosophers say about Reality is often as disappointing as a sign you see in a shop window, which reads: Pressing Done Here. If you brought your clothes to be pressed, you would be fooled; for the sign is only for sale.[97]

A Ta-Hui interpretation would likely focus on the phrase Pressing Done Here as an example of a watō revealing the fundamental paradoxicality concerning a sign-indicator that has no meaning or background (signified-referent) and thereby reflects the trap inherent in conceptual thinking which mistakes the bifurcations of discursive consciousness (Skt. vijñāna) for the holistic insight of genuine wisdom (prajñā). The sign does not and cannot deliver the results it promises. It entices the mind to pursue its supposed reservoir of meaning but only leads to a recognition of thorough-going meaninglessness. The moment when the mind considers how it has been betrayed or has led itself into this mockery is a turning point to freedom from dependence upon signs. The disappointment and distrust with all material (or advertising) signs and linguistic designations gives way to a sense of release from an appetitive interest in examining the content and meaning of "dead words." As long as one insists on grappling with the sign, making sense of the phrase Pressing Done Here is like trying to swallow an iron rod. But in causing liberation from such a preoccupation, it functions as a tasteless "live word."

A Dōgen interpretation of the anecdote begins as an extension of Ta-hui's approach and culminates in a view stressing the erasure of a central, single, unifying signified in favor of shifting perspectives that is in some ways opposite to *watō* practice. As seen in Chapter 3, Dōgen's approach to religious symbols is influenced by a number of factors in Japanese religiosity, including Tendai and esoteric Buddhism, and medieval lyricism and Shinto ritualism. The combined impact of these elements is Dōgen's notion that each and every aspect of the universe in its daily activity preaches the Dharma verbally or nonverbally, and therefore "mountains and rivers themselves are the sounds of the *sūtra*" (*sansuikyō*). Dōgen's hermeneutic approach seems to be striving for a middle way between sacramentalism and iconoclasm, metaphor and criticism, *mythos* and *logos*. He maintains the necessity of perpetually "explaining the Way" (*dōtoku*) through "disclosing mind/disclosing nature" (*sesshin sesshō*), and he clearly and consistently affirms rather than denies the efficacy of all forms of discourse including anecdotes, parables, metaphors, and logical analysis as well as metonymic, paradoxical, and ironic discourse as essential means of revealing the experience of enlightenment. In KS "Muchū-set-sumu," he maintains that words creatively used are not "figures of speech" (*hiyu*) in the sense of setting up distinctions between figurative and literal, or tropical and mimetic, but the "true form of reality" (*shohō jissō*). Yet Dōgen does not overlook the critical and subversive aspect of language whose foundation is the insubstantiality of nothingness-nothingness or no-Buddha-nature. Ta-hui emphasizes the *power of doubt*, or the "ball of doubt" which is designed to concentrate all aspects of human frustration with the perplexities of life into a single event forcing a breakthrough to *satori*.[98] Dōgen, on the other hand, stresses the *power of disclosure* to continuously unfold multiple meanings stemming from a surplus at the inexhaustible source. As Dōgen writes in the following waka which subverts the conventional meaning of its title, "No reliance on words and letters" (*furyū monji*) by stressing continuous discourse rather than silence: "Not limited/By language/[Dharma] is ceaselessly expressed;/So, too, the way of letters/Can display but not exhaust it."[99]

Dōgen's approach to the Kierkegaard parable probably highlights the point that the phrase Pressing Done Here is indeed disclose the truth even if it is a partial, misleading, or even contradictory truth. That is, the sign is an expression of the truth that there is no particular, fixed truth, but always a connection between words themselves and relative or contextually based truths. If assumed to represent a single absolute truth, Dōgen might agree with Ta-hui's view that live words are meaningful only in their meaninglessness; the sign points to something that cannot be pointed to and in so doing shows the futility of all pointers. Thus Pressing Done Here would seem to represent the inverse of the *Diamond Sūtra* dictum: no-truth is truth and therefore no-truth. But whereas Ta-hui uses this paradox to make the case for the hopelessness of language, Dōgen reaches a radically different conclusion by uncovering other, multiple levels beyond paradoxicality. If seen in terms of its relative context, the sign invariably holds meaning: in a sign shop it is a sample product, and in a dry-cleaning shop it is either a description (if on the inside wall), which is mimetic, or an advertisement (if on the outside door) that functions metaphorically. Beyond that, the verbal image of the sign Pressing Done Here in the anecdote holds a symbolic import because it invites the reader to identify metonymically with an existential feeling the author conveys. Subjective response transforms the sign into a symbol, which according to Tillich is an indicator that allows participation in what it symbolizes. This understanding now reverses, but does not lose sight of Ta-hui's ironic view so that words are meaningless because of their inherent meaningfulness.

Furthermore, for Dōgen there are no half-truths. In his synechdochic doctrine of "total penetration of a single dharma" (*ippō gūjin*), each and every aspect as the true form of reality reveals without partiality or limitation the truth of the whole: "A full [instance of] being-time half known is a half being-time fully known."[100] Pressing Done Here, then, is the complete truth or full disclosure of reality. It is not an absurdity and it only disappoints those minds which bring to it deluded expectations. The verbal sign does deliver because it fulfills what the mind really needs, which is not a matter of cleaning or repairing a material object but spiritual purification and elevation through a unity of subjective awareness and objective expression. In that light, Dōgen argues that the most basic paradox of language and thought embedded in the use of kōans is, "Only the painted rice cake (*gabyō*) satisfies hunger."[101] That is, the so-called illusion of metaphorical wordplay and symbolism is the reality of truth. According to Ricoeur, "In no way does poetic imagination reduce itself to the power of forming a mental picture of the unreal; the imagery of sensory origin merely serves as a vehicle and as material for the verbal power whose true dimension is given to us by the oneiric and the cosmic. As Bachelard says

[*La Poétique de l'espace*, 7], the poetic image 'places us at the origin of articulate being'; the poetic image 'becomes a new being in our language, it expresses us by making us what it expresses.'"[102] Pressing Done Here therefore is not an antisymbol or a necessary barrier to enlightenment but has a metaphorical quality encompassing metonymy completely containing and fully revelatory of realization. Metaphor in the broadest tropical sense, Ricoeur suggests, can be "compared to stereoscopic vision where the different concepts may be said to come together to give the appearance of solidity and depth."[103] Dōgen might concur with Ricoeur's distinction, which would represent the converse of Ta-hui's view, between "dead" metaphors whose strength is dissipated by repetition and contrivance (perhaps as in the *watō* when it becomes a mechanical gimmick) and "live" metaphors which spring from an ever inventive and creative source of inspiration.[104]

"Does the Dog Have Buddha-nature?": Alternative Paradigms

The "Busshō" fascicle offers the clearest demonstration of the constructive and deconstructive elements in the KS. "Busshō" is by far the longest and most complex fascicle, and thus the one with the most sustained and consistent argumentation on a single doctrinal topic. Here, Dōgen examines over a dozen kōans concerning causality, temporality, language, life-and-death, illusion, and practice in regard to the Buddha-nature. He refutes numerous misconceptions which hypostatize the Buddha-nature as either an objectifiable entity or a supramundane transcendence, a teleological goal or a prior possession, something in time or beginningless and eternal, a reality beyond illusion or an idealistic projection. These misconceptions tend to identify truth with the mundane world or presuppose a realm beyond concrete existence, thereby violating the middle path. Dōgen seeks to subvert and to replace the delusions with positive notions encompassing a unity of opposites, such as *shitsuu* or "whole-being" which overcomes the apparent conflict between anthropocentrism and transcendence, *shingen* or the "manifesting body" (overcoming cosmology and substantiality), *gyō* or "activity" (teleology and potentiality), *setsu* or "symbolic disclosure" (ineffability and reason), *mujō* or "impermanence" (time and eternity), *i* or "dependence" (causation and liberation), and *gabyō* or the "painted rice cake" (reality and illusion). In that light, Dōgen disputes Pai-chang, who suggests that freedom from extreme views is gained through the denial of each by saying that "to preach sentient beings have . . . or have not the

Buddha-nature disparages Buddha." In contrast Dōgen argues, "Despite such disparagement, you cannot avoid explaining something. . . . Although it disparages, is the Buddha-nature disclosed, or not? If the Buddha-nature is disclosed, it is penetrated by the teacher and at the same time it is heard by the listener."[105]

Like most of the KS fascicles, "Busshō" does not have a clear, linear design reflecting a logical progression of ideas. But the theme that emerges underlying its various refutations is the issue of having and not having, or the being and nothingness of the Buddha-nature. Of the fourteen sections in the fascicle,[106] half deal directly with this topic, including the commentary on the Mu kōan. Dōgen indicates that the question of having is grounded on being (u), and the question of not having is grounded on nothingness (mu), based on the fact that the Sino-Japanese words u and mu have a double meaning. Beyond that, he maintains in analyzing several dialogues between the fourth and fifth patriarchs that the nothingness of "no-Buddha-nature" (mu-busshō) is the fundamental concern of Zen attainment pervading Chao-chou's Mu. No-Buddha-nature is not the denial of the existence of Buddha-nature because "no is a touchstone to express emptiness; emptiness is the foundation of expressing no."[107] Dōgen asks rhetorically, "Isn't the being of whole-being (shitsuu) based on the nothingness of nothingness-nothingness (mu-mu)?"[108] On the other hand, no-Buddha-nature does not merely represent an ironic affirmation since the categories of affirmation and negation must be subverted and broken through. The average person, he maintains, in hearing of the doctrine of the Buddha-nature, fails to consider what it truly means and remains preoccupied with "such things as the existence or non-existence of Buddha-nature."[109] But Dōgen stresses that to comprehend the truth of no-Buddha-nature, "one must not think of it in terms of the nothingness of being and nothingness, but ask 'What is this very Buddha-nature?'"[110] Thus, by the time Dōgen considers the Mu kōan in the thirteenth section of the fascicle, he has developed a hermeneutics of mu embracing yet sublating the topics of denial, negation, nonexistence, nothingness, and emptiness in terms of the direct, immediate yet continuing experience of no-Buddha-nature.

As Dōgen and others suggest, the Mu response to the question of the dog's Buddha-nature is perplexing and subject to various interpretations. In the Chao-chou dialogue, the initial query, "Does the dog have the Buddha-nature or not?," is generally seen as an unfortunate idle, speculative question begging to be rebuffed or dismissed about whether a being that lacks self-reflective consciousness possesses the potential to be enlightened. If limited to the mimetic level, the question should be refuted by a simple "no." But Dōgen comments, "The meaning of this question must be clarified. It neither asks whether the dog has or does not have the Buddha-nature. It is a question of whether an iron [enlightened] man continues to practice the Way."[111] He argues that the question is so challenging and penetrating that Chao-chou is taken aback and feels threatened. When the query is somewhat stubbornly restated (after Chao-chou answers *Mu* to the first question) as "All sentient beings have the Buddha-nature, why not the dog?," Dōgen argues, "The real meaning of this is, if all sentient beings are nothingness (*mu*), the Buddha-nature must be nothingness, and the dog must be nothingness as well. The real meaning is such, the dog and Buddha-nature manifest nothingness as such[ness]."[112] That is, Dōgen rereads the question, "Why does not the dog have [the Buddha-nature]?" as the statement, "the dog is such nothingness," or "the dog is no[-Buddha-nature]." Therefore, the supposedly deluded question—when seen from the standpoint of tropical discourse—discloses in a way equal to the master's enlightened response the wellspring of nothingness and suchness from which the tropological significance of all expressions derive.

The *Mu* response has various "negative" implications, including: no, what a foolish question for the Buddha-nature is not a possession and a dog cannot be enlightened; or it may ironically convey a "diamond-cutting" and "lion's roaring" silence putting an end to all speculation. *Mu* can also paradoxically indicate an affirmation in that there is no Buddha-nature apart from concrete existence symbolized by the dog, and therefore from the standpoint of emptiness, of course, the dog and each and every phenomenon is buddha. According to Dōgen's transmimetic comment in his *juko* on this kōan in EK-9 no. 73, "A dog is itself nothing other than a dog, and the Buddha is himself nothing other than the Buddha/In this realm there is no dichtomy of 'yes' and 'no' . . . " Ta-hui, who referred to this kōan at least twenty times in his writings, interprets *Mu* as the prime example of the shortcut or *watō* technique. He sees "this one word [as] the weapon which smashes all types of wrong knowledge and wrong conceptualization,"[113] leading the conceptual mind to the brink of collapse beyond which lies the abyss of nonconceptual truth. According to Ta-hui:

> This one character is the rod by which many false images and
> ideas are destroyed in their very foundations. To it you should

add no judgement about being or non-being, no arguments, no
bodily gestures. . . . Words have no place here. Neither should
you throw this character away into the nothingness of emptiness
. . . continually stir it [this kōan] around the clock.[114]

He emphasizes that while concentrating on the Mu during all occasions
and activities, one should feel the supreme doubt of perplexity and frustration until the ten defects have been conquered and the breakthrough to
satori is attained. The ten defects originally suggested by Ta-hui and
elaborated upon by Korean Zen master Chinul are (to paraphrase): (1)
thinking of Mu in terms of yes and no, (2) relating it to doctrine, (3)
pondering it logically, (4) considering it as a wordless gesture, (5) evaluating the meaning of the word, (6) approaching it through silent illumination, (7) viewing it as a product of meditation, (8) examining it through
literary analysis, (9) taking it to be true nonexistence, (10) relating it to
the original, inherent potentiality for awakening.[115] Ta-hui's watō appears
to be similar to the contemplative prayer recommended by the anonymous
author of the medieval Christian mystical text, The Cloud of Unknowing,
who argues that "it is quite sufficient to focus your attention on a single
word such as sin or God (or another one you might prefer) and without the
intervention of analytical thought allow yourself to experience directly the
reality it signifies. The one syllable prayer is like crying out 'help!' or 'fire!'"
But The Cloud warns, "Do not use clever logic to examine or explain this
word to yourself nor allow yourself to ponder its ramifications. . . . I do not
believe reasoning ever helps in the contemplative work. That is why I
advise you to leave these words whole. . . . When you think of sin, intend
nothing in particular but only yourself, though nothing particular in
yourself either."[116]

Hung-chih comments on the Mu kōan in case no. 18 of his Juko
Hyakusoku collection of one-hundred cases with poetic commentary used
as the basis for the SH. Hung-chih's interpretation seems to indicate a
different direction than Ta-hui by stressing that the Mu is not a truth to be
contemplated without conceptualization but an expression based on and
springing forth from the experience of enlightenment:

It is not realized by no-mind (mu-shin) or known with-mind
(u-shin). Because it circulates freely throughout the veins and
speech of the unbounded, true person, there is no place it does
not penetrate.[117]

The approach suggested by Hung-chih may have been a key influence on Dōgen's contention that the *watō* method creates subtle yet devastating dichotomies between means and end, practice and realization, and illusion and truth. Hung-chih suggests a synechdochic perspective on the freely circulating function of the kōan. However, the interpretation of Ju-ching, who Dōgen cites as his only authentic teacher (aside from Śākyamuni), does not seem to diverge significantly from Ta-hui's explanation of the *Mu* as a method of surpassing conceptualization through concentrating on a conceptually unresolvable puzzle. According to Ju-ching:

> In Chao-chou's expression *Mu* uttered in response to the question of the dog's Buddha-nature, the word *Mu* is an iron broom used to sweep aside delusions. As one sweeps, countless delusions are exposed; the more sweeping, the more delusions. One must sweep away all conceptualizations that even this broom cannot reach. Sit erect and vigilant day and night without taking your attention off [the kōan]. Suddenly, the broom breaks open the great, empty sky and the myriad distinctions are fully penetrated.[118]

Yet the final line may be different than Ta-hui in suggesting that discursive thought is an avenue rather than obstacle to realization, an expression that metonymically penetrates each and every barrier.

Dōgen's approach to the *Mu* kōan is distinctive in several respects. First, as indicated above, Dōgen grounds the discussion of *Mu* in terms of the doctrine of no-Buddha-nature, which he says causes a "reverberating echo circulating through Chao-chou," and related notions of nothingness and emptiness. *Mu* is one of the multiple ways of expressing no-Buddha-nature which must not be absolutized but explored through alternative possibilities. Dōgen also highlights Chao-chou's affirmative response *U*, which he interprets in terms of being-Buddha-nature. The doctrine of being-Buddha-nature, however, is not a possession or an inherent potentiality that exists in contrast to no-Buddha-nature. Of Chao-chou's *U*, he writes that it

> is not the "has" posited by the Sarvāstivādans [an early Buddhist school of "realism"]. . . . The being of buddha is the being of Chao-chou. The being of Chao-chou is the being of the dog. The being of the dog is being-Buddha-nature.[119]

Consistent with his interpretation of saindhava, Dōgen argues that Chao-chou answered both Mu and U because these terms are interchangeable yet distinct ways of expressing no-Buddha-nature. In addition, Dōgen comments on Chao-chou's ironic answer, "It is because a dog has karmic consciousness," given in response to the disciple's restatement of the initial question, "All sentient beings have the Buddha-nature, why not the dog?" Dōgen interprets Chao-chou's reply in positive terms. Since causality is inseparable from noncausality, the existence of karma indicates that the problem of the dog's Buddha-nature is oriented in terms of "the nothingness of the dog and the nothingness of the Buddha-nature."[120] This phrase (kushi-mu, busshō-mu nari) can also be read as "no-dog and no-Buddha-nature," "dog-nothingness and Buddha-nature-nothingness," or "dog-Mu and Buddha-nature-Mu."

In some ways, Dōgen's approach to the Mu kōan is similar to Ta-hui, especially when he suggests that "this Mu has the power of the sun to melt rocks."[121] Dōgen seems to concur with Ta-hui's refutation of some of the ten defects, such as (1), (4), and (10), but he clearly and willingly violates others, including (7), (8), and (9). Dōgen's argument appears to be: Is it reasonable or even desirable to use words such as Mu (or in The Cloud of Unknowing, sin or God) that are loaded with so many levels of meaning and implication reflecting the historical development of doctrine only in order to defeat thought and discourse? Isn't it preferable to explore the polysemy of such words while remaining free from commitment to any particular meaning? This is the "language of samādhi,"[122] or the playful (asobiteki) expressions of awakened consciousness. Subversion is liberating in a sense parallel to Derrida's view of the repetition of language: "Its freedom is to exploit every latent connection, every associative bond, every phonic, graphic, semiotic, and semantic link, every relation of whatever sort which exists among signifiers, in order to set forth the power of repetition in all its productivity, inventiveness, and freedom."[123] Dōgen's critique of the watō approach thus reflects several concerns. Philosophically, he seeks to establish firmly the middle way encompassing the oneness of means and end, practice and realization, activity and anticipation without any subtle gap separating these apparent opposites. Psychologically, Dōgen emphasizes the interplay of thought and thoughtlessness in order to open up all possible approaches to enlightenment experience. From the standpoint of religious language, he values the deconstructive function of metonymic symbol extending from metaphor through irony as semantic and nonsemantic modes of disclosing the nothingness of nothingness. Dōgen's emphasis on the boundless variety of expressions by glossing Chinese ideograms with puns in terms of Japanese pronunciations has a Joycean quality in which "certain incomprehensible words . . . come to be fraught with many meanings and values and with a strange beauty for the initiate when he discovers that they are derived from [obscure languages'] words disfigured by aberrant consonants, and enriched by secret allusions to possible puns when they are spoken aloud and very fast."[124] Furthermore Dōgen's use of metonymy straddling the boundary between words and wordlessness, or polysemous expression and the casting aside of discourse recalls Derrida's metonymic punning in the essay "White Mythology" on the phrase *"plus de metaphore."* This French expression means at once "more metaphor" and the "end of metaphor." As translator Alan Bass notes, "this idea is related to the 'general economy' of metaphor . . . [in which] 'profit' produces 'loss': *more* metaphor, the extra turn of speech, becomes *no more* metaphor, the missing turn of speech."[125]

Conclusions: Does the Kōan Have Buddha-Nature?

Considered in light of the problematics of mythology and demythology, and textuality and untextuality, the Zen dialogue at its best self-reflectively and self-correctively shows an awareness of the need for different, provisional modes of discourse based on the appropriate level of understanding. It thus encompasses and fosters the interaction between mythicization, supported by the first three tropes, especially metaphor, and demythicization reflecting the last three tropes, especially irony, with metonymy as the fulcrum for flexible shifting between all levels. Thus, the dialogue attains the self-surpassing, transcendental quality that Nishitani stresses is inherent in Zen discourse: it is *trans*formational in capturing the spontaneous moment of attainment of *satori, trans*missional as the main symbol of lineal succession, *trans*positional in viewing the masters as interchangeable pieces of the puzzle of discourse, *trans*linear in expressing an approach to temporality beyond ordinary sequence, and *trans*actional in engaging the audience's active participation. Furthermore, the effectiveness of the Zen master in meeting these ends is due largely to the *trans*gressive quality of his repartee which "engenders incurable disease by violating propriety and infecting purity"[126]—that is, the supposed purity of logic, grammar, and common sense.

One way of interpreting the relation between mythology and demythology, narrative history and transhistory, polemics and philosophy in the discourse of Zen chronicles and dialogues is to refer to Roland Barthes' radical rereading of the Tower of Babel account from a postmodern stand-point that suggests a Zen attitude. "Thus the Biblical myth is reversed," Barthes writes, "the confusion of tongues is no longer a punishment, the subject gains access to bliss by the cohabitation of languages *working side by side*: the text of pleasure is a sanctioned Babel."[127] In this view, Babel represents not a condemnation to a labyrinth of deception and folly but the freedom of exploring multiple perspectives—it is the opportunity to leave things unnamed or to self-reflectively question the naming process by exploiting the creative potential of the self-supassing parallactic shifting of tropes. That is, myths contain the possibility of their own reversal. For Aristotole, *mythos* is the style of discourse that establishes the meaning of *logos*, but for Zen discourse *mythos* and *logos* are used to constantly undercut one another. For Zen, the ever-present reversibility of myths used for persuasion is perhaps the greatest of all antimyths seeking liberation and thus no myth at all. This recalls White's emphasis on authentic discourse as seeking a middle ground between the conceptually overdetermined and the conceptually underdetermined. "On the contrary," according to White, "discourse, if it is genuine discourse—that is to say as *self*-critical as it is critical of others—will radically challenge [these extremes]. It throws all 'tactical' rules into doubt, including those originally governing its own formation. . . . Discourse always tends toward metadiscursive reflexiveness. This is why every discourse is always as much about discourse itself as it is about the objects that make up its subject matter."[128] It seems that while Zen does not necessarily have exclusive privilege in regard to the attain-ment of transhistory, it also need not be defensive concerning the role of narratology in the way it presents its own history. Rather, the intersection between Nishitani's philosophy of Zen and postmodernism lies in their shared emphasis on constructing a discourse for which "meaning is always in the process of forming, deforming, and reforming,"[129] so that it reaches a continuing state of "metadiscursive reflexiveness."[130]

However, the problematical history of Zen indicates that the rituali-zation and reification of kōans as paradigmatic cases has at times left its discourse vulnerable either to excessive rigidity or to overflexibility. If the dialogues are so open-ended as to allow shifting and multiple perspectives, on what basis can standards and guidance be established without self-con-tradiction or hypocrisy? In *The Temple of the Golden Pavilion*, Mishima Yukio focuses on the potentially fatal flaw of the kōan used in Zen training. Throughout the book, several kōans, especially "Nan-ch'üan kills the cat," are given idiosyncratic and seemingly distorted readings by key characters to justify their questionable motives; for example, the Father Superior of the temple uses the "cat" kōan to explain away the tragedy of war and his own lack of leadership during times of hardship, and the disabled social misfit Kashiwagi uses it to defend his exploitation of beautiful women. Near the end of the book, the miserable anti-hero Mizoguchi is about to commit the tragic act of burning down the hauntingly beautiful temple because he is obsessed with how it betrays his sense of ugliness and self-loathing. Mizoguchi's motives are based largely on his overly literal interpretation of Lin-chi's dictum "If you see the buddha, kill the buddha." But Mizoguchi briefly meets Father Zenkai while he visits the temple. In contrast to the secretive and corrupt Father Superior, Zenkai appears to Mizoguchi as an authentic teacher who is able to see into his heart without making judgment or causing suspicion, and whose clarity of character nearly persuades Mizoguchi to give up on his destructive folly. Zenkai exhibits "the gentleness of the harsh roots of some great tree that grows outside a village and gives shelter to the passing traveler."[131] He is not like "[Zen masters who] are apt to fall into the sin of never giving a positive judgment on anything for fear of being laughed at later in case they have been wrong . . . [or] the type of Zen priest who will instantly hand down his arbitrary decision on anything that is discussed, but who will be careful to phrase his reply in such a way that it can be taken to mean two opposite things."[132]

Both Dōgen and Ta-hui are sensitive and seek to avoid the kind of counter-productive spiritual predicament in which the study of traditional cases can easily result if metaphor is taken literally and flexibility, spontaneity, and ambiguity degenerate into arbitrary, whimsical, misleading pronouncements. They are equally wary of an overemphasis on enigma as an end in itself, which "can lead us to a perception of the *mise en abime*, a nauseating void of signifers in which a nihilistic abandonment to free play and arbitary will seems the only appropriate strategy."[133] Both thinkers agree on the need to firmly criticize the approaches of original enlightenment, naturalism, and silent illumination, which may stress subitization without the need for sustained, authentic praxis. The issue in comparing these thinkers is not whether Dōgen accepted or rejected the kōan in taking a position that is polarized in relation to the latter. Rather, within the context of trying to revive and refashion the kōan tradition, two distinct views arose of how to minimize the kinds of problems Mishima describes. Ta-hui warns that thinking itself which invariably results in the ten defects must be conquered by trying to spit out the tasteless live word; one word is sufficient to the task. For Dōgen, all words are touchstones to articulate the nothingness of no-Buddha-nature; language is the play of *samādhi*. Kōans are not seen as either merely compatible with or replacing *sūtras* but as the essential nature of the symbol-making process encompassing parable and paradox, tautology and metaphor, syntactical meaning and nonsemantic wordplay (puns, homophones, onomatopoeia, etc.).

The differences in approach can also be seen by interpreting Franz Kafka's famous parable in *The Trial*, "Before the Law."[134] According to Kafka, a "man from the country" comes to the door of the Law begging for admittance but is denied entrance by an intimidating doorkeeper who counsels, "It is possible, but not at this moment." Unlike Bodhidharma, who is said to have sat in concentration for nine years, the man continues to wait but without real purpose, trying to cajole and even to bribe the doorkeeper, all to no avail. Finally, near the end of his life, the man sees a radiance streaming inextinguishably from the door of the Law and asks the doorkeeper, "Everyone strives to attain the Law, how does it come about, then, that in all these years no one has come seeking admittance but me?" The doorkeeper responds, "No one but you could gain admittance through this door, since this door was intended for you. I am now going to shut it." Ta-hui would likely see the doorkeeper as an embodiment of the necessary obstacle or impenetrable barrier of the *Mu watō* which forces the conceptual mind into exhaustion and eventual collapse. The death of the man from the country represents the demise of rationality, requiring a sudden leap beyond all doorways into the Law. The paradox for Ta-hui is that the man has wasted his efforts on a path of hopeless futility. Dōgen, however, interprets the paradoxicality in terms of the doorkeeper's final pronouncement: there are an infinite number of doors but each person must find the key to the one that is appropriate to him. The man from the country never realizes that he has always been at the door containing the light or the truth of the Law. Instead of idly waiting or focusing on his frustration, the man should have tried to negotiate his way through the gateless gate (*mu-monkan*) by engaging earlier in the parallactical discursive process that inspired his final illuminative question.

The conventional account of Zen history which suggests that the kōan is useful and meaningful only in demonstrating the uselessness and meaninglessness of words leading to the psychodynamics of doubt and transformation may be applicable to Ta-hui's Rinzai Zen. However, it is misleading not only for understanding Dōgen's approach but for understanding how both thinkers branch off from the roots of the tradition. For the conventional view emphasizing *watō*, a fixation with logic must be overcome by paradoxical expressions teleologically ever approaching silence to demonstrate the importance of psychological experience. But for a decentric literary account, logic is surpassed in terms of a continuing hermeneutic process of parallactic tropological shifting without any sense of an inevitability of order or sequence.

At the same time, it must be recognized that there are several limitations in this assessment of the tradition. First, both Dōgen and Ta-hui, as well as their predecessors Hung-chih and Yüan-wu in addition to dozens of other Sung Zen masters, were remarkably diverse in their literary creativity and productivity. Each composed multiple genres, and there remains considerable debate about what constitutes their primary genius and contribution to Buddhist thought. For example, the recent scholarly school of "critical Buddhism" (hihan bukkyō) has argued that Dōgen's strength is not his philosophical wordplay, which is considered to be a mask or a sign of immaturity, but his later monastic or instructional writings that seem more consistent and clear on the issue of causality. Second, any methodological attempt to analyze, classify, or categorize kōans may violate the metadiscursive and persistently self-disruptive quality of the discourse that it is seeking to capture. Therefore, it is necessary to comment self-critically on our discourse about Zen discourse in order to prevent an overly neat and systematic packaging of categories. Consider the following Lin-chi dialogue:

> The Master asked a monk, 'Sometimes a shout is like the Diamond King's jewel sword, sometimes a shout is like a golden haired lion crouching on the ground, sometimes a shout is like a probing pole or reed shade; sometimes a shout does not function as a shout: how do you understand?' The monk hesitated, whereupon the Master shouted.[135]

Would Dōgen, who was not known for his shouting, look upon the first three definitions of the shout as metaphorical and the final as ironic, or would he maintain that the abrupt concluding shout, or shouting about not-shouting, is metonymic? Or would he not-shout about the shout about not-shouting? As Harold Bloom argues, poems have meaning but "the meaning of a poem can only be another poem [or] a range of poems.[136]" In light of the above examination of the Mu and other cases, if the question is posed, "Does the kōan for Dōgen have the Buddha-nature?", it must also be asked, does the Buddha-nature have kōans, do kōans really have (or really are) kōans, and does Buddha-nature really have (or really is) the Buddha-nature? To paraphrase (by substituting the word "kōan" for "sentient beings" in the original) Dōgen's rhetorical comment to Ta-kuei, who said that "all sentient beings have no Buddha-nature":

> You explain that all kōans are no-Buddha-nature. But you do not explain that all Buddha-natures are no-kōan, or that all Buddha-natures are no-Buddha-nature. How could you expect to realize even in your dreams that all buddhas are no-Buddha-nature? You must see things more clearly![137]

Appendix I
Translations of Kana Shōbōgenzō Fascicles

Introduction

This section provides a translation of three KS fascicles that are particularly important for understanding Dōgen's method of interpreting source dialogues and kōan cases: "Kattō," which challenges the conventional hierarchical, teleological reading of the Bodhidharma "skin, flesh, bones, marrow" dialogue by citing a Chao-chou dialogue on Bodhidharma; "Ōsaku-sendaba," which alludes to the Bodhidharma case and also uses with very different aims and styles many of the same anecdotes that appear in HR no. 92 on the the notion of "a king requesting offerings of saindhava"—it highlights the main differences between the KS text and the standard Sung era kōan collections; and "Shinfukatoku," which reinvents the dialogue and wordplay between Te-shan and the old woman who refuses to sell him rice cakes because he fails to explain a key passage from the *Diamond Sūtra*.

ENTANGLED VINES:
A TRANSLATION OF THE KS "KATTŌ" FASCICLE

It was only bodhisattva Mahākāśyapa who, at a sermon on Vulture Peak, received the authentic transmission of the supreme wisdom of the treasury of the true Dharma-eye from Śākyamuni. This authentic transmission from Śākyamuni was then transmitted through successive generations to the twenty-eighth patriarch, the venerable Bodhidharma. Bodhidharma came to China and transmitted the supreme wisdom of the treasury of the true Dharma-eye directly to the great teacher, Cheng-tsung P'u-chüeh, who became the second patriarch.

The twenty-eighth patriarch [in India] is referred to as the first patriarch in China, and the twenty-ninth patriarch is referred to as the second patriarch, according to the lineal system in China. The first patriarch received the authentic transmission through instruction directly from the venerable Prajñātara, and his transmission in turn became the root for the branches and leaves [symbolizing various Zen schools and doctrines].[1] Generally, although all Buddhist sages in their training study how to cut off entanglements (*kattō*) at their root, they do not study how to cut off entanglements by using entanglements. They do not realize that entanglements entangle entanglements. How little do they know what it is to transmit entanglements in terms of entanglements. How rarely do they realize that the transmission of the Dharma is itself an entanglement. Few have as yet heard of or practiced the way [of transmission]. How can anyone genuinely realize [the Dharma]?[2]

My late master [Ju-ching] once said: "The vine of a gourd coils around the vine of a[nother] gourd like a wisteria-vine." I have never heard this saying from anyone else of the past or present. The first time I heard this was from my late master. When he said, "the vine of a gourd coils around the vine of a[nother] gourd," this refers to studying the buddhas and patriarchs directly from the buddhas and patriarchs, and to the transmission of the buddhas and patriarchs directly to the buddhas and patriarchs. That is, it refers to the direct transmission from mind-to-mind (*ishin-denshin*).[3]

> The twenty-eighth patriarch said to his disciples, "As the time is drawing near [for me to transmit the Dharma to my successor], please tell me how you express it."
>
> Tao-fu responded first, "According to my current understanding, we should neither cling to words and letters, nor abandon them altogether, but use them as an instrument of the Tao (*dō-yō*)."
>
> The master responded, "You express my skin."
>
> Then the nun, Tsung-chih, said, "As I now see it, [the Dharma] is like Ananda's viewing the Buddha-land of Akshobhya, seeing it once and never seeing it again."
>
> The master responded, "You express my flesh."
>
> Tao-yu said, "The four elements are emptiness, and the five

skandhas are non-being. But in my view, there is not a single dharma to be expressed."

The master responded, "You express my bones."

Finally, Hui-k'o prostrated himself three times, and stood [silently] in his place.

The master said, "You express my marrow."[4]

Hui-k'o became the second patriarch as a result of this, and he received the transmission of the Dharma as well as the transmission of the sacred robe.

You must study the first patriarch's saying, "You express my skin, flesh, bones, and marrow," as the way of the patriarchs. All four disciples heard and realized this saying all at once. Hearing and learning from it, they realized the skin, flesh, bones, and marrow of the liberated body-mind, or the skin, flesh, bones, and marrow of the casting off of body-mind (*shinjin datsuraku*). You should not interpret the teachings of the patriarchs and masters from only a single specific viewpoint. It is a complete manifestation without partiality. However, those who do not fully understand the true transmission think that "because the four disciples had different levels of insight, the first patriarch's saying concerning the 'skin, flesh, bones, and marrow' represents different degrees in recognizing the superficiality or depth [of understanding]. The skin and flesh are further [from the truth] than the bones and marrow." Thus, they say that [Bodhidharma told Hui-k'o] that he "expressed the marrow because the second patriarch's understanding was superior." But interpreting the anecdote in this manner is not the result of studying the buddhas and patriarchs or of realizing the true patriarchal transmission.

You should realize that the first patriarch's expression "skin, flesh, bones, and marrow" does not refer to the superficiality or depth [of understanding]. Although there may remain a [provisional] distinction between superior and inferior understanding, [each of the four disciples] expressed the first patriarch in his entirety. When Bodhidharma says "you express my marrow" or "you express my bones," he is using various pedagogical devices that are pertinent to particular people, or methods of instruction that may or may not apply to particular levels of understanding. It is the same as Śākyamuni's holding up an *udambara* flower [to Mahākāśyapa], or the transmitting of the sacred robe. What Bodhidharma said to the four disciples is fundamentally the selfsame expression. Although it is fundamentally the selfsame expression, since there are necessarily four ways of understanding it, he did not express it in one way alone. But even though

each of the four ways of understanding is partial or one-sided, the way of
the patriarchs ever remains the way of the patriarchs.

As a rule, the teaching of a master must be adjusted so that it is
appropriate for [each one of] his disciples. For example, in order to instruct
one of his four disciples the first patriarch said, "You express my skin." But,
if after the second patriarch there were hundreds of thousands of disciples,
there would also be hundreds of thousands of appropriate ways of explaining [the Dharma]. There would be an inexhaustible number [of explana-
tions]. Because he was speaking with four disciples, Bodhidharma only used
the four provisional expressions, "skin," "flesh," "bones," and "marrow," and
although there were other possible expressions Bodhidharma did not
choose to use them. For instance, he could have said to the second
patriarch, "You express my skin." But even if Hui-k'o had been told, "You
express my skin," he still would have received the transmission of the
treasury of the true Dharma-eye and become the second patriarch. "Expressing skin" or "expressing marrow" does not refer to the superiority or
inferiority [of understanding.]. Also, Bodhidharma could have said, "You
express my marrow," to Tao-fu, Tao-yu, or Tsung-chih. He must be able to
transmit the Dharma even to someone who expresses [only] the skin. The
body-mind of the patriarchs is the patriarchs' skin, flesh, bones, and
marrow. The marrow is not closer [to the Dharma], and the skin is not
further [from the Dharma].[5]

If someone is currently studying with an [authentic] Dharma-eye and
receives the seal, "You express my skin," that really signifies that they are
expressing the complete patriarch. There is the patriarch whose skin
permeates his entire body, the patriarch whose flesh permeates his entire
body, the patriarch whose bones permeate his entire body, and the patriarch
whose marrow permeates his entire body. There is the patriarch whose
mind permeates his body, the patriarch whose body permeates his body,
and the patriarch whose mind permeates his mind. There is the patriarch
who permeates the [other] patriarchs, and the patriarch whose body permeates all selves. When the patriarchs appear and teach hundreds of
thousands of disciples, they often explain, "You express my skin." Although
the explanations given to the hundreds of thousands use the expression
"skin, flesh, bones, and marrow," you must realize that the masters of the
way may use the expression "skin, flesh, bones, and marrow" but without
regard for the matter of signifying superficiality or depth. If there were six
or seven disciples studying with the first patriarch, he might say "You
express my mind," or "You express my body." He might also say, "You express

my buddha," "You express my eyeballs," or "You express my realization."
The term "you" may refer [nondualistically] either to the master [Bodhidharma] or to [the disciple] Hui-k'o. One must also study very carefully the meaning of the term "expression."

You should realize that when you express me, then I express you, expression expresses both me and you, and expression expresses both you and me. In studying the body-mind of the first patriarch, you must realize the oneness of the interior and the exterior [dimensions]. If we do not realize that his whole body permeates his body, then we have not realized the domain of the manifestation of the buddhas and patriarchs. Expressing the skin is expressing the bones, flesh, and marrow. Expressing the bones, flesh, and marrow is expressing the skin, flesh, face, and eyes.[6] It is none other than the awakening of the true body experienced throughout the entire ten directions of the universe, and [the realization of] the skin, flesh, bones, and marrow. In this way, you express my robe and you express the Dharma. Therefore, through the ec-static experience of expressing the way, masters realize an unimpeded mutuality with their disciples. And through the ec-static experience of receiving the path to liberation, disciples realize an unimpeded mutuality with their masters. The unimpeded mutuality of masters and disciples is the entanglement of buddhas and patriarchs, and the entanglement of buddhas and patrarichs is the realization of the skin, flesh, bones, and marrow. Śākyamuni's holding up an *udambara* flower and winking his eye is itself an entanglement, and Mahākāśyapa's wise smile is itself the skin, flesh, bones, and marrow.

You must realize that because the seed of an entangled vine has the capacity for liberation, it produces the branches, leaves, blossoms, and fruit that coil around the entangled vines. Because these [parts of vines] are at once thoroughly surrounding and free from being surrounded by each other, the entangled vine is the spontaneous realization of buddhas and patriarchs, or the spontaneous realization of the kōan (*kōan-genjō*).

> The great teacher Chao-chou once said to his disciples, "Mahākāśyapa transmitted [the Dharma] to Ananda. You must explain to me, to whom did Bodhidharma transmit it?"
>
> A monk responded, "Everyone knows it was the second patriarch who expressed the marrow. Why even ask such a question?"
>
> Chao-chou said, "Don't slander Hui-k'o."
>
> Chao-chou further said, "Bodhidharma also said, 'A person

of superficial understanding expresses my skin, and a person of deeper understanding expresses my bones.' You must tell me, what does a person of even deeper understanding express?"

The disciple responded [to Chao-chou], "Isn't it expressing the marrow?"

Chao-chou said, "You must know only the skin. This old teacher has no reliance (furyū) on marrow."

The disciple asked, "What is the meaning of marrow?"

Chao-chou said, "If you ask such a question, you have not yet even expressed the skin."[7]

Therefore, you must realize that when "you have not yet even expressed the skin," it is also the case that "you have not yet even expressed the marrow."[8] Expressing the skin is expressing the marrow. We must reflect on the meaning of "you have not yet even expressed the skin." When the disciple said, "Isn't it expressing the marrow?," Chao-chou immediately responded, "You must know only the skin. This old teacher has no reliance on marrow." His interpretation that expressing the skin is a matter of nonreliance on the marrow is the true meaning of expressing the marrow. Therefore, the monk said, "Everyone knows it was the second patriarch who expressed the marrow. Why even ask such a question?" Just at the moment "Mahākāśyapa transmitted the Dharma to Ananda," Ananda's body was fully transformed into Mahākāśyapa and Mahākāśyapa's body was fully transformed into Ananda. However, whenever there is a transmission from person to person, there is usually some kind of change in the face, eyes, skin, flesh, bones, and marrow. That is why Chao-chou said, "You must explain to me, to whom did Bodhidharma transmit it?" Bodhidharma in transmitting the Dharma is already Bodhidharma, and the second patriarch who expressed the marrow is also already Bodhidharma. In studying the meaning of this, the Buddha Dharma not yet [realized] is the Buddha Dharma realized right now. If that were not the case, there would be no Buddha Dharma realized right now. You must reflect on this quietly, attain it for yourself, and teach it to others.

[Chao-chou citing Bodhidharma said]: "A person of superficial understanding expresses my skin, and a person of deeper understanding expresses my bones. You must tell me, what does a person of even deeper understanding express?" Whether or not [the understanding] is superficial or has depth, it reflects the clarity of spiritual insight. In the case of superficiality, the skin, flesh, bones, and marrow are all superficial, and in the case of depth, the skin, flesh, bones, and marrow all have depth. Therefore, what the four disciples of Bodhidharma studied in various ways was beyond even the innumerable [levels of] skin, flesh, bones, and marrow. It is not the case that the marrow should be considered the highest level. There are at least thirty-five [other dimensions] beyond the marrow.[9]

The old master Chao-chou's instruction is the way of the buddhas. But it is not well understood by a number of monks, including Lin-chi, Te-shan, Ta-wei, and Yün-men, among others. They cannot even imagine it in their dreams, let alone express it clearly. If it were explained to them, they would be surprised and perplexed.

Hsüeh-tou Ming-chüeh said, "Chao-chou and Mu-chao were old masters." The sayings of the "old masters" are authentic evidence of the Buddha Dharma as well as of their own personal realization. Great teacher Hsüeh-feng Chen-chüeh also referred to "old master Chao-chou." [Both Hsüeh-tou and Hsüeh-feng] praised [Chao-chou] as an old master. Thus they considered him an old master who surpassed the buddhas and patriarchs of past and present. Therefore, the meaning of the entanglements of skin, flesh, bones, and marrow has become the standard set by old master [Chao-chou]'s saying in his lecture to his monks, "You express me." You must carefully examine this standard.

Furthermore, the reports that the first patriarch returned to India are unfounded. Although Sung-yen is said to have seen him there, this is untrue. How could Sung-yen have seen the works of the first patriarch? The truth of the matter is that after he entered *parinirvāṇa* the first patriarch's ashes were interred on Mt. Hsiung-erh in China.

This instruction for an assembly of monks (jishu) *was delivered on the seventh day of the seventh month in 1242 at Kannondōri Kōshōhōrinji Temple in Uji-gun, Yawashiro. It was transcribed on the third day of the third month in 1243 at the chief disciple's quarters of Kippōji Temple in Yoshida-gun, Echizen, by Ejō.*

A KING REQUESTS SAINDHAVA: A TRANSLATION OF THE KS "ŌSAKUSENDABA" FASCICLE

Words and wordlessness:
Like tangled vines to a tree,
Feeding a mule to feeding a horse,
Or water to clouds.

In the same vein, the *Mahāparinirvāṇa Sūtra* states the following:

> The World-Honored One [Śākyamuni] said, "It is just like when
> a king [of the land of Saindhava] tells his retainer to 'bring me
> saindhava.' There are four items all known as 'saindhava.' The
> first is salt, the second is a chalice, the third is water, and the
> fourth is a horse. These are four different things, but each shares
> the same name. If the king wants to wash his face and hands, he
> is offered the saindhava of water. If the king wants to eat a meal,
> he is offered the saindhava of salt. If the king wants to have a
> drink after eating, he is offered the saindhava of a chalice. And
> if the king wants to go for a ride after he has finished his meal,
> he is offered the saindhava of a horse. A wise retainer under-
> stands the four inner meanings of the king's words."[10]

The mutuality involved in the king's requests and the retainer's
offerings has been practiced for a long time, and it closely resembles the
transmission of the sacred robe in Buddhism. Since Śākyamuni himself has
commented on this topic, all of his descendants should reflect on its
meaning. All those who study are practicing the saindhava in the same way
as Śākyamuni, but those who do not practice it in this way must strengthen
their efforts to make the first step of authentic practice. The saindhava was
already being practiced by buddhas and patriarchs long before it was
disclosed, partially, to royal families.

One time old master Hung-chih of Mt. T'ien-t'ung in Ching-yüan-fu
in Sung China entered the lecture hall and instructed his followers:

> A monk said to Chao-chou, "What will you do when asked
> for saindhava?"
> Chao-chou folded his hands over his chest and bowed.
> Hsüeh-tou commented [on this topic], "When salt is re-
> quested, I will offer a horse."[11]

Hung-chih also said, "Hsüeh-tou was a great priest who lived a hundred
years ago, and Chao-chou was an old master whose life spanned one
hundred and twenty years. If Chao-chou's answer were right then Hsüeh-
tou would be wrong, and if Hsüeh-tou were right then Chao-chou would
be wrong. Which answer is better?" Hung-chih commented on this in the
following way: "If one of these responses were wrong, it would be one
thousand *ri* from the other one. Expressing is like beating the grass to
frighten a snake, and not expressing is like burning money to exorcise the

demons.[12] Neither [response] wanders into an open field. [Both] are like Chu-ti holding up one finger."[13]

When my former teacher [Ju-ching of Mt. T'ien-t'ung], an old master, entered the lecture hall he frequently referred to "old master Hung-chih." However, my former teacher was the only one who referred to old master Hung-chih as an old master. In Hung-chih's time there was another monk named Ta-hui Tsung-kao of Mt. Ching, who is said to have been in the lineage of Nan-yüeh. Most people during the Sung era thought Ta-hui the equal of Hung-chih. Some even considered Ta-hui to be superior. This error was due to the fact that monks and laypersons alike in Sung China studied superficially, did not possess an insight into the way, and had not yet acquired knowledge of self or others.[14]

Hung-chih's comments reflect a true understanding. We must study the meaning of old master Chao-chou's "folding his hands over his chest and bowing." Did this gesture represent "the king's requesting saindhava" or "the retainer's offering saindhava"? We must also study the significance of Hsüeh-tou's response, "When salt is requested, I will offer a horse." "I will offer a horse" is both the king requesting saindhava and the retainer offering a saindhava. When Śākyamuni requested saindhava, Mahākāśyapa smiled. When Bodhidharma requested saindhava, his four disciples offered him a horse, salt, water, and a chalice. We must study why it was that when a horse, or salt, or water, or a chalice were requested as saindhava, [any one of] the disciples [may have] offered [only] a horse or [only] water.[15]

One day when Nan-ch'üan saw Teng-yin-feng coming, he pointed to a pitcher of water and said, "The pitcher is an object. It contains some water. Bring the water over to this old priest without moving the object." Teng-yin-feng brought the pitcher over to Nan-ch'üan and poured the water all over him. Nan-ch'üan remained silent.

Nan-ch'üan requested water, which came from the dried-up sea, and Teng-yin-feng offered a chalice or a pitcher he used to pour out every drop of water. Nevertheless, we must study the water in the object and the object in the water. Was it the water that was being moved, or was it the object that was being moved?

> The great teacher Hsiang-yen was asked by a monk, "What is it when a king asks his retainer for saindhava?"
> Hsiang-yen responded, "Come over here."
> The monk went over there, and Hsiang-yen said, "Don't be such a fool!"[16]

However, we could ask, did Hsiang-yen's command, "Come over here," indicate a king requesting saindhava or a retainer offering it? Just try to answer that question!

Furthermore, when "the monk went over there," did that indicate that Hsiang-yen was requesting saindhava, receiving saindhava being offered, or expressing another, more fundamental concern? If he were not expressing a more fundamental concern, we could not understand the meaning of his saying, "Don't be such a fool." If he did not have a more fundamental concern, the monk he called over would not have appeared so foolish. Although Hsiang-yen's response stems from an understanding built up during an entire lifetime, we should not be concerned [that the monk failed]. It is like a general who has lost a battle but is proud in defeat. Generally, [the buddhas and patriarchs] explain the [mutuality] of the request and the offering of saindhava in extremely subtle ways, such as pointing to black and calling it yellow, in order to reveal the nature of an enlightened vision.[17] Who can say that holding a staff or a fly whisk is not a type of saindhava? On the other hand, are there not those [who are supposedly specialists but] who do not know how to fasten the bridge to the base of a *koto* or how to tighten the strings of a *koto* to just the right degree?[18]

> One time when the World-Honored one sat on a dais [to preach the Dharma, before uttering even a word], Mañjuśrī struck the gavel [to signal the end of the discourse] and said, "When seen clearly the teaching of the king of Dharma is just like this: this is the teaching of the king of Dharma."[19]

> Zen master Hsüeh-tou commented on this:

> If only one sage [in the assembly] understood
> The real meaning of the teaching of the king of Dharma;
> If only one of them had realized the value of saindhava
> Would Mañjuśrī have needed to strike the gavel?

Hsüeh-tou's comment means that striking a single blow of the gavel while exerting one's entire body, whether or not one actually strikes a gavel, is the casting off (*datsuraku*) of the striking of the gavel. If this is the case, then the gavel is itself saindhava. And [Mañjuśrī] is already such a person [who realizes saindhava], and all of the wise sages present are the recipients of his saindhava, because "the teaching of the king of Dharma is just like this." All activity and expression throughout twenty-four hours is nothing other than requesting saindhava. All activity and expression throughout twenty-four hours is nothing other than offering saindhava. When you request a fist you receive a fist, and when you request a flywhisk you receive a flywhisk.

However, because in Sung China the senior monks in all the districts are pretentious, they cannot imagine this in their wildest dreams. What a pity! The way of the patriarchs is on the decline. Do not avoid taking up the most challenging studies for it is up to you to transmit the lifeblood of the buddhas and patriarchs. For example, when we are asked what the buddha is, we may answer "this very mind itself is buddha" (*sokushin-ze-butsu*), but what does this mean? Is it not [an example of] saindhava? You must carefully study "this very mind itself is buddha." How few are there who truly understand the meaning of saindhava.

This instruction for an assembly of monks was delivered on the twenty-second day of the tenth month in 1245 at Daibutsuji Temple in Echizen.

UNGRASPABLE MIND:
A TRANSLATION OF THE KS "SHINFUKATOKU" FASCICLE

Śākyamuni once said: "Past mind is ungraspable, present mind is ungraspable, and future mind is ungraspable."[20]

This represents the practice of the buddhas and patriarchs. We attain awareness of past, present, and future in terms of the ungraspable mind. But this only occurs by virtue of our [ordinary] self-awareness. Our self[-awareness] is none other than the ungraspable mind. Discursive, discriminative thinking right now is the ungraspable mind. Our whole body abiding throughout this very twenty-four hours is the ungraspable mind. By entering on the path of the buddhas and patriarchs, one merges into the ungraspable mind. If one has not yet entered the path of the buddhas and patriarchs, then he or she will not be able to see, hear of, or attain the ungraspable mind. Even those who are learned in the *sūtra* and *śāstra* literature are unable to even dream about it.

There is a familiar example of this doctrine involving Zen master Te-shan Hsüan-chieh, who claimed to be an expert in the *Diamond Sūtra*, and who thought of himself as "the king of the *sūtra*."[21] Te-shan was especially proud [of his knowledge of the commentary on the *Diamond Sūtra* by a monk named] Chin-lung Tao-chi. He also boasted of having written twelve volumes of commentary and of being an unsurpassed lecturer [on the *Diamond Sūtra*]. Te-shan was a prominent figure in the path of scholastic Buddhism. However, upon hearing that the supreme Dharma was being transmitted [through patriarchal transmission] directly from generation to generation in the Southern school he became jealous, and eventually he traveled over hill and dale carrying his writings on the *sūtra* to see firsthand the southern district. On the way, he heard that master Lung-t'an was slated to preach to an assembly of monks, and he decided to join that group. While taking a rest by the side of the road, he was greeted by an old woman also resting there.

> Te-shan asked her, "Who are you?"
> She responded, "I am an old woman selling rice cakes."
> He said, "I'll take some rice cakes."
> She said, "Venerable priest, why do you want them?"
> He said, "I am hungry and need some refreshments (*ten-shin*)."
> She said, "Venerable priest, what are you carrying in your bag?"
> He said, "Haven't you heard I am 'the king of the *Diamond Sūtra*.' I have thoroughly penetrated all of its levels of meaning. Here I have my notes and commentaries on the scripture."
> Hearing this the old woman said, "I have one question. Venerable priest, may I ask it?"
> He said, "Go ahead and ask it."
> She stated, "I have heard it said that according to the *Diamond Sūtra*, past mind is ungraspable, present mind is ungraspable, and future mind is ungraspable. So, where is the mind (*shin*) that you wish to refresh (*ten*) with rice cakes? Venerable priest, if you can answer, I will sell you a rice cake. But if, venerable priest, you cannot answer, I will not sell you any rice cake."[22]

Te-shan was struck speechless, and the old woman got up abruptly and left without selling Te-shan a single rice cake.

It is truly pitiable that someone who had written voluminous commentaries and lectured for so many years [on the *Diamond Sūtra*] was outsmarted so easily by such an unassuming old woman, and was unable to answer even a single, simple question about the scripture. This anecdote shows that there is a world of difference between a seeker who hears the true Dharma by seeing and learning directly from a true master and someone who has not yet heard the true Dharma or even seen a true master. It was only after he received the transmission of the Dharma from Lung-t'an that Te-shan was able to say for the first time that "a painted rice cake (*gabyō*) cannot satisfy hunger."

When we consider the contextual conditions (*innen*) of the encounter between the old woman and Te-shan, it seems clear that Te-shan must have been unenlightened at the outset of their dialogue. Even after he became a disciple of Lung-t'an, he probably still felt intimidated by the old woman's question. Te-shan probably always remained a follower after this incident and was unable to attain the status of an "old master" who has realized a self-surpassing enlightenment. But even though the old woman was able to reduce Te-shan to silence on that particular occasion, it is not clear whether or not she was actually a truly enlightened person. Based on their dialogical exchange, it seems that the old woman thought that the phrase "ungraspable mind" only refers to the "ungraspability or unreality of mind." If Te-shan had been more skillful, he could have adroitly surpassed her. Had he been able to surpass her, then the evidence for her own true enlightenment would have been more apparent. But since Te-shan was not yet the [truly enlightened] Te-shan, it seems that the old woman may not have yet been a truly enlightened person at this point either.[23]

Currently in Sung China, many dimwitted [monks] are quite superficial and foolish in responding so unfavorably to Te-shan while at the same time lavishly praising the old woman's wisdom. But it is not unreasonable to doubt [her understanding]. When Te-shan was unable to answer, why didn't she say to him, "Venerable priest, if you cannot answer my question, try asking me a question to see if I can answer you." In that case, if she had been able to express her own understanding in answering Te-shan's [hypothetical] question in such a way that he felt directly encountered [by her insight], then it would be clear that she was a truly enlightened person. For although she raised [such a powerful] question, she did not express [her own understanding during the dialogue]. Throughout history, it has never been the case that someone who did not express even a single word [of their own understanding] was considered to be truly enlightened. Of course it has always been considered useless folly for someone like Te-shan to engage in self-promotion. But, the old woman's failure to express her own understanding is also problematic.

Let us try to consider what Te-shan should have said in this situation.[24] When the old woman asked her question, he could have retorted, "If you say so, then don't bother to sell me any rice cakes." That would have been an effective response. Or he could have asked her,

As past mind is ungraspable, present mind is ungraspable, and future mind is ungraspable, where is the mind (*shin*) that now makes the rice cakes used for refreshment (*ten*)?

In that case, the old woman could confront Te-shan by saying,

You know only that one cannot refresh the mind with a rice cake. But you do not realize that the mind refreshes the rice cake, or that the mind refreshes [or liberates] the mind (*kokoro no kokoro o tenzuru*).

Hearing this, Te-shan would undoubtedly feel bewildered. At that point, she should offer him three rice cakes by saying to the perplexed Te-shan, "[Here is one rice cake each for] the past ungraspable mind, the present ungraspable mind, and the future ungraspable mind." If he should fail to reach out his hand to take the rice cakes, she should slap him with one of the rice cakes and say, "You ignorant fool, don't be so absent-minded." If Te-shan should then give a good reply, the old woman would be able to feel satisfied [about his understanding]; otherwise, she would need to instruct him further. According to the original anecdote, the old woman left abruptly although she did not intend to humiliate Te-shan. On the other hand, he did not ask her, "I cannot answer your question, what would you say?" Therefore, neither the old woman nor Te-shan were able to adequately hear or express the past ungraspable mind, the present ungraspable mind, or the future ungraspable mind.

After this incident, Te-shan continued to struggle to attain an awakening experience. If he had diligently trained with and absorbed the teaching of Lung-t'an for a long time, perhaps he would have attained a true awakening and received the transmission of the jewel. His experience of seeing Lung-t'an blow out a candle in the dark was not sufficient for him to receive the transmission of the lamp. This highlights the point that monks in training (*unsui*) must study with utmost diligence, for [Te-shan's] casual manner is not satisfactory to attain the way of the buddhas and patriarchs. As a rule, [to realize] the ungraspable mind is to imbibe and to savor a painted rice cake (*gabyō*).

This instruction for an assembly of monks was delivered during the summer training period of 1242 at Kannondōri Kōshōhōrinji Temple in Uji-gun, Yawashiro.

Appendix II
On the Mana Shōbōgenzō

KŌAN CASE CHART FOR MANA SHŌBŌGENZŌ

Introduction

The aim of the following chart is to demonstrate the intra- and inter-textuality of the MS text in relation to Dōgen's others texts as well as to the prominent texts in Sung China which served as the basis for his citation of kōans. The chart lists three items: the titles of each of the three hundred MS kōan cases; Dōgen's texts in which some mention or discussion of the case appears; and the Sung texts which probably were the source of his citations, especially the KD, SR, and ST. For the list in the first column (titles) I have consulted in addition to the Japanese text in Kawamura Kōdō's SSK and in the DZZ II two English translations: an unpublished translation by Francis Cook, and Hisao Inagaki, *A Glossary of Zen Terms* (Kyoto: Nagata Bunshodo, 1991), 463–84. The list of Dōgen's texts in the second column is a translation with minor changes from the SSK, 267–301. The third column listing of Sung texts is translated from the same passage in SSK with some additions selected from Ishii Shūdō's CZS, 561–70. Immediately below is a list of abbreviations for the titles of Dōgen's texts and the texts of Sung Zen. The fascicle titles that are listed in the second column of the main chart all refer to Dōgen's KS text; an asterisk indicates that the kōan citation may be referred to indirectly or may appear in an irregular version of the fascicle that is not included in some modern editions. The order of the texts listed in the third column is based on

Kawamura's judgment of the primary and secondary influences on the formation of the MS; Ishii's list puts more emphasis on the ST than does Kawamura's list. Note that the major kōan collections, the *Hekiganroku*, *Shōyōroku* and *Mumonkan*, are not included in the list of Sung texts; the first text was apparently not a source for MS cases, and the latter two texts were published in Japan after the composition of the MS. Unfortunately, the *Mana Shōbōgenzō Sanbyakusoku: Goi-Sakuin* edited by the Sōtō-shū Shūgaku Kenkyūjō (Tokyo, 1993) was released too late for me to consult it.

Abbreviations of Dōgen's Texts:

CS	*Nihonkoku Echizen Eiheiji Chiji Shingi*
EK	*Eihei Kōroku*, 10 fascicles
EK-9	*Eihei Kōroku*, ninth fascicle
G	*Gakudōyōjinshū*
KS	*Kana Shōbōgenzō*, 92 fascicles
MS	*Mana Shōbōgenzō*, or *Shōbōgenzō Sanbyakusoku*, 300 cases
SZ	*Shōbōgenzō Zuimonki*, 6 fascicles
T	*Tenzokyōkun*
WS	*Waka Shū*

Abbreviations of Sung Zen Texts:

DR	*Daie (Ta-hui) Roku*
DS	*Daie (Ta-hui) Shōbōgenzō*
ER	*Engo (Yüan-wu) Roku*
JR	*Jōshū (Chao-chou) Roku*
KD	*Keitoku Dentōroku*
KF	*Katai Futōroku*
KZ	*Kenchū Seikoku Zokutōroku*
NR	*Nyojō Roku*
OR	*Ōbaku (Huang-po) Roku*
RR	*Rinzai (Lin-chi) Roku*
SJ	*Setchō (Hsüeh-tou) Juko Hyakusoku*
SR	*Shūmon Rentōeyō*
ST	*Shūmon Tōyōshū*
TK	*Tenshō Kōtōroku*
TR	*Tōzan (Tung-shan) Roku*
WK	*Wanshi (Hung-chih) Kōroku*

MS Case Titles	Dōgen's Texts (cases cited in)	Sung Texts (sources)
	MS I (*Jōkan*)	
1. Ch'ing-yüan picks up his *hossu*	Butsudō, Mitsugo, Kokū*, EK-9 (18)	DS, SR, KD, ST
2. Pai-chang's reason for sitting down in silence	EK 2, 6, -9 (44)	SR, KD, ST
3. Nan-ch'üan's water buffalo	EK 2	DS, KD, SR
4. Head monk Liang interviews Ma-tsu	Kokū*	KD, SR, ST
5. Why the ten thousand dharmas are nondependent	—	SR, WK, ER, ST
6. Lang-yeh's "Pure original nature"	Keiseisanshoku*, EK-9 (46)	WK, ER, KF
7. Yang-shan's "It is not that enlightenment does not exist"	Daigo*, EK-9 (47)	WK, KD, SR
8. Nan-ch'üan's "Polishing a tile and beating the cart"	Zazenshin, Kokyō*, EK-9 (38), SZ 3	KD, DS, SR
9. Prime Minister P'ei-hsü responds "Yes"	Gyōji I*, EK-9 (48)	KD, SR
10. Ch'ing-yüan responds to the question about "[Bodhidharma's] coming from the west"	EK-9 (49)	SR, ST
11. Chao-chou's "Losing the mind in confusion"	EK-9 (43)	JR, ST
12. Tung-shan's "Going beyond buddha"	Bukkōkōji, EK-9 (50)	KD
13. T'ou-tzu's "Swallowing two or three [moons]"	Juki*, EK-9 (17)	KD, SR
14. Kuei-shan's "Blue is not yellow"	Genjōkōan*, Yuibutsu yobutsu*, EK-9 (40)	SR, ST
15. Hsüan-sha's "One bright pearl"	Ikka myōjū, Jippō*, EK 1, -9 (41)	DR, SR
16. Ch'ang-sha's "Transforming the self [into the mountains, rivers, and great earth]	Keiseisanshoku*, EK-9 (42)	WK, ER, SR
17. Hsiang-yen attains great enlightment on hearing the sound of a stone striking bamboo	Gyōji I, Menjū, Keiseisanshoku, Bendōwa*, SZ 5, 3, EK 6, 8, -9 (62)	SR, KD

*Indicates the case may be referred to indirectly or may appear in an irregular version of the fascicle not included in some modern editions.

MS Case Titles	Dōgen's Texts (cases cited in)	Sung Texts (sources)
18. Nan-ch'üan meets the land[-deity]	Gyōji I, EK-9 (63)	SR, KD, ST
19. Nan-ch'üan's "Everyday mind is Tao"	Shinjingakudō*, Bukkōjōji*	SR, KD, ST
20. Ch'ang-sha's "Stop illusory thinking"	Busshō*, SZ 2, 7, EK-9 (65)	DS, SR, ST
21. Pan-shan's "Cut off a slice of the best [meat]"	EK-9 (67)	SR, DS, ST
22. P'u-hua rings the bell	Zazenshin, Kaiinzammai, Kokyō, Henzan*	DS, ST
23. Yang-shan's "High places and low places are equal"	Arakan*, T*, EK-9 (66)	KD
24. Ta-sui's "Fire blazing at the end of the kalpa"	Daigo, Den'e, Bukkyō*, SZ 1, EK-9 (83)	KD, SR, ST
25. Ti-tsang fasts for Hsüan-sha	—	SR, ST
26. Hsi-ching's "An [alms-giver] treading on Vairocana's head"	—	KD
27. Lin-chi is enlightened by the blows from Huang-po's staff	Gyōji (1)*, Butsudō*, EK 7, 8, -9 (51)	KF, KD, SR, DS, RR
28. Hsiang-yen's "Dragon singing in a withered tree"	Ryūgin*	SR, ST
29. Chien-yüan's "Dead or alive"	EK 2, CS	SR, KD, DS, ST
30. Ts'ao-shan's "Not following the path"	Shisho*	ER, KD
31. Te-shan's "Thirty blows for not getting out of the boat"	—	ER, KD
32. Ta-yüan's "Prior to the birth of your father and mother"	—	ER, KD, SR
33. Ts'ao-shan's "Falling down [but getting up] without depending on the ground"	Immo*	KD
34. Yün-chu's, "The World-Honored One's intimate words"	Mitsugo*	KD, SR
35. T'ou-tzu's charioteer possessing ten bodies [of buddha]	EK-9 (54)	SR, ST
36. Te-hai's "Assembly on Vulture Peak"	—	KD
37. Kan-feng's "One straight path to nirvāṇa"	Jippō*	SR, WK, DS, ST

MS Case Titles	Dōgen's Texts (cases cited in)	Sung Texts (sources)
38. Hsüeh-feng's "Turning the wheel of the great Dharma"	Ikka myōju, Kannon, SR, ST	
39. Tao-fu's "Buddha Dharma at the new year"	Busshō*, EK 1	SR, OR
40. San-sheng pushes a monk in front of [of Pao-shou]	—	ER
41. Shih-t'ou's "Ask the center pillars"	Busshō, Raihaitokuzui, EK 5	SR, KD
42. Ching-ch'ing's reason for thirty blows	Henzan	SR, ST
43. Kuei-tsung cuts a snake in two	—	SR, KD, ST
44. Ta-kuei's "I can spare you the trouble"	SZ 6*	SR, KD, ST
45. Hsüan-sha's "Teaching the three vehicles in [twelve] divisions"	Bukkyō	KD
46. Chao-chou's "East gate, west gate"	Sangai yuishin*, Henzan*, EK-9 (21)	DR
47. Ta-kuei's "Do not be ungrateful to others"	—	SR, ST
48. Hsüan-sha writes nothing on the page	—	KD, SR, ER
49. Tung-shan's "Did you reach the peak?"	—	KD, SR, ST, TR
50. Shih-lou's reason for having no earlobes	—	KD, SR, ST
51. Nan-ch'üan's "When Niu-t'ou had not yet met [the fourth patriarch]"	—	SR, DR
52. San-sheng's "The golden scale fish passes through the net"	Kokyō*	SR, DR, ST
53. Ch'ing-yüan's and Shih-t'ou's "Great tripiṭika, small tripiṭika"	Bukkyō*	ER, KD
54. Pai-chang once again visits Ma-tsu	EK 1, -9 (82)	ER, KD, DR
55. Tung-shan's "Which of three [Buddha-]bodies preaches the Dharma"	Menju, Jinzū, Henzan*	DS, KD, SR, TR, ST

MS Case Titles	Dōgen's Texts (cases cited in)	Sung Texts (sources)
56. Ta-kuei donates three bolts of silk	—	SR, ST
57. Nan-ch'üan's "Where wisdom cannot reach"	Kankin*, Bukkōjōji, EK-9 (61)	KD, SR, ST
58. Shih-shuang's "Nothing concealed in the entire universe"	Busshō, Gyōbutsuigi, Zazenshin, Juki, T	SR, ST
59. Ts'ao-chi's "I do not understand the Buddha Dharma"	Kenbutsu*, EK 8	DR, SR, ST
60. Hsüeh-feng constructs a seamless monument	Juki*	DS, KD, SR, ST
61. Ta-kuei turns his face to the wall	Jinzū*, Arakan*	SR, KD, ST
62. Tung-shan's "Disclosing mind, disclosing nature"	Sesshin sesshō	SR, TR, ST
63. Pao-fu's "Which venerable master have you met?"	—	KD, SR
64. Nan-ch'üan's "The clean jar is the container"	Ōsakusendaba*	SR, KD
65. Kuei-tsung's "I have one-taste Zen"	—	ER, KF, SR, DS
66. Yüeh-shan's "A calf bears a child"	—	ER, KD, SR, KF
67. Chao-chou's "Go wash your bowls"	EK 6	DR, SR, WK
68. Yang-shan sticks his hoe in the ground and clasps his hands in front of him	—	KD, SR, ST
69. Mu-chou's "A hundred families use it daily"	Yuibustu yobutsu*	DR
70. Ts'ao-shan's "Eating the ever abiding sprouts"	Hōsshō, Jippō, Kajō, Udonge, Jishō-zammai, Gyōji	DR, DS, ST
71. Ts'ui-wei's dialogue on the meaning of [Bodhidharma's] coming from the west	Menju, Keiseisanshoku*, EK-9 (36)	KD, SR
72. Tung-shan's "Going beyond buddha"	Bukkōjōji*	KD, SR, DS
73. Pi-mo-yen's "You shall die from my pitchfork even if you express it"	—	DS, KD, SR, ST

MS Case Titles	Dōgen's Texts (cases cited in)	Sung Texts (sources)
74. Chao-chou finishes chanting the *sūtras*	Kankin*	DR
75. Yen-t'ou's reason for sitting while the kalpa arrives	Kaiinzammai*	DR, SR
76. Ta-kuei's "No mind is the Way"	—	SR, ST
77. Hsing-k'ung's "Disclosing ten feet long [is better than one foot]"	Gyōji I*, Dōtoku*, EK 1, 7	SR, KD, ST
78. Tung-shan's reason for eating the fruit	—	SR, DS, TR, ST
79. Yüeh-shan ascends his seat and then waits awhile	Kankin, EK 7, 8	WK
80. Chao-chou's "There is Buddha, there is no Buddha"	SZ 6	WK, SR, JR
81. Yün-men's "Everyone has a radiance within"	Gyōbutsuigi*, Kūge*	ER
82. Tung-shan's "No grass grows for ten thousand *ri* all around"	Gyōbutsuigi*, Ango*	ER, TR, DS
83. Yün-yen holds up his broom	Juki*, EK-9 (12)	SR, DS, KD, ST
84. Yün-yen's "Not even a single word"	—	KD, SR, ST
85. Chüan-ming's "When a hair bores many holes"	Kūge*	SR, ST
86. Yüeh-shan's "You can wash this [infant buddha]"	—	ER, SR
87. Nan-ch'üan's pat on the back	EK-9 (79)	DR
88. Layman P'ang's "The clear meaning of the patriarch"	Gyōbutsuigi, EK 1, 4, 8, -9 (9)	SR, ST
89. Shih-shuang's "This side and that side"	—	ST
90. Chia-shan sees the ferryman	Muchū-setsumu*, Sansuikyō*, EK 8, -9 (10, 22, 28)	DS, SR, ST
91. Huang-po's single staff	EK 1	?
92. San-sheng's "Coming forth and and not coming forth"	Kokyō*, Uji*, Gyōbutsuigi*	WK, SR, DS
93. Seng-mi's holding a needle	—	SR, ST

MS Case Titles	Dōgen's Texts (cases cited in)	Sung Texts (sources)
94. Yün-chu's "It is not contained anywhere"	—	KD
95. Yün-men's disclosing [the Dharma] in accord and in opposition to [time and audience]	—	SJ
96. P'u-hua kicks over the dining table	Jinzū	DR, ER, KF, SR, ST
97. Su-shan offers some money	Shinjingakudō, Kobusshin	DS, SR
98. Tung-shan is not well	—	WK
99. (Layman P'ang's) "Original person who is not obscured"	—	DS, DR, SR, ST
100. Yün-men's "Going beyond the Dharmakāya"	—	ER, SR
MS II (*Chūkan*)		
101. [Ta-hui] Nan-yüeh's "To say it is like a thing [misses it]"	Busshō, Shinjingakudō*, Gyōbutsuigi*, Gyōji*, Immo*, Juki*, Menju, Bukkyō, Butsudō, Bukkyō, Kenbutsu*, Henzan*, Senjū, Jishō-zammai, Bendōwa, EK 5, 7, 8, -9 (59)	KF, KD
102. Pai-chang's "Not obsuring causality"	Ikka myōjū*, Raihaitokuzui*, Daishugyō, Arakan*, Jinshininga, SZ 2, EK 1, 5, -9 (77)	DS, SR, TK, KF, ST
103. Ta-kuei's "Tearing apart the past and present"	Shisho*	SR, ST
104. Lung-t'an [first lights then] blows out a candle	Shinfukatoku*, EK-9 (24)	DS
105. Yün-yen's "Hands and eyes all over the body"	Kannon	SR, WK, ER, ST
106. Lung-t'an makes cake for a living	EK-9 (24)	KD, DS
107. Yün-men's "The light does not penetrate"	—	WK, SR, DS
108. Ma-tsu's "Chi-tsang's head and Hui-hai's head"	Daigo*, EK-9 (78)	WK, SR
109. Hsüeh-feng's "The breadth of the world [is ten feet]"	Kokyō	SR, KD, ER, ST

MS Case Titles	Dōgen's Texts (cases cited in)	Sung Texts (sources)
110. Ta-kuei's disciples expressing themselves in words	—	SR, ST
111. Fa-yen's "The fountainhead is obstructed"	Kōkyō, Gyōbutsuigi	KD, SR, ST
112. Hsüan-sha's "The triple world is mind only"	Kobusshin*, Sangai yuishin*	KD, SR, ST
113. Pao-fu's reason for blocking his eyes and ears	—	KS, KD, SR, ST
114. Chao-chou's "Does the dog have Buddha-nature?"	Busshō, G, EK 6, 7, 8 -9 (73)	WK, SR
115. Ta-kuei's "Sentient beings have no Buddha[-nature]"	Busshō, EK-9 (39)	SR, ST
116. Ta-hui's "A [Buddha-] image reflected in a mirror"	Kōkyō*, EK 5	TK, KD, DS, SR
117. Master Yüan-t'ao's "Explanation of the primordial mirror"	Kōkyō*	KD
118. Yang-shan's "Ask one question, receive ten answers"	Gyōji*, Bukkōjoji*	SR, ST
119. Chao-chou's "The oak tree in the garden"	Hakujushi*, EK 6, 7, 8, -9 (45)	SR, DR, ST
120. Chin-shan's "Arising and not arising"	EK 1	WK, KD, SR
121. Ma-ku cuts grass with a hoe	SZ 1	DS, SR, ST
122. Hsüan-tse's "Fire attendant"	Bendōwa, SS, EK 1, 4	WK, KD, SR, DS
123. Pao-che [Ma-tsu] "There is no place [the wind] does not circulate"	Genjōkōan	SR, ST
124. Shen and Ming drawing a fishnet	EK-9 (70)	SR, DS, ST
125. Ts'ao-shan's "It is like a donkey seeing a well"	Busshō*, Shoaku makusa*, Bukkōjōji*, EK 5	WK
126. Ta-tien remains silent for a long time	Busshō*	SR, ST
127. Mañjuśrī's "Three in front and three behind"	Busshō*	DR, NR
128. Pai-chang's gate for entering the ultimate reality	Kannon*	KD, SR, ST
129. Yüeh-shan on not-thinking	Zazengi, Zazenshin*, EK 5, 7	KD, SR, ST

MS Case Titles	Dōgen's Texts (cases cited in)	Sung Texts (sources)
130. Ta-kuei's "Sixty pails of donkey's milk"	EK 1	KD, SR, DS
131. Hui-ch'iu's "[The master's] flesh is still warm"	Shinjingakudō*, Kūge*, Kattō*, EK-9 (37)	KD, SR, ST
132. Pen-jen's "Sound itself is no-sound"	—	ER, SR, DS, ST
133. Chao-chou examines an old woman	Shinfukatoku*	ER, KD, WK
134. Kuei-shan's "Is the weather cold, or are people cold?"	—	KD, ER, SR
135. Chao-chou throws a tile [into the fire] to make a jewel	Shinjingakudō, Zazenshin	ER, KD, SR
136. Chao-chou's discourse on the great death	—	WK, DR, DS
137. Hsüeh-feng's "Not even a flake [of snow] remains"	EK 1, 5	SR, ST
138. Chao-chou's "Brightness and darkness"	—	KD
139. Yang-shan's "The doctor reads the *sūtra*"	Busshō*, Gyōbutsuigi*, Kenbutsu*	SR, ST
140. The Third Patriarch's "You already have no mind"	SZ	SR, ST
141. The World-Honored One ascends his seat, and Mañjuśrī raps the gavel	EK 3	SR
142. Yang-shan thrusts out a pillow	—	KD, DS, SR, ST
143. Tao-k'ai explains the intentions of the buddhas and patriarchs	Kajō, EK-9 (57)	SR, KF
144. Hsüan-sha says "Is that so?"	—	SR, ST
145. Te-shan's "Asking a question is itself to blame"	—	SR, ST
146. The Sixth Patriarch says "It is your mind that is moving"	Immo*, Raihaitokuzui*, EK-9 (8)	KD, TK, SR
147. Lin-chi's "True man without rank"	Kūge, Uji, Sesshin sesshō*	WK, KD, TK, SR, RR
148. Yün-yen's "Insentient beings preach the Dharma"	Mujō seppō*, EK 6, -9 (52)	KD

MS Case Titles	Dōgen's Texts (cases cited in)	Sung Texts (sources)
149. Hsüeh-feng's "A thin strip of arable land"	—	SR, ST
150. Ta-chi raises his eyebrows and blinks his eyes	Uji*	SR, DR, DS, ER
151. Yüeh-shan's "Do not change even if the country is overthrown"	—	SR, KD
152. Ta-cheng points to a stone lion	—	SR, KD
153. Pai-ling puts on his bamboo rain hat	—	KD, SR
154. Nan-ch'üan's "This [sickle] cuts well"	Sansuikyō*, EK 8, -9 (81)	WK, SR
155. Ling-yün is enlightened on seeing the peach blossoms in bloom	Bendōwa, Keiseisanshoku*, Udonge*, SZ , 3, 5, WS, EK 6, -9 (72)	DS, KD, SR
156. Ling-yün on donkeys and horses	Gyōji*, Uji*, Shoaku makusa, EK-9 (29)	DS, SR, KD
157. Kuei-shan's "Expressing and not expressing it"	Busshō, Shinjingakudō, Gyōbutsuigi, Kattō	WK
158. Yün-men's dust-mote samādhi	EK 6, 8	WK, SR, ER
159. Su-tsung is possessed of the ten bodies	—	KD, SR
160. [The demon] Nalakuvara crushes his bones and returns them to his father	—	KD
161. Shih-shih's "Such are the buddhas of the three periods"	—	ER
162. Yün-men's "On the tips of a hundred blades of grass"	—	ER, DR
163. Hsüan-sha builds a seamless monument	Juki*	KD, SR, DS, ST
164. Lin-chi's "Ask [the two Zen guests] in the Dharma Hall"	—	SR, ST
165. The World-Honored One did not speak a word	—	KD, SR
166. Yün-men's "When birth and death arrive"	—	ER

MS Case Titles	Dōgen's Texts (cases cited in)	Sung Texts (sources)
167. Lin-chi's "[The demon] perishes with the blind donkey"	Butsudō*	WK, KD, TK, SR
168. Ta-kuei's "Wondrous, pure and radiant mind"	Shinjingakudō*, Sokushin-zebutsu*, SZ 2	SR, ST
169. Mahākāśyapa's "Topple over the flagpole"	Bendōwa, EK 3, 8	SR, ST
170. The non-Buddhist philosopher asks for neither words nor no-words	Shime*	SR, WK, DS, ER, ST
171. Fa-yen's "Not knowing is the point"	EK 1, -9 (16)	KD, WK
172. Tung-shan's "Buddha is three pounds of flax"	SZ 5, T, EK-9 (68)	KF, ER, SR, DS
173. The emperor welcomes the Buddha's relics	Kōmyō	SR, ST
174. The World-Honored One celebrates the seven primordial buddhas	—	SR, ST
175. Chien-yüan sits in a paper tent	—	WK, SR
176. Hsüeh-feng's "Innumerable dead men"	—	WK, SR
177. Tsu-chao's "Whose successor are you?"	—	WK, SR
178. Lin-chi sees Huang-po reading a *sūtra*	—	RR, KD, SR, ST
179. Shih-shuang's "Not a single person understands thoroughly"	Shinjingakudō	SR, KD, ST
180. Shui-yen asks about the originally abiding principle	—	WK, KD, SR
181. Nan-ch'üan cuts a cat in two	SZ 2, EK-9 (76)	WK, KD, SR
182. Pai-chang is enlightened seeing a wild duck	T	SR, TK, SR
183. The hermit's "The valley stream is deep; the ladle is long"	Gyōji I*, Dōtoku, EK-9 (71)	DS, SR, ST
184. Yün-yen's "Stop, stop"	—	KD, SR
185. Yün-chi's "Within the matrix of the Tathāgata"	—	WK, KD, ER, SR

MS Case Titles	Dōgen's Texts (cases cited in)	Sung Texts (sources)
186. Ho-shan's "Learning and beyond learning"	—	SR, ST
187. Chin-feng eats half a cake	—	SR, ST
188. Kuei-tsung raises his fist	Gyōji II*, Juki*	KD, SR, ST
189. Ch'ing-ch'i's "The thief is in your family"	EK-9 (74), EK 10	KD, DS, SR, ST
190. Ma-tsu's "Six ears not in accord"	—	ER, KD, SR
191. Shih-t'ou's "Not expressing or knowing it"	Bukkōjōji*, EK 1	KD
192. Chang-ch'ing's "Seeing forms, seeing mind"	Bukkōjōji*	KD
193. Shih-shuang's "Everything you see is *bodhi*"	—	KD, SR
194. Ts'ao-shan's "It harbors the ten thousand things"	Kaiinzammai.	KD, SR, TR
195. Nan-ch'üan's "The way is not outside ordinary things"	—	KD, SR
196. Lung-ya's "Like a thief breaking into an [empty] room"	—	KD, SR, DS
197. Kuei-shan first presents an air of dignity	—	DR, SR
198. Shen-shan and Tung-shan cross the river	—	DR, SR, TR
199. Hsui-ching's place where weeds do not grow	—	KD, TK, SR, ST
200. Shiu-yen's "What period is this?"	—	SR, ST
	MS III (*Gekan*)	
201. Bodhidharma's "Skin, flesh, bones, marrow"	Kattō, Ōsakusendaba, EK 1, 7	KD, SR
202. Huang-po's "You are all dregs-eaters"	EK 1	WK, TK, KD
203. Hsüan-sha's "Saving things and benefitting beings"	EK-9 (34)	SR, WK
204. Tung-shan's "Dead snake in the road"	Kankin	WK, SR

MS Case Titles	Dōgen's Texts (cases cited in)	Sung Texts (sources)
205. Ts'ui-wei's "Come here past the back-rest"	—	WK, ER, KD, SR
206. Shih-t'i's "Entering the hall for purification"	—	WK, SR
207. Lin-chi's "You are an ordinary person"	Busshō*	SR, TK, RR, ST
208. Yün-men's "I still have ninety days of food money"	Ango*	SR, ER
209. Ta-kuei writes five words on the left side	Busshō*, T, EK-9 (69)	KD, SR, ST
210. The National Teacher [Nan-yüeh]'s "Come here past the water pitcher"	—	WK
211. Ts'ao-shan's "It is a matter of course"	—	WK, SR
212. Ti-tsang's "Sowing the fields and harvesting rice"	EK 6	WK, SR
213. Tao-wu's "An equally enlightened one understands at once"	—	SR, ST
214. Feng-hsüeh's "This old man from the country will knit his eyebrows"	—	SR, WK, ST
215. T'ien-t'ung answers like this	—	DS, KD, SR, ST
216. Lin-chi's "Can you sell this one?"	—	RR, WK, KD
217. Lin-chi's "I'll spare you a beating"	Raihaitokuzui	SR, KD, TK, ST
218. Hsüeh-feng's "Attaining the way at Ao-shan"	EK-9 (15)	SR, ST
219. Kuei-shan sends a letter and a mirror	—	SR, ST
220. Tung-shan shakes his sleeves and departs	—	SR, KD, ST
221. Chiu-feng's "A man who thoroughly transmits words"	—	SR, ST
222. Lung-shan's "Two clay bulls enter the sea"	—	DS, SR, ST
223. Ma-tsu leaves out the salt and pickles	EK 1, 8	KD, SR

MS Case Titles	Dōgen's Texts (cases cited in)	Sung Texts (sources)
224. Yen-kuan's "What *sūtras* and commentaries do you study?"	—	KD, ST
225. Tung-shan's "Heat and cold do not reach there"	Shinjū, EK-9 (74)	WK, KF, SR
226. Tsao-shu strikes the sitting mat three times	—	SR, ST
227. Ch'i-hsien's "This old monk just looks"	—	KD
228. Yün-yen's "Just tell him"	EK 7	KD, WK, ST
229. Lo-han raises the *hossu*	—	KD, SR, ST
230. Ta-kuei strikes a wooden fish gong	—	KD, SR
231. Yün-men's "If you have not yet entered"	—	ER
232. Shih-t'ou has nothing to do with it	—	ER
233. Chao-chou says three times, "Drink your tea"	Kajō*	SR, KZ, WK
234. Ch'ang-sha's "When Shih-t'ou was a novice monk"	Kaiinzammai*	KD, ST
235. Shih-ku's "Where does the reverend nun live?"	—	SR, ST
236. Chang-ching's "Advancing one step is delusion"	—	SR, ST
237. Ch'ing-yüan's "I have not even sought for the holy truth"	Henzan*, EK-9 (19)	SR, KD, DR, ST
238. Chih-men's "I have this power"	—	SR, ST
239. Chao-chou's "Loading and unloading"	EK 4	KD, DS, SR
240. Ching-feng's case [of the bright jewel in the palm of your hand]	EK 4	SR, ST
241. Hsüan-sha hears the sound of a swallow	Shohō jissō*	SR, ST
242. Liang-shan's "This is a painting by retired scholar Wu"	—	SR, DS, ST
243. Hsiang-yen's thousand foot overhanging cliff	Soshi seiraii*, EK-9 (87)	DS, KD, SR, ST

MS Case Titles	Dōgen's Texts (cases cited in)	Sung Texts (sources)
244. Ma-ku's "Which is the true eye?"	—	TK, SR, DS, ST
245. Chu-ti holds up one finger	Henzan*, SZ 5, EK 3	KD, DS, ST
246. Yang-shan's one day of chanting the *sūtra*	—	SR, KD, ST
247. Shui-yen calls out, "Master"	—	SR, DR
248. Shih-kung's "Have you grasped empty space?"	Kokū*, EK-9 (53)	KD, SR
249. Nan-ch'üan's "Not mind, not buddha"	Arakan*	WK
250. Ts'ao-shan's "Eyebrows and eyes are not acquainted"	—	KD
251. Tao-wu's "When you leave this leaky shell"	—	KD, SR
252. Fa-yen's "You are Hui-chao"	EK-9 (84)	SR, DR
253. The World-Honored One holds up a flower and Mahākāśyapa smiles	Butsudō, Menju*, Udonge*, EK-9 (1)	SR, DR
254. Fa-yen's "Forms arise from the formless"	—	WK
255. Lin-chi raises his *hossu*	Kenbutsu*	RR, TK, SR
256. Ch'ang-sha's "Harvesting water and rice"	—	ER
257. Yün-men's "Attaining enlightenment on hearing sounds"	Kannon*, SZ 3	ER, SR
258. Nan-ch'üan's "Buddha view, Dharma view"	—	ER, SR
259. Pa-chiao's "When there is a question, there is an answer"	—	KD, DR
260. Ts'ao-shan's "No way out"	EK-9 (56)	KD, ER, TR
261. Yün-men composes a verse	—	KD
262. Ts'ao-shan's "Ouch, ouch!"	—	SR, ST
263. Ch'ang-shih throws down his brush	—	DS, KD, SR, ST
264. Pao-ying strikes the monk and he leaves the hall	—	DR, SR, DS, ST

MS Case Titles	Dōgen's Texts (cases cited in)	Sung Texts (sources)
265. Shui-liao suddenly attains enlightenment	—	DS, SR, ST
266. Ta-kuei summons the head training monk	CS	KD
267. Pai-chang's "He has no means of livelihood"	—	KD, SR, ST
268. Wei-cheng spreads apart his two hands	—	SR, KD, ST
269. Shou-shan's "Is the bamboo stick in accord or not in accord [with reality]"	—	SR, DS, TK, SR
270. Ch'ang-sha's "This monk can recite [a *dhāraṇī*]"	—	KD, SR, ST
271. Huang-po's "Doing what is necessary for the monks"	—	SR, ST
272. Chin-feng's "Adding frost to the snow"	Hotsubodaishin*	SR, ST
273. Lo-shan draws near and bows	—	SR, DS, ST
274. Chin-feng holds up a pillow	—	SR, DS, ST
275. The imperial attendant enters the hall and asks a question	—	KF, DS, ST
276. Tung-shan asks whether the water is deep or shallow	—	KD, SR, ST
277. Yen-yang's "Not relying on a single thing"	Bukkōjōji	WK, DS
278. Ma-tsu's "Mind itself is buddha"	Gyōji I*, EK 4, 8, -9 (75)	ER, KD
279. Ta-kuei's "Great activity, great functioning"	—	ER, SR
280. Yün-men's "I'll spare you sixty blows"	—	KD, ER, SR
281. Chao-chou examines two hermits	—	ER, SR
282. Hsüan-sha draws a circle	—	ER, WK, SR
283. Hsüeh-feng's "Cold water in an old mountain stream"	Kobusshin*, Kattō*	WK, ER, SR, DS, ST

MS Case Titles	Dōgen's Texts (cases cited in)	Sung Texts (sources)
284. Hsi-yüan's "Let's discuss the two errors"	—	ER, SR
285. Shu-shan's "Matters concerning the Dharmakāya	Shinjingakudō, Ryūgin*	ER, SR, DS
286. Ching-ch'ing's discourse on attaining enlightenment on hearing the sound of raindrops	Ikka myōjū, EK 1	ER, SR, WK
287. Hsüeh-feng turns the great Dharma wheel	Gyōbutsuigi*	ER, WK
288. Chao-chou's "Four great elements and five aggregates"	Busshō*, Menju*, EK 1	ER, SR, WK
289. Tao-wu consoles a family	Busshō*, Kaiinzammai*, CS, EK 2, 4	ER, SR, JR
290. Hsüeh-feng's "[I met them at] Wang-chou and Wu-shih"	Kōmyō, EK 6	ER, KD, WK, SR
291. Chao-chou's "Holding firmly to heaven and earth"	Gyōbutsuigi*, EK 4	WK, DR
292. Chia-shan's "No thing before the eyes"	—	WK
293. Nan-ch'üan's "Swarthy servant and white bull"	EK-9 (35)	WK, KD, SR
294. San-sheng's "It is nameless from time immemorial"	Kokyō	WK, SR
295. Yün-men's "Mysteriously abiding in this mountain shape"	—	WK
296. Fa-yen's two words, "sound" and "form"	EK 1	WK, KD
297. Lung-ya's "If a black tortoise could explain it"	Menju*	WK, KD, SR
298. Chang-ch'ing's "The Tathāgata's wordless [preaching]"	EK-9 (64)	KD, WK, DS
299. Wu-hsieh's "If you don't agree I'll leave"	Muchū-setsumu*, EK-9 (31)	ER, KD, SR
300. Lin-chi's "Is this an ordinary person or a sage?"	—	KD, RR

Masters Most Frequently Cited in the MS

Master	Case No.
Ch'ang-sha	16, 20, 234, 256, 270
Chao-chou	11, 46, 67, 74, 80, 114, 119, 133, 135, 136, 138, 233, 239, 281, 288, 291
Ch'ing-yüan	1, 10, 53, 237
Fa-yen	111, 171, 252, 254, 296
Hsiang-yen	17, 28, 243
Hsüan-sha	15, 25, 45, 48, 112, 144, 163, 203, 241, 282
Hsüeh-feng	38, 60, 109, 137, 149, 176, 218, 283, 287, 290
Huang-po	27, 91, 178, 202, 271
Kuei-shan	14, 134, 157, 197, 219
Kuei-tsung	43, 65, 188
Lin-chi	27, 147, 164, 167, 178, 207, 216, 217, 255, 300
Ma-tsu	4, 54, 108, 123, 190, 223, 278
Nan-ch'üan	3, 8, 18, 19, 51, 57, 64, 87, 154, 181, 195, 249, 258, 293
Pai-chang	2, 54, 102, 128, 182, 267
Śākyamuni (The World-Honored One)	141, 165, 174, 253
San-sheng	40, 52, 92, 294
Shih-shuang	58, 89, 179, 193
Shih-t'ou	41, 53, 191, 232, 234
Ta-kuei	44, 47, 56, 61, 76, 103, 110, 115, 130, 168, 209, 230, 266, 279
Tao-wu	213, 251, 289
Ts'ao-shan	30, 33, 70, 125, 194, 211, 250, 260, 262
Tung-shan	12, 49, 55, 62, 72, 78, 82, 98, 172, 198, 204, 220, 225, 276
Yang-shan	7, 23, 68, 118, 139, 142, 246
Yüeh-shan	66, 79, 86, 129, 151
Yün-men	81, 95, 100, 107, 158, 162, 166, 208, 231, 257, 261, 280, 295
Yün-yen	83, 84, 105, 148, 184, 228

Glossary of Sino-Japanese Terms, Names and Titles

Terms

asobiteki—playful (expressions)　遊び的

bendō—discrimination or practice of the way　辦道

bunke—branch (of Zen houses)　分家

busshō—Buddha-nature　仏性

ch'ing-t'an (J. seidan)—neo-Taoist colloquies　清談

chinsō—Zen portraits　頂相

chūkan—middle section (of *Mana Shōbōgenzō*)　中間

daigo—great awakening　大悟

daijō-ki—Mahayana mind　大乘機

daisan—Zen formal lectures　大参

daishi—great teacher　大師

danka—parish system　檀家

densetsu—legend　伝説

dentōroku—transmission of the lamp histories　伝燈録

deshi—disciples　弟子

dōji—simultaneity　同時

277

dōtoku—expressing the way　道德

dō-yō—instrument of the Tao　道用

ei-in-bon—photo-fascimile edition　影印本

en—relations, conditions　緣

engi—dependent origination　緣起

engo—relational word　緣語

fumai-inga—not obscuring causality　不昧因果

furaku-inga—not falling into causality　不落因果

furyū monji—non-reliance on words and letters　不立文字

fusetsu—Zen sermons; universal explantions　普說

gabyō—painted rice cake　画餅

gekan—final section (of MS)　下卷

genjōkōan—spontaneous realization of the kōan　現成公按

goke—five houses　五家

goku no nenryo—discourse is thought　語句の念慮

goroku—recorded sayings　語錄

gyō—activity　行

gyōji—sustained practice　行持

gyōji-dōkan—circulation of the way through sustained practice
　　行持道環

gyōroku—Zen travels or pilgrimage　行錄

hankyō—classification of teachings　判教

hattō—Dharma Hall　法堂

henkai fuzōzō—nothing concealed throughout the entire universe
　　偏界不曾藏

hihan bukkyō—critical Buddhism　批判仏教

hiyu—metaphor　比喩

hōben—skillful means　法弁

hōjō—abbot's quarters　方丈

hongaku shisō—original enlightenment thought　本覺思想

honjaku—fundamental standpoint　本迹

honkadori—allusive variation　本歌取リ

honrai no memmoku—original face　本来の面目

hsin-ch'en—(cast off) dust from the mind　心塵

i—dependence　依

ichinen sanzen—three thousand moments in a single thought　一念三千

immo—suchness　恁麼

innen—cause-effect; context　因緣

ippō gūjin—total penetration of a single dharma　一法究尽

ishin-denshin—transmission from mind-to-mind　以心伝心

jakugo—capping phrases　著語

jiji muge—interpenetration of things and things　事々無礙

jinen-gedō—naturalist heresy　自然外道

jiriki—self-power　自力

jishu—Zen informal lectures　示衆

jobun—preface　序文

jōdō—entering the hall and ascending the high seat to present a lecture
　上堂

jōkan—first section (of MS)　上卷

juko—poetic commentary　頌古

junbiteki—preparatory　準備的

kaki mo tsukubeki—writing must exhaust　かきもつくべき

kakuzen mushō—just emptiness, nothing sacred　廓然無聖

kanben—examinations　勘辦

kanbun—Chinese writing　漢文

kanji—Chinese characters　漢字

kanjin-shaku—interpretation based on contemplation of mind　観心釈

kanjō—transmission ceremony　灌頂

kanna-zen—kōan introspection　看話禅

kannō dōkō—spiritual communion　感応道交

kattō—entangled vines　葛藤

ke—Zen house or family　家

kenshō—seeing into one's own nature　見性

ki—dynamism　機

kien-mondō—*satori* encounter dialogue　機縁問答

kigen kiko—strange words, extraordinary gestures　奇言崎行

kikan—pedagogical opportunities　機関

kōan (C. kung-an)—Zen instructional dialogues　公按

kōan-roku—kōan collections and commentaries　公按録

kobutsu—old master or buddha　古仏

kojin—individual style　個人

kōjō—self-surpassing; "excelsior"　向上

kokoro—heart-mind　心

kokoro no kokoro o tenzuru—the mind refreshes (or liberates) the mind
　　心の心をずる

kokyō—primordial mirror　古鏡

kosoku-kōan—paradigmatic cases　古則公按

koto—things　事

kotoba—words, language　言葉

kotodama—soul of words　言魂

kufū—method　工夫

kyōge betsuden—special transmission outside the teachings (or scriptures)
　　教外別伝

kyōryaku—temporal passage　経歴

kyōten—scriptures, *sūtras*　経典

kyōzen itchi—oneness of Zen and teachings　教禅一致

menpeki—wall-gazing　面壁

mikkyō—esoteric Buddhism　秘教

mokushō-zen—silent illumination　默照禅

mu—no, nonbeing, nothingness　無

mu-busshō—no-Buddha-nature　無仏性

muchū-setsumu—disclosing a dream within a dream　夢中說夢

mui no shinjin—true person of no rank　無位の眞人

muji no ji—wordless word　無字の字

mujō—impermanence　無常

mujō-busshō—impermanence Buddha-nature　無常仏性

mumonkan—gateless gate　無門関

mu-mu—nothingness-nothingness　無々

munen—no thought　無念

mushin—no-mind　無心

nembutsu (C. nien-fo)—Pure Land chant　念仏

nenko—prose commentary　拈古

nenryo no goku—thought is discourse　念慮の語句

nihonjinron—Japanism　日本人論

nikon—moment　而今

nyo-nyo—suchness　如々

omote no go—surface words　表の語

ryōhō—Zen travels　旅方

sansuikyō—mountains and rivers *sūtras*　水山経

satori—sudden enlightenment　悟

sesshin sesshō—disclosing mind, disclosing nature　說心說性

setsu—symbolic disclosure　說

shaku—commentary, interpretation   釈

shih-tai-fu—scholar-officials   士大夫

shikan—cessation-contemplation   止観

shikantaza—just-sitting, zazen-only   只管打坐

shinfukatoku—ungraspable mind   心不可得

shingen—manifesting body   身現

shinjin datsuraku—casting off body-mind   身心脱落

shitsunai—abbot's quarters   室内

shitsuu—whole-being   悉有

shōbōgenzō—treasury of the true Dharma-eye   正法眼蔵

shōden no buppō—right transmission of the Buddha Dharma   正伝の仏法

shohō jissō—true form of all dharmas   諸法実相

shōjō-ki—Hinayana mind   小乗機

shōjō no shu—practice in realization   証上の修

shomu—various nothings   諸無

shōsan—Zen informal lecture   小参

shū—Zen lineage   宗

shūkyō-setsuwateki—sacred narrative   宗教説話的

shushō ittō—oneness of practice-realization   修証一等

sokushin-zebutsu—this very mind itself is buddha   即心是仏

soshi-zen—patriarchal Zen   祖師禅

taigi—great doubt   大疑

taimitsu—esoteric Tendai Buddhism   台秘

taishi—great death   大死

tamashii—soul, spirit   魂

tegami—letters of instruction   手紙

teisho—sermon on kōan   提唱

tengo—turning word   転語

ten-shin—rice-cake, or refreshing the mind　点心

tera no engi—temple formation legend　寺の縁起

tōdatsu—penetrate　透脱

tōshi-roku—lamp historical texts　燈史錄

u—yes, being, presence　有

ui-jinen—actively natural　有爲自然

ui no shinjin—true person with rank　有爲の眞人

uji—being-time　有時

unsui—clouds and water; a monk　雲水

u-shin—with-mind　有心

watakushi nashi—selfless　わたくしなし

watō—head-word or main phrase　話頭

yamabushi—mountain ascetism　山伏

yō—essential point　要

yojō—suggestive overtones of meaning　余情

yūgen—profound mystery　幽玄

yuibutsu-yobutsu—only between buddha and buddha　唯仏與仏

zazen　坐禅

zenki—total dynamism　全機

zettai mu—absolute nothingness　絕対無

zettai shukan—absolute subjectivity　絕対習慣

Names (with Japanese equivalents of some Chinese names)

Chao-chou (J. Jōshū)　趙州

Chen-hsieh　眞歇

Chih-yi　智顗

Ching-te-ssu　景德寺

Chi-tsang　吉藏

Chung-feng Ming-pen　中峰明本

Chu-ti　俱胝

Daijōji　大乘寺

Dainichi Nōnin　大日能忍

Daiō Kokushi　大應国師

Daitō Kokushi　大燈国師

Daruma-shū　達曆宗

Dōgen　道元

Echizen　越前

Eiheiji　永平寺

Eisai　榮西

Eishōin　永唱院

Ejō　懷奘

Ennin　圓仁

Fen-yang (J. Fun'yō)　汾陽

Gien　義演

Gikai　義介

Hakuin　白隱

Hōnen　法然

Honkō Katsudō　本光瞎堂

Hsiang-yen　香嚴

Hsüeh-feng (J. Seppō)　雪峰

Hsüeh-tou (J. Setchō)　雪竇

Huang-po (J. Ōbaku)　黃蘗

Hua-yen (J. Kegon)　華嚴

Hui-chung　慧忠

Hui-k'o　慧可

Hui-neng (J. Enō)　慧能

Hung-chih (J. Wanshi)　宏智

Hung-chou　洪州

Jōkōji　成高寺

Ju-ching (J. Nyojō)　如淨

Kōshōji　興聖寺

Lin-chi (J. Rinzai)　臨濟

Lung-t'an (J. Ryūtan)　龍潭

Ma-tsu (J. Basō)　馬祖

Menzan Zuihō　面山瑞方

Miroku　彌勒

Myōzen　明全

Nan-ch'üan　南泉

Nan-yüan　南院

Nan-yüeh (J. Nangaku)　南嶽

Nichiren　日蓮

Pai-chang (J. Hyakujō)　白丈

San-sheng　三聖

Seng-chao　僧肇

Shen-hsiu　神秀

Shen-hui　神會

Shigetsu Ein　指月慧印

Shih-t'ou　石頭

Shinran　親鸞

Shinpōji　眞法寺

Shōshin　正眞

Sōtō (C. Ts'ao-tung)　曹洞

Ta-hui (J. Daie)　大慧

Ta-kuei　大潙

Tao-hsin　道信

Tao-sheng　道生

Te-shan (J. Tokusan)　德山

T'ien-t'ung (J. Tendō)　天童

Tsung-mi　宗密

Tung-shan (J. Tōzan)　洞山

Wan-sung　萬松

Yang-chi　楊岐

Yüan-wu (J. Engo)　圜悟

Yün-men (J. Unmon)　雲門

Titles (with Chinese equivalents of some Japanese titles)

Bendōwa　辨道話

Busshō　仏性

Daie Roku (C. Ta-hui lu)　大慧錄

Daishugyō　大修行

Den Hōbōki (C. Chuan fa-pao chi)　伝法寶紀

Denkōroku　傳光錄

Eihei Kōroku　永平広錄

Engo Goroku (C. Yüan-wu yü-lu)　圜悟語錄

Fukanzazengi　普観坐禅儀

Fun'yō Roku (C. Fen-yang lu)　汾陽錄

Gakudōyōjinshū　学道用心集

Gekisetsuroku　擊節錄

Goke Goroku (C. Wu-chia yü-lu)　五家語錄

Gotō Egen (C. Wu-teng hui-yüan)　五燈會元

Gyōji　行持

Hachidainingaku　八大人覺

Hekiganroku (C. Pi-yen lu)   碧巌録

Hōkyōki   宝慶記

Hōrinden (C. Pao-lin chuan)   宝林伝

Ichiya Hekiganroku   一夜碧巌録

Immo   恁麼

Jinshin-inga   深信因果

Jishō-zammai   自証三昧

Kana Shōbōgenzō   仮字正法眼蔵

Kattō   葛藤

Keitoku Dentōroku (C. Ching-te chuan-teng lu)   景徳伝燈録

Kenbutsu   見仏

Kenchū Seikoku Zokutōroku (C. Chien-chung ching-kuo hsü-teng lu)
    建中靖国続燈録

Kenzeiki   建撕記

Kokyō   古鏡

Kōsōden (C. Kao-seng-chuan)   高僧伝

Mana Shōbōgenzō   眞字正法眼蔵

Menju   面授

Mumonkan (C. Wu-men kuan)   無門関

Nempyō Sanbyakusoku Funogo   拈評三百則不能語

Ōsakusendaba   王索仙陀婆

Rekidai Hōbōki (C. Li-tai fa-pao-chi)   歴代法宝記

Rinzai Roku (C. Lin-chi lu)   臨済録

Sanbyakusoku Juko   三百則頌古

Sansuikyō   山水経

Sesshin sesshō   説心説性

Setchō Juko Hyakusoku (C. Hsüeh-tou sung-ku pai-tse)   雪竇頌古百則

Shike Goroku (C. Ssu-chia yü-lu)   四家語録

Shinekiroku　請益錄

Shinfukatoku　心不可得

Shisho　嗣書

Shizen Biku　四禅比丘

Shōbōgenzō (C. Cheng-fa yen-tsang)　正法眼蔵

Shōbōgenzō Sanbyakusoku　正法眼蔵三百則

Shōbōgenzō Zuimonki　正法眼蔵随聞記

Shōyōroku (C. Ts'ung-jung lu)　從容錄

Shūkyō to wa nanika　宗教とわ何か

Shūmon Rentōeyō (C. Tsung-men lien-teng hui-yao)　宗門聯燈会要

Shūmon Tōyōshū (C. Tsung-men tung-yao chi)　宗門統要集

Sodōshū (C. Tsu-t'ang chi)　祖堂集

Sō Kōsōden (C. Sung kao-seng-chuan)　宋高僧伝

Ta-hsüeh　大學

Tajintsū　他心通

Teiho Kenzeiki　訂補建撕記

Tenshō Kōtōroku (C. T'ien-sheng kuang-teng lu)　天聖廣燈錄

Wanshi Goroku (C. Hung-chih yü-lu)　宏智語錄

Zazenshin　坐禅箴

Zazenyōjinki　坐禅用心記

Zen-en Shingi (C. Ch'an-yüan ch'ing-kuei)　禅苑清規

Zenki　全機

Zoku Kōsōden (C. Hsü kao-seng-chuan)　続高僧伝

Notes

Chapter 1. Text and Untext

1. SZK, 105–8.

2. Richard DeMartino, "The Human Situation and Zen Buddhism," in *Zen Buddhism and Psychoanalysis*, ed. Erich Fromm, D. T. Suzuki, and Richard DeMartino (New York: Harper, 1960), 144.

3. KS "Kattō," I, 427; see CZW, 62–67.

4. Ibid., I, 425.

5. The original dialogue appears in KD 5, TSD 51:240.

6. See KS "Zazenshin," "Kokyō," MS no. 8, EK-9 (38), SZ 3.

7. KS "Kokyō," I, 254; see CZW, 124–30.

8. Manabe Shunshō, in introductory material for *Ei-in-bon Shōbōgenzō*, ed. Manabe and Kawamura Kōdō (Tokyo: Juniseiki Gurafikusu, 1993). This beautiful edition, printed on paper and with binding that preserve the look and feel of a medieval text, sells for 1,770,000 yen (over $10,000).

9. See KS "Gyōji" and also *Hōkyōki* in DZZ II.

10. I am referring to what has become the standard edition of KS fascicles, but there is a significant controversy concerning the number of fascicles according to Dōgen's original intentions and as found in medieval manuscripts. There are also KS versions containing twelve, twenty-eight, sixty, seventy-five, and ninety-five fascicles. One of the main aims of the SSK is to demonstrate the viability of the sixty-fascicle edition. The oft-cited passage in which Dōgen supposedly expressed a desire to compose one hundred fascicles was written posthumously by Ejō and is included as an appendix to the KS "Hachidainingaku" fascicle.

11. See ZD, 198–99.

12. The *Nempyō Shōbōgenzō Sanbyakusoku Funogo* is not included in the standard collection of Sōtō writings, the *Sōtō Shū Zensho*, but it is included in the supplementary collection, the *Zoku Sōtō Shū Zensho*. See *Sōtō Shū Kankei Bunken Mokuroku* (Tokyo: Sōtō Shūmujō, 1990).

13. See SSK and CZW, 38ff.

14. These are published by the Sōtō sect in the continuously released multi-volume (over twenty-five volumes so far) edition of *Shōbōgenzō* texts, the *Shōbōgenzō Shūsho Taisei* (Tokyo: Taishūkan, 1978–). Since the publication of the SSK, there is a new Muromachi MS manuscript included in the above text. See also Kawamura, "Shōbōgenzō," *Dōgen no Chosaku*, ed. Kagamishima Genryū and Tamaki Koshirō (Tokyo: Shunjūsha, 1980); and "Kanazawa Bunkojōzō 'Shōbōgenzō,' Kanken," in *Dōgen*, ed. Kawamura and Ishikawa Rikizan (Tokyo: Yoshikawa Kobunkan, 1985).

15. For a discussion of how this title also appears in other Sung Zen texts, see Takeshi James Kodera, *Dogen's Formative Years in China* (Boulder: Prajna Press, 1980), 167 n. 288.

16. SSK, 4.

17. CZW, 14–19 and 572.

18. Ibid., 537 and 23–24.

19. In HR, trans., I, vii. For a discussion of the multifarious uses of kōans in later Sōtō sect, see William Bodiford, *Sōtō Zen in Medieval Japan* (Honolulu: University of Hawaii Press, 1993).

20. Heinrich Dumoulin, *Zen Buddhism: A History*, 2 vols. (New York: Macmillan, 1988–90), II [Japan], 73.

21. For a bibliographical discussion of recent approaches to Dōgen studies in English see "Editor's Introduction," in Masao Abe, *A Study of Dōgen: His Philosophy and Religion*, ed. Steven Heine (Albany: SUNY Press, 1992), 1–10.

22. This approach, which will be discussed in detail in Chapter 2, is influenced by many postmodern theorists including Barthes, Foucault, Lyotard, Taylor, Tracy and White (whose works are cited below), and also seems parallel to what Meir Sternberg describes in *The Poetics of Biblical Narrative* (Bloomington: Indiana University Press, 1985), 15. In his work on Biblical criticism, Sternberg makes a fundamental distinction that can be applied to other scriptural traditions, including Zen, between "source-oriented analysis," which deals primarily with historical (in the conventional historiographical sense) and social scientific concerns, and "discourse-oriented analysis," focusing on literary and textual interpretive issues relative to what Foucault calls "effective history." For a discussion of the role of literary criticism specifically in relation to Zen, see John Maraldo, "Is There Historical Consciousness Within Ch'an," *Japanese Journal of Religious Studies* 12/2–3 (1985), 141–72.

23. Tzvetan Todorov, *Genres in Discourse* (Cambridge: Cambridge University Press, 1990), 8–10.

24. See Fromm, "Psychoanalysis and Zen Buddhism," in *Zen Buddhism and Psychoanalysis*, 77–141.

25. Suzuki, *Mysticism: Christian and Buddhist* (New York: Collier, 1957), 36. For a discussion of how Martin Buber and Gershom Scholem comment on kōans in light of Jewish mysticism see Dumoulin, *Zen Enlightenment: Origins and Meaning* (New York and Tokyo: Weatherhill, 1979), 74–76. Another interesting discussion of Zen and mysticism is in Robert Gimello, "Mysticism and Meditation," in *Mysticism and Philosophical Analysis*, ed. Steven Katz (New York: Oxford University Press, 1978), 170–79.

26. Jacques Derrida, *Of Grammatology*, cited in John W. Murphy, *Postmodern Social Analysis and Criticism* (Westport, CT: Greenwood Press, 1989), 23.

27. Haruo Shirane, "Lyricism and Intertextuality: An Approach to Shunzei's Poetics," *Harvard Journal of Asiatic Studies* 50/1 (1991), 71, citing Julia Kristeva, *Desire in Language: A Semiotic Approach to Literature and Art* (Oxford: Basil Blackwell, 1980), 66.

28. Roland Barthes, "From Work to Text," in *Textual Strategies: Perspectives in Post-Structuralist Criticism*, ed. Josue V. Harari (Ithaca: Cornell University Press, 1979), 76, 74.

29. Luis Gomez, "D. T. Suzuki's Contribution to Modern Buddhist Scholarship," in *A Zen Life: D. T. Suzuki Remembered*, ed. Abe (New York and Tokyo: Weatherhill, 1986), 90–94.

30. Edward Said, "The Text, the World, the Critic," in *Textual Strategies*, 183, 188.

31. Hayden White, *Tropics of Discourse: Essays in Cultural Criticism* (Baltimore: Johns Hopkins University Press, 1978).

32. John R. McRae, *The Northern School and the Formation of Early Ch'an Buddhism* (Honolulu: University of Hawaii Press, 1986), 76.

33. Judith Berling, "Bringing the Buddha Down to Earth: Notes on the Emergence of *Yü-lu* as a Buddhist Genre," *History of Religions* 21/7 (1987), 61. The fact that Berling refers to "all language or silence" in this passage does not appear to lessen the emphasis on ineffability in the sense that nothing expresses the way of Zen.

34. Peter N. Dale, *The Myth of Japanese Uniqueness* (New York: St. Martin's Press, 1986).

35. An example is Michihiro Matsumoto, *The Unspoken Way: Haragei, Silence in Japanese Business and Society* (Tokyo: Kodansha, 1988).

36. Roy Andrew Miller, *Japan's Modern Myth: The Language and Beyond* (New York: Weatherhill, 1982), 85.

37. Dale S. Wright, "Rethinking Transcendence: The Role of Language in Zen Experience," *Philosophy East and West* 42/1 (1992), 113–38.

38. See Dumoulin, *Zen Buddhism: A History* I [India and China], 12 n. 5.

39. The ST text is not in either the TSD or the ZZ collections, but has been reprinted from a Toyo Bunka library edition—I examined a copy at the Komazawa University library in summer 1992.

40. SZK, 93–104 and 351ff.

41. See Martin Collcutt, *Five Mountains: The Rinzai Zen Monastic Institution in Medieval Japan* (Cambridge, MA: Harvard University Press, 1981), 194ff.

42. See Shibata Dōken, *Dōgen no Kotoba* (Tokyo: Yuzankaku Shuppan, 1978), 126–29. While these terms are not necessarily used interchangeably in all situations or contexts, they do refer to the same basic style and method of Zen discourse.

43. Miriam Levering, "Ta-hui and Lay Buddhists: Ch'an Sermons on Death," in *Buddhist and Taoist Practice in Medieval Chinese Society, Buddhist and Taoist Studies* II, ed. David W. Chappell (Honolulu: University of Hawaii Press, 1987), 183.

44. SSK, 358ff.

45. The SSK supports the viability of the sixty-fascicle edition.

46. William F. Powell, *The Record of Tung-shan* (Honolulu: University of Hawaii Press, 1986), 5.

47. These ideas were discussed with Prof. Ishii during the summer of 1992.

48. Suzuki, *Essays in Zen Buddhism*, First Series (New York: Grove Press, 1961), 177.

49. See Arthur F. Wright's discussion of *kōsōden* literature in *Studies in Chinese Buddhism*, ed. Robert M. Somers (New Haven: Yale University Press, 1990).

50. See SZS, and McRae, "Encounter Dialogue and the Transformation of the Spiritual Path in Chinese Ch'an," *Paths to Liberation: The Mārga and Its Transformations in Buddhist Thought*, ed. Robert N. Buswell, Jr. and Robert M. Gimello (Honolulu: University of Hawaii Press, 1991), 341.

51. Dōgen's lyrical poetry is included in the EK tenth fascicle and in his *Waka Shū*; see Heine, *A Blade of Grass: Japanese Poetry and Aesthetics in Dōgen Zen* (New York: Peter Lang, 1989).

52. Yanagida Seizan, "The 'Recorded Sayings' Texts of Chinese Ch'an Buddhism," in *Early Ch'an in China and Tibet*, ed. Whalen Lai and Lewis R. Lancaster (Berkeley: Buddhist Studies Series, 1983), 185–205.

53. For a discussion on the relation between Japanese familism and patriarchalism and Zen lineage see Francis Hsu, *Iemoto: The Heart of Japan* (New York: Schenkman, 1975), 166.

54. Paul Ricoeur, *Interpretation Theory: Discourse and the Surplus of Meaning* (Fort Worth: Texas Christian University, 1974).

55. Ōgawa Kōkan, *Chūgoku Nyoraizō Shisō Kenkyū* (Tokyo: Nakayama Shobō, 1976), 437.

56. MMK, trans., 19.

57. KS "Busshō," I, 54; see CZW 294–99.

58. CZW, 609, presents a comprehensive chart of masters and their cases cited in the MS.

59. KS "Shinfukatoku," I, 108.

60. Paul de Man's definition as cited in Jonathan Culler, *The Pursuit of Signs: Semiotics, Literature, Deconstruction* (Ithaca: Cornell University Press, 1981), 197.

61. KS "Shinfukatoku," I, 110.

62. Ibid., 109.

63. Ibid., 111.

64. Ibid., 111.

65. On the multibranched nature of the tradition see T. Griffith Foulk, "The Ch'an School and Its Place in the Buddhist Monastic Tradition," Ph.D. diss., University of Michigan, 1987. For a critical view of the use of this metaphor from the standpoint of French literary criticism on the "rhizome" metaphor, see Bernard Faure, "The Daruma-shū, Dōgen, and Sōtō Zen," *Monumenta Nipponica* 42/1 (1987), 25–55.

66. Robert E. Buswell, Jr., "The 'Short-cut' Approach of K'an-hua Meditation," in *Sudden and Gradual: Approaches to Enlightenment in Chinese Thought*, ed. Peter N. Gregory (Honolulu: University of Hawaii Press, 1987), 322 and 356. (Although I disagree somewhat with his conclusions concerning the development of the kōan tradition, Buswell's excellent scholarship has greatly influenced my understanding of this period in the history of Zen.) On the development of the kōan tradition see Furuta Shōkin, "Kōan no Rekishiteki Hatten

Keitai ni okeru Shinrisei no Mondai," in *Bukkyō no Kompon Shinri*, ed. Miyamoto Shōson (Tokyo: Sanseidō, 1956), 807–40. For a more popular appraisal of the tradition, see Akizuki Ryōmin, *Kōan* (Tokyo: Chikuma Shobō, 1987). See also, CZW, 20–28.

67. Kazuaki Tanahashi, ed. and trans., *Moon in a Dewdrop: Writings of the Zen Master Dōgen* (San Francisco: North Point, 1985), 22 and 16.

68. See Furuta, "Kōan no Rekishiteki," for a discussion of many of these terms; also *Zengagku Daijiten* (Tokyo: Taishūkan, 1978).

69. CZW, 14ff.

70. Noted by Robert M. Gimello, "Mārga and Culture: Learning, Letters, and Liberation in Northern Sung Ch'an," *Paths to Liberation*, 412 n. 3, from Mu-an's *Sōte Jien*, ZZ 113:132a11–16.

71. Julian F. Pas, trans., *The Recorded Sayings of Ma-tsu* (Lewiston/Queenston: Edwin Mellen, 1987), 41.

72. Gimello, "Echoes of the *Platform Scripture* in Northern Sung Ch'an," in *Fo Kuang Shan Report of the International Conference of Ch'an Buddhism* (Taipei: Fo Kuang, 1990), 143.

73. MMK, trans., xv.

74. Maraldo, "Is There Historical Consciousness," 166.

75. Dumoulin, *Zen Buddhism: A History*, I, 181, 249.

76. Buswell, "The 'Short-Cut' Approach of *K'an-hua* Meditation," 345.

77. McRae, *The Northern School*, 73–80.

78. McRae, "Shen-hui and the Teaching of Sudden Enlightenment in Early Ch'an Buddhism," in *Sudden and Gradual: Approaches to Enlightenment in Chinese Thought*, ed. Peter Gregory (Honolulu: University of Hawaii Press, 1987), 230.

79. Foulk, "The Ch'an School," 3.

80. Ibid., 92 (emphasis added).

81. Pas, *The Recorded Sayings*, 29 (emphasis added).

82. Kenneth Ch'en, *Buddhism in China* (Princeton: Princeton University Press, 1964), 356.

83. On the causes and consquences of the 845 suppression under Emperor Wu-tsung see Ch'en, *Buddhism in China*, 363–64; Stanley Weinstein, *Buddhism Under the T'ang* (Cambridge: Cambridge University Press, 1987), 114–36; Dumoulin, *Zen Buddhism: A History* I, 211–13; Jacques Gernet, *A History of Chinese Civilization* (Cambridge: Cambridge University Press, 1972), 294–96.

84. Ch'en, *Buddhism in China*, 353.

85. See for example KS "Menju."

86. For Dōgen, the arising of the thought of enlightenment (or arousing of the bodhi-seeking mind, *hotsubodaishin*) is coterminous with the realization of enlightenment. Furthermore, he argues that arousal, realization, *bodhi*, and nirvāṇa are different aspects of the coming into and going out of existence of the selfsame, holistic moment of being-time (*uji*); see Heine, *Existential and Ontological Dimensions of Time in Heidegger and Dōgen* (Albany: SUNY Press, 1985).

87. On the other hand, recent studies in the scholarly movement at Komazawa

University reassessing East Asian Buddhism, including Dōgen's thought, in light of Indo-Tibetan Buddhism, known as "critical Buddhism" (*hihan bukkyō*) tend to refute syncretism with Taoist naturalism as non-Buddhist. See Hakamaya Noriaki, *Hongaku Shisō Hihan* (Tokyo: Daizō Shuppan, 1989), *Hihan Bukkyō* (Tokyo: Daizō Shuppan, 1990), *Dōgen to Bukkyō: Junikanbon Shōbōgenzō no Dōgen* (Tokyo: Daizō Shuppan, 1992); and Matsumoto Shirō, *Engi to Kū—Nyoraizō Shisō* (Tokyo: Daizō Shuppan, 1989).

88. Chung-yüan Chang, *Original Teachings of Ch'an Buddhism* (New York: Vintage, 1969), 91–92.

89. Yoshizu Yoshihide, "Hijiri no Ningenkan to Mondō ni yoru Satori," *Buddha Kara Dōgen E*, ed. Nara Yasuaki (Tokyo: Daizō Shuppan, 1992), 131–42.

90. Philip Kapleau, "The Private Encounter with the Master," in *Zen: Tradition and Transition*, ed. Kenneth Kraft (New York: Grove Press, 1988), 51.

91. ZD, 10.

92. Suzuki, *Essays in Zen Buddhism*, Second Series, 230ff.

93. In ZD, 5.

94. Carl Bielefeldt, *Dōgen's Manuals of Zen Meditation* (Berkeley: University of California Press, 1988), 98. For a historical study of Chinese religious influences on the development of Zen, see Chōichi Abe, *Chūgoku Zenshūshi no Kenkyū* (Tokyo: Seishin Shobō, 1963).

95. Gregory, *Tsung-mi and the Sinification of Buddhism* (Princeton: Princeton University Press, 1991), 180.

96. John C. H. Wu, *The Golden Age of Zen* (Taiwan: United, 1975), 52.

97. Pas, *The Recorded Sayings*, 5.

98. Arthur F. Wright, *Studies in Chinese Buddhism*, 26.

99. In Walpola Rahula, *What the Buddha Taught* (New York: Grove Press, 1959), 14.

100. For example, on the question of what happens after death the Buddha is silent because the question is unedifying; and on the question such as "will I die?," the answer is "yes" because the question is factual but does not disclose new information or significant interpretation. The Buddha's aim is to inspire the disciple to ask the pragmatic soteriological question, "How do I become enlightened (transcend suffering) prior to the inevitability of death?"

101. For diagrammatic representations of some of these and other doctrines see Paul Swanson, *Foundations of T'ien-t'ai Philosophy* (Berkeley: Asian Humanities Press, 1989), 358–65.

102. KS "Gabyō," I, 287.

103. Berling, "Bringing the Buddha Down to Earth," 75.

104. McRae, "Shen-hui and the Teaching of Sudden Enlightenment," 229.

105. Gregory, "Introduction," in *Sudden and Gradual: Approaches to Enlightenment in Chinese Thought*, 7.

106. Charles W. Fu, "The Underlying Structure of Metaphysical Language: A Case Examination of Language and Chinese Philosophy" (unpublished paper, revised version in *Journal of Chinese Philosophy* 6 [1979], 338–66).

107. Suzuki, *Essays in Zen Buddhism*, First Series, 164 (emphasis added).

108. Arthur F. Wright, *Buddhism in Chinese History* (Stanford: Stanford University Press, 1959), 46. Another important concise literary unit especially in the chronicles is the poem or *gāthā* marking *satori*, succession, or death.

109. Daniel K. Gardner, "Modes of Thinking and Modes of Discourse in the Sung: Some Thoughts on the *Yü-lu* ('Recorded Conversations') Texts," *Journal of Asian Studies* 50/3 (1991), 586.

110. David Pollack, *The Fracture of Meaning: Japan's Synthesis of China from the Eighth through the Eighteenth Centuries* (Princeton: Princeton University Press, 1986), 19.

111. Ishii, "Recent Trends in Dōgen Studies," *Komazawa Daigaku Kenkyū Nempō* 1 (1990), 263. However, this comment does not appear sensitive to the criticism that an over-emphasis on "Japanese uniqueness" obfuscates an understanding of the historical development of the tradition.

112. Eido T. Shimano, "Zen Kōans," in *Zen: Tradition and Transition*, 70.

113. Ta-hui, trans. Buswell, *The Korean Approach to Zen: The Collected Works of Chinul* (Honolulu: University of Hawaii Press, 1983), 338.

114. In ZD, 5.

115. Ibid., 35.

116. Burton Watson, trans., *The Complete Works of Chuang Tzu* (New York: Columbia University Press, 1968), 304.

117. Daniel Boyarin, *Intertextuality and the Reading of Midrash* (Bloomington: University of Indiana Press, 1990), 116.

118. Attributed to Yün-chü in KD (TSD 51:335c19), cited in Bielefeldt, *Dōgen's Manuals*, 145 (slightly altered).

119. According to Berling, "'Texts' in this sense includes not only written documents but also oral tradition, myths, and rituals that encode and present the story of the tradition" ("Bringing the Buddha Down to Earth," 57).

120. Mark C. Taylor, *Erring: A Postmodern A/Theology* (Chicago: University of Chicago Press, 1984), 179.

121. Herman Ooms, "Review of David Pollack, *The Fracture of Meaning*," in *Harvard Journal of Asiatic Studies* 49/1 (1989), 279.

122. Harold Bloom, *The Anxiety of Influence* (New York: Oxford University Press, 1973). Although Bloom indicates that he is referring only to poets and poetry in his analysis, it is possible to extrapolate from his argument in a way applicable to the Zen literary tradition.

Chapter 2. Mythology and Demythology

1. Bielefeldt, "Recarving the Dragon: History and Dogma in the Study of Dōgen," in *Dōgen Studies*, ed. William R. LaFleur. (Honolulu: University of Hawaii Press, 1985), 24.

2. McRae, *The Northern School*, 7–9.

3. Bielefeldt, "Recarving the Dragon," 47.

4. Robert H. Sharf, "Occidentalism and the Zen of Japanese Nationalism," Annual Meeting of the American Academy of Religion, Kansas City, November 1991.

5. Michel Foucault, "Truth and Power," in *A Foucault Reader*, ed. Paul Rabinow (New York: Pantheon, 1984), 74.

6. See Eric Hobsbawm and Terence Ranger, eds., *The Invention of Tradition* (Cambridge: Cambridge University Press, 1983). This collection deals primarily with non-religious traditions.

7. Freidrich Nietzsche, as cited in Culler, *The Pursuit of Signs*, 204.

8. See Nishitani's essay, "Bukkyō ni okeru 'Kōjō' no Tachiba," in *Zettai Mu to Kami*, ed. Jan van Bragt (Tokyo: Shunjūsha, 1981), 150–94.

9. Nishitani's critique of Christianity at once resembles and yet is nearly opposite to Mircea Eliade's study of the relation between Christian doctrine and mythology. Like Nishitani, Eliade criticizes Christianity for not recognizing its rootedness in circular time, but he identifies the true source of "cosmic Christianity" with the myth and rites of renewal that establish the inseparability of cosmology and eschatology; this source is retained though camouflaged in millennialist and hagiocentric seasonal festival worship. See Eliade, *Myth and Reality* (New York: Harper, 1963). Nishitani, however, argues from the other direction that Christian cosmology-eschatology in the sense that the end of history is foreshadowed by the beginnings (for example, a holocaust by water to root out evil near the start sets up the need for a final conflagration by fire) never overcomes naive mythology; see *Religion and Nothingness* (Berkeley: University of California Press, 1982), 213. For the relation between fertility mythology and Buddhist contemplation as seen in Japanese religion, see Heine, "From Rice Cultivation to Mind Contemplation: The Meaning of Impermanence in Japanese Religion," *History of Religions* 30/4 (1991), 374–403.

10. Nishitani, *Religion and Nothingness*, 211.

11. Ibid., 272.

12. Abe, "Will, Śūnyata, and History," in *The Religious Philosophy of Nishitani Keiji*, ed. Taitetsu Unno (Berkeley: Asian Humanities Press, 1989), 289.

13. KS "Bendōwa," I, 20.

14. KS "Gyōji," I, 165.

15. The similarity between Blake and Dōgen has been pointed out by Joan Stambaugh, *Impermanence is Buddha-nature: Dōgen's Understanding of Temporality* (Honolulu: University of Hawaii Press, 1990), 32–33.

16. McRae, *The Northern School*, 7–8.

17. Philip B. Yampolsky, trans., *The Platform Sūtra of the Sixth Patriarch* (New York: Columbia University Press, 1967), 13. Yampolsky also notes (67) that, similar to the case of Śākyamuni, when Hui-neng died on a date he himself predicted to his disciples, "Mountains tumbled . . . rivers ran dry, and the birds and monkeys cried in anguish."

18. Faure, "Bodhidharma as Textual and Religious Paradigm," *History of Religions* 25/3 (1986), 187–98.

19. For example, the standard modern biographies of Dōgen have been increasingly challenged by revisionist studies that penetrate many of the traditionally accepted myths of his birth, upbringing and career in Buddhism. The main Sōtō sectarian biography is the

Kenzeiki in Kawamura, *Eihei Kaizan Dōgen Zenji Gyōjō: Kenzeiki* (Tokyo: Taishūkan Shoten, 1975). The main modern studies are Ōkubo Dōshū, *Dōgen Zenji Den no Kenkyū* (Tokyo: Chikuma Shobō, 1966) and Takeuchi Michio, *Dōgen* (Tokyo: Yoshikawa Kobunkan, 1962); also see Kodera for a review of traditional sources. One of the major revisionist studies is Nakaseko Shōdō, *Dōgen Zenji Den Kenkyū* (Tokyo: Kokusho Kankōkai, 1979).

20. Yün-Hua Jan, "Buddhist Historiography in Sung China," *Zeitschrift der Deutschen Morgenlhandischen Gesellschaft* 114 (1964), 362. Yanagida in SZS also carefully traces the history of this process.

21. On the "golden age" debate see Buswell, "The 'Short-cut' Method," 359 n. 8.

22. On the idea of Zen inventing itself see Pas, *The Recorded Sayings*, 42, "These examples [of Indian encounter dialogues] derive from Ch'an histories, written after Ma-tsu's time, and are typically Chinese. According to Yanagida, one may conclude that all Ch'an masters about whom similar anecdotes have been transmitted, belong to Ma-tsu's school, and that their recording started from his time."

23. Jan, "Buddhist Historiography," 367–68.

24. Yampolsky, *The Platform Sūtra*, 4–5.

25. Buswell, *The Formation of Ch'an Ideology in China and Korea: The Vajrasamādhi-Sūtra, a Buddhist Apocryphon* (Princeton: Princeton University Press, 1989), 43–44.

26. Faure, *The Rhetoric of Immediacy* (Princeton: Princeton University Press, 1991), 68.

27. Bodiford, "Dharma Transmission in Sōtō Zen: Manzan Dōhaku's Reform Movement," *Monumenta Nipponica* 46/4 (1991), 423–24.

28. See Faure, *The Rhetoric of Immediacy*, and Sharf, "The Idolization of Enlightenment: On the Mummification of Ch'an Masters in Medieval China," *History of Religions* 32/1 (1992), 1–31.

29. See the discussion of Dōgen's monastic rules and instructions on washing, brushing teeth, etc. in Hee-Jin Kim, *Dōgen Kigen— Mystical Realist* (Tucson: University of Arizona Press, 1975), 234–52.

30. See Dumoulin, *Zen Buddhism: A History*, II, 137–43.

31. See Foucault's essay on Nietzsche and "effective history," "Nietzsche, Genealogy, History," in *A Foucault Reader*, 76–100.

32. The traditional sources strive to present an "arborescent" paradigm of lineage—that is, one based on the family tree model [a different use of the term arborescent than that given in Chapter 1]—that betrays a sequential teleology; see Faure, "The Daruma-shū, Dōgen, and Sōtō Zen," 54.

33. McRae, "The Story of Early Ch'an," in *Zen: Tradition and Transition*, ed. Kenneth Kraft (New York: Grove Press, 1988), 138–39. An example of a study that seems to follow the "string of pearls" approach (which seems to correspond to what Nietzsche refers to as "monumentalistic" history) is Wu, *The Golden Age of Zen*.

34. Bielefeldt, *Dōgen's Manuals of Zen Meditation*, 131–32.

35. One of the most persuasive responses is on "Dōgen as founder of a religious sect" by Etō Sokuō, *Shūso toshite no Dōgen Zenji* (Tokyo: Iwanami Shoten, 1944).

36. Thomas Cleary, in SH, trans., xxxvii.

37. Suzuki, *Studies in Zen* (New York: Delta, 1955), 135; Suzuki argues that Hu Shih "may know a great deal about history but nothing about the actor behind it." Actually, Suzuki and Hu Shih are less at odds than they appear in that the former often demonstrates his sensitivity to historical issues and the latter still seeks an understanding of the essence of Zen. Their real debate is whether Zen is "conscious and rational" (Hu Shih) or "irrational and not explainable by intellectual analysis" (Suzuki). On the other hand, nearly forty years later it appears the Hu Shih "won" the debate because of the tremendous development of historical studies of Zen and a general sense (perhaps not as valid as it seems) that Suzuki overlooked these matters.

38. Jan, "Buddhist Historiography," 369.

39. Takayuki Nagashima, *Truth and Fabrications in Religion* (London: Arthur Probsthain, 1978), 327.

40. See Faure, "Bodhidharma as Textual and Religious Paradigm."

41. Faure, "The Daruma-shū, Dōgen, and Sōtō Zen," 53 (emphasis added).

42. Maraldo, "Is There Historical Consciousness," 161.

43. Ibid., 162–63.

44. See for example Suzuki, *Essays in Zen Buddhism* (Second Series) 227–53. For an essay on Dōgen stressing literary or stylistic themes, see Hee-Jin Kim, "'The Reason of Words and Letters'—Dōgen and Kōan Language," in *Dōgen Studies*, 54–82; Kim's study is based on works by Kagamishima Genryū and Terada Tōru.

45. A quotation originally from Pope Pius XII, cited by Patrick W. Skehan in the Preface to Addison G. Wright, *Midrash: The Literary Genre* (Staten Island: Alba House, 1967), 8.

46. Sternberg, *The Poetics of Biblical Narrative*, 15.

47. Boyarin, *Intertextuality*, 117.

48. Ibid., 118.

49. White, *Tropics of Discourse*, 88.

50. Barthes, *S/Z*, trans. Richard Miller (New York: Hill and Wang, 1974), 10.

51. Foucault, "What is an Author?", in *Foucault Reader*, 107.

52. White, *Tropics of Discourse*, 51.

53. Ibid., 96.

54. Both Scholes and Ionesco are cited in Murphy, *Postmodern Social Analysis and Criticism* (Westport, CT: Greenwood Press, 1989), 2 and 28.

55. Barthes, *S/Z*, 5. See the opening passage of the book for a somewhat ambivalent reference to Buddhist contemplation.

56. See Faure, "Bodhidharma as Textual and Religious Paradigm"; see also Nagashima, who argues that he has proven the "nonexistence" of Hui-neng but nevertheless considers the sixth patriarch significant as a "symbol" (327).

57. SZS, 17–18. Also cited in Maraldo, "Is There Historical Consciousness," 154.

58. See Wright, *Midrash: The Literary Genre*.

59. Paul Ricoeur, *The Symbolism of Evil* (Boston: Beacon, 1967), 15.

60. Cited in ibid., 15.

61. Paul Tillich, *Systematic Theology* (Chicago: University of Chicago Press, 1951), I, 239.

62. T. P. Kasulis, *Zen Action/Zen Person* (Honolulu: University of Hawaii Press, 1981), 104ff. Some of the scholars who have analyzed early Buddhist thought from the standpoint of modern psychology include Herbert Guenther, Lama Govinda, Rune Johansson, Padmiri DeSilva and Nolan Pliny Jacobson. See Nathan Katz, ed., *Buddhist and Western Psychology* (Boulder: Prajna, 1983).

63. KS "Busshō," I, 46.

64. KS "Genjōkōan," I, 36.

65. See Kasulis, *Zen Action/Zen Person*, 142ff.

66. Wu, *The Golden Age of Zen*, 99.

67. Ibid., 94–95 (emphasis added).

68. Cited in Ronald L. Burr, "Lin-chi on 'Language-Dependence,' An Interpretive Analysis," in *Early Ch'an in China and Tibet*, 221.

69. Cited in Fu, "Heidegger and Zen on Being and Nothingness: A Critical Essay in Transmetaphycial Dialectics," in *Buddhist and Western Philosophy*, ed. Katz (New Delhi: Sterling, 1981), 188, from *Zen no Goroku*, 6 (Tokyo: Chikuma Shobō, 1970), 80.

70. See David Reynolds, *Flowing Bridges, Quiet Therapies: Japanese Psychotherapies, Morita and Naikan* (Albany: State University of New York Press, 1989).

71. Sandra Wawrytko, "Zen and Western Psychotherapy: Nirvanic Transcendence and Samsara Fixation," *Chung-Hwa Buddhist Journal* 4 (1991), 452.

72. Abe, "The Self in Jung and Zen," *The Eastern Buddhist* 18/1 (1985), 66.

73. In addition, studies in the area of clinical psychology include: Victor E. Krynicki, "The Double Orientation of the Ego in the Practice of Zen," *American Journal of Psychoanalysis* 40/3 (1980), 239–68; Robert L. Woodfolk, "Psychophysiological Correlates of Meditation," *Archives of General Psychiatry* 32 (1975), 1326–33; Eido Tai Shimano and Donald B. Douglas, "Research in Zen," *American Journal of Psychiatry* 132/12 (1975), 1300–02; Nathaniel Ross, "Affect as Cognition: With Observations on the Meanings of Mystical States," *International Review of Psycho-Analysis* 2 (1975), 79–93.

74. Suzuki, *Zen Doctrine of No Mind* (New York: Weiser, 1973), 124.

75. Stanley Tambiah, "A Performative Approach to Ritual," *Proceedings of the British Academy*, 65, 113–69 (New York, Oxford University Press, 1981), 141, cited in Faure, *The Rhetoric of Immediacy*, 296.

76. The second and third stages seem to correspond to three stages of contemplation in Chuang Tzu: forgetting, fasting of the mind, and free and easy wandering.

77. Rollo May, *The Courage to Create* (New York, Bantam, 1975).

78. See Gomez, "D. T. Suzuki's Contribution to Modern Buddhist Scholarship."

79. Suzuki, *On Indian Mahayana Buddhism*, ed. Edward Conze (New York: Harper and Row, 1968), 242.

80. Kim makes this distinction in "'The Reason of Words and Letters.'"

81. Ricoeur, *The Symbolism of Evil*, 61.

82. Victor Turner, *Dramas, Fields and Metaphors* (Ithaca, NY: Cornell University Press, 1974), 46–48, 291–92.

83. Powell, *The Record of Tung-shan*, 17, 15.

84. Robert Ellwood, *Introducing Religion—From Inside and Out* (Englewood Cliffs: Prentice-Hall, 1983), 99–125.

85. Dumoulin, *Zen Enlightenment*, 74–76.

86. See Elie Wiesel, *Souls on Fire* (New York: Vintage, 1972).

87. Sōiku Shigematsu, *A Zen Forest: Sayings of the Masters* (New York: Weatherhill, 1981), 15.

88. LaFleur, *The Karma of Words: Buddhism and the Literary Arts in Medieval Japan* (Berkeley: University of California Press, 1983), 21.

89. See Maraldo, "Is There Historical Consciousness," for discussion of this point.

90. David Tracy, *Plurality and Ambiguity: Hermeneutics, Religion, Hope* (San Francisco, Harper and Row, 1989), 57.

91. Ibid., 45.

Chapter 3. Inter- and Intra-Textuality

1. DZZ II, 3. A similar question is posed in the *Kenzeiki*: "Both exoteric and esoteric Buddhism teach the primal Buddha-nature [or Dharma-nature] and the original self-awakening of all sentient beings. If this is the case, why then have the buddhas of all ages had to awaken the longing for and seek enlightenment by engaging in ascetic practice?", in *Sōtō Shū Zensho* (Tokyo: Kōmeisha, 1929–39), 17:16a.

2. SZ, 192.

3. KS "Jishō-zammai," II, 250.

4. KS "Kenbutsu," II, 158.

5. Kim, *Dōgen Kigen—Mystical Realist*, 42 (slightly modified).

6. KS "Shisho," I, 441–42.

7. EK 1.

8. KS "Gyōji," I.

9. In Kawamura, *Eihei Kaizan Dōgen Zenji Gyōjō: Kenzeiki*, 24–25.

10. See Kagamishima, *Tendō Nyojō Zenji no Kenkyū* (Tokyo: Shunjūsha, 1983).

11. Kodera, *Dogen's Formative Years in China*, 74.

12. *Swampland Flowers: The Letters and Lectures of Zen Master Ta-hui*, trans. Christopher Cleary (New York: Grove Press, 1977), 131, 127.

13. Ibid., 85.

14. *Cultivating the Empty Field*, trans. Taigen Daniel Leighton (San Francisco: North Point Press, 1991), 53, TSD 48:100.b.

15. Ibid., 39–40.

16. Bielefeldt, *Dōgen's Manuals*, 2. Elsewhere, in the introductory chapter, Bielefeldt points out the historical conditioning involved in the formulation of the conventional view of this polarization.

17. SZ, 261–62.

18. KS "Sansuikyō," I, 335–36 (emphasis added). See also Kim, "'The Reason of Words and Letters,'" 56–57. The last sentence of my translation differs from Kim's.

19. In Kawamura, *Kenzeiki*, 87; Heine, *A Blade of Grass*, 91.

20. On the rivalry, see Bielefeldt, "Recarving the Dragon," and Faure, "Daruma-shū, Dōgen, and Sōtō Zen."

21. KS "Jishō-zammai," I, 249.

22. Kagamishima, *Dōgen to sono Shūhen* (Tokyo: Daitō Shuppansha, 1985), 318–20.

23. Another version is included in EK-9.

24. See Ōgawa, *Chūgoku Nyoraizō Shisō Kenkyū*, 441ff.

25. KS "Kattō," I, 427.

26. Buswell, *The Korean Approach to Zen* (Honolulu: University of Hawaii Press, 1983), 253 n.1, numbers 9 and 10 may have been devised by Chinul.

27. Bielefeldt, *Dōgen's Manuals*, 99–101.

28. KS "Jinshin-inga," II, 435–37.

29. MMK, trans., 39.

30. C. J. Jung, "Foreword," in D. T. Suzuki, *An Introduction to Zen Buddhism* (New York: Grove Press, 1964), 20.

31. Levering, "Ta-hui and Lay Buddhists," 196.

32. One of the arguments of the *"hihan bukkyō"* [see Chapter 1, n. 87] scholarship has been to argue that Dōgen only truly understood and expressed the meaning of impermanence and causality in his later twelve-volume edition of the *Shōbōgenzō* (a separate text included in the ninety-two fascicle version). See especially Hakamaya's works; also Kagamishima Genryū and Suzuki Kakuzen, ed., *Jūnikanbon Shōbōgenzō no Shomondai* (Tokyo: Daizō Shuppan, 1991).

33. See Abe, *A Study of Dōgen*, 160–61.

34. This issue is based on the discrepancy between two phrases, "casting dust off the mind" and "casting off body-mind," which sound identical in Japanese though not in Chinese, the language of the original conversation. See Heine, "Dōgen Casts Off 'What': An Analysis of *Shinjin Datsuraku*," *Journal of the International Association of Buddhist Studies* 9/1 (1986), 53–70.

35. See *Cultivating The Empty Field*.

36. Takasaki Jikidō and Umehara Takeshi, *Kobutsu no Manabi* (Tokyo: Kodokawa Shoten, 1963), 59–62, 190–93.

37. Kurebayashi Kōdō, *Dōgen Zen no Honryū* (Tokyo: Daihōrinkaku, 1978), 58–69.

38. See KS "Shizen Biku."

39. SZ, 243–44; the reference in this passage could be to a T'ang era master named Ta-hui, but Mizuno argues that this is not the case based on another reference to the Sung Ta-hui shortly after this.

40. See Chapter 1, n. 15.

41. ZD, 199.

42. SZ, 50.

43. KS "Gyōji," I, 221.

44. See Dumoulin, *Zen Buddhism: A History*, II, 129–47.

45. See Tamura Yoshirō, "Critique of Original Awakening Thought in Shōshin and Dōgen," *Japanese Journal of Religious Studies* 11/2–3 (1984), 243–66; and *Kamakura Shin-Bukkyō Shisō no Kenkyū* (Kyoto: Heirakuji Shoten, 1965).

46. Kagamishima, *Tendō Nyojō no Kenkyū*, 48–52.

47. CZW, 560–68.

48. Dōgen and Keizan were known by the sect as *taiso* ("great patriarch") and *kōso* ("high patriarch"), respectively.

49. John Daido Loori, *Mountain Record* 3/4 (Spring 1990), 88.

50. Keizan is primarily known for creating a syncretism of Dōgen's "pure" Sōtō with esoteric Buddhism and other elements of Japanese religiosity in addition to kōan studies that may have been influenced by the Daruma school. KS "Gyoji" is similar in style to Keizan's text.

51. SZ 112, 126–27. On the other hand (SZ, 117), "It is useless to preach to deluded people by reading from recorded sayings or kōan [collections], or by observing the actions of ancient masters. . . . Clarify the great matter by practicing zazen only . . ."

52. Bloom, *The Anxiety of Influence*, 30. Again, the use of a Bloomian hermeneutic here must be qualified by the fact that Bloom insists he is dealing only with poets, not prose authors or other kinds of writers or artists, in the period "after the flood," that is, in modern, industrial societies; similarly, as Bob Dylan has said of Woody Guthrie, "He was my last idol because he was my first idol." Nevertheless, it is possible to extrapolate from Bloom's argument in a way applicable to the Zen literary/lineal tradition.

53. Vincent B. Leitch, *Deconstructive Criticism: An Advanced Introduction* (New York: Columbia University Press, 1983), 137.

54. Bloom, *The Anxiety of Influence*, 5.

55. Ibid., 14–16.

56. Levering, "Ch'an Enlightenment for Laymen: Ta-hui and the New Religious Culture of the Sung," Ph.D. diss., Harvard University (1978), 6.

57. Bielefeldt suggests that the *watō* was directed primarily for laypersons and not for monks, but Buswell sees the method from the standpoint of its impact on Korean Zen as the highest and most persuasive form of Zen training.

58. Some of the main scholarship on this includes Tamura; Yamauchi Shun'yū, *Dōgen Zen to Tendai Hongaku Hōmon* (Tokyo: Daizō Shuppan, 1986); Ikeda Rosan, *Dōgengaku no Yōran* (Tokyo: Daizō Shuppan, 1990).

59. Powell, *The Record of Tung-shan*, 11.

60. Richard John Lynn, "The Sudden and Gradual in Chinese Poetry Criticism: An Examination of the Ch'an-Poetry Analogy," in Peter N. Gregory, ed., *Sudden and Gradual*, 381.

61. Joseph Kitagawa, *On Understanding Japanese Religion* (Princeton: Princeton University Press, 1987), 45–49.

62. DKK, 121–37.

63. Daigan Matsunaga and Alicia Matsunaga, *Foundation of Japanese Buddhism*, 2 vols. (Tokyo: Buddhist Books International, 1978) I, 184.

64. Kasulis, "Truth Words: The Basis of Kūkai's Theory of Interpretation," in *Buddhist Hermeneutics*, ed. Donald S. Lopez, Jr. (Honolulu: University of Hawaii Press, 1988), 262.

65. TSD 34:1ff.

66. See Heine, *A Blade of Grass*, 13–15, 61–66.

67. Pollack, *The Fracture of Meaning*, 19.

68. R. A. Miller, "The 'Spirit' of the Japanese Language," in *Journal of Japanese Studies* 3/2 (1977), 264. See also the article on Japanese Religion in *Encyclopedia of Religion*, ed. Eliade (New York: Macmillan, 1987), vol. 7, 555–56.

69. Ki no Tsurayuki, editor's introduction, in *Nihon Koten Bungaku Zenshū* (Tokyo: Kogakukan, 1971), vol. 7.

70. Nishitani, *Religion and Nothingness*, 178.

71. Cited in Buswell, "The 'Short-cut' Approach," 350.

72. Kagamishima, *Dōgen Zenji to sono Shūhen*, 318–20.

73. Prof. Kawamura discussed some of these issues with me during the summer of 1992.

74. CZW, 572.

75. Pas, *The Recorded Sayings*, 31 (citing Yanagida).

76. See Yanagida, "Dōgen to Chūgoku Bukkyō," *Zen Bunka Kenkyūjō Kiyō* 13 (1984), 7–128.

77. CZW, 572. Other sources, according to Ishii's counting, include the DR (11 cases), DS (7), SR (7), *Tenshō Kōtōroku* (3), *Setchō Juko Hyakusoku* (3). No cases are cited directly from the HR.

78. Kagamishima, "Dōgen Zenji no In'yō Tōshi-Goroku nitsuite: Mana *Shōbōgenzō* o Shiten toshite," *Komazawa Daigaku Bukkyōgakubu Kenkyū Kiyō* 45 (1987), 1–3.

79. According to Kawamura, Dōgen did not just randomly jot down Zen dialogues and anecdotes in the MS, but systematically developed a method of expression involving the connection between the MS and KS.

80. Kagamishima, "Dōgen Zenji no In'yō Tōshi-Goroku nitsuite: Mana Shōbōgenzō," 6–12.

81. DKK, 72–78.

82. Leitch, *Deconstructive Criticism*, 161.

83. ZD, 199.

84. SSK, 334.

85. Gregory, "Tsung-Mi and the single word "awareness" (*chih*)," *Philosophy East and West* 35/3 (1985), 265.

86. See Chung-yüan Chang, *Original Teachings of Ch'an Buddhism* (New York: Vintage, 1969), 306–11.

Chapter 4. Narratology and Tropology

1. Wu, *The Golden Age of Zen*, 210. Yet, despite echoing the *watō* approach, Wu's personal comment, in disagreement with Suzuki, criticizes Ta-hui's "post-golden age" Sung style as lacking the freshness of T'ang dialogues (296–97).

2. See Jan Nattier, *Once Upon a Future Time: Studies in a Buddhist Prophecy of Decline* (Berkeley: Asian Humanities Press, 1991), 19–21.

3. McRae, "Encounter Dialogue and the Transformation," 353.

4. Yampolsky, *The Platform Sūtra*, 8–9; also see SZS.

5. Foulk, "The Legacy of Vinaya in Modern Japanese Zen," Second Chung-Hwa International Conference on Buddhism, Taiwan, July 1992.

6. Te-shan is from the Shih-t'ou lineage, and Lin-chi is from the Ma-tsu lineage.

7. Yampolsky, *The Platform Sūtra*, 7.

8. John Jorgenson, "The 'Imperial' Lineage of Ch'an Buddhism: The Role of Confucian Ritual and Ancestor Worship in Ch'an's Search for Legitimation in the Mid-T'ang Dynasty," *Papers on Far Eastern History* 35 (1989), 96.

9. Yanagida, "The Life of Lin-chi I-hsüan," *Eastern Buddhist* 5/2 (1972), 70.

10. SZK, 105–8; Yanagida, "Dōgen to Chūgoku Bukkyō," 50–75.

11. SZS, 190; see also Pas, *The Recorded Sayings*, 29.

12. See McRae, *The Northern School*.

13. The sources for the list are ZD, 333–479; CZS; SSK; Yanagida, *Zengaku Goroku II* (Tokyo: Chikuma shobō, 1974).

14. Buswell, "Chinul's Ambivalent Critique of Radical Subitism in Korean Sōn," *Journal of the International Association of Buddhist Studies* 12/2 (1989), 44.

15. Tracy, *Plurality and Ambiguity*, 45.

16. Todorov, *Genres in Discourse*, 19.

17. Berling, "Bringing the Buddha Down to Earth," 58.

18. Ibid., 59.

19. Ibid., 69.

20. Yampolsky, *The Platform Sūtra*, 141–43.

21. Yanagida, "The 'Recorded Sayings' Texts of Chinese Ch'an Buddhism," 189.

22. KS "Zenki," I, 275.

23. See Nakamura Hajime, *Shin Bukkyō Jiten* (Tokyo: Seishin Shobō, 1979).

24. Ian Reader, *Religion in Contemporary Japan* (Honolulu: University of Hawaii Press, 1991), 41.

25. SSK, 4.

26. On the playfulness of the face-to-face encounter in Socratic-Platonic dialogues, see John Sallis, *Being and Logos: The Way of Platonic Dialogue* (Pittsburgh: Duquesne University Press, 1975), 12–22.

27. Dale Wright, "Historical Understanding in the Ch'an Transmission Narratives," presented at the Annual Meeting of the American Academy of Religion in New Orleans, November 1991. Wright carefully explains how the Zen sense of family spirit and choosing heirs is influenced by traditional Chinese patterns of ancestral worship.

28. Jean-François Lyotard, *The Postmodern Condition: A Report on Knowledge* (Minneapolis: University of Minnesota Press, 1984), 19–22.

29. Barthes, *The Pleasure of the Text* (New York: Hill and Wang, 1975). In a similar way Foucault comments on the "author-function" in "What is an Author?", 108ff.

30. Todorov, *Genres in Discourse*, 31.

31. Wallace Martin, *Recent Theories of Narrative* (Ithaca, NY: Cornell University Press, 1986), esp. 112ff dealing with Tomaschevsky, Barthes, Chatman.

32. This point, influenced by Plato, is made in Seymour Chatman, *Story and Discourse: Narrative Structure in Fiction and Film* (Ithaca, NY: Cornell University Press, 1978).

33. The theories concerning rite of passage and heroism usually describe three stages: departure either by choice or calling, liminality or crossing the threshhold to fulfillment, and reincorporation or return to a social context to apply the lessons learned during attainment. See, for example, Turner, *The Ritual Process: Structure and Anti-Structure* (Chicago: Aldine, 1969), 94ff. On the relation between narrative and heroism White writes (88), "a historical narrative is not only a reproduction of the events reported in it, but also a complex of symbols which gives us directions for finding an icon of the structure of those events in our literary tradition."

34. For a discussion of some of the similarities in the accounts of Te-shan and Lin-chi, see Yanagida, "The Life of Lin-chi I-hsüan," 73.

35. An interesting contemporary account of the Zen quest is in Morinaga Sōkō, "My Struggle to Become a Zen Monk," in *Zen: Tradition and Transition*, 13–29.

36. For this phrase see Ricoeur, *Time and Narrative*, 3 vols. (Chicago: University of Chicago Press, 1984) III, 220.

37. Maraldo, "Is There Historical Consciousness," 165. Also Yampolsky discusses how Shen-hui established Bodhidharma's robe as a symbol of the transmission of the Dharma, in *The Platform Sūtra*, 27.

38. Faure, "Bodhidharma," 190, which is influenced by Foucault's essay, "What is an Author?"; Foucault writes, "The author's name manifests the appearance of a certain discursive set and indicates the status of this discourse within a society and a culture" (107). See also Tracy, *Plurality and Ambiguity*, 45; and White, *Tropics of Discourse*, 88ff.

39. Powell, *The Record of Tung-shan*, 5, 7.

40. Ibid., 6.

41. Berling, "Bringing the Buddha Down to Earth," 81 (Japanese equivalents added); the passage suggests a different distinction between *jōdō* and *shōsan*.

42. David Damrosch, "Leviticus," *The Literary Guide to the Bible*, ed. Robert Alter and Frank Kermode (Cambridge, MA: Harvard University Press, 1987), 73.

43. McRae, *The Northern School*, 74.

44. According to the Zen dictum cited above which initially appeared during the Sung (1108) dynasty but is attributed to Bodhidharma, "A special transmission outside the teachings/Without reliance on words or letters" (*kyōge betsuden/furyū monji*). The "correct" lineage was associated with the Southern School, and southern China was where Buddhism had long established positive social connections; see also Weinstein, *Buddhism Under the T'ang*, 4.

45. For an explanation of a Hindu view of the guru-sisya relationship, see William Cenkner, *A Tradition of Teachers: Sankara and the Jagadgurus Today* (Delhi: Motilal, 1983), esp. 15–19.

46. See Levering, "Ch'an Enlightenment for the Laymen," on the role of Ta-hui in propogating Rinzai Zen amongst the literate elite.

47. See Daniel Overmyer, *Folk Buddhist Religion: Dissenting Sects in Late Traditional China* (Cambridge, MA: Harvard University Press, 1976), 176ff.

48. Yampolsky, *The Platform Sūtra*, 27. H Neill McFarland discusses the "iconoclastic iconography" and "iconographic iconoclasm" associated with Buddhism in *Daruma: The Founder of Zen in Japanese Art and Popular Culture* (Tokyo: Kodansha, 1987), 47–56.

49. The last instance is cited in Buswell, "Ch'an Hermeneutics: A Korean View," in *Buddhist Hermeneutics*, 238.

50. HR, trans., I, 72.

51. Kim, *Dōgen Kigen—Mystical Realist*, 45.

52. *The Recorded Sayings of Ch'an Master Lin-chi Hui-chao of Chen Prefecture*, trans. Ruth Fuller Sasaki (Kyoto: The Institute for Zen Studies, 1975), 22 (trans., 40), TSD 47:506b.

53. Tung-shan, in Powell, *The Record of Tung-shan*, 14.

54. Chung-ying Cheng, "On Zen (Ch'an) Language and Zen Paradoxes," *Journal of Chinese Philosophy* 1/1 (1973), 91.

55. Ibid., 90.

56. ZD, xi–xii.

57. MMK, trans., 19.

58. For the notion of "metonymic displacement" see Damrosch, "Leviticus," 73.

59. Cleary, in SH, trans., xxxiii.

60. Wu, *The Golden Age of Zen*, 95–96.

61. For example, MMK nos. 24 and 32.

62. See Tracy, *Plurality and Ambiguity*, 92. On its role in Zen contemplative literature see Heine, "The Flower Blossoms 'Without Why': Beyond the Heidegger-Kuki Dialogue on Contemplative Language," *Eastern Buddhist* 23/2 (1990), 60–86. Nietzsche also can be interpreted as attempting "to transcend an ironic apprehension of the world in order to arrive at a restored metaphoric contact with reality . . ." that has something of the carnivalesque about it, in Dominick LaCapra (commenting on White's reading of Nietzsche), *Rethinking Intellectual History: Texts, Contexts, Language* (Ithaca, NY: Cornell University Press, 1983), 77.

63. See Taitetsu Unno, "Emptiness and Reality in Mahayana Buddhism," in *The Religious Philosophy of Nishitani Keiji*, 312ff.

64. See Joseph Faulkner, *Sociology of Humor* (St. Paul: West, 1987).

65. Steve Odin, "Derrida and the Decentered Universe of Chan/Zen Buddhism," *Journal of Chinese Philosophy* 17 (1990), 84.

66. Umberto Eco, "The Semantics of Metaphor," as cited in Culler, *The Pursuit of Signs*, 199–200.

67. White, 5. See also David E. Klemm, "Toward a Rhetoric of Postmodern Theology: Through Barth and Heidegger," *Journal of the American Academy of Religion* 55/3 (1987), 443–69.

68. I have translated "express" rather than the more conventional "attain" in Bodhidharma's responses because this suggests the present/active rather than future/receptive nature of discourse, and also because the term is used in that sense in KS "Dōtoku" or "Expressing (*toku*) the Way (*dō*)."

69. From the Ma-tsu *goroku* as cited in Wu, *The Golden Age of Zen*, 94–95.

70. On the debate among tropical theorists about the priority of metaphorical or metonymic thinking see Culler, *The Pursuit of Signs*, 200ff.

71. Yanagida, "Dōgen to Chūgoku Bukkyō," notes that in the KS "Raihaitokuzui" text composed in 1240 ("Kattō" was written in 1243) Dōgen used the term marrow to refer to the essence of the Dharma, and he also frequently repeats "skin, flesh, bones, marrow" as almost a kind of *watō*.

72. See KS "Bendōwa" and KS "Sokushin-zebutsu."

73. KS "Ōsakusendaba," II, 296.

74. KS "Kattō," I, 428.

75. MMK, trans., 292 (slightly revised), TSD 48:298.a.

76. Ibid., 215.

77. Paul Reps, trans., *Zen Flesh, Zen Bones* (New York: Penguin, 1957), 71.

78. KS "Immo," I, 226–27.

79. See Faure, *The Rhetoric of Immediacy*, 114, for this term.

80. Kenneth Kraft, *Eloquent Zen: Daitō and Early Japanese Zen* (Honolulu: University of Hawaii Press, 1992), 5.

81. Leighton, "Review of *The Book of Serenity*, trans. Thomas Cleary," *Eastern Buddhist* 24/1 (1991), 141.

82. HR, trans., I, 8.

83. See Cleary, trans., *Shōbōgenzō: Zen Essays by Dōgen* (Honolulu: University of Hawaii Press, 1986), 6, on comparing the KS and kōan collections. Another appropos comment by Yüan-wu in HR, trans., I, 12: "It was all because [Chao-chou] never had so many calculating judgements: he could pick up sideways and use upside-down, go against or go with, having attained great freedom."

84. HR, trans., III, 589.

85. Cited from KS "Ōsakusendaba," II, 296.

86. KS "Ōsakusendaba," II, 297 (emphasis added).

87. KS "Kokyō," I, 248–49.

88. HR, trans., II, 359.

89. HR, trans., I, 35.

90. KS "Kokyō," 249.

91. Ta-hui, in *Dai Sho*, ed. Araki Kengō (Tokyo: Chikuma Shobō, 1969), 65, 68, 113, 225; and in *Swampland Flowers*, 86, 88; see also Chün-fang Yü, "Ta-hui Tsung-kao and Kung-an Ch'an," *Journal of Chinese Philosophy* 6 (1979), 211–35.

92. Cited in Suzuki, *Essays in Zen Buddhism*, Second Series, 105, 109.

93. See Kim, "The Reason of Words and Letters," for a detailed discussion of some of these categories; see also DKK, 31–83.

94. KS "Muchū-setsumu," I, 311; another oft-cited example of this rhetorical technique is in KS "Sokushin-zebutsu."

95. John Dominic Crossan, *The Dark Interval: Towards a Theology of Story* (Sonoma, CA: Eagle Books, 1988), 104.

96. Ibid., 105.

97. Soren Kierkegaard, *Either/Or*, 2 vols. (Garden City, NY: Doubleday, 1959), I, 31.

98. Buswell, "The 'Short-cut' Approach," 352–56.

99. In Kawamura, *Kenzeiki*, 86; Heine, *A Blade of Grass*, 98.

100. KS "Uji," I, 259.

101. KS "Gabyō," I, 287.

102. Ricoeur, *Freud and Philosophy: An Essay on Interpretation* (New Haven and London: Yale University Press, 1970), 15–16.

103. Ricoeur, *Interpretation Theory*, 56.

104. Ibid., 52.

105. KS "Busshō," I, 64. Some of the following discussion is included in Heine, "Does the Kōan Have Buddha-Nature?," *Journal of the American Academy of Religion* 58/3, 357–87.

106. According to Kodera, "The Buddha Nature in Dōgen's *Shōbōgenzō*," *Japanese Journal of Religious Studies* 4/4 (1977), 267–98.

107. KS "Busshō," I, 52.

108. Ibid., I, 52.

109. Ibid., I, 54.

110. Ibid., I, 54.

111. Ibid., I, 68.

112. Ibid., I, 69.

113. Cited in Buswell, *The Korean Approach to Zen*, 338.

114. Cited in Dumoulin, *Zen Buddhism: A History*, I, 258.

115. Cited in Buswell, *The Korean Approach to Zen*, 337–38, 373–74; and in Hee-sung Keel, *Chinul: The Founder of the Korean Son Tradition* (Berkeley: Berkeley Buddhist Studies Series, 1984), 148.

116. William Johnston, ed., *The Cloud of Unknowing* (Garden City, NY: Doubleday, 1973), 94.

117. In Ōgawa, *Chūgoku Nyoraizō Shisō Kenkyū*, 446.

118. In Kagamishima, *Tendō Nyojō no Kenkyū*, 282.

119. KS "Busshō," I, 69–70.

120. Ibid., I, 70.

121. Ibid., I, 69.

122. Katsuki Sekida, *Zen Training: Methods and Philosophy* (New York and Tokyo: Weatherhill, 1972), 99.

123. John D. Caputo, *Radical Hermeneutics: Repetition, Deconstruction, and the Hermeneutic Project* (Bloomington: Indiana University Press, 1987), 142.

124. Eliade, *Myth and Reality*, 189.

125. Derrida, *The Margins of Philosophy*, trans. Alan Bass (Chicago: University of Chicago Press, 1982), 219.

126. Taylor, *Erring*, 117.

127. Barthes, *The Pleasure of the Text*, 3–4.

128. White, *Tropics of Discourse*, 4.

129. Taylor, *Erring*, 179.

130. But to avoid this high-minded language by paraphrasing the brooding, rebellious Marlon Brando character in the film *The Wild One*, if asked what his metadiscursive reflexiveness is reflecting upon, the Zen master might respond coolly, "Waddaya got?"

131. Yukio Mishima, *The Temple of the Golden Pavilion* (New York: Perigee, 1959), 244.

132. Ibid., 245.

133. W. J. T. Mitchell, *Iconology: Image, Text, Ideology* (Chicago: University of Chicago Press, 1986), 29.

134. Franz Kafka, *The Trial* (New York: Knopf, 1956), 267–69.

135. Cited in HR, trans., I, 57.

136. Bloom, *The Anxiety of Influence*, 95. The range extends from a precursor poem or poems, the poem we write as our reading, the rival poem, the poem that never got written, or that should have been written, and the composite poem.

137. KS "Busshō," I, 64.

Appendices

1. In the opening passages of the fascicle, Dōgen's primary concern is to evoke lineal transmission.

2. This paragraph contains the heart of Dōgen's reinterpretation of the term *kattō* from indicating illusion to suggesting the self-entangling/dis-entangling potentiality of discourse.

3. Other doctrines used by Dōgen to express this ideal are *kannō dōkō* (spiritual communion) and *yuibutsu-yobutsu* ("only between buddha and buddha").

4. Original dialogue appears in KD 5, TSD 41:240, and also is included in MS no. 201. See SZK for the textual history of the passage. I have translated "you express . . ." in Bodhidharma's responses rather than the conventional "you have attained . . ." because that seems in accord with Dōgen's active/dynamic interpretation.

5. Here Dōgen defeats the conventional hierarchical interpretation.

6. One response is equal to and penetrates all other possible responses.

7. This is the second case cited in the fascicle, culled from the *Jōshū Roku*, which Dōgen uses to support his undermining of the conventional interpretation of the Bodhidharma case.

8. According to Dōgen's reading, the skin must come before the marrow, and this stage cannot be skipped over so that if the marrow has not been attained, neither has the skin.

9. An emphasis on the arbitrary convention of "four" stages or levels and on the potentiality for multiple, innumerable dimensions of discourse.

10. Cited from HR no. 92.

11. Although the anecdote is attributed to Hsüeh-tou, it does not appear in the HR's commentary.

12. These expressions are symbols of futility.

13. In MMK no. 3 and MS no. 245.

14. An example of Dōgen's use of partisan polemics directed against Ta-hui.

15. One offering is sufficient to satisfy all requests based on the principle of nondifferentiation and interpenetration of particularity and universality.

16. Also cited in HR no. 92.

17. An emphasis on the exchangeability of possible responses.

18. These concrete, vernacular images suggest the importance of self-modulating, self-correcting discourse.

19. Cited in HR no. 92 and a similar version is in no. 67, MS no. 141, SH no. 1.

20. A paraphrase of the *Diamond Sūtra*.

21. See Wu, *The Golden Age of Zen*, for the legend of Te-shan who began his career as an expert in the *Diamond Sūtra* and "traveled south" to defeat the Southern school's iconoclastic, anti-scriptural standpoint but was eventually enlightened by Lung-t'an (150ff).

22. Cited in HR no. 4.

23. This emphasis on the unenlightened status of Te-shan and the old woman is the opposite of Dōgen's usual strategy in interpreting the dialogues where he stresses that both parties are enlightened at the outset of the encounter.

24. Thus begins Dogen's novel interpretation and extended wordplay.

Bibliography

Abe, Chōichi, *Chūgoku Zenshūshi no Kenkyū*. Tokyo: Seishin Shobō, 1963.

Abe, Masao, *A Study of Dōgen: His Philosophy and Religion*, ed. Steven Heine. Albany: SUNY Press, 1992.

Akizuki, Ryōmin, *Kōan*. Tokyo: Chikuma Shobō, 1987.

Ban, Tetsugyu, *Gendai Mumonkan*. Tokyo: 1980.

Barthes, Roland, *The Pleasure of the Text*. New York: Hill and Wang, 1975.

————. *S/Z*, trans. Richard Miller. New York: Hill and Wang, 1974.

Benoit, Herbert, *The Supreme Doctrine: Psychological Studies in Zen Thought*. New York: Viking, 1955.

Berling, Judith, "Bringing the Buddha Down to Earth: Notes on the Emergence of *Yü-lu* as a Buddhist Genre," *History of Religions* 21/7 (1987), 57–88.

Bielefeldt, Carl, "Recarving the Dragon: History and Dogma in the Study of Dōgen," in *Dōgen Studies*, ed. William R. LaFleur. Honolulu: University of Hawaii Press, 1985, 21–53.

————. *Dōgen's Manuals of Zen Meditation*. Berkeley: University of California Press, 1988.

Bloom, Harold, *The Anxiety of Influence*. New York: Oxford University Press, 1973.

Bodiford, William, "Dharma Transmission in Sōtō Zen: Manzan Dōhaku's Reform Movement," *Monumenta Nipponica* 46/4 (1991), 423–51.

————. *Sōtō Zen in Medieval Japan*. Honolulu: University of Hawaii Press, 1993.

Boyarin, Daniel, *Intertextuality and the Reading of Midrash*. Bloomington: University of Indiana Press, 1990.

Burr, Ronald L., "Lin-chi on 'Language-Dependence,' An Interpretive Analysis," in *Early Ch'an in China and Tibet*, ed. Whalen Lai and Lewis Lancaster. Berkeley: Berkeley Buddhist Studies Series, 1983, 207-27.

Buswell, Robert E., Jr., "Chinul's Ambivalent Critique of Radical Subitism in Korean Sōn," *Journal of the International Association of Buddhist Studies* 12/2 (1989).

————. *The Formation of Ch'an Ideology in China and Korea: The Vajrasamādhi-Sūtra, a*

Buddhist Apocryphon. Princeton: Princeton University Press, 1989.

———. *The Korean Approach to Zen: The Collected Works of Chinul*. Honolulu: University of Hawaii Press, 1983.

———. "The 'Short-cut' Approach of *K'an-hua* Meditation: The Evolution of a Practical Subitism in Chinese Ch'an Buddhism," in *Sudden and Gradual: Approaches to Enlightenment in Chinese Thought*, ed. Peter N. Gregory. Honolulu: University of Hawaii Press, 1987.

——— and Robert M. Gimello, ed., *Paths to Liberation: The Mārga and Its Transformations in Buddhist Thought*. Honolulu: University of Hawaii Press, 1991.

Campbell, Joseph, *The Power of Myth*, with Bill Moyers. New York: Doubleday, 1988.

Caputo, John D., *Radical Hermeneutics: Repetition, Deconstruction, and the Hermeneutic Project*. Bloomington: Indiana University Press, 1987.

Cassirer, Ernst, *Language and Myth*. New York: Dover, 1946.

Cenkner, William, *A Tradition of Teachers: Sankara and the Jagadgurus Today*. Delhi: Motilal, 1983.

Chang, Chung-yüan, *Original Teachings of Ch'an Buddhism*. New York: Vintage, 1969.

Chappell, David W., ed., *Buddhist and Taoist Practice in Medieval Chinese Society, Buddhist and Taoist Studies* II. Honolulu: University of Hawaii Press, 1987.

Chatman, Seymour, *Story and Discourse: Narrative Structure in Fiction and Film*. Ithaca, NY: Cornell University Press, 1978.

Ch'en, Kenneth, *Buddhism in China: A Historical Survey*. Princeton: Princeton University Press, 1964.

Cheng, Chung-ying "On Zen (Ch'an) Language and Zen Paradoxes," *Journal of Chinese Philosophy* 1/1 (1973), 77–102.

Cheng, Hsueh-li, "Psychology, Ontology and Zen Soteriology," *Religious Studies* 22 (1986), 459–72.

Cleary, Thomas, trans., *Sayings and Doings of Pai-chang*. Los Angeles: Center Publications, 1978.

———. trans., *Timeless Spring: A Sōtō Zen Anthology*. Tokyo and New York: Weatherhill, 1980.

———. trans., *Transmission of Light: Zen in the Art of Englightenment* by Zen Master Keizan. San Francisco: North Point Press, 1990.

——— and Cleary, J. C., trans., *The Blue Cliff Record*, 3 vols. With a foreword by Maezumi Taizan Roshi. Boulder: Shambala, 1977.

Collcutt, Martin, *Five Mountains: The Rinzai Zen Monastic Institution in Medieval Japan*. Cambridge, MA: Harvard University Press, 1981.

Crossan, John Dominic, *The Dark Interval: Towards a Theology of Story*. Sonoma, CA: Eagle Books, 1988.

Culler, Jonathan, *On Deconstruction: Theory and Criticism after Structuralism*. Ithaca, NY: Cornell University Press, 1982.

———. *The Pursuit of Signs: Semiotics, Literature, Deconstruction*. Ithaca, NY: Cornell University Press, 1981.

Dainihon Zoku Zōkyō. Kyoto: 1905–12.

Dale, Peter N., *The Myth of Japanese Uniqueness.* New York: St. Martin's Press, 1986.

Damrosch, David, "Leviticus," in *The Literary Guide to the Bible,* ed. Robert Alter and Frank Kermode. Cambridge, MA: Harvard University Press, 1987.

Derrida, Jacques, *The Margins of Philosophy,* trans. Alan Bass. Chicago: University of Chicago Press, 1982.

Dilworth, David, *Philosophy in World Perspective: A Comparative Hermeneutic of the Major Trends.* New Haven: Yale University Press, 1989.

Dōgen, *Dōgen Zenji Zenshū,* 2 vols., ed. Ōkubo Dōshū. Tokyo: Chikuma Shobō, 1969 and 1970.

———. *Eihei Kōroku,* ed. Yokoi Yūhō. Tokyo: Sankibō, 1978.

———. *Shōbōgenzō Zuimonki,* ed. Mizuno Yaoko. Tokyo: Chikuma Shobō, 1963.

———. *Shōbōgenzō,* 2 vols., ed. Terada Tōru and Mizuno Yaoko. Tokyo: Iwanami Shoten, 1970.

———. *Shōbō-genzō,* trans. Yūhō Yokoi. Tokyo: Sankibō, 1986.

———. *Shōbōgenzō: Zen Essays by Dōgen,* trans. Thomas Cleary. Honolulu: University of Hawaii Press, 1986.

Dumoulin, Heinrich, *Zen Enlightenment: Origins and Meaning.* New York and Tokyo: Weatherhill, 1979.

———. *Zen Buddhism: A History,* 2 vols. New York: Macmillan, 1988–90.

Eliade, Mircea, *Encyclopedia of Religion.* New York: Macmillan, 1987.

———. *Myth and Reality.* New York: Harper, 1963.

Entralgo, Pedro Lain, *The Therapy of the Word in Classical Antiquity.* New Haven: Yale University Press, 1970.

Etō, Sokuō, *Shūso toshite no Dōgen Zenji.* Tokyo: Iwanami Shoten, 1944.

Faulkner, Joseph, *Sociology of Humor.* St. Paul: West, 1987.

Faure, Bernard, "Bodhidharma as Textual and Religious Paradigm," *History of Religions* 25/3 (1986), 187–98.

———. "The Daruma-shū, Dōgen, and Sōtō Zen," *Monumenta Nipponica* 42/1 (1987), 25–55.

———. *The Rhetoric of Immediacy: A Cultural Critique of Ch'an/Zen Buddhism.* Princeton: Princeton University Press, 1991.

Fo Kuang Shan Report of the International Conference of Ch'an Buddhism. Taipei: Fo Kuang, 1990.

Foucault, Michel, *A Foucault Reader,* ed. Paul Rabinow. New York: Pantheon, 1984.

———. *The Order of Things: An Archaeology of the Human Sciences.* New York: Pantheon, 1970.

Foulk, T. Griffith, "The Ch'an School and Its Place in the Buddhist Monastic Tradition." Ph.D. dissertation, University of Michigan (1987).

Fromm, Erich, D. T. Suzuki, and Richard DeMartino, *Zen Buddhism and Psychoanalysis.* New York: Harper, 1960.

Fu, Charles W., "The Underlying Structure of Metaphysical Language: A Case Examination of Language and Chinese Philosophy" (unpublished paper, revised version in *Journal of Chinese Philosophy* 6 [1979], 338–66).

Furuta, Shōkin, "Kōan no Rekishiteki Hatten Keitai ni okeru Shinrisei no Mondai," in *Bukkyō no Kompon Shinri*, ed. Miyamoto Shōson. Tokyo: Sanseidō, 1956.

Gardner, Daniel K., "Modes of Thinking and Modes of Discourse in the Sung: Some Thoughts on the *Yü-lu* ('Recorded Conversations') Texts," *Journal of Asian Studies* 50/3 (1991), 574–603.

Gimello, Robert M., "Mysticism and Meditation," in *Mysticism and Philosophical Analysis*, ed. Steven Katz. New York: Oxford University Press, 1978, 170–99.

Gomez, Luis, "D.T. Suzuki's Contribution to Modern Buddhist Scholarship," in *A Zen Life: D. T. Suzuki Remembered*, ed. Masao Abe. New York and Tokyo: Weatherhill, 1986, 90–94.

Gregory, Peter N., "Tsung-Mi and the Single Word 'Awareness' (*chih*)," *Philosophy East and West* 35/3 (1985), 248–69.

Hakamaya, Noriaki, *Hongaku Shisō Hihan*. Tokyo: Daizō Shuppan, 1989.

———. *Hihan Bukkyō*. Tokyo: Daizō Shuppan, 1990.

———. *Dōgen to Bukkyō: Junikanbon Shōbōgenzō no Dōgen*. Tokyo: Daizō Shuppan, 1992.

Hakeda, Yoshito S., trans., *Kūkai: Major Works*. New York: Columbia University Press, 1972.

Hanson, Chad, *Language and Logic in Ancient China*. Ann Arbor: University of Michigan Press, 1983.

Harari, Josue V., ed., *Textual Strategies: Perspectives in Post-Structuralist Criticism*. Ithaca, NY: Cornell University Press, 1979.

Harootunian, H. D., *Things Seen and Unseen*. Chicago and London: University of Chicago Press, 1988.

Hartman, Geoffrey H. and Sanford Budick, ed., *Midrash and Literature*. New Haven: Yale University Press, 1986.

Heine, Steven, *A Blade of Grass: Japanese Poetry and Aesthetics in Dōgen Zen*. New York: Peter Lang, 1989.

———. "Does the Kōan Have Buddha-Nature? The Zen Kōan as Religious Symbol," *Journal of the American Academy of Religion* 58/3 (1990), 357–87.

———. "Dōgen Casts Off 'What': An Analysis of *Shinjin Datsuraku*," *Journal of the International Association of Buddhist Studies* 9/1 (1986), 53–70.

———. *Existential and Ontological Dimensions of Time in Heidegger and Dōgen* (Albany: SUNY Press, 1985).

———. "From Rice Cultivation to Mind Contemplation: The Meaning of Impermanence in Japanese Religion," *History of Religions* 30/4 (1991), 374–403.

———. "The Flower Blossoms 'Without Why': Beyond the Heidegger-Kuki Dialogue on Contemplative Language," *Eastern Buddhist* 23/2 (1990), 60–86.

Hobsbawm, Eric, "Introduction: Inventing Traditions," in *The Invention of Tradition*, ed. Eric Hobsbawm and Terence Ranger. Cambridge: University of Cambridge Press, 1983.

Hsu, Francis, *Iemoto: The Heart of Japan*. New York: Schenkman, 1975.

Ikeda, Rosan, *Dōgengaku no Yōran.* Tokyo: Daizō Shuppan, 1990.

Inagaki, Hisao, *A Glossary of Zen Terms.* Kyoto: Nagata Bunshodo, 1991.

Ishii, Shūdō, *Chūgoku Zenshūshi Wa: Mana Shōbōgenzō ni Manabu.* Kyoto: Zen Bunka Kenkyūjō, 1988.

———. "Recent Trends in Dōgen Studies," *Komazawa Daigaku Kenkyū Nempō* 1 (1990), 219–64.

———. *Sōdai Zenshūshi no Kenkyū.* Tokyo: Daitō Shuppansha, 1987.

Jan, Yün-hua, "Buddhist Historiography in Sung China," *Zeitschrift der Deutschen Morgenlhandlischen Gesellschaft* 114 (1964), 360–81.

———. "Buddhist Self-Immolation in Medieval China," *History of Religions* 4/2 (1965), 243–68.

———. "Tsung-mi: His Analysis of Ch'an Buddhism," *T'oung Pao* 58 (1972), 1–50.

Johnston, William, ed., *The Cloud of Unknowing.* Garden City, NY: Doubleday, 1973.

Jorgenson, John, "The 'Imperial' Lineage of Ch'an Buddhism: The Role of Confucian Ritual and Ancestor Worship in Ch'an's Search for Legitimation in the Mid-T'ang Dynasty," *Papers on Far Eastern History* 35 (1989), 89–133.

Kafka, Franz, *The Trial.* New York: Knopf, 1956.

Kagamishima, Genryū, "Dōgen Zenji no In'yō Tōshi-Goroku nitsuite: Mana Shōbōgenzō o Shiten toshite," *Komazawa Daigaku Bukkyōgakubu Kenkyū Kiyō* 45 (1987), 1–14.

———. *Dōgen Zenji to In'yō Kyōten-Goroku no Kenkyū.* Tokyo: Mokujisha, 1974.

———. *Tendō Nyojō Zenji no Kenkyū.* Tokyo: Shunjūsha, 1983.

———. *Dōgen to sono Shūhen.* Tokyo: Daitō Shuppansha, 1985.

——— and Suzuki Kakuzen, ed., *Jūnikanbon Shōbōgenzō no Shomondai.* Tokyo: Daizō Shuppan, 1991.

——— and Tamaki Koshirō, ed. *Dōgen no Chosaku.* Tokyo: Shunjūsha, 1980.

Kasulis, Thomas P., "Truth Words: The Basis of Kūkai's Theory of Interpretation," in *Buddhist Hermeneutics,* ed. Donald Lopez. Honolulu: University of Hawaii Press, 1988.

———. *Zen Action/Zen Person.* Honolulu: University of Hawaii Press, 1981.

Katz, Nathan, ed., *Buddhist and Western Philosophy.* New Delhi: Sterling, 1981.

———. ed. *Buddhist and Western Psychology.* Boulder: Shambala, 1983.

Kawamura, Kōdō, *Eihei Kaizan Dōgen Zenji Gyōjō: Kenzeiki.* Tokyo: Taishūkan, 1975.

———. *Shōbōgenzō no Seiritsu Shiteki no Kenkyū.* Tokyo: Shunjūsha, 1987.

——— and Ishikawa Rikizan, ed., *Dōgen.* Tokyo: Yoshikawa Kobunkan, 1985.

Keel, Hee-sung, *Chinul: The Founder of the Korean Son Tradition.* Berkeley: Berkeley Buddhist Studies Series, 1984.

Keller, Carl, "Mystical Literature," in *Mysticism and Philosophical Analysis,* ed. Steven Katz. New York: Oxford University Press, 1978.

Kierkegaard, Soren, *Either/Or,* vol. 1. Garden City, NY: Doubleday, 1959.

Kim, Hee-jin, *Dōgen Kigen: Mystical Realist.* Tucson: University of Arizona Press, 1975.

———. "'The Reason of Words and Letters': Dōgen and Kōan Language," in *Dōgen Studies,* ed. William LaFleur. Honolulu: University of Hawaii Press, 1985.

————. "Review of Dōgen's Manuals of Zen Meditation by Carl Bielefeldt," Eastern Buddhist 23/1 (1990), 141–46.

Kitagawa, Joseph, On Understanding Japanese Religion. Princeton: Princeton University Press, 1987.

Klemm, David E., "Toward a Rhetoric of Postmodern Theology: Through Barth and Heidegger," Journal of the American Academy of Religion 55/3 (1987), 443–69.

Kodera, Takeshi James, Dogen's Formative Years in China. Boulder: Prajna Press, 1980.

————. "The Buddha Nature in Dōgen's Shōbōgenzō," Japanese Journal of Religious Studies 4/4 (1977), 267–98.

Kraft, Kenneth, Eloquent Zen: Daitō and Early Japanese Zen. Honolulu: University of Hawaii Press, 1992.

————. Zen: Traditions and Transition. New York: Grove Press, 1988.

Kristeva, Julia, Desire in Language: A Semiotic Approach to Literature and Art. Oxford: Basil Blackwell, 1980.

Krynicki, Victor E., "The Double Orientation of the Ego in the Practice of Zen," The American Journal of Psychoanalysis 40/3 (1980), 239–48.

Kurebayashi, Kōdō, Dōgen Zen no Honryū. Tokyo: Daihōrinkaku, 1978.

LaCapra, Dominick, Rethinking Intellectual History: Texts, Contexts, Language. Ithaca, NY: Cornell University Press, 1983.

LaFleur, William R., The Karma of Words: Buddhism and the Literary Arts in Medieval Japan. Berkeley: University of California Press, 1983.

Leighton, Taigen Daniel, trans., Cultivating the Empty Field. San Francisco: North Point Press, 1991.

————. "Review of The Book of Serenity, trans. Thomas Cleary," Eastern Buddhist 24/1 (1991), 140–42.

Leitch, Vincent B., Deconstructive Criticism: An Advanced Introduction. New York: Columbia University Press, 1983.

Levering, Miriam, "Ch'an Enlightenment for Laymen: Ta-hui and the New Religious Culture of the Sung." Ph.D. dissertation, Harvard University (1978).

————. "Ta-hui and Lay Buddhists: Ch'an Sermons on Death," Buddhist and Taoist Practice in Medieval Chinese Society, ed. Chappell, 181–209.

Luk, Charles, Ch'an and Zen Teaching, Second Series. Berkeley: Shambala, 1971.

Lynn, Richard John, "The Sudden and Gradual in Chinese Poetry Criticism: An Examination of the Ch'an-Poetry Analogy," in Sudden and Gradual: Approaches to Enlightenment in Chinese Thought, ed. Peter N. Gregory. Honolulu: University of Hawaii Press, 1987.

Lyotard, Jean-François, The Postmodern Condition: A Report on Knowledge. Minneapolis: University of Minnesota Press, 1984.

Ma, Y. W., "Themes and Characterization in the Lung-t'u Kung-an," T'oung Pao 59 (1973), 179–202.

Manabe, Shunshō and Kawamura Kōdō, ed., Ei-in-bon Shōbōgenzō. Tokyo: Juniseiki Gurafikusu, 1993.

Maraldo, John, "Is There Historical Consciousness Within Ch'an?," Japanese Journal of Religous Studies 12/2–3 (1985), 141–72.

Martin, Wallace, *Recent Theories of Narrative*. Ithaca, NY: Cornell University Press, 1986.

Matsumoto, Michihiro, *The Unspoken Way: Haragei, Silence in Japanese Business and Society*. Tokyo: Kodansha, 1988.

Matsumoto, Shirō, *Engi to Kū—Nyoraizō Shisō*. Tokyo: Daizō Shuppan, 1989.

Matsunaga, Daigan and Alicia, *Foundation of Japanese Buddhism*, 2 vols. Los Angeles and Tokyo: Buddhist Books International, 1978.

May, Rollo, *The Courage to Create*. New York, Bantam, 1975.

McFarland, H. Neill, *Daruma: The Founder of Zen in Japanese Art and Popular Culture*. Tokyo: Kodansha, 1987.

McRea, John R., "Encounter Dialogue and the Transformation of the Spiritual Path in Chinese Ch'an," *Paths to Liberation: The Mārga and Its Transformations in Buddhist Thought*, ed. Robert N. Buswell, Jr. and Robert M. Gimello. Honolulu: University of Hawaii Press, 1991.

———. *The Northern School and the Formation of Early Ch'an Buddhism*. Honolulu: University of Hawaii Press, 1986.

———. "Shen-hui and the Teaching of Sudden Enlightenment in Early Ch'an Buddhism," *Sudden and Gradual: Approaches to Enlightenment in Chinese Thought*, ed. Peter N. Gregory. Honolulu: University of Hawaii Press, 1987.

Miller, Roy Andrew, *Japan's Modern Myth: The Language and Beyond*. New York: Weatherhill, 1982.

Mishima, Yukio, *The Temple of the Golden Pavilion*. New York: Perigee, 1959.

Mitchell, W. J. T., *Iconology: Image, Text, Ideology*. Chicago: University of Chicago, 1986.

Miura Isshū and Ruth Fuller Sasaki, *The Zen Kōan*. New York: Harcourt Brace Javonovich, 1965.

———. *Zen Dust: The History of the Kōan Study in Rinzai (Lin-chi) Zen*. New York: Houghton Mifflin, 1966.

Mountain Record 3/4 (Spring 1990).

Murphy, John W., *Postmodern Social Analysis and Criticism*. Westport, CT: Greenwood Press, 1989.

Nagashima, Takayuki, *Truths and Fabrications in Religion*. London: Arthur Probsthain, 1978.

Nakamura, Hajime, *Shin Bukkyō Jiten*. Tokyo: Seishin Shobō, 1979.

Nakaseko, Shōdō, *Dōgen Zenji Den Kenkyū*. Tokyo: Kokusho Kankōkai, 1979.

Nattier, Jan, *Once Upon a Future Time: Studies in a Buddhist Prophecy of Decline*. Berkeley: Asian Humanities Press, 1991.

Nishitani, Keiji, "Bukkyō ni okeru 'Kōjō' no Tachiba," in *Zettai Mu to Kami*, ed. Jan van Bragt. Tokyo: Shunjūsha, 1981.

———. *Religion and Nothingness*. Berkeley: University of California Press, 1982.

Odin, Steve, "Derrida and the Decentered Universe of Chan/Zen Buddhism," *Journal of Chinese Philosophy* 17 (1990) 61–86.

Ogata, Sohaku, trans., *The Transmission of the Lamp: Early Masters*. Wolfeboro, NH: Longwood Academic, 1988.

Ōgawa, Kōkan, *Chūgoku Nyoraizō Shisō Kenkyū*. Tokyo: Nakayama Shobō, 1976.

Ōkubo, Dōshū, *Dōgen Zenji Den no Kenkyū*. Tokyo: Chikuma Shobō, 1966.

Ooms, Herman, "Review of *The Fracture of Meaning: Japan's Synthesis of China from the Eighth through the Eighteenth Centuries* by David Pollack," *Harvard Journal of Asiatic Studies* 49/1 (1989) 266–82.

Overmyer, Daniel, *Folk Buddhist Religion: Dissenting Sects in Late Traditional China*. Cambridge, MA: Harvard University Press, 1976.

Pas, Julian F., trans., *The Recorded Sayings of Ma-tsu* (from Dutch translation by Bavo Lievens). Lewiston/Queenston: Edwin Mellen, 1987.

Pollack, David, *The Fracture of Meaning: Japan's Synthesis of China from the Eighth through the Eighteenth Centuries*. Princeton: Princeton University Press, 1986.

Powell, William F., trans., *The Record of Tung-shan*. Honolulu: University of Hawaii Press, 1986.

Reader, Ian, *Religion in Contemporary Japan*. Honolulu: University of Hawaii Press, 1991.

Red Pine, trans., *The Zen Teaching of Bodhidharma*. San Francisco: North Point Press, 1989.

Reps, Paul, trans., *Zen Flesh, Zen Bones*. New York: Penguin, 1957.

Reynolds, David, *Flowing Bridges, Quiet Therapies: Japanese Psychotherapies, Morita and Naikan*. Albany: State University of New York Press, 1989.

Ricoeur, Paul, *Freud and Philosophy: An Essay on Interpretation*. New Haven: Yale University Press, 1970.

———. *Interpretation Theory: Discourse and the Surplus of Meaning*. Fort Worth: Texas Christian Univ. Press, 1974.

———. *The Rule of Metaphor: Multidisciplinary Studies of the Creation of Meaning in Language*. Toronto and Buffalo: University of Toronto Press, 1975.

———. *The Symbolism of Evil*. Boston: Beacon Press, 1967.

———. *Time and Narrative*, 3 vols. Chicago: University of Chicago Press, 1984.

Rosenberg, Bruce A., *The Art of the American Folk Preacher*. New York: Oxford University Press, 1970.

Sallis, John, *Being and Logos: The Way of Platonic Dialogue*. Pittsburgh: Duquesne University Press, 1975.

Sasaki, Ruth Fuller, trans., *The Recorded Sayings of Ch'an Master Lin-chi Hui-chao of Chen Prefecture*. Kyoto: The Institute for Zen Studies, 1975.

Schloegl, Irmgard, trans., *The Zen Teaching of Rinzai*. Berkeley: Shambala, 1976.

Scholem, Gershom, "The Name of God and the Linguistic Theory of the Kabbala," *Diogenes* 79 (1972), 59–80; 80 (1972), 164–94.

Scholes, Robert and Kellogg, Robert, *The Nature of Narrative*. New York: Oxford University Press, 1966.

Sekida, Katsuki, *Two Zen Classics: Mumonkan and Hekiganroku*, ed. A. V. Grimstone. New York and Tokyo: Weatherhill, 1977.

———. *Zen Training: Methods and Philosophy*. New York and Tokyo: Weatherhill, 1975.

Sekiguchi, Shindai, *Daruma Daishi no Kenkyū*. Tokyo: Shunjūsha, 1957.

Sharf, Robert H., "The Idolization of Enlightenment: On the Mummification of Ch'an Masters in Medieval China," *History of Religions* 32/1 (1992), 1–31.

———. "Occidentalism and the Zen of Japanese Nationalism," presented at the Annual Meeting of the American Academy of Religion, Kansas City, November 1991.

Shibata, Dōken, Dōgen no Kotoba. Tokyo: Yuzankaku Shuppan, 1978.

Shibayama, Zenkei, Zen Comments on the Mumonkan. New York: Mentor, 1974.

Shibe, Ken'ichi, "Tenkei Shūgaku to Mondaiten—'Kōan' Kōtei," Shūgaku Kenkyū 29 (1987), 219–24.

Shigematsu, Sōiku, trans., A Zen Forest: Sayings of the Masters. New York and Tokyo: Weatherhill, 1981.

Shimano, Eido, Golden Wind: Zen Talks, ed. Janis Levine. Tokyo: Japan Publications, 1979.

Shirane, Haruo, "Lyricism and Intertextuality: An Approach to Shunzei's Poetics," Harvard Journal of Asiatic Studies 50/1 (1991), 71–85.

Shōbōgenzō Shūsho Taisei. Tokyo: Taishūkan, 1978– .

Sōtō Shū Kankei Bunken Mokuroku. Tokyo: Sōtō Shūmujō, 1990.

Sōtō Shū Zensho. Tokyo: Kōmeisha, 1929–39.

Stambaugh, Joan, Impermanence is Buddha-nature: Dōgen's Understanding of Temporality. Honolulu: University of Hawaii Press, 1990.

Sternberg, Meir, The Poetics of Biblical Narrative: Ideological Literature and the Drama of Reading. Bloomington: Indiana University Press, 1985.

Suzuki, D. T., An Introduction to Zen Buddhism, with a Foreword by C. G. Jung. New York: Grove Press, 1964.

———. Essays in Zen Buddhism (Second Series). London: Rider, 1970.

———. Mysticism: Christian and Buddhist. New York: Collier, 1957.

———. On Indian Mahayana Buddhism, ed. Edward Conze. New York: Harper and Row, 1968.

———. Studies in Zen. New York: Delta, 1955.

———. Zen Doctrine of No Mind. New York: Weiser, 1973.

Swanson, Paul, Foundations of T'ien-t'ai Philosophy. Berkeley: Asian Humanities Press, 1989.

Ta-hui, Daie Sho, ed., Araki Kengo. Tokyo: Chikuma Shobō, 1969.

———. Swampland Flowers, Letters and Lectures of Zen Master Ta-hui, trans. Christopher Cleary. New York: Grove Press, 1977.

Taishō Shinshū Daizōkyō. Tokyo: 1914–22, esp. vols. 34, 47–52.

Takao, Giken, Sōdai Bukkyōshi no Kenkyū. Tokyo: Hyakugaen, 1973.

Takasaki, Jikidō and Umehara Takeshi, Kobutsu no Manabi. Tokyo: Kodokawa Shoten, 1963.

Takeuchi, Michio, Dōgen. Tokyo: Yoshikawa Kobunkan, 1962.

Tamura, Yoshirō, "Critique of Original Awakening Thought in Shōshin and Dōgen," Japanese Journal of Religious Studies 11/2–3 (1984), 243–66.

———. Kamakura Shin-Bukkyō Shisō no Kenkyū. Kyoto: Heirakuji Shoten, 1965.

Tanabe, George J., Jr. and Willa Jane Tanabe, ed. The Lotus Sūtra in Japanese Culture. Honolulu: University of Hawaii Press, 1989.

Tanahashi, Kazuaki, ed. and trans., Moon in a Dewdrop: Writings of Zen Master Dōgen. San Francisco: North Point, 1985.

Taylor, Mark C., Erring: A Postmodern A/theology. Chicago: University of Chicago Press, 1984.

Tillich, Paul, Systematic Theology. Chicago: University of Chicago Press, 1951.

Todorov, Tzvetan, Genres in Discourse. Cambridge: Cambridge University Press, 1990.

Tracy, David, Plurality and Ambiguity: Hermeneutics, Religion, Hope. San Francisco: Harper and Row, 1987.

Turner, Victor, Dramas, Fields, and Metaphors. Ithaca, NY: Cornell University Press, 1974.

———. The Ritual Process: Structure and Anti-Structure. Chicago: Aldine Publishing Co., 1969.

Ui, Hakuju, Zenshūshi Kenkyū. Tokyo: Iwanami, 1935.

Unno, Taitetsu, ed., The Religious Philosophy of Nishitani Keiji. Berkeley: Asian Humanities Press, 1989.

van Gennep, Arnold, Rites of Passage. Chicago: University of Chicago Press, 1960.

Watson, Burton, trans., The Complete Works of Chuang Tzu. New York and London: Columbia University Press, 1968.

Wawrytko, Sandra, "Zen and Western Psychotherapy: Nirvanic Transcendence and Samsara Fixation," Chung-Hwa Buddhist Journal 4 (1991), 451–95.

Weinstein, Stanley, Buddhism under the T'ang. Cambridge: Cambridge University Press, 1987.

White, Hayden, Tropics of Discourse: Essays in Cultural Criticism. Baltimore: Johns Hopkins University Press, 1978.

Wiesel, Elie, Souls on Fire. New York: Vintage, 1972.

Wright, Addison G., Midrash: The Literary Genre. Staten Island: Alba House, 1967.

Wright, Arthur F., Buddhism in Chinese History. Stanford, CA: Stanford University Press, 1959.

———. Studies in Chinese Buddhism, ed. Robert M. Somers. New Haven: Yale University Press, 1990.

Wright, Dale S., "Historical Understanding in the Ch'an Transmission Narratives," presented at the Annual Meeting of the American Academy of Religion, New Orleans, November 1990.

———. "Rethinking Transcendence: The Role of Language in Zen Experience," Philosophy East and West 42/1 (1992), 113–38.

Wu, John C. H., The Golden Age of Zen. Taiwan: United, 1975.

Yamauchi, Shun'yū, Dōgen Zen to Tendai Hongaku Hōmon. Tokyo: Daizō Shuppan, 1986.

Yampolsky, Philip B., trans., The Platform Sūtra of the Sixth Patriarch. New York: Columbia University Press, 1967.

———. trans., The Zen Master Hakuin: Selected Writings. New York: Columbia University Press, 1971.

Yanagida, Seizan, "Dōgen to Chūgoku Bukkyō," Zen Bunka Kenkyūjō Kiyō 13 (1984), 7–128.

———. Shoki Zenshū Shisho no Kenkyū. Kyoto: Hōzōkan, 1967.

———. "The Life of Lin-chi I-hsüan," Eastern Buddhist 5/2 (1972), 70–94.

―――. "The 'Recorded Sayings' Texts of Chinese Ch'an Buddhism," in *Early Ch'an in China and Tibet*, ed. Whalen Lai and Lewis R. Lancaster. Berkeley: Berkeley Buddhist Studies Series, 1983.

―――. *Zengaku Goroku II*. Tokyo: Chikuma shobō, 1974.

Yoshizu, Yoshihide, "Hijiri no Ningenkan to Mondō ni yoru Satori," in *Buddha Kara Dōgen E*, ed. Nara Yasuaki. Tokyo, Daizō Shuppan, 1992.

―――. *"En" no Shakaigaku*. Tokyo: Bijitsu Sensho, 1987.

Yü, Chün-fang, "Ta-hui Tsung Kao and *Kung-An* Ch'an," *Journal of Chinese Philosophy* 6 (1979), 211–35.

Zengagku Daijiten. Tokyo: Taishūkan, 1978.

Index